APOCALYPTIC PATIENCE

In Memoriam:
Vasili Arkhipov 1962
Stanislav Petrov 1983

Also Available from Bloomsbury

The Selected Writings of Jan Patocka, ed. by Erin Plunkett and Ivan Chvatík
The Phenomenology of Questioning, Joel Hubick

APOCALYPTIC PATIENCE

Mystical Theology / Gnosticism / Ethical Phenomenology

Andrew Shanks

BLOOMSBURY ACADEMIC
LONDON • NEW YORK • OXFORD • NEW DELHI • SYDNEY

BLOOMSBURY ACADEMIC
Bloomsbury Publishing Plc, 50 Bedford Square, London, WC1B 3DP, UK
Bloomsbury Publishing Inc, 1359 Broadway, 12th Floor, New York, NY 10018, USA
Bloomsbury Publishing Ireland, 29 Earlsfort Terrace, Dublin 2, D02 AY28, Ireland

BLOOMSBURY, BLOOMSBURY ACADEMIC and the Diana logo are
trademarks of Bloomsbury Publishing Plc

First published in Great Britain 2024
This paperback edition published 2026

Copyright © Andrew Shanks, 2024

Andrew Shanks has asserted his right under the Copyright, Designs and
Patents Act, 1988, to be identified as Author of this work.

Cover design by Charlotte Daniels
Cover image © Gloria in Excelsis. Obcanske Forum!. Poster. 1989,
Pavel Beneš (Printed and published) (© DACS 2024)

All rights reserved. No part of this publication may be: i) reproduced or transmitted in any form, electronic or mechanical, including photocopying, recording or by means of any information storage or retrieval system without prior permission in writing from the publishers; or ii) used or reproduced in any way for the training, development or operation of artificial intelligence (AI) technologies, including generative AI technologies. The rights holders expressly reserve this publication from the text and data mining exception as per Article 4(3) of the Digital Single Market Directive (EU) 2019/790.

Bloomsbury Publishing Plc does not have any control over, or responsibility for, any third-party websites referred to or in this book. All internet addresses given in this book were correct at the time of going to press. The author and publisher regret any inconvenience caused if addresses have changed or sites have ceased to exist, but can accept no responsibility for any such changes.

A catalogue record for this book is available from the British Library.

Library of Congress Cataloging-in-Publication Data
Names: Shanks, Andrew, 1954- author.
Title: Apocalyptic patience / Andrew Shanks.
Description: 1. | London : Bloomsbury Academic, 2024. |
Includes bibliographical references and index.
Identifiers: LCCN 2023058365 (print) | LCCN 2023058366 (ebook) |
ISBN 9781350410602 (hardback) | ISBN 9781350410664 (paperback) |
ISBN 9781350410633 (epub) | ISBN 9781350410619 (ebook)
Subjects: LCSH: Patočka, Jan, 1907–1977.
Classification: LCC B4805.P384 S53 2024 (print) | LCC B4805.P384 (ebook) |
DDC 199/.437–dc23/eng/20240308
LC record available at https://lccn.loc.gov/2023058365
LC ebook record available at https://lccn.loc.gov/2023058366

ISBN:	HB:	978-1-3504-1060-2
	PB:	978-1-3504-1066-4
	ePDF:	978-1-3504-1061-9
	eBook:	978-1-3504-1063-3

Typeset by Integra Software Services Pvt. Ltd.

For product safety related questions contact productsafety@bloomsbury.com.

To find out more about our authors and books visit www.bloomsbury.com
and sign up for our newsletters.

CONTENTS

INTRODUCTION	1
A moment of truth	1
'Grand narrative'?	4
Synopsis	13

Part I
THE TWO SIDES OF THE EQUATION

Chapter 1	
THE SOLIDARITY OF THE SHAKEN: JAN PATOČKA'S ARGUMENT	19
The Heretical Essays	19
Two species of truth	28
Chapter 2	
THE KINGDOM OF GOD: ABRAHAMIC RELIGION, ITS HISTORIC ORIGINS IN A DILEMMA	33
Three species of religion	33
Abraham / Moses: Amos / Hosea	35
De Trinitate	42

Part II
RECOIL FROM EVANGELISTIC IMPATIENCE:
MYSTICAL THEOLOGY / GNOSTICISM

Chapter 3	
'MYSTICAL THEOLOGY'	49
'Dionysius the Areopagite'	49
Meister Eckhart	62
Niffarí	72
Chapter 4	
DECADENCE OF 'MYSTICISM'	85
'Mysticism' of Church and sect	86
'Mysticism' deracinated	93

Chapter 5
'GNOSTICISM' 101
   The question regarding divine 'almightiness' 101
   Kabbalah 106
   Böhme 109
   'Gnostic return in modernity?' 117

Part III
PHILOSOPHY AND CATHOLICITY: ETHICAL PHENOMENOLOGY

Chapter 6
PHILOSOPHIC MEDITATION ON THE 'PATHOS OF SHAKEN-NESS' 127
   Kierkegaard 128
   Levinas 136
   Løgstrup 144

Chapter 7
SHAKEN-NESS, MINUS CATHOLICITY 155
   Heidegger 155
   Strauss 164
   Adorno 172
   Arendt 174

Chapter 8
SHAKEN-NESS, PLUS CATHOLICITY: HEGEL, AND BEYOND 185
   Desegregated *'Sittlichkeit'* 185
   From Hegel to Patočka: The transition to 'third modernity' 202
   Twenty-first-century *Geist* 206

Notes 213
Bibliography 248
Index 260

INTRODUCTION

A moment of truth

In early January 1990 it so happens that I was in Prague, as part of a little group of Western European church-related peace activists, under the aegis of the Dutch Inter-Church Peace Council, meeting Czech human rights defenders, church-related supporters of the dissident Charter 77 movement.

The expedition had been planned several months before. But, quite unexpectedly to most observers and with astonishing speed, in the meantime a revolution had occurred. Over the previous seven weeks, the Communist regime in Czechoslovakia, like all the other Communist regimes of Central Europe, had simply collapsed. The people we were meeting were both exhilarated and exhausted. Everywhere, on the streets, there were posters: '*Havel na Hrad*', 'Havel to the Castle' – left over from the emergency election, a few days previously, of Václav Havel, the leading spokesman of Charter 77, to be president of the newly liberated nation. After over four decades of more or less totalitarian rule, a regime, which up until a few months ago had appeared absolutely fixed in place, was gone. In vast numbers the people had come out on the streets, and jingled their keys. With almost no violence, Charter 77 – which had never presumed to act as a political party aspiring to a direct share in governance – had nonetheless miraculously prevailed. Shabby multitudes filled the information centre of Civic Forum, the newly formed, broad-based revolutionary organization, to which it had given birth. The beautiful city was as if transfigured.

> *I have thus with my own eyes, once, witnessed a clear visitation of the kingdom of God.*

Party politicians and journalists, of course, trumpeted a great triumph of West over East, throughout Central Europe, of which the events in Prague were a crucial part. I have no interest in any such merely propagandist notion. On the contrary: I would argue that the moment of truth here precisely consisted in a local overthrow of propaganda-thinking *as such*; caught at a weak point, the whole idolatrous enterprise in principle being dealt a blow.

A moment of truth – it was, inevitably, ephemeral. There ensued a rapid transition, from the old normality of Communist dictatorship, to the new normality of liberal multi-party democracy. That is, from the former, truly lethal banality – to another, milder banality. Straight away, overcrowded prisons were so far as possible emptied. The result was a crime wave. Then, over the ensuing years, many of the most enterprising youngsters left, as now they could, to pursue more promising opportunities overseas. The economy failed to boom. Fresh resentment started to fester.

And yet – for that one brief moment, there, in the interlude, it was: a visitation. It is the nature of the kingdom of God to flicker just ever so briefly into sight, a will-o'-the wisp; but, in so doing, to light up whole vistas of history.

So: how to follow through?

§

I am inclined to speak in New Testament terms of the 'kingdom of God', because I am a priest. But of all European nations the Czechs are, in fact, one of the most secularized.

Jan Hus, based at the Charles University in Prague, had been the second great forerunner of the Protestant Reformation; following John Wycliffe in England. Though Hus was burnt at the stake in 1415, his followers were undaunted; five successive anti-Hussite 'crusades' failed to crush them; and by the mid-fifteenth century, theirs was firmly established as the dominant form of church life in Bohemia as a whole. But in 1620 the Holy Roman Emperor Ferdinand II had led yet a further Roman Catholic assault, culminating in the decisive defeat of the Hussites at the battle of White Mountain; in the immediate aftermath of which, the great majority of the Bohemian nobility went into exile. Their lands were confiscated and given to German-speaking Roman Catholics, whilst the remaining proto-Protestant population was placed under great pressure to convert. Nowadays, insofar as they have any religion, most Czechs are Roman Catholic. But the contrast with their generally far more devout Polish neighbours could not be greater. Whereas Polish Roman Catholicism is reinforced by its close identification with Polish nationalism – traditionally embattled both against the Orthodox Russians to the east and against the Lutheran Prussians to the west – Czech Roman Catholicism, as a violently imposed German import, has enjoyed no such advantage.

Our little group attended the church of the leading Charter 77 priest, Father Václav Malý. At the height of the upheaval, he had addressed a large crowd in Wenceslas Square, which was dangerously seething with rage against the riot police for the heavy-handed tactics they had at first used. He had brought representatives of the police before them, to apologize. Then he had led the crowd in the Lord's Prayer: 'Forgive us our sins as we forgive those who sin against us … ' In this somewhat theatrical way, he had helped ensure the velvety nature of the so-called 'Velvet Revolution'. And there was certainly quite a fervent mood in church the day we were there.

However, the fact remains that Charter 77 itself was a thoroughly secular organization.

What had triumphed in this 'Velvet Revolution'? Václav Havel, for his part, employed a secular formula, deriving from the work of the philosopher Jan Patočka, with whom, amongst others, he had co-founded Charter 77, some twelve years earlier. (Patočka had then been arrested and, aged seventy, died following his interrogation.) In a text dating from 1984 Havel put it like this:

> When Jan Patočka wrote about Charter 77, he used the term '*solidarity of the shaken*'. He was thinking of those who dared resist impersonal power and to confront it with the only thing at their disposal, their own humanity. Does not the perspective of a better future depend on something like an international community of the shaken which, ignoring state boundaries, political systems, and power blocs, standing outside the high game of traditional politics, aspiring to no titles and appointments, will seek to make a real political force out of a phenomenon so ridiculed by the technicians of power – the phenomenon of human conscience?[1]

§

The 'solidarity of the shaken': one might define it as *solidarity founded, purely and simply, on the mutual recognition of the most thoughtful, as such*. Not necessarily the most correct – not necessarily the most articulate – but those who most deeply, and most honestly, *care*. Or: it is that which empowers the most radically thoughtful openness to others, embattled against even the most repressive closure. Just that – a solidarity without any other essential qualification. In this book I want, so far as I can, to give substance to this initially nebulous ideal. Moreover, I want to argue that the solidarity of the shaken, enacted, *is* the kingdom of God; and, conversely, that the kingdom of God *is* the solidarity of the shaken, enacted.

To affirm that the solidarity of the shaken is the kingdom of God is to say that it is a *sacred* ideal; indeed, properly the most sacred of all. Infusing older sacred traditions at their best, it is the proper telos of their revelatory evolution, to inspire it ever more effectively.

To affirm that the kingdom of God is the solidarity of the shaken is to suggest that it is just what appears in events comparable, for example, to the 1989 Velvet Revolution in Czechoslovakia; insofar as that Revolution was an authentic outcome of the work of Charter 77. The kingdom of God is the deepest level of potential moral truth energizing traditional sacred tradition, but, as the solidarity of the shaken, also forever overflows the confining particularity of any particular such tradition. It overflows into the secular domain, transfiguring it. Such, in a nutshell, is my argument.

And my aim in what follows is, then, to sketch something of *the history of the emergence of the possibility of that twofold insight, in all of its potential fullness, rendered richly explicit*.

'Grand narrative'?

But – an argument attempting to evoke a supremely authoritative, and universally valid, moral ideal, by tracing the global history behind it: is that not a *'grand narrative'*? And has not the twentieth century, especially, taught us the wisdom of, in Jean-François Lyotard's phrase, a generalized postmodern 'incredulity towards grand narratives'?

Well, yes, what I intend is just that, an unabashed essay in grand-narrative thought; a bid, so far as possible, to mobilize the rich inspirational power of that genre. Only, it is by no means the sort of grand narrative that Lyotard for instance had in mind. Lyotardian postmodernism arose in the first instance out of recoil, on the radical left, from *Marxist* grand narrative; disillusionment then extended to include all other forms of grand narrative liable, like the Marxist one, to inform manipulative propaganda projects, justifying tyrannical violence in the name of Progress. Marxist grand narrative became manipulative, in essence surely, because of the way it purports to predict the future: *guaranteeing* the eventual global triumph of the movement it celebrates. This guarantee has certainly proved effective – even to a quite astonishing degree! – as a means of boosting partisan morale. But insofar as its morale-boosting power comes to be valued more than any inhibitory moral scruple, it tends to legitimate all manner of coercion. For, in this case, the entirely desirable final outcome of History being pre-determined, nothing else seems to matter other than that one should work to accelerate its advent, as much as one can. *Such* grand narrative is in the end nothing more than an argument for impatience; and hence, for violence.

However, the grand narrative that I have in mind is not predictive. It is purely retrospective: tracing the emergence of a possibility of thought that has *already* arrived. There are, here, no guarantees for the future. And moreover, this is a reading of what Kant called 'Universal History' beginning from a moment of truth that was, to a quite striking degree *non*-violent; precisely the overthrow of a violent bully-regime, which claimed to be Marxist.

§

I am not the first to attempt a grand-narrative interpretation of what happened, across Central Europe, in late 1989. Francis Fukuyama's work *The End of History and the Last Man* is another such. First published in 1992, Fukuyama's pyrotechnic work was much more of an immediate response. I do not agree in every respect with Fukuyama's argument, but I do think one has to admire its sheer brio.

In a certain sense, Fukuyama suggests, the events of 1989 are a confirmation of the 'End of History'. Obviously, by the 'End of History' he does not mean an end of momentous historical events. The actual beginning of the 'End' that he has in mind pre-dates 1989 by some two centuries. But he is no by means denying the world-historical momentous-ness of what has occurred in the interim – or of what is liable to occur in the future. Only, as he sees it, the point is that the events of 1989 are momentous above all by virtue of the way in which they serve to clarify the meaning of the earlier 'End', which they help complete.

The 'End' he is talking about is the final rendering-possible of a supremely authoritative, and not to be surpassed, perception of general direction in human affairs. As Fukuyama sees it there are two basic aspects to this.[2] On the one hand, there is the discovery of *the* supremely efficient method of ordering economic life: namely, modern free-market capitalism. On the other hand, there is the discovery of *the* broad type of ideal political order: namely, modern liberal democracy. In the long run, he thinks, these two goals serve to define true Progress. To my mind, this is much too closely related to the standard 'Western' propaganda-reading of the events. But Fukuyama is building here on the foundations laid by Alexandre Kojève, originally in his famous lectures on Hegel, delivered at the École des Hautes Études in Paris from 1933 to 9.[3] As a portrait of Hegel, these lectures are to a very large degree fictional. As a fresh form of grand-narrative thought they are, however, undeniably electrifying!

Thus, as Kojève tells the tale, the End of History crucially involves the notion of universal human rights, understood as a revolutionary principle of absolute validity, transcending, and wherever necessary negating, ancient custom. What has 'ended' – once and for all, for those with the eyes to see it – is, in short, History as a principle of moral inertia; the grip of the past, in that sense. The first state actually governed according to such a radically anti-traditional ideology was the French Revolutionary Republic. After the violent chaos of that Republic, the Napoleonic Empire then developed a second, internally altogether more stable version of the same: as this regime melded the ideological promise of universal human rights with the self-assertion of Napoleon's own formidable ego. In 1806 Napoleon defeated the Prussian army at the battle of Jena. On October 13, the day before the battle, he entered Jena. A philosophy lecturer at the university there wrote, in a letter to a friend:

> I saw the Emperor – this world-soul – riding out of the city on reconnaissance. It is indeed a wonderful sensation to see such an individual, who, concentrated here at a single point, astride a horse, reaches out over the world and masters it … this extraordinary man, whom it is impossible not to admire …[4]

The lecturer was Hegel, who was at that time just putting the finishing touches to his masterpiece the *Phenomenology of Spirit*, the very text on which Kojève was subsequently to deliver his lectures. And, as Kojève sees it, Hegel's *Phenomenology of Spirit* is nothing other than the definitive working-through, in theory, of the End of History which Napoleon symbolically embodied in practice.

Kojève expresses this thought with a great, mischievous flourish of messianic hyperbole, which goes far, far beyond Hegel's own momentary admiration of that 'world-soul astride a horse'. 'Napoleon,' he writes

> completes the course of the historical evolution of humanity. He is the human *Individual* in the proper and full sense of the word; because it is through *him*, through *this* particular man, that the "common cause," the truly universal cause, is realized; and because this particular man is recognized, in his very particularity by all men, universally. The only thing he lacks is *Self*-Consciousness; he *is*

the perfect Man, but he does not yet *know* it, and that is why Man is not fully 'satisfied' in him alone. He cannot *say* of himself all that I have just said.

Now, I have said it because I read it in the *Phenomenology*. Therefore it is Hegel, the author of the *Phenomenology*, who is somehow Napoleon's Self-Consciousness. And since the perfect Man, the Man fully 'satisfied' by what he *is*, can only be a Man who *knows* what he is, who is fully *self-conscious*, it is Napoleon's existence as *revealed* to all men in and by the *Phenomenology* that is the realized ideal of human existence ...[5]

Now, Hegel does not in fact make any such absurd claim, on his own behalf, in the *Phenomenology*! But what Kojève *does* find there, which Fukuyama further develops, is a theoretical basis for thinking about the historical emergence of the concept of universal human rights.[6]

Fukuyama differs from Kojève, inasmuch as the latter saw no *fundamental* difference, in relation to the End of History, between the free-market capitalism of the cold-war West and the communism of the East: as both blocs equally appealed – even if perhaps with different emphases and with different degrees of hypocrisy – to universal human rights. It was just that appeal, in itself, which fascinated Kojève.[7] Fukuyama, by contrast, takes sides, with the West against the newly defeated East. He takes sides with Charter 77, for instance, as it campaigned against the Czech government on the basis of that government's being a signatory to the 1975 Helsinki Accords: urging compliance with Article VII in particular, which was precisely an affirmation of universal human rights.

Still, he does follow Kojève's reading of Hegel, and he does locate the beginning of the End of History in the same period, the same developments.

§

Fukuyama blithely ignores the postmodernist critique of grand narrative in the work of Lyotard and others. But his grand narrative is not manipulative in Marxist fashion. For whilst he fundamentally celebrates the End of History, as Marx does, he also introduces a qualifying critical note associated with Nietzsche's dismal notion of the 'last man'.

This engagement with Nietzsche arises out of Fukuyama's discussion of the Platonist notion of '*thymos*', 'spiritedness'. Thus, Plato in the *Republic* distinguishes between three 'parts' of the soul, three species of desire.[8] The first is *appetite*: immediate desire for material goods simply valued for their own sake, that is, hunger, thirst and everything akin. The second is *reason*: desire shaped by training, complex calculation, detached contemplative wisdom; hence, refined taste, strategic enterprise. The third is *thymos*. This includes all forms of desire informed by self-esteem. It is more urgently impassioned than the desire of pure reason; less immediate, more reflective, than crude appetite. Depending on the circumstances, *thymos* may manifest either as pride or as shame. Insofar as one does not feel one's own self-esteem to be matched by the esteem one receives from others, it becomes indignation. It may take shape as ambition; may be moralized, at one level, as a jealous concern for one's personal honour; or, at another level, may be sublated into all manner of fierce dedication to an ethical ideal.

Plato's concern, in the *Republic*, is with the potential usefulness of thymotic passion in the governance of the ideal state. The prime characteristic of those belonging to the sovereign class in this utopia is of course their philosophic rationality, but they will not be lacking in well-controlled *thymos*, by way of a supplement. And then the philosopher-rulers need *enforcers*: loyal military, loyal police, loyal lower-level administrators of every kind. In order that this loyalty be reinforced, there is needed a moral culture which infuses it with *thymos*. On the one hand, *thymos* has to be subordinated to reason; on the other hand, reason – struggling with the inertia of mere appetite in the population at large – has so far as possible to be allied with *thymos*. Fukuyama, however, inverts Plato's argument: inasmuch as he is concerned – not so much with the role of *thymos* in stiffening a system of rule – but rather, quite to the contrary, with *thymos* as a potential stimulus to justified rebellion, from below, *against* reactionary government. That is to say, precisely the elementary demand for freedom driving the revolutionary events of 1989.

He distinguishes two basic different forms of *thymos*; for which he coins the useful terms '*isothymia*' and '*megalothymia*'. *Isothymia*: the thymotic demand of the hitherto oppressed to be recognized as equal in proper dignity to their oppressors. *Megalothymia*: the thymotic claim of nonconformist individuals, as such, to have what they see as their own particular vocation in life duly respected.

When Hegel set out to develop a pioneering grand narrative of emergent 'freedom' – the progressive religious, political and philosophic rolling back of the 'lord / bondsman' relationship, along with everything deriving from it – what he intends is, in effect, nothing other than a comprehensive survey of *isothymia* at work. And the revolutionary events of 1989 might well be described, in essence, as a volcanic eruption of *isothymia*.

Václav Havel captures the suppressed simmering of this volcano, just prior to its eruption, in his parable of the greengrocer:

> The manager of a fruit and vegetable shop [somewhere in Communist Czechoslovakia] places in his window, among the onions and carrots, the slogan: 'Workers of the World, Unite!' Why does he do it? What is he trying to communicate to the world? Is he genuinely enthusiastic about the idea of unity among the workers of the world? Is his enthusiasm so great that he feels an irrepressible impulse to acquaint the public with his ideals? Has he really given more than a moment's thought to how such a unification might occur and what it would mean? …

Surely not! In reality, the greengrocer is addressing a message, first and foremost, to his immediate boss. He is saying:

> I, the greengrocer XY, live here and I know what I must do. I behave in the manner expected of me. I can be depended upon, and am beyond reproach. I am obedient and therefore I have a right to be left in peace.

But, of course, the message has to be encoded and delivered indirectly. For

> if the greengrocer had been instructed to display the slogan, "I am afraid and therefore unquestioningly obedient," he would not be nearly as indifferent to its semantics, even though the statement would reflect the truth. *The greengrocer would be embarrassed and ashamed to put such an unequivocal statement of his own degradation in the shop window, and quite naturally so, for he is a human being and thus has a sense of his own dignity.* To overcome this complication, his expression of loyalty must take the form of a sign which, at least on its textual surface, indicates a level of disinterested conviction. It must allow the greengrocer to say, "What's wrong with the workers of the world uniting?" Thus, the sign helps the greengrocer to conceal from himself the low foundations of his obedience, at the same time concealing the low foundations of power. It hides them behind the façade of something high.[9]

The greengrocer's hypothetical 'embarrassment' and 'shame', his underlying 'sense of his own dignity', are the work of *thymos* within him. And the 'something high' behind which he is hiding is, 'on its textual surface', an *isothymotic* ideology: the slogan he displays urges loyalty to a project theoretically promoting one particular strategic approach to universal human rights. But its true function is to help neutralize any actual *isothymotic* rebellion on the greengrocer's part, by obscuring – even as it confirms – his abjection. In this sense, Havel writes, he is 'living within a lie'.

Like all parables, although Havel does not use theological language, this is a picture of what it means for the kingdom of God to arrive; as the story ends with a reversal. So:

> Let us now imagine that one day something in our greengrocer snaps and he stops putting up the slogans merely to ingratiate himself. He stops voting in elections he knows are a farce. He begins to say what he really thinks at political meetings. And he even finds the strength in himself to express solidarity with those whom his conscience commands him to support. In this revolt the greengrocer steps out of living within the lie. He rejects the ritual and breaks the rules of the game. He discovers once more his suppressed identity and dignity. He gives his freedom a concrete significance. His revolt is an attempt to *live within the truth*.

In sharp contrast to the propaganda fiction of 'Workers of the World, Unite!' he is now committed to the solidarity of the shaken. Naturally, this being Communist Czechoslovakia, there is an immediate price to pay:

> He will be relieved of his post as manager of the shop and transferred to the warehouse. His pay will be reduced. His hope of a holiday in Bulgaria will evaporate ...[10]

But the greater the sacrifice, the clearer grows the moral authority of the now dissident greengrocer's testimony.

The End of History as envisaged by Kojève and Fukuyama is the enthroning of *isothymia* as prime inspiration of a globally dominant moral ideology. (The terminology is Fukuyama's, but the thought it serves to express is shared by both.) Only – what follows from that enthronement? Is it the sort of mere lip-service to *isothymia* represented by the little slogan in the still subservient greengrocer's window? Or is it the actual *isothymia* which was eventually to explode in the events of 1989? As I have said, the ironically, and provocatively, self-professed 'Stalinist' Kojève was quite blasé about the difference here; Fukuyama, by contrast, much less so. And at the same time Fukuyama is, also, much more ready openly to question shallower forms of *isothymia* in the name of *megalothymia*. He draws on Nietzsche to do so.

The key Nietzschean text in this regard is the Prologue to *Thus Spoke Zarathustra*. Like Jesus – but after ten years rather than just forty days – the bombastic prophet of Nietzsche's fantasy emerges from his desert retreat. Having been away for so long, he needs to re-learn some things that in his seclusion he had forgotten. And in the Prologue, he learns two immediate lessons. First, he encounters an old other-worldly saint, living in ascetic solitude, and praising God. Zarathustra is amazed: this man has not heard that God is dead! How could there still be such people? Then, secondly, he arrives in a town and starts to address the crowd in the market square. He delivers three discourses to them. The first two are lyrical celebrations of the *Übermensch*: the symbol precisely of *megalothymia* pushed to an ultimate extreme; wisdom understood as an ultra-individualistic sheer contempt for the human herd. Finally, in the third discourse, Zarathustra speaks of the 'last man', the most complete opposite to the *Übermensch*.

The 'last man' is the ultimate product of the End of History. *Isothymia* having triumphed, so decisively as to remove any perceived need for further struggle, the 'last man' is one in whom *thymos* itself has, largely, lapsed altogether. It is, as it were, burnt out. In the world of the 'last men', accordingly,

> Nobody grows rich or poor any more: both are too much of a burden. Who still wants to rule? Who obey? Both are too much of a burden.
>
> No herdsman and one herd. Everyone wants the same thing, everyone is the same: whoever thinks otherwise goes voluntarily into the madhouse.
>
> 'Formerly all the world was mad,' say the most acute of them and blink.
>
> They are clever and know everything that has ever happened: so there is no end to their mockery. They still quarrel, but they soon make up – otherwise indigestion would result.
>
> They have their little pleasure for the day and their little pleasure for the night: but they respect health.
>
> 'We have discovered happiness,' say [the Last Men] and blink.[11]

For Zarathustra this is a ghastly nightmare. But the crowd listening to him shouts out and interrupts: 'Give us this last man, O Zarathustra, make us into this last man! You can have the *Übermensch*!' And they laugh.

§

Fukuyama by no means goes all the way with Nietzsche. He is well aware of the dangers inherent in unchecked *megalothymia*; as Nietzsche seems not to be. After all, he has seen how Nietzsche's thought was co-opted into Nazi and Fascist propaganda, as mere flattery of the arrogant. Indeed, he remains, first and foremost, a celebrant of liberal-democratic *isothymia*. And yet he, so to speak, sprinkles a little Nietzschean *megalothymia* on top of his argument – by way of a spicy corrective.

I must say, I think it is good that he does so. For the propaganda-ethos of liberal democracy surely always *is* all too liable to incubate complacent banality. And whilst the danger of unchecked *isothymia*, its proneness to degenerate into mere herd morality, is far milder than the danger of unchecked *megalothymia* – as this, by contrast, allies itself to the ethos of gang (a)morality – it is clear that a world of 'last men', as portrayed by Nietzsche, would scarcely manage to rise to the unprecedented challenges of twenty-first-century human survival. Thus, Fukuyama's invocation of Nietzsche does, in my view, add a certain necessary extra level of nuance to his conception of the End of History.

Nevertheless, I would argue, there still remains one rather large area of unfortunate fuzziness in Fukuyama's analysis as a whole. Namely: *his view of religion*.

Fukuyama presents his view of religion as the Hegelian view. But it is not! Rather, it is a rehashed and somewhat toned-down version of Kojève's interpretation of Hegel on religion, and this is in fact a gross *mis*-interpretation. Kojève's interpretation has pedigree: it belongs to the tradition stemming from Feuerbach. It brings Hegel quite close to Nietzsche. However, it drastically oversimplifies, and misses what, to my mind, is of real interest here. What the Hegelian grand narrative tracks is the evolution of a core existential truth-'content' which remains deeply religious to the end. I will come back to this at greater length in Chapter 8. Suffice to say here: the evolution in question accomplishes a greatly deepened awareness of the intrinsic *ambivalence* of religious thinking, as a 'form' for that 'content'; but the religious 'form' still continues to be necessary, alongside the philosophic 'form', in order to disseminate their shared 'content' as widely and as powerfully as possible. Thus, the essential inter-relationship of religious 'form' and existential 'content', in itself, abides, whilst what changes is just how it is appreciated, theoretically. Kojève distorts this, inasmuch as *his* 'Hegel' sees religion in general, and Christianity in particular, as being simply superseded by philosophy. The cult of Napoleon, as a sort of secularizing messiah, which Kojève attributes to 'Hegel', is nowhere to be found in Hegel's actual writings. Instead, Hegel sees 'modernity', the third and culminating epoch of 'the Germanic world', as being inaugurated by quite a different figure:

a simple monk who was conscious that [the authentically sacred] is to be found in the deepest recesses of the heart, in the absolute ideality of inwardness, who was clearly aware of present conditions, and whose deepest heart was distressed by the distortion of the truth.[12]

Namely: the pugnacious *theologian*, Martin Luther.

According to Kojève's 'Hegel', in Fukuyama's words, Christianity plays a key progressive role in Universal History inasmuch as

> the Christian God *recognizes* all human beings universally, recognizes their individual human worth and dignity. The Kingdom of Heaven, in other words, presents the prospect of a world in which the *isothymia* of every man – though not the *megalothymia* of the vainglorious – will be satisfied.

And yet (Fukuyama goes on) the immediate theological form of Christian faith also irrecoverably distorts this promise. For

> the problem with Christianity ... is that it remains just another slave ideology, that is, it is untrue in certain crucial respects. Christianity posits the realization of human freedom not here on earth but only in the Kingdom of Heaven [understood in quite other-worldly terms]. Christianity, in other words, had the right *concept* of freedom, but ended up reconciling real-world slaves to their lack of freedom by telling them not to expect liberation in this life. According to Hegel, the Christian did not realize that God did not create man, but rather that man had created God. He created God as a kind of projection of the idea of freedom, for in the Christian God we see a being who is the perfect master of himself and of nature. But the Christian then proceeded to enslave himself to this God that he himself created. He reconciled himself to a life of slavery on earth in the belief that he would be redeemed later by God, when in fact he could be his own redeemer. Christianity was thus a form of *alienation*, that is, a new form of slavery where man enslaved himself to something that he himself created, thereby becoming divided against himself.[13]

An admirably crisp little summary – but very misleading! For Fukuyama is clearly thinking here of Kojève's rather brisk reading of the passage in the *Phenomenology of Spirit* discussing '*das unglückliche Bewußtsein*'; literally translatable as 'the Unhappy Consciousness' (although I prefer 'the Unatoned State of Mind').[14] This, though, is not a discussion of Christianity *per se*, at all. It is illustrated by allusions to Christian history. What these allusions however serve to illustrate is a very widespread corruption which is by no means confined to Christianity; that indeed is *why* they are only allusions. At this stage of the *Phenomenology* Hegel is discussing purely trans-cultural phenomena. By '*das unglückliche Bewußtsein*' Hegel means the mentality of *any* rigidified self-righteousness; *any* dogmatic mere repression of questioning thought; *any* appeal to supposedly sacred principle, designed to vindicate inner servility. It is in fact just what the truth of the Christian gospel, in his view, *overthrows*. Only, the point is to recognize its slipperiness. It can never be simply expelled. This is a corruption which is forever liable to affect not only every form of belief in God, but also, in principle, every form of non-theistic religion, every form of atheist ideology still appealing to sacred principles as such. The only truly effective prophylactic against it is to hold nothing sacred. But then that, for Hegel, is just another form of corruption: the principled frivolity of nihilistic 'scepticism'.

Hegel illustrates his discussion of *das unglückliche Bewußtsein* with allusions to Christian history just because he himself remains a devout (not just a pretend) Christian. As a Christian philosopher, he seeks to highlight the ineradicable ambiguity of orthodox faith: both its essential truth-potential, as therapy for this corruption, yet also its continual liability to re-corruption by the very ill that it is in principle intended to cure. It is not 'Christianity' that Hegel is talking about in the passage Fukuyama intends; it is, on the contrary, the most basic potential corruption of the sacred in any form, including (even) the Christian form. Nor, though, does Hegel consider it a simple matter to distinguish true Christianity from its corruption. On the contrary, he is intent on the most searching possible corporate self-criticism; criticism from within. This ambivalence is what renders him so very much more interesting, as a religious thinker, than his professed 'radicalizer' Feuerbach, for instance. Kojève, in representing him as a mere proto-Feuerbachian atheist, misses the point entirely; and here, alas, is Fukuyama following suit.

Let us go back to Jan Patočka. In a short text drafted shortly before his death, and dated the actual day of the launch of Charter 77, Patočka writes:

> If human development is to match the possibilities of technical, instrumental reason, if a progress of knowledge is to be possible, humankind needs to be convinced of the unconditional validity of principles which are, in that sense, "sacred," valid for all humans and at all times, and capable of setting out humanity's goals. We need, in other words, something that in its very essence is not technological, something that is not merely instrumental: we need a morality that is not merely tactical and situational but absolute.[15]

I am embarking on an essay in grand narrative, precisely tracking the emergent ideal of the solidarity of the shaken as a *sacred* principle. I think that this will, of necessity, involve far more of a concern with the history of religious thought than is evident in Fukuyama's work. For it is in dialogue with traditional religion that a feeling for the sacred is rendered imaginatively richest; poetically most vivid. It will in fact involve a sustained probing at the problematics of *das unglückliche Bewußtsein*, as evidenced by that history. For what else, after all, is the solidarity of the shaken if not the actual practice required in order that we should be healed from *das unglückliche Bewußtsein*?

Synopsis

Had not the good people at Bloomsbury Publishing deemed it too cryptic (no doubt they are right) I would have called this book '*A Moment and Its Meaning*'. The historic 'moment' in question being the weeks leading up to early January 1990, in Central Europe. And the 'meaning', how that 'moment' properly appears in grand-narrative perspective.

But, rather than the cryptic, the ostensibly oxymoronic. I have ended up, instead, with a paradox: '*Apocalyptic Patience*'. We are so used to associating the 'apocalyptic' with prophecies of supposedly imminent cataclysmic events; a genre of thinking in which the evocation of moral urgency jostles with panic; and hence with the very utmost prophetic *im*-patience. Yet, the original meaning of the Greek term '*apokalypsis*' is, simply, 'revelation': the historic rendered transparent to the eternal; in other words, theological grand narrative, in general. And not *all* such grand narrative need be panicky.

On the contrary, I want to argue that appropriate patience is a basic virtue of any truly good grand-narrative thought. Indeed, the story that I want to tell has, in essence, to do with a progressive overcoming of pathological im-patience, chiefly in two distinct forms. On the one hand, that form of impatience which constitutes the chief blockage to the solidarity of the shaken within Abrahamic religious tradition: namely '*evangelistic impatience*'. And on the other hand, that form of impatience which constitutes the most sophisticated distraction, obstructing the articulation of the solidarity of the shaken in secular, trans-confessional terms: namely, '*philosophic impatience*'. The kingdom of God / solidarity of the shaken is, as I would see it, *ultimately* a twofold achievement of patience; patient openness to the as-yet-unthought, un-ventured, on both sides of the equation between the two concepts. What I am attempting here, in short, is nothing less than a systematic account of the tremendous potential power – for both good and evil – of faith in God, a suggested mapping of its whole force-field; as illuminated by a commitment to such patience.

The argument falls into three Parts. *Part One* is an initial expansion of the equation at the heart of it: the solidarity of the shaken = the kingdom of God. So, Chapter 1 focuses on the theoretical context of Jan Patočka's conception of the solidarity of the shaken, in his *Heretical Essays on the Philosophy of History*. And Chapter 2 discusses the genealogy of the concept of the kingdom of God, tracing its origins back to the properly *historical* (i.e. non-legendary) eighth century BCE source of Abrahamic religious tradition, the moment it becomes something quite different in kind from the other sacred cults of the time. Here is the beginning of the grand narrative with which I am concerned; extending Patočka's grand narrative, jumping yet deeper into history.

And then there comes another jump. (Grand narrative, in general, is an art of intellectual leaping and bounding, between linked, but often very diverse topics.) The equation, the kingdom of God = the solidarity of the shaken, is already latent, as a possibility, in the origins of Abrahamic tradition. But the disease of evangelistic impatience conceals it. (Note: I say 'evangelistic' here, not 'evangelical'. This is not a partisan argument ...) In *Part Two* I discuss two strands within the tradition which, I think, may very well be regarded as originating in critical response to evangelistic impatience, a desire to counter its malign effects; and so as anticipatory, albeit incomplete, contributions to the sacralization of the solidarity of the shaken. Namely: *'mystical theology'* and *'gnosticism'*.

However, these are still confessional modes of thought, and the solidarity of the shaken is a purely *trans*-confessional ideal. It transcends the solidarity of the faithful, as such. And so, in order for it to be fully conceptualized, in itself, it requires the development of an appropriate, autonomously philosophic milieu. This is what I mean by *'ethical phenomenology'*; the main topic of *Part Three*. Only, I want to argue: the solidarity of the shaken, in its equation with the kingdom of God, still remains a sacred ideal, which therefore requires – even as it transcends confessional boundaries – maximum integration into the devotional life of authentically (small 'c') catholic, that is, ideally isothymotic religious communities; whichever, in any particular case, is nearest to hand. But in order for this to be possible everything depends on philosophy being healed of its own endemic disease of philosophic impatience. Just as evangelistic impatience exalts solidarity among orthodox believers to the exclusion of the solidarity of the shaken, so philosophic impatience exalts the solidarity of an intellectual elite, as such, to equivalently exclusive effect. And 'ethical phenomenology', then, is a name for the prime contemporary context, within philosophy, for tackling this disease.

'Mystical theology' / 'gnosticism' / 'ethical phenomenology': the story towards which I am edging juxtaposes these heterogeneous elements. It is an attempt to think them, notwithstanding their heterogeneity, systematically together.

Part Two, thus, sketches a twofold traditional resistance, *within* Abrahamic religion, to evangelistic impatience inasmuch as the impatient evangelist is naturally tempted to exploit potential converts' appetite (a) for cheap certainty, and (b) for wish-fulfilling, distorted conceptions of divine almightiness. Mystical theology critically confronts the former appetite; gnosticism, the latter appetite. These are very different strategies, seldom if ever combined, and yet I would suggest that, deep down, both alike are modes of resurgent shaken-ness, challenging the typically rigidified, narrow dogmatism of evangelistic impatience. In Chapter 3, I present mystical theology in this light, with particular reference to the pseudonymous, probably Syrian, late fifth- or early sixth-century writer Saint *'Dionysius the Areopagite'* who coined the term; its origins in the pagan Neo-Platonist tradition whose greatest figure was *Plotinus* (c. 204–70 CE); its Christian culmination in the thought of *Meister Eckhart* (c. 1260–c. 1328); and then, by way of contrast, the work of the great proto-Sufi poet *Muhammad ibn ʿAbd al-Jabbaar ibn al-Hasan an-Niffarí* (died c. 965). In Chapter 4, I trace what I argue is the decline of 'mystical theology' proper into the various later phenomena self-designated as 'mysticism'. And in Chapter 5, I present my general hypothesis regarding 'gnosticism', with a particular focus on its least sectarian forms: the *Kabbalist tradition* within Judaism and the maverick Christian thought of *Jakob Böhme* (1575–1624).

In Part Three, on the other hand, I am concerned with a set of philosophic initiatives emergent within post-Enlightenment secularity. My starting point here is what I term ethical 'pathos of shaken-ness', as something abstractly considered, in the sense of not yet being incorporated into any organized solidarity strategy: for instance, in the thought of *Søren Kierkegaard, Emmanuel Levinas*, and *Knud Løgstrup*. This is the topic of Chapter 6. After which, in Chapter 7, I go on to confront the problematics – with regard to solidarity-building – of philosophic impatience, at its most sophisticated; the way that such impatience tends, quite dogmatically, to preclude any true participation by philosophers in the properly catholic (isothymotic) religious matrix for solidarity of the shaken. *Martin Heidegger* is a prime, tragic twentieth-century example. But I also discuss *Leo Strauss*'s admiration for Heidegger – Strauss, playful advocate of 'Platonist philosophic politics' – even as Heidegger, the great critic of Plato, recoils after the debacle of 1933–4 into a professedly altogether a-political outlook. What these two thinkers nonetheless have in common is, in my terms, precisely a radical identification of the highest wisdom with the most intransigent, pure philosophic impatience; such impatience at its most seductive. And then, as well – for a counter-balance to the right-wing philosophic impatience of Heidegger and Strauss – I consider *Theodor Adorno*'s, likewise seductive, left-wing version of the same. Against all three, I appeal in the first instance to *Hannah Arendt*'s very different reading of the lessons in twentieth-century history; her anti-Platonist, but equally anti-Heideggerian, and anti-Marxist, revindication of 'isonomous' politics.

Finally, in Chapter 8 I go on to consider *Hegel*'s systematic project of reconciling philosophy with (again, small 'c') catholic religion. My own point of view, as elaborated here, may well be termed 'neo-Hegelian'. Albeit – as I, in conclusion, go on to discuss – in some ways *very* 'neo'! But how, after all, could it be otherwise; in view of the accumulated historical experience of the intervening two centuries … ?

Part I

THE TWO SIDES OF THE EQUATION

Chapter 1

THE SOLIDARITY OF THE SHAKEN: JAN PATOČKA'S ARGUMENT

The Heretical Essays

Jan Patočka's major work, in which he introduces the concept of the 'solidarity of the shaken', is entitled *Heretical Essays in the Philosophy of History*; completed in 1975, and at first privately circulated in samizdat form around what was shortly afterwards to evolve into the Charter 77 sub-culture.[1] It is, itself, a series of essays in grand narrative: ironically 'heretical', by the standards of the orthodox Marxist grand narrative constituting the official ideology of the ruling Czechoslovak Communist Party. Not that he, for his part, had ever professed to be any sort of a Marxist. There is nothing sectarian about his 'heresy'. To the contrary!

It contains six essays. By 'history' here Patočka does not just mean everything that has ever happened in the human past. But in Essay One he begins to clarify what he does mean, by discussing what, significantly, is *not* 'history': (a) the non-historic '*natural world*', that is, the ever-abiding background to history; (b) the world of *pre-history*, as recorded in ancient annals, or reflected in ancient myths. So, how is that which belongs to 'history' properly to be differentiated from its background in the natural world? And at what exact point does 'history' proper emerge from pre-history? In Lecture One, Patočka suggests an initial answer to these questions with reference to Heidegger on 'openness': 'history' for him, by definition, begins precisely where an accentuated 'openness' of thought starts to render the world 'problematic'. It is the rendering 'problematic' of what had previously been each individual's straightforward communion with their ancestors; of the straightforward immortality that consists in membership of species and tribe; of the straightforward closed-down sacredness of what is customary *merely as such*.

In Essay Two, he goes on to elaborate upon this. He begins from a doctrine that he had already developed in several previous writings: a distinction between what he calls the 'three fundamental movements of human life'.[2] First, he argues, there is the movement of '*acceptance*'. Here we have that basic orientation to the past with which the very earliest notions of the sacred are exclusively preoccupied: a cultivated sense of belonging; being rooted in a tradition; both accepting it and being accepted into it. This first movement, of course, persists into historical religion; but it is not yet, in itself, necessarily historical. Then, there is the second movement, which he calls the movement of '*defence*'. Primarily oriented to the present, this is the impulse to defend one's community against immediate threats. Like the movement of acceptance, again, the movement of defence is also a prime source of morality. Another name for it, Patočka remarks, might be 'the movement of self-surrender'; inasmuch as the defence of the community essentially involves each individual member, wherever necessary, working for the common good. And yet, neither is this second movement – any more than the first – what makes history historical. But, rather: history arises from a fundamental transformation of the twofold morality deriving from acceptance and defence, by the outworking of another, third movement, which is equally beyond them both. Thus, what generates history, in the strict sense, is an impulse no longer simply confined to the sacredness of the past, or to the needs of the present; but, on the contrary, fundamentally opened up to the future, in a way that calls into question all traditional understandings, not only of that sacredness but also of those needs. He calls it, simply, the movement of '*truth*'.

As a philosopher, Patočka is especially interested in the breakthrough-moment marked by the original emergence of philosophy, culminating in the work of Plato. However, he couples the breakthrough of philosophy with the contemporary, purely *political* ethos of Ancient Athenian democracy; or, better, 'isonomy'. That is, the celebration of free-spirited civic activism, as the very noblest of vocations. He alludes, here, to Hannah Arendt. Not that he altogether follows Arendt, as she polemically advocates the ethos of isonomous politics *as opposed to* that of philosophy, in general; thereby reversing the traditional philosophic privileging of the contemplative over the active life.[3] Nevertheless, he is quite strikingly critical of his two prime philosophic mentors, Husserl and Heidegger: inasmuch as, whereas both Husserl and Heidegger 'speak of philosophy *alone* as the starting point and, in a sense, the core of history', he does not.[4] Indeed, he is clear that he, for his part, is advocating a 'deeply different' conception of history from theirs. For Husserl had discussed the philosophy of history, in his unfinished 1936 work *The Crisis of European Sciences and Transcendental Phenomenology*, solely in terms of the history of philosophy.[5] And whereas, like Heidegger, Patočka reaches back behind Plato to engage with Herakleitos, there is a sense in which he does so in a yet more radically anti-Platonist way. For as an advocate of the solidarity of the shaken he is decisively emancipated – as Heidegger after all is not – from the age-old confusion between philosophy as love of wisdom and philosophy as ideology of the educationally privileged; the class-ideology of solidarity *among philosophers* as such that Leo Strauss celebrated as 'Platonist' politics.

I have discussed this elsewhere.[6] And, as I have said, I will also come back to the issues illustrated by the Heidegger / Strauss relationship in Chapter 7.

Herakleitos however, for Patočka, represents a form of philosophy still untainted by that confusion, which only emerges later; classically, in Plato's work. So, for instance, consider his dictum:

We need to know that *polemos* [literally, war] is *xunos* [what is common], and that *eris* [literally, conflict] is *diké* [the right], and that everything takes place through *eris* and its impetus.[7]

For Herakleitos, *xunos* ['what is common'] means something like the universal truth, beyond merely subjective opinion; or, precisely, the proper basis for an ideal form of solidarity.[8] In what sense can this, then, be identified with *polemos*? Surely, in the same sense that 'the right' is identifiable with *eris*: in this context, '*polemos*' and '*eris*' are precisely two terms for the process of being *shaken* – by whatever means – into critical thought, a fundamental revaluation of values. (They are indeed names for what Hegel calls '*Geist*', 'Spirit', in its character as sheer dialectical energy, or the power of the negative, considered in the most general terms.) As Patočka puts it:

> *polemos* is at the same time [both] that which constitutes the *polis* and the primordial insight which makes philosophy possible.[9]

Herakleitos is thinking *equally*, Patočka suggests, of the lively public exchange of ideas among the free-spirited citizens of an isonomous *polis*, and of the all-questioning process of philosophical enquiry. In which case, he goes on,

> *Polemos* is not the destructive passion of a wild brigand but is, rather, the creator of unity. The unity it founds is more profound than any ephemeral sympathy or coalition of interests; adversaries meet in the shaking of a given meaning, and so create a new way of being human – perhaps the only mode that offers hope amid the storm of the world: the unity of the shaken but undaunted.
>
> Thus Herakleitos sees the unity and the common origin of philosophy and the *polis*.
>
> [And] therewith the question of the origin of history seems decided.[10]

'History' proper, for Patočka, originates in the beginnings of the process that will eventually unfold towards a real solidarity of the shaken, as such; wherever those beginnings are to be found. Solidarity of the shaken partly coincides with solidarity among true philosophers, inasmuch as philosophy is one channel for shaken thought; but is, at the same time, also a much broader, more catholic ideal. It is indeed quite distinct from any solidarity among philosophers merely on the basis of their shared self-interest, as an educational elite class.

Essay Three, then, is framed as a discussion of the basic question: 'Does history have a meaning?' Patočka's answer, already implicit in his discussion of historical origins, is clearly going to be yes. But let us be clear about the exact meaning of 'meaning' in this case. 'History', as he puts it, 'differs from prehistoric humanity *by the shaking of accepted meaning*'.[11] This very much includes the continual shaking of accepted ideas about the meaning of history. Such shaken-ness elicits ideological resistances: modes of dogmatism, which are in essence an expression of wilful inertia; bids to subdue the intrinsic negativity of history. As the *polis*-ethos, philosophy's original partner, runs out of energy, philosophy itself starts to mutate into metaphysical dogma. The competing schools launched by Plato, Démokritos, and then also Aristotle no longer represent pure disciplines of shaken-ness; they become battle-grounds, between conservatives seeking, in general, to hold 'accepted meaning' firm and critics (those whom Hegel, in general, calls 'stoics' and 'sceptics') regarded by the conservatives as nihilists. And neither are those critics, yet, true thinkers of the solidarity of the shaken, since they uphold no real principle of organized solidarity. Later on, again, in the context of the Roman Empire, the dogmatic ideology of Christendom becomes a grand-narrative-shaped force of repression, subduing the initial history-intensifying power-to-shake of the Christian gospel. And then, in the wake of the Enlightenment, there appear a range of 'scientific', secular successor-ideologies to that of Christendom, similarly repressive of genuine open-mindedness; notably including, for example, vulgar Marxism. All the while, though, the history-driving energies of, in Heraklitean terms, *polemos* and *eris* are constantly at work, dissolving what these dogmatisms seek to construct. For Patočka, on the other hand, it is clear, the true ideal consists *neither* in any would-be history-subduing dogma – *nor* in mere dogmatic nihilism, affirming ultimate meaninglessness – but, rather, in something altogether more demanding than either. Thus, as he puts it:

> From this perspective, history would not [after all] represent the gradual unfolding of the meaninglessness of the universe, at least not necessarily, and [notwithstanding all its negativity] it might perhaps even be possible for humankind to bring about a meaningful existence consistent with it – [if only] on condition of a gigantic conversion, or of an unheard-of *metanoein*.[12]

What is required is, thus, nothing less than a 'gigantic conversion': *from fearing shaken-ness – to embracing, and honouring it.* 'Actually', he writes,

> we are dealing only with the uncovering of meaning that can never be explained as a thing [in the sense that a dogma is a 'thing'], which cannot [in other words] be mastered, delimited, grasped positively, and dominated, but which is present only in the *seeking* of being.[13]

And for him this 'uncovering' is, indeed, precisely the very definition of what, in principle, we ought to hold sacred.

At the beginning of Essay Four he cites Hegel; on the lost, because no longer effective, 'holiness' of the Holy Roman Empire; an institution still lingering on into the period of Hegel's youth, but only as a manifestly lost cause.[14] For Hegel, the question was, how to find some new, more workable expression for the underlying ideal which had foundered here? That is: the ideal of a more than merely small-town political culture, truly capable of inspiring loyalty, not just as a channelling of economic self-interest but, on the contrary, as representing a real, corporate quest for moral truth. And Patočka – citizen of Prague, that great historic city of the Holy Roman Empire – also endorses this. Trapped within the stagnant (post)-totalitarianism of the Brezhnev-era Soviet Empire, he conjures up a glittering counter-ideal of 'Europe'.[15] This is not just the neo-liberal, bureaucratic ethos of the European Union. But it is 'Europe' as a culture essentially dedicated to 'care for the soul'.[16] By 'care for the soul', or 'the care to *be*' (i.e. to be what one is inwardly called to be) he means an ideal partly grounded in philosophy, and partly in Christian faith; but essentially embattled, today, against a rival impulse, largely stemming as he sees it from the sixteenth century, which he calls 'the care to *have*', or 'care for the external world and its conquest', the dominant tendency of the secular world as such, at its most civilized, alike on either side of the Iron Curtain.[17]

I say 'at its most civilised' – for at least, on the other hand, the 'care to have', in itself, remains a principle of sober rationality. There are also far worse possibilities than this, which have, of course, become quite spectacularly manifest in the twentieth century. And Essays Five and Six, next, bring to the fore the ultimate phenomena of twentieth-century 'decadence'.

Thus, Essay Five defines the term. 'Decadence', for Patočka, is first and foremost a general name for what is generated by *boredom*, at its most malign. It is an essentially *escapist* impulse. To go back to his analysis of the 'three fundamental movements of human life', what 'decadent' culture offers is, in the first instance, sheer escape from the humdrum monotony so often involved in the necessary movement of '*defence*': 'the everyday', the world of 'forced labour'. On the one hand, it is thus a wholesale flight from that profane reality: a plunging into the orgiastic, the demonic, the drugged, the deeper reaches of Plato's cave, in the *Republic*; where all real responsibility is abrogated. On the other hand, it is, at the same time, just as much a basic refusal to engage with the authentically sacred – that is, what is generated, first, by the movement of '*acceptance*' and then, more or less transfigured, by the movement of '*truth*'. Indeed, the authentically sacred is essentially medicine against decadence. In prehistoric cultures, this medicine is derived from the movement of 'acceptance' as mediated by communion with the ancestors. Later, more truly historical cultures, insofar as they are governed by 'care for the soul', rightly identify the sacred with the movement of 'truth' deriving from moments of shaken-ness. But 'decadent' cultures, by contrast, are not motivated by any of the three 'movements of life'. They are, on the contrary, dedicated to that which is most *deadly* for the soul. In such self-indulgent cultures there is neither 'acceptance' nor 'truth': that is, neither any genuine, rooted continuity from the past, nor any authentic, future-oriented open-mindedness. But, insofar as the spirit of 'decadence' finally prevails, it gives rise to a savage cult of 'Force', and a correspondingly ruthless practice of propaganda; more or less mixed with the basic technocratic 'care to have', systematically exalted over any 'care of the soul'. In short, it becomes totalitarian.

And yet, there is a sense in which, the worse things get, the greater the actual chance for the 'gigantic conversion' of which Patočka dreams; or at any rate some real movement towards it, by way of revulsion.

Essay Six, finally, is concerned with that countervailing chance. This Essay is entitled 'Wars of the Twentieth Century and the Twentieth Century as War'. And underlying the argument is a basic contrast between two possible approaches, initially to the interpretation of the First World War, and then also to the interpretation of all the other conflicts flowing from that catastrophe, right down to 1975, when Patočka was actually writing. In the first place, there are all those interpretations that are essentially framed in terms of conventional, party-political ideology: nationalist, fascist, liberal, socialist, communist – the whole spectrum, including every mixture and variation. These he groups together as interpretations according to the values of '*the day*'. Such thinking, in general – inasmuch as it is largely designed for propaganda purposes – tends to invoke a banal and sentimental prospect of 'progress'; represented in terms designed to stir up relatively unthinking popular enthusiasm for governmental, or oppositional, projects. And it is, from the outset therefore, quite unfitted to learn anything, of any real value, from the actual, difficult realities in question. But then, by contrast to this, there is another depth of thinking, truly opened up towards the revelatory actuality of 'war and death': a meditation on twentieth-century history, far rather, as 'an epoch of *the night*'.

So, thinking of the government propaganda on both sides of the First World War, Patočka remarks:

> It was the forces of the day which for four years sent millions of humans into hellfire.[18]

And, reflecting on the post-war peace movement, he sees it as an essentially ambivalent phenomenon. For whilst, at one level, it represented at least a glimpse of 'something "eschatological", something like the end of all the values of the day' – at another, once again altogether more propagandist level, it also '[bent] eschatology back to the "mundane" level, and [used] in the service of the day what [properly] belonged to the night and to eternity'.[19]

Everything, he argues, depends upon our learning – on the contrary – to remain absolutely faithful to the revelation, here, belonging 'to the night and to eternity'. In other words: to the intense sheer shaking-power inherent in the remembered 1914–18 '*experience of the front*'.

> The grandiose, profound experience of the front with its line of fire [he writes] consists in its evocation of the night in all its urgency and undeniability.[20]

Indeed,

> The motives of the day which had [on the contrary] evoked the will to war are consumed in the furnace of the front line, if that experience is intense enough that it will not yield again to the forces of the day. Peace transformed into a will to war could objectify and externalize humans as long as they were ruled by the day, by the hope of everydayness, of a profession, of a career, simply possibilities

for which they must fear and which feel threatened. Now, however, comes the upheaval, shaking that peace and its planning, its programmes and its ideas of progress indifferent to mortality. All everydayness, all visions of future life pale before the simple peak on which [the exalted front-line combatants] find themselves standing. In face of that, all the ideas of socialism, of progress, of democratic spontaneity, of independence and freedom appear impoverished, neither viable nor tangible.[21]

This is 'the night' he means: finding oneself stranded in a place of darkness where *propaganda* can, quite simply, no longer function; inasmuch as all the all-too-obvious 'day-time' prejudices to which it appeals, and on which it depends, have ceased to shine.

But he asks:

Why has this grandiose experience, [of the sort that is] alone capable of leading humankind out of war into a true peace, *not* [in actual fact] had a decisive effect on the history of the twentieth century, even though humans have been exposed to it twice for four years [*sic*], and were truly touched and transformed thereby?[22]

Why is there not more evidence of the 'gigantic conversion' actually beginning, that such trauma, in principle, helps make possible? In particular, he wonders, why is there not yet an altogether more effective challenge to the 'smouldering' persistence of the Cold War? Well, he himself was just about to help launch just such a challenge, in Prague. Nevertheless, the question remains. It is the challenge with which, above all, he wishes to leave us.

Charter 77 had not yet been launched; yet already Patočka is pondering the ideal ethos of such a movement. Again, he asks:

How can the 'front-line experience' acquire the form that would make it a factor of history? Why is it not [yet] becoming that?[23]

He has illustrated the 'front-line experience' with particular reference, as it happens, to the testimony of two First World War soldiers: the French Jesuit priest and theologian, Pierre Teilhard de Chardin and the German literary philosopher Ernst Jünger. However, he remarks, the trouble is that, in the form described by Teilhard and Jünger, this experience still remains so very much a phenomenon of private subjectivity. It is an experience of shaken *individuals*, as such – those who have been 'shaken in their faith in the day', that is, radically liberated from any worldview compatible with propagandist norms – only, without as yet any corresponding form of organized solidarity.[24] In the end, the need is for actual *movements* embodying the solidarity of the shaken.

Such movements will necessarily be limited in their practical ambitions. At most, perhaps,

> the solidarity of the shaken can say "no" to the measures of mobilization which make the state of war permanent. It will not offer detailed positive programmes for government but will speak, like Socrates' *daimonion*, far rather in warnings and prohibitions. It can and must create a spiritual authority, become a spiritual power that could drive the warring world to some restraint, rendering some acts and measures impossible.[25]

Charter 77, for its part, offered no 'positive programme': it was a human rights campaign, not an embryo political party. But, just by virtue of that restraint, it was able to recruit all sorts of Czech and Slovak individuals, united simply in their desire for open political debate, of which they were deprived. It really did represent something like an all-encompassing solidarity of the shaken, in that context. The solidarity of the *shaken*: again, be it noted, not just of *philosophers*. Patočka is very clear about the desirability of including the widest possible range of people. He especially aspires to reach out to

> the 'technical intelligentsia' ... researchers and those who apply research, inventors and engineers ... [t]o shake the everydayness of the fact-crunchers and routine minds, to make them aware that their place is on the side of *the front* and not on the side of even the most pleasing slogans of the day which in reality call to war, whether they invoke the nation, the state, classless society, world unity, or whatever ... [26]

However, Charter 77 was, in the event, a movement which derived tremendous energy from its quite *unconditional* openness, and general inclusiveness.

§

Indeed, Charter 77 was a singularly pure embodiment of the solidarity of the shaken. Its participants had just two things in common: they were all citizens of Czechoslovakia; and they were the people, in that society, who *cared* enough to take action, calling for freedom of debate, freedom of artistic expression, freedom of religion. Had the regime been *fully* totalitarian, as it had been in the 1950s, and not just the decaying 'post-totalitarian' monster that it actually was, the movement would have been crushed altogether, from the outset. Had the regime been more liberal, the moral energy concentrated here would have been dissipated, into dozens of different political enterprises. (As, in fact, happened after 1989.)

The solidarity of the shaken is the least *natural* of solidarities. It is far easier to organize solidarity on the basis of shared belonging to a particular nation, a particular place, a particular ethnicity, a particular linguistic group, a particular gender-identity, a particular socio-economic category; sharing in a particular orthodoxy, political or religious.

This is why the solidarity of the shaken needs its own grand narrative. It needs a grand narrative in the same way that an individual person needs a life-story, establishing their identity. The role of such grand narrative is to give the solidarity of the shaken a definite shape in corporate memory; and so, to reinforce it, hopefully render it more resilient. It is not dependent on any particular *version* of its grand narrative. The grand narrative may be philosophically and/or theologically sophisticated; it may be quite crude. Never mind. What is ideally required is just a great multi-cultural confluence of different versions.

On the other hand: because the solidarity of the shaken is so difficult to organize, it also tends to be ephemeral. And this is indeed a problem. *Therefore, it surely does need, so far as possible, to be grafted into the much more durable solidarity of a stable, deep-rooted popular culture of the sacred.* From a philosophic point of view, any such culture will do. Let it be whatever is most readily to hand.

As for Patočka himself: he was not a religious man. He was never, in fact, a member of any church. His biographer Erazim Kohák notes that 'in the 1950s ... he is said to have come close to joining the Czech Brethren Protestant Church ... [And] again, in the 1970s, [he] is said to have come close to a formal conversion to Catholicism ... Yet [he] never took the formal step of a conversion, and, in a private lecture he gave in 1974, "Christianity and the 'Natural' World", he lets the hearer know why: his pre-reflective life-world, the "natural" world of his life, simply did not include the experience of God'.[27] At the heart of Essay Five in the *Heretical Essays*, however, is an enigmatic passage discussing the historic achievements of Christianity. Christian faith, Patočka argues, represents not only an effective popularization, but also an 'abysmal deepening' of the Platonic notion of the soul.[28] Thus, 'Christianity remains thus far the greatest, unsurpassed but also un-thought-through human outreach that enabled humans to struggle against decadence'.[29]

And note also the argument of a paper he delivered at an international philosophical congress held at the Black Sea resort of Varna, in Bulgaria, in 1973. Although Patočka was already at that point under close surveillance by the secret police, he was rather surprisingly allowed to leave Czechoslovakia, to attend this Communist Party supervised congress. (A lapse, it seems, on the part of authorities.) But that he was only allowed to deliver one small part of the paper, and that it was excluded from the subsequently published proceedings of the conference, is less surprising.

The paper is scholarly, yet really quite daring in the circumstances. It is entitled 'The Dangers of Technicisation in Science according to E. Husserl and the Essence of Technology as Danger according to M. Heidegger'.[30] In it, Patočka actually tackles two main themes. First, the double theme advertised in the title: (a) Husserl's insistence on the need for an intellectual culture that maintains a real, critical independence from the ethos of technocracy; (b) Heidegger's incorporation of the same sort of critical concern into a larger vision of history. The 'danger' in question here is essentially the sheer banality of spirit promoted by the economic dynamics of industrial mass society; the malignity of which is indeed at work in both totalitarian and liberal-democratic societies, but most of all in the former. And then, secondly, the paper also addresses the theme of 'sacrifice': both the involuntary sacrifice of the economically exploited – or of those who suffer as victims of modern high-tech warfare – and also the voluntary sacrifice of those who rise up in resistance, precisely, to the general 'danger' he has been discussing.

This was written before the launch of Charter 77. Nevertheless, Patočka is clearly already thinking of the prospective sacrifices liable to be involved in any such dissident project. And then he very briefly turns towards theology. He observes the singular radicality of that form of voluntary sacrifice, which, in its purest form, serves no merely 'technical' or utilitarian purpose – but, on the contrary, is motivated by a spirit of protest, precisely, against the danger of a culture altogether reduced to just such purposes. From the point of view of an essentially 'technical' ideology, such sacrifice thus appears quite pointless:

> It is not a sacrifice for something or for someone, even though in a certain sense it is a sacrifice for everything and for all. In a certain essential sense, it is a sacrifice for nothing, if thereby we mean that which is no existing particular.

Properly understood – he goes on – it is just what Christ represents in his crucifixion:

> Such an understanding of sacrifice might basically be considered that in which Christianity differs from those religions which conceive of the divine always as a power and a force, and of a sacrifice as the activity which places this power under an obligation. Christianity, as we might perhaps think, placed at the centre a radical sacrifice in the sense of the interpretation suggested above and rested its cause on the maturity of the human being. The divine in the sense of the suprahuman, the suprahuman in the sense of turning away from ordinary everydayness, rests precisely in the radicality of sacrifice. Perhaps it is in this sense that we need to seek the fully ripened form of demythologised Christianity.[31]

The political context in which Patočka was writing confers on these words of his a truly rich significance.

However, he never goes on to undertake the sort of sustained philosophical engagement with Christian theology towards which he is gesturing in this text. The notion of 'demythologized Christianity' comes, of course, from the theological work of Rudolf Bultmann. But Bultmann – despite making friendly overtures towards philosophy, as represented by Martin Heidegger – remains essentially a pure biblical theologian. He is not yet, after all, moving towards a grand-narrative conception of the solidarity of the shaken, from the theological side.[32]

There remains a gap here, which I want to try and fill.

Two species of truth

So, what does the 'shaking' in the solidarity of the shaken?

In pre-theological grand-narrative terms it is the forever restless impulse of thought that Hegel calls '*Geist*'. The philosophic narrative at which Hegel works is essentially a tale of the self-revelatory self-realization of *Geist*, in and through the shaken-ness of humanity. And – whilst Patočka's narrative, shaped as it is by an altogether different historic context, is quite independent of Hegel's – Hegel, too, surely envisages his story-telling as an ideal philosophico-religious basis for solidarity in shaken struggle.

What allows the shaking; welcomes it; resonates with it?

With prime reference to the Socratic origins of philosophy, Patočka's preferred term for this internalizing process is 'care for the soul'.[33]

And what is it, then, that *Geist* demands? What is the response that authentic care of the soul serves to articulate? What, for the solidarity of the shaken, is always the supreme criterion?

Let us call it: '*truth-as-openness*' – decisively elevated to its proper pre-eminence, in the order of the sacred, over the general quest for '*truth-as-correctness*'. Indeed, this elementary distinction – between truth-as-openness, properly pre-eminent, and truth-as-correctness, properly subordinate – is, it now appears, inscribed within the very physiology of our brains.

Here I am drawing on the work of my friend Iain McGilchrist.[34] Part One of McGilchrist's book *The Master and His Emissary* establishes the neuro-scientific groundwork of his argument; foundational to the grand-narrative sketch of Part Two; and this is further developed both epistemologically and metaphysically in the two volumes of *The Matter with Things*. As McGilchrist's work richly illustrates, the two cerebral hemispheres each have a whole range of different specialized skills, and complementary jobs to do. They constantly collaborate. And yet, it is remarkable in fact how little actual criss-cross connection the *corpus callosum* which physically divides them from one another permits. Where either hemisphere is disabled by injury or (for instance, in the treatment of some forms of epilepsy) surgically switched off, it becomes evident just how different the characteristic worldview of each is. And, crucially, each has quite a different basic orientation to truth.[35]

By 'truth-as-openness' I mean the truth-ideal of the right cerebral hemisphere; by 'truth-as-correctness', the truth-ideal of the left cerebral hemisphere.

Truth-as-openness essentially involves *a quality of character*: an ideal disposition, relating well to others, with empathy and consequent insight; the skills of the good teacher, the wise counsellor or, more generally, the perceptive observer of the world at large. It is patiently attentive, disclosive truth; the dissolving of wilful, lazy self-deception.

Truth-as-correctness, by contrast, is a quality of well-framed *propositions, considered in themselves*.

One cannot *capture* truth-as-openness in propositions: everything, from this point of view, always depends on *who* is speaking, and *to whom*. What counts is the appropriateness of the interaction. Truth-as-correctness is less slippery, because it is abstracted from the affective aspect of any conversational context. The right hemisphere registers the rich, overflowing actuality of what is actually *present*; the left *re*-presents it in such a way as to reduce it to order. So, it likes to apply abstract, theoretical categories; it measures and calculates; it is instinctively utilitarian. This utilitarian sub-self is primarily interested in control: a correct representation of natural phenomena is what is needed in order to subdue them technologically, a correct application of the law gives structure to governance, a correct reading of other people's motives and responses enables one to manipulate them. Truth-as-openness, however, is the antithesis to manipulation.

The specific skills of the left hemisphere may well be out-competed by artificial intelligence. But the *emotional* intelligence of the right hemisphere is just what can never be artificially replicated, at any depth. As the work of the left hemisphere is crucial for survival, evolution has invested it with a great deal of pleasure. At the humblest level: consider for example the puzzles one finds in newspapers and magazines. These are little treats for the left hemisphere, offering a few moments of respite from the stresses of right-hemisphere life. Or, again, I for my part am addicted to the left-hemisphere pleasure involved in writing books. But in Part Two of *The Master and his Emissary* McGilchrist surveys the history of Western civilization, as a field of constant battle between right-hemisphere wisdom and grandiose left-hemisphere hubris.

The right hemisphere, he argues, is the true 'Master', when it comes to moral authority and hence what is sacred. The rightful role of the left hemisphere, in this regard, is to be the Master's 'Emissary'; an aid in communicating the Master's will, no more. And yet, all too often the Emissary has *usurped* the Master's authority. Instead of correctly, at the deepest level, recognizing the right-hemisphere ideal of perfect truth-as-openness as the very essence of the sacred, the Usurper's culture incorrectly sacralizes some form or other of supposed moral, metaphysical and historiographical truth-as-correctness; the group-think of a human herd or a gang, internalized as a rigid dogmatism, not just diverting from truth-as-openness, but actually suppressing it. The Usurpation may be dressed up in religious terms – no religious tradition is immune, certainly no large-scale one – or it may be dressed up in the most purely secularist terms. Either way, the result is a manipulative project of mind-control.

Hegel, again, speaks to this. He of course pre-dates any knowledge of brain-hemisphere function. But what he calls '*Geist*' is, in effect, nothing other than the impulse of the right hemisphere. His name for the impulse of the left hemisphere (prior to, though not precluding, its corruption) is '*Verstand*'. And in his account of '*das unglückliche Bewußtsein*' he is describing the after-effects of the Usurpation. What McGilchrist speaks of as the rightful 'Master' has for Hegel already become the 'subjugated' sub-self; what McGilchrist speaks of as the hubristic 'Emissary' is for Hegel the despotic 'master' sub-self, the Usurper, rigidified *Verstand*, repressing *Geist*. As for the 'care for the soul' of which Patočka speaks: this is the philosophic form of therapy, aiming at a wholesale restoration of the proper order which the Usurpation disrupts.

What I witnessed in immediately post-revolutionary Prague was not just the overthrow of one particular, especially dreary, tyrannical regime. It was an epiphany of the kingdom of God, inasmuch as the fallen regime represented the Usurpation in general. The solidarity of the shaken is, quite simply, a coming-together of those who have been decisively shaken *out of* the complacencies of *das unglückliche Bewußtsein*; and *into* dissident action, against the Usurpation.[36]

As a grand-narrative thinker, I am concerned with the gradual, multi-layered historic emergence of a certain intellectual possibility. Namely: the possibility of a thinking which (a) radically identifies the properly sacred, in theory, with all that contributes to release from the Usurpation of das unglückliche Bewußtsein; *and which (b) then sets out to develop the most effective possible mode of solidarity-practice, on just that basis.*

Chapter 2

THE KINGDOM OF GOD: ABRAHAMIC RELIGION, ITS HISTORIC ORIGINS IN A DILEMMA

Three species of religion

And now let us go beyond Patočka's grand narrative, to delve back a little more deeply into the sacred origins of 'shaken' thought; right to the very earliest recorded stirrings, in fact, of the latent possibility of the solidarity of the shaken, understood as a sacred ideal.

I have suggested that, in order to reinforce it, render it durable, such solidarity needs, so far as possible, to be grafted into a stable, deep-rooted culture of the sacred; whichever one is closest to hand. For pure, deracinated secularity lacks the poetic, catholic bonding power ideally required. But are all stable, deep-rooted traditions of the sacred equally capable of serving this purpose?

I will not presume to say 'equally' – or to judge between them in abstract fashion – for how, after all, could anyone be well enough informed to do so? But, at their best, all the great traditions of the sacred originating in what Karl Jaspers called the 'Axial Age' of world history, between the eighth and third centuries BCE, may I think very well be seen as therapeutic projects of 'care for the soul'; strategies of thoughtful resistance to the Usurpation; celebration, and cultivation, of sovereign truth-as-openness.

Thus, as I have argued elsewhere, there are surely three basic species of such religious strategy: in the sense of three different critical orientations of the sacred towards ruling power; upholding the deep-mind atoning impulse of *Geist*, against the split-mind superficiality of *das unglückliche Bewußtsein*, and the associated *libido dominandi* (crass 'lust for domination') which it informs.[1]

- One strategy emerges in China, with the Confucian envisioning of the ideal gentleman, or *junzi* (alternatively transcribed as *chün tzu*). The *junzi* is a ruler; that is to say, just the sort of person most exposed to the temptations of an excessive will to control the world, the desire to domineer, typically characteristic of the Usurper sub-self. Yet, his defining characteristic as a *junzi* is just his conscientious overcoming of such surface-self temptation. So, the *junzi*'s style of ruling is characterized above all by a highly ritualistic honouring of truth-as-openness, even as he still continues in office. And

the Confucian tradition originates, first and foremost, as that ritualizing of the deep mind. Taking 'politics' in the narrowest sense – as a term specifically for the gaining, and implementation, of executive power over a state, a region, or a city – one might call it '*intra*-political religion'.
- A second form of strategy emerges in upanishadic India, taoist China, philosophic Greece – which, by contrast, one might call '*pre*-political religion'. For it centres on the ideal of the world-renouncing sage, as one who subdues the domineering natural impulse of the surface-self, very differently, by so far as possible withdrawing altogether from political temptation; and even from any great controlling power within their domestic world. Therefore, in such religious traditions the prime champion of the deep mind is the solitary contemplative; the dweller in silence.
- A third form of strategy – let us call it '*anti*-political religion' – first emerges in the Middle East. In this case, the prime champion of the deep mind is the prophet; who confronts and challenges the corrupted, domineering rulers of the world in the name of God. The rulers of this world seek to advance the shallow interests of their surface-selves, not least, by propaganda offering their subjects a share in their reflected glory. But the prophet represents, in principle, an infinitely higher authority than that possessed by any this-worldly regime; decreeing compassion. And that decree then endlessly collides with the rulers' propaganda.

I am talking here about the *core distinctive truth-potential* of each species, in remedying the Usurpation. Thus, in the case of Confucianism, this potential is simply what would appear in the governance of an authentic Confucian state. But, although rulers have of course repeatedly attempted to draw sacred legitimacy from all sorts of other religious tradition, I make so bold as to suggest that there is, at the deepest ideal level, a certain intrinsic self-contradiction in the notion of Buddhism, say, as being primarily the ideology of a state; of Hinduism (at any rate, Hinduism still preserving some genetic connection to the spirit of the *Upanishads*) as being primarily the ideology of a state; of Judaism, Christianity or Islam, as being primarily the ideology of a state – where sectarian confessional-state-building has been elevated to the be-all and end-all of true piety. Which is not to deny that there may also be growths of genuine, non-sectarian intra-political religion *within* primarily pre-political or anti-political religious contexts; just as there may be elements of pre-political religion flourishing within primarily intra-political or anti-political religious cultures; or (as in the case of Mahatma Gandhi, say) elements of anti-political religion emergent within a primarily pre-political religious culture.

Nevertheless, the *core* in each case remains the core.

As I would use the term, 'religion' strictly speaking means whatever authentically belongs to any one of these three great families of therapeutic sacred tradition. In this sense, prior to the Axial Age there was no religion. There was a plethora of sacred practices essentially conceived, not at all as challenging the inner dividedness of the surface-self, *das unglückliche Bewußtsein*, but on the contrary as catering to that servile mentality; expressing its own perception of its interests; invoking supernatural aid towards the fulfilment of those interests. But there was not yet any religion. In general, authentic religion needs to be decisively distinguished from mere *sacred ideology*, both that which precedes the advent of religion and also that in which the outer forms of authentic religious tradition have, to all intents and purposes, been emptied out, and re-occupied, now, by the very energies which those traditions began by trying to expel. For religion, after all, works by being ambiguous: thereby allowing people to connect into it at all different levels of sophistication. However, this means that the Usurpation itself is also endlessly reproducible in outwardly religious form. Sacred ideology may well be quite orthodox, and invested with the very utmost sincerity; yet in its obsession with mere dogmatic moral, metaphysical and historiographical truth-as-correctness, it is nonetheless fundamentally governed by just the sort of shallow will-to-domineer, the closed-mindedness that the religious tradition in question was originally meant to overcome.

Abraham / Moses: Amos / Hosea

One might, I think, well say that the grand narrative that I am intent on exploring actually belongs to a *second* Axial Age, beginning in the early nineteenth century and still very much underway; Hegel, in his role as pioneering philosophic student of comparative religion, being in fact its first great thinker.[2] Whereas the first Axial Age gave birth, for the first time, to a multitude of properly religious traditions, the second Axial Age sees the explicit development of criteria rendering it possible, for the first time, to see the underlying potential complementarity of all these various traditions, in their critical essence.

As a Christian priest, on the other hand, I am naturally interested, first and foremost, in anti-political religion. This indeed is the species most immediately equipped for – and, at the same time, most urgently in need of – a grand-narrative opening-up towards the solidarity of the shaken, as it spins its tales of divine revelation. Insofar as it is corrupted by *das unglückliche Bewußtsein*, it generates stunted forms of grand narrative: Haredi, Salafi or Protestant Fundamentalist versions, affirming divine revelation to have been a process definitively concluded long ago; and reactionary Roman Catholic or Eastern Orthodox versions, simply identifying divine revelation with the evolving official dogma of the institutional church as such. What is ultimately needed, I want to argue, by way of healing here is the richest possible grand narrative of *ongoing* divine revelation, *channelled by all manner of means*. In short: revelation in a multitude of different forms, yet *essentially identifiable* as including *whatever* may be said to point towards the ultimate telos, the solidarity of the shaken.

A truly universal grand narrative of this kind must therefore begin with an acknowledgement of *anonymous* divine revelation, so defined, in non-theistic forms of intra-political and pre-political religion. But in this work, I will concentrate especially on the history of the original, and most widespread, family of anti-political, theistic religious traditions: that which in principle embraces all Jews, Muslims and Christians alike; namely, the '*Abrahamic*' family.

§

The inner servility of *das unglückliche Bewußtsein* in individuals generates *herd morality* in groups; its inner despotism generates *gang morality*. Once upon a time, before any of the three species of 'religion', in the strict sense, existed – but only primitive sacred ideology – the sole forms of morality that could flourish were herd morality or gang morality. Herd morality and gang morality are two forms of moralized corporate egoism, both in effect excluding any wider appreciation for truth-as-openness. Perhaps René Girard is right, and every culture of sacralized herd or gang morality *originates* in the ultimate antithesis to truth-as-openness: the dream-transfigured remembrance of some prehistoric, primal act, or acts, of scapegoat-murder. Who can say? At all events, it is all too imaginable.

The earliest beginnings of an anti-political religious challenge to herd / gang morality are to be found in the literature of the Ancient Hebrews. Thus, as Girard remarks, among ancient literary traditions it is uniquely in Hebrew literature that we hear the voices of scapegoat victims, protesting the injustice of their treatment by herd and gang, colluding together: in the writings of the prophets, the protest represented, above all, by *Deutero-Isaiah*'s depiction of the 'suffering servant'; repeatedly, also, resurgent in the *Psalms*; and in the book of *Job*.[3]

This, then, is where the history of the possibility of a true solidarity of the shaken begins.

Abraham is the legendary figure representing the moment when Ancient Hebrew religion began decisively to diverge from the typical sacred-ideological cultures of the surrounding world: the very earliest stirring towards the solidarity of the shaken here. He is introduced as a wanderer, departing first from his birthplace, Ur of the Chaldees, in lower Mesopotamia; then, after an extended stay at Haran in south-eastern Anatolia, heading south and spending time in Egypt; before finally settling in Canaan. His various departures may well be seen as symbolizing the fresh cultural otherness he embodies, leaving the sacred-ideological world behind. Four times God comes to Abraham, to seal a covenant with him: first, just before he departs from Haran, *Genesis* 12.1-3; then, following the blessing he receives from the priest-king Melchizedek, *Genesis* 15; then yet again, at greater length, in *Genesis* 17.1-22. But the covenant-story which is surely crucial is that of the 'binding' (*akedah* in Hebrew) of his son Isaac, in *Genesis* 22.1-19.

In each of its iterations, the divine covenant with Abraham includes a promise of innumerable descendants. Yet Abraham's wife Sarah is barren; and it takes a miracle for her only son Isaac to be born, long after she has passed normal child-bearing age. Twice this birth is prophesied (*Genesis* 17.15-22; 18.9-15). Sarah laughs, finding it incredible. Nevertheless, it happens! And the child Isaac is naturally all the more beloved because he appears irreplaceable. Then, however, God addresses Abraham and gives him the most appalling instructions: to take his son out into the desert, and sacrifice him there, as a burnt offering. Abraham obeys. On arrival at the appointed place, he binds his beloved son; lays him on the altar; lifts the knife ... And only then, at the very last moment, does an angel intervene, with a ram to sacrifice instead (*Genesis* 22.1-18).

What on earth did the original author of this story – and what did its subsequent editors – intend by it?

There are two basic possible ways of reading it which relate directly to Abraham's prime symbolic role as the notional father of anti-political religion. The difference between them has to do with how the figure of Isaac is understood: whether (a) as primarily in his victimhood representing the typical *cruelty* of herd / gang morality towards the outcast from the herd, symbolized by the sacred-ideological practice of child-sacrifice; or else (b) as primarily in his role as heir representing all the *hopes* of Hebrew herd / gang morality, which hang upon his survival, which God teasingly endangers. Thus:

(a) There is plenty of evidence to suggest that the practice of sacrificing the first-born child may have been quite widespread in Canaan (ancient Palestine) as a whole, and not least amongst the Hebrews themselves.[4] It might be as an emergency response to a crisis: as in *Judges* 11.29-40, the story of Jephthah and the sacrifice of his daughter; or, again, as in *2 Kings* 3.26-27, the story of the King of Moab and the sacrifice of his son (said to have been highly effective as a magical intervention in his war against Israel!) At other times it appears to have been a more routine ritual. The topheth, or child cemetery, in the valley of Ben-Himmon, near Jerusalem, was notorious as a place where children were made to 'pass through fire'. This is denounced in *Leviticus* 18.21 and 20.2-5; *Deuteronomy* 12.29-31; *Jeremiah* 7.31 and 19.1-6. It is reported, as a scandal, that Ahaz, the king of Judah (*c.* 732–*c.* 716) did it to his sons: *2 Kings* 16.3; *2 Chronicles* 28.3. Also that Manasseh, king of Judah (*c.* 687–*c.* 643) did the same to his son: *2 Kings* 21.6; *2 Chronicles* 33.6. It is unclear whether or not the phrase 'pass through fire' necessarily refers to full child-sacrifice, or just to some other ritual; and the charred remains of children which archaeologists have unearthed may simply be a consequence of cremation after death. But see *Ezekiel* 16.20-2; 20.25-6; 23.39: texts quite unambiguously deploring ritual child-sacrifice amongst the Hebrews. Moreover, we know that ritual child sacrifice was also carried out by the Phoenicians, on a large scale, at Carthage, and at their other settlements in Malta, Sicily, and Sardinia; and the Phoenicians largely originated from Canaan.

Still more striking, however, is the evidence of child-sacrifice having been practised in the name of the Hebrew god Yahweh himself. See in particular *Ezekiel* 20.25-6. Here the prophet, writing in the early sixth century BCE, represents Yahweh confessing:

> I gave them statutes that were not good and ordinances by which they could not live. I defiled them through their very gifts, in their offering up all their firstborn, in order that I might horrify them, so that they might know that I am the LORD.

Compare *Exodus* 13. 1-2, and 22. 29(b)-30; ambiguous texts, but quite possibly relics preserved from that earlier time of 'horror'. In *Leviticus* the children ritually 'passed through fire' (in the valley of Ben Himmon?) are described either as having been 'given to Molech', or 'given to the molech'. Scholarly opinion is divided: does this word refer to a pagan deity – or is it just a name for the forbidden ritual itself? Was the ritual, indeed, intended as an offering to Yahweh?

And does the story of the 'binding of Isaac', then, originate as an occasion for meditation on the evolution of the Yahwistic conception of God, away from the magic cruelty of child-sacrifice in particular; hence, ideally, away from the cruelty of herd / gang morality in general?[5] In which case – as the rabbis of the Gemara in the Babylonian Talmud argued – God never intended Abraham to obey his command.[6] Abraham, that is to say, *ought* to have protested, and rebelled, from the outset.

It would indeed be rather odd if the story did not refer to this general context. And yet – such a reading scarcely seems to fit with the actual conclusion in *Genesis* 22: 16-17, where Yahweh, on the contrary, commends Abraham precisely for *not* having protested, *not* having rebelled; but for simply having obeyed …

(b) Abraham, in fact, obeys without so much as a murmur. He obeys even though what God is demanding from him spells the imminent end of his people: the nascent human herd held together by the patriarchal authority he was hoping to hand down to his son. From the point of view of herd / gang morality, this obviously makes no sense at all. But, in obeying as he does, he makes it clear that he knows the truth of God to be far greater than any form of herd / gang morality will allow; far greater, one might surely say, than any mere idolatrous projection of *das unglückliche Bewußtsein*.

This second reading of the story is less specific in its ethical implications than the first reading which concentrates on the immediate cruelty of child-sacrifice; but is, at the same time, implicitly far wider-ranging. Abraham follows the dictates of his conscience, even though they seem absurd. He obeys, even though he cannot justify doing so with any argument ever likely to persuade the ordinary protagonists of herd / gang morality. Because he does not know how to, he does not even attempt to justify himself to anyone else. The terrible divine commandment is therefore, for him, a great burden of secrecy, to be borne in silence. Kierkegaard, writing under the pseudonym 'Johannes de Silentio', celebrates the deep inwardness of faith which, to him, Abraham accordingly represents.[7] And Derrida, also, celebrates this silence.[8]

But, although the story read along such lines is without question sublime, the sheer cruelty of God's action, with regard both to Abraham and to Isaac, obviously remains problematic.

§

The first reading of the Abraham story is too limited in its immediate criticism only of a singularly cruel manifestation of herd / gang morality. The second reading is bolder, pitting Abraham against herd / gang morality *as such*; yet fails really to explain the moral rationale of divine transcendence. This failure is intrinsic to the legendary nature of the story, in that it abstracts the action from any political context. One can scarcely explain the origin of anti-political religion, as such, in a political vacuum.

But now, let us shift from legend to history. Let us turn from the *legendary* father of anti-political religion, Abraham, to its *actual, historic founder*: namely *the prophet Amos*, in the mid-eighth century BCE.

Amos, for the first time in history it seems, introduces something completely missing in sacralized herd / gang morality: a furious isothymotic demand for 'legal justice (*mishpat*) and moral righteousness (*tsedaqah*)', on the part of the rich, towards the poor. That is to say: an emphatic identification of God's will with the imperatives of perfect truth-as-openness; embattled against material self-interest and class distinction. It is indeed an isothymotic demand delivered with the most extravagantly megalothymotic chutzpah!

The gods of sacralized theistic herd / gang morality have three elementary characteristics. First, they promise various utilitarian benefits to the devout herd as a whole and to each of its devout individual members separately: fertility, healing, success in war and so forth. Second, by way of repayment for these benefits, and as insurance for the future, they demand liturgical flattery; aesthetically bonding the herd together. Third, as back-up to coercive law and order, they enjoin respect for their priests, and for the rulers of the herd, that gang, in general. In the book of *Amos*, all this has changed. Yahweh, as represented here, promises no utilitarian benefits to the herd and its members, but only all manner of catastrophes, evoked with great poetic brio, meant to shake them out of their complacency. He absolutely rejects any liturgical flattery, saying to his own devout worshippers:

> I hate, I despise your festivals,
>   and I take no delight in your solemn assemblies.
> Even though you offer me your burnt offerings and grain offerings,
>   I will not accept them;
> and the offerings of well-being of your fatted animals
>   I will not look upon.
> Take away from me the noise of your songs;
>   I will not listen to the melody of your harps.
> But let justice roll down like waters,
>   and righteousness like an ever-flowing stream.
>
> (*Amos* 5.21-4)

Compare, for instance, *Proverbs* 21. 3: 'To do righteousness and justice is more acceptable to the LORD than sacrifice' (also, *Proverbs* 15.8, 21.27). The book of *Proverbs* cannot be at all accurately dated; this little saying may indeed pre-date

Amos in origin, it may post-date *Amos*, we do not know. But in any case, set it alongside *Amos*, and how pallid, how trite by contrast it appears! What is new in *Amos* is just the sublimely incandescent ethical sheer rage pervading the whole book. And then in Chapter 7: 10-17 the prophet is shown in bitter conflict with Amaziah, the priest of Bethel, that is, the leading cleric in the northern kingdom of Israel; after Amaziah has accused him of seeking to subvert the rule of king Jeroboam II. Amos curses Amaziah: not only will Jeroboam be killed in battle, and Amaziah, along with all the ruling class of Israel, be sent into exile; but also, his sons and daughters will be slaughtered, and his wife will end up as a common prostitute. Yes, this is ugly! But, equally: a vivid echo, from a breakthrough moment. There is no reason to suppose that Amaziah and his class were any more corrupt than such privileged classes generally tend to be. What *is* unprecedented, however, is the ultra-demanding moral standard to which Amos is holding them.

Amos is the first of the Hebrew writing prophets. Discount the element of fictional back-projection in texts written long after Amos's own day, and there is no real indication that, before his breakthrough, the worship of Yahweh was, to any serious degree, different in kind from the worship of the other tribal gods of that world. Perhaps it was already characterized by certain aesthetic eccentricities. This is hard to assess. But, even if so, there is no evidence at all of corresponding *ethical* difference.

As with all the texts of Hebrew Scripture, the book of *Amos* has clearly evolved somewhat in the process of its transmission. The closing lines for instance, *Amos* 9.11-15, look like a later addition: a promise of future salvation tacked onto a text which is otherwise quite devoid of any such hopeful promise. And no doubt the other material has also been edited, and recomposed, a number of times over. However, the text as a whole has qualities of sustained literary brilliance, and thematic consistency, which tend to justify the supposition that it very largely does cohere; and that a good deal of it does, indeed, go back to the very early time indicated in the epigraph, describing it as 'the words of Amos … which he saw [*sic*] concerning Israel in the days of King Uzziah of Judah and in the days of King Jeroboam son of Joash of Israel, two years before the earthquake' (1.1).[9]

Moreover, this supposition also helps explain another feature of the book of *Amos*. Namely: the remarkable lack of emphasis, in it, on the theme so dominant in the rest of Hebrew prophetic literature, namely *the need to worship Yahweh alone*. Amos may well be presumed to have spurned the syncretistic worship of other gods. However, that is not the main pioneering thing he wants to say. The prophets after him belong to a milieu of militant 'Yahweh-alone-ism'; but it is in fact quite surprising how little the later editors of *Amos* have done to impose that ideology onto its text. Amos pre-dates the Yahweh-alone-ist movement; helps set the scene for it; but, very interestingly, does not yet belong to it.

§

Amos bears megalothymotic witness to pure isothymotic shaken-ness. There is no element of *das unglückliche Bewußtsein* in his thinking; no conventional endorsement of any sort of herd / gang morality. His prophecy is one great, thunderous surge of *Geist*. Consider, though, that thunder. As represented by Amos, God thunders, relentlessly; rages, relentlessly; menaces, relentlessly. This relentlessness is I guess a symptom of acute frustration on the prophet's part, resulting from his isolation. Amos is the very epitome of a shaken poet-thinker; but (discounting the later addition of 9.11-15) he has not yet found his way to the sort of hope that would surely require an effective *solidarity* of the shaken, for its development.

The thunderous intensity, here, of God's demand for 'justice and righteousness', is simply infinite, inchoate. What is lacking any programme of specific reforms, on the basis of which a large-scale solidarity movement might be coherently organized.

And *that* then is what the Yahweh-alone-ist movement provides. Around the central demand that the Hebrew people should abandon their age-old practice, shared with all other nations back then, of worshipping different gods for different purposes, and henceforth worship Yahweh alone, this movement develops a whole set of other, subsidiary prescriptions; as set out in the legislative parts of *Exodus*, *Leviticus*, *Numbers* and *Deuteronomy*.

The great historic pioneer of the Yahweh-alone-ist movement was a younger contemporary of Amos: the second writing prophet, *Hosea*. Just as Amos's role as a pioneer is concealed behind the legend of Abraham, so Hosea's role is concealed behind the legend of Moses. For this was a world in which authority correlated with antiquity: the more ancient, the better. But the texts which speak of Moses as the great recipient of Yahweh-alone-ist law were written over an extended period considerably later than Hosea. They are legends back-projected into the immemorial past. There is, in fact, no real evidence of a Yahweh-alone-ist movement existing prior to Hosea. The prophet Elijah is an earlier, ninth century BCE figure, who is said to have battled on behalf of Yahweh, as the Hebrews' national god, against the worship of Baal at the royal court of Israel. But Elijah is of somewhat doubtful historicity. And, whilst he is presented as a hero by the post-Hoseanic Yahweh-alone-ist historians who tell us about him, his reforming ambitions appear much more limited than those of Hosea. The Yahweh-alone-ism initiated by Hosea was not only concerned with what went on at the royal court. Hosea's demand is that *no one* who worships Yahweh should ever worship any other god.

Contrast the thunder of God in *Hosea* with the thunder of God in *Amos*. In the case of *Hosea*, this is no longer just a venting of frustration. It is a hope-filled impatience for controlling power, to implement reform. Here God rages in the persona of a jealous husband, whose wife, the people of Israel, is guilty of adultery with other gods; a disturbing eruption of violent patriarchal rhetoric.

Nevertheless, there is also a clear continuity between *Hosea* and *Amos*. For, after all, *why* worship only Yahweh? Surely, this must imply that Yahweh is true God, by nature quite unlike all other gods. And where else did that idea of Yahweh's uniqueness originate, if not in the prophecy of *Amos*?

§

I have seen, with my own eyes, a coming of the kingdom of God! In Prague, January 1990: encountering the exhaustion, yet also the elation, of people there who had hitherto been long-term dissidents, but now were dissidents no longer, since the system had changed. I have seen the solidarity of the shaken, for a moment, triumphant.

Again: what imaginative resources does our culture provide for the articulation of this solidarity-ideal, *as the very essence of the sacred*? What other deeper-rooted memories do we – the Jewish, Christian, Muslim inheritors of Abrahamic anti-political religious tradition – need to cultivate?

I think we need to reframe our whole sense of revelation-history, going right back to the dialectic interplay between *Amos* and *Hosea*. So much of Hebrew Scripture – the Pentateuch, the history books, the Prophets – is, in essence, campaign literature of the Yahweh-alone-ist movement launched, it appears, by Hosea: a great religious solidarity-building venture with a core-potential to channel the radical shaken-ness of what one might well call the '*Amos* impulse'. This indeed is where the New Testament concept of the 'kingdom of God' ultimately originates.

But Yahweh-alone-ism was also, right from the outset, beset by ambivalence. Thus, whereas Amos is uncompromising in his repudiation of old-fashioned herd / gang morality, the Yahweh-alone-ist project was, by contrast, radically ambivalent in this regard. Battling to gain power, YHWH-alone-ist preachers were immediately liable to become, themselves, a holy gang, deploying a fanatical rhetoric of holy warfare, with a view to policing a herd-like consensus among the Hebrew people. A movement with ineradicable, rich potential to open towards the solidarity of the shaken, Yahweh-alone-ism could not exclude such deflection. In the event of which, it represented an advance only in the sense of introducing a salutary element of latent self-contradiction into its sacred ideology.

Yes, the pure shaken-ness of the *Amos* impulse does indeed cry out for strategic embodiment in some form of effective, and enduring, organized solidarity. But then – conversely – the need is for organized solidarity which remains in the fullest sense faithful to the pure *Amos* impulse. And the sheer intransigence of the *Amos* impulse renders that virtually impossible. This, surely, is the founding *dilemma* of Abrahamic moral culture, in general. Right at the heart of Abrahamic tradition, as a result, there is an intractable instability, constantly powering its evolution. The story which, historically, begins with Amos and Hosea is ongoing to this day: through Yahweh-alone-ism, and on, into Rabbinic Judaism, Christianity in all its many branches, Islam in all its many branches, and the secular humanism of the Judaeo-Christian-Islamic world.

How are we to capture the true revelatory quality of this evolution *as a whole*? How is the story best told, with a view to helping push it forward? What aspects stand out? That, in short, is my topic in what follows.

De Trinitate

I am interested in the whole of religious history, considered as the self-revelation of *Geist*, the drive to truth-as-openness. But since I am a Christian theologian, let me also frame the matter in specifically Christian, Trinitarian terms. Not that I am claiming, by this, any intrinsic superiority for Christian faith. The revelation of ideal truth-as-openness, after all, fundamentally serves to relativize any such claim to competitively sacralized confessional truth-as-correctness. Far rather however, I want briefly to consider, at this point, how the dogma of the Trinity may itself be understood as a systematic, Christian-confessional framework for the, in itself trans-confessional, history of *Geist*.

Abstracted from any particular political struggles, there are indeed five modes of solidarity-building immediately in play here: solidarity among Christians as such; solidarity among Jews as such; solidarity among Muslims as such; solidarity among philosophers as such; and the solidarity of the shaken. I want to affirm the prime authority of the solidarity of the shaken; not as displacing any of the others, but rather growing within them. Historically, each of the other four has at times played a crucial role in the implicit development of the solidarity of the shaken as a possibility; and they still surely must, so far as possible, continue to nurture it, in ever more explicit fashion. (Again, the same goes for all the other various sacred traditions stemming from the Axial Age.) And yet, the solidarity of the shaken, by definition, transcends their temptations: the temptations of xenophobia forever plaguing all forms of religious tradition; the temptations of intellectual snobbery forever plaguing all forms of philosophic tradition.

I want to address the history of that transcendence. In a sense, this is to venture a fresh account of what Hegel, provocatively, terms 'absolute knowing'.

§

It is of course unfortunately true that, as formulated by the Council of Nicaea, the doctrine of the Trinity has been twisted into a set of dogmatic claims regarding metaphysical truth-as-correctness. *In its origins* however, it surely reflects an essential three-fold-ness in the early Church's wrestling with the demands of truth-as-openness.

At one level, the three divine Persons simply correspond to three placings of God in the gospel story. But to confine one's understanding of the dogma to this first, superficial level is the error of the 'Sabellian' heresy. For orthodox Christian theology, God is triune in all eternity. Why? Because God's three-in-oneness is in fact the objective correlate of Christian theology's primordial, and abiding, three-in-oneness as an intellectual discipline. Right from the beginning, divine revelation has always been refracted to Christian theologians through three basic *problem-clusters*:

- As regards 'First-Person theology': In the early Church, there was the general problem of how to reconcile the narrative and lyrical culture of Hebrew Scripture with the analytical, debating culture of Greek philosophy. The early theologians were men trained in the schools of philosophy; but pagan philosophers like Celsus scorned what they saw as the crudity of Hebrew Scripture. There was a natural antagonism there, which the theologians had to overcome. 'First-Person theology' was, to begin with, a matter of learning to be both literally and metaphorically *bi*-lingual in this context: the First Person of the Trinity being 'Father' to both Jew and Greek. Nowadays, in the richly cosmopolitan environment of modernity, the ideal theologian is metaphorically *multi*-lingual. Yet, the basic task remains the same: 'First-Person theology', as I would understand it, is a matter of re-affirming the specific truth-potential of anti-political, or prophetic, religion generally – the primordial truth of the *Amos* impulse – in dialogue both with other religious traditions, intra-political or pre-political, and likewise also with the traditions of secular existentialism as such. One might say, it is encounter with 'God, Convenor of the Tribes'.

- As regards 'Second-Person theology': The thinkers of the early Church had the problem of interpreting what, *in practical terms*, it meant to see God in the resurrection of a crucified dissident. How to tell the story, incorporate it into liturgy? How to preach it; spread the gospel of salvation for which it stands? How to interpret its ethical and political implications, its fundamental challenge to the crucifying regime, and to all other such regimes? 'Second-Person theology' is grounded in the injunction, 'Go therefore and make disciples of all nations' (*Matthew* 28.19). It is the dominant intellectual context for the New Testament as a whole. And it remains dominant in more strictly Bible-focused forms of theology, such as Barthian dogmatics or Bultmannian 'demythologization', to this day. Here, we encounter 'God, our Judge'.

- As regards 'Third-Person theology': This originally emerges, in the New Testament, from the problems involved in the early Christians' being obliged to invent a whole new set of authority-structures, a whole new spiritual ethos for the Church. Thus, whereas 'Second-Person theology' is outward-looking, evangelistic, 'Third-Person theology' is far more a matter of institutional introspection. All internal debate concerning the criteria for authority within the Church belongs in the first instance to 'Third-Person theology': all challenges to the establishment; all fresh authority-claims, based on such initially unlicensed charisms as visions, miracles, oracular inspiration, eloquent enthusiasm, scholarly erudition or sheer critical thoughtfulness. Hence, by contrast to 'Second-Person theology', which is ideally promotional strategy for radical, shaken isothymia, 'Third-Person theology', at its best, is a critical appropriation of radical, shaken megalothymia. ('First-Person theology' may be either: depending on what it absorbs from its non-Christian conversation-partners.) In principle, 'Third-Person theology' reviews Church history in its entirety; not just the gospel aspect of that history, but also the corruption; asking what has gone wrong. It is a therapeutic discipline, of chastened corporate self-knowledge; endlessly intent on beginning all over again. Through it, we encounter 'God, Mending Spirit / now and for evermore. Amen.'

Of course, all three divine Persons play a role in each of these domains, inasmuch as they mutually embrace. Such is the principle of *perichorēsis*: the difference between the domains is simply a matter of shifting focus. Nor is 'First-Person theology' always *explicitly* presented as discourse with a primary focus on God the Father;

'Second-Person theology', as discourse with a primary focus on God the Son; or 'Third-Person theology', as discourse with a primary focus on God the Holy Spirit. The identity of each domain is not determined merely by frequency of sacred name-checking. What counts, far rather, is just the underlying triangularity of Christian theology as a systematic whole.

Trinitarian dogma begins to form in this triangularity; and was then decisively shaped by a struggle, climaxing in the fourth century, over the widespread tendency to subordinate the Second and Third Persons to the First. This, I think, needs to be understood very much as a form of sublated class struggle: 'First-Person theology' being premised on an education in philosophy, and hence associated with the social privilege implied by such an education, God the Father was, in effect, tacitly regarded as God for sophisticated intellectuals; God the Son and God the Holy Spirit, as God for the Christian masses. In its final, obsolescent, Arian form, explicitly subordinationist theology had, it is true, lost the elitist edge apparent in earlier forms (as represented for example by Origen); Arianism appears to represent little more than a persistence of intellectual inertia, rendered factional. But to affirm the equality of the three Persons was to begin with, surely, a matter of insisting on the proper class-transcending catholicity of the Church.

In this sense, the three domains of theology are equal. Yet, as I have said, the primary original growth-point of Christian thought was in 'Second-Person theology'; which still remains the most basic foundation of Christian faith as a distinctive phenomenon, within the Abrahamic family of religions.

§

Observe: in neo-Hegelian terms, each of the three Trinitarian domains is a battlefield, on which *Geist*, the drive to perfect truth-as-openness, is engaged with differing manifestations of *das unglückliche Bewußtsein*.

Elsewhere, I have tried to analyse this in terms of a struggle against three basic forms of dishonesty.[10] Thus, 'First-Person theology' is essentially embattled against '*dishonesty-as-banality*'. Its logical priority derives from this being the most primitive species of dishonesty, sheer thoughtlessness; against which such theology seeks to build all manner of alliances. 'Second-Person theology' is essentially embattled against '*dishonesty-as-manipulation*'. The Roman imperial institution of crucifixion, transfigured by the crucifixion of Christ, becomes the ultimate symbol of manipulative dishonesty in general. And Christian evangelism, at its best, is then pitched as a rebellious vindication of honesty in those terms. 'Third-Person theology' is essentially embattled against '*dishonesty-as-disowning*'. It is the Church's owning of its own corporate sin, in relation to *Geist*; its training in collective repentance; its continually renewed owning of its need for change.[11]

The sap of Abrahamic tradition, originally deriving from Hosea's appropriation of *Amos*, flows into Christian theology first and foremost by way of 'Second-Person theology'. The work of 'Second-Person theology' is to invest it into vigorous fresh poetic growth. And 'First-Person theology' may, also, be said to have pre-Christian origins. Namely: in the thought of Philo, the Jewish philosopher of Alexandria, who was an older contemporary of Jesus. For Philo is already negotiating between the truth of Hebrew scripture and the truth of Platonism. 'Third-Person theology' on the other hand, inasmuch as it consists in ecclesiastical self-criticism, arrives a little later.

Nevertheless, it is the simultaneity of all three pressures, right from the early days of Christian theology, which is registered by the dogma. Why did nothing at all similar emerge in Rabbinic Judaism, or in Islam? Partly, of course, this was due to polemical rivalry with Christianity. But note, also, the early pressure of 'First-Person theology' in Christendom. In Rabbinic Judaism, by contrast, there were no significant immediate successors to Philo; and in Islam, philosophy did not enter upon the scene until well after the *umma* had been established.

§

In order that Christianity should best go on to serve as a matrix, more generally, for the solidarity of the shaken it is necessary, first, that it be well established in its own right: spread to the widest possible extent across diverse cultures; in imaginative terms, rendered as ebullient as possible. 'Second-Person theology', dominant in the New Testament, is by definition strategy for Christian evangelism: building the solidarity of Christians with Christians. The narrative that I want to explore here *presupposes* the rich truth-potential of 'Second-Person theology' at its best.

Moreover, 'Second-Person theology' is also a latent presence, lighting up the background to the critique of philosophic impatience, which is my central theme in Part Three; with epic / lyric / dramatic power.

Yet, in order that Christ should be truly recognized as the ideal embodiment, not only of the confessional solidarity of Christians with Christians but also, in and through that, still more significantly, of the trans-confessional solidarity of the shaken as such, we need, in addition, other qualities of thought which belong far rather to good 'Third-Person theology', and to good 'First-Person theology'; qualities serving essentially as prophylaxis against, or therapy for, evangelistic impatience – which originates as a disease of 'Second-Person theology'.

There are, to be sure, other common Christian diseases chiefly associated with the other domains. In the case of 'Third-Person theology': an un-catholic spirit of boasting which may, at worst, be positively sectarian. And in the case of 'First-Person theology': automatic mere assimilation to the ethos of the surrounding secular world. Both these subsidiary types of disease tend to weaken one's resistance to the temptations primarily stemming from evangelistic impatience. But, in Trinitarian terms, my next step is to consider the potential contribution of 'Third-Person theology', at its best, to healing us from the spiritual sickness that remains hardest of all to detect for a thinking narrowly confined to 'Second-Person theology'. This is the topic of Part Two.

And then in Part Three I enter the domain of 'First-Person theology'; considered as a secularizing re-contextualization of the critique in Part Two.

Part II

RECOIL FROM EVANGELISTIC IMPATIENCE:
MYSTICAL THEOLOGY / GNOSTICISM

Chapter 3

'MYSTICAL THEOLOGY'

'Dionysius the Areopagite'

So: how has it, as a matter of historical fact, become possible to think the equation, the kingdom of God = the solidarity of the shaken?

The final movement towards a fully explicit conception of the solidarity of the shaken, in all its proper sacred-ness, belongs to post-Enlightenment philosophy; partnered first of all by Abrahamic religious tradition, and then by other religions.

Take the case of Christianity in particular, from this point of view. Christianity clearly does have rich poetic potential to contribute. Thus, the solidarity of the shaken is solidarity based upon nothing other than a shared dedication to the ideal of perfect truth-as-openness. Christ – precisely, one might say, as a prime symbol of perfect truth-as-openness – is crucified by the protagonists of closed-mindedness: gang, mob and herd, conjoined. Christian faith however affirms that God has vindicated him. The Crucified Dissident, a second, only marvellously less embittered, Amos, is revealed as our Saviour …

Alas though, Christian history – like the history of religion in general, but Christian history not least – is one long story of backsliding from this truth-potential. Why? Above all, due to a recurrent disease. Namely: evangelistic impatience.

For, evangelistic impatience exalts, not truth-as-openness, but on the contrary some sacralized form of supposed moral, metaphysical and historiographical truth-as-correctness; informing, not the solidarity of the shaken, but rather a solidarity of 'true believers'. It preys upon the universal, elementary, all too human craving to feel oneself in settled possession of sacred truth-as-correctness; to the exclusion of the forever unsettling, *shaken* urge to truth-as-openness. This craving may simply manifest as moral indolence: not wanting to be bothered by the challenge of other points of view. Or it may be aggressive: a delight in clever polemic, winning arguments, as a game. Or, perhaps: a delight in sheer hatred of the other, an excuse for abandoning civilized inhibition, letting off steam, or worse. I am talking about a broad spectrum of desires on which the impatient evangelist can play – in each case alike, essentially by identifying salvation with the *fetishization* of some supposed form of supreme truth-as-correctness, 'knowing' God in that sense. In other words: by converting a tradition, the real truth-potential of which consists in the religious honouring of perfect truth-as-openness, solidarity of the shaken, into a mere sacred ideology, a set of pleasurably rigidified closures, instead. This is what *das unglückliche Bewußtsein*, in all its forms, neurotically loves. Evangelistic impatience thrives on its appeal to *das unglückliche Bewußtsein*, the ubiquitous mentality of gangs, mobs and human herds, in general.

Where, then, within Christian theology do we find any real push-back against evangelistic impatience? Consider, first, the work of 'Dionysius (or Denys) the Areopagite' – or 'Pseudo-Dionysius'.

§

Dionysius the Areopagite is not an especially charming writer. His style tends to be somewhat drily schematic. However, the authority he accrued, first in Byzantium, and then in the mediaeval West, was not only due to the twofold confusion of his identity – as his choice of pseudonym disguised his actual late fifth- or early sixth-century date, and caused him to be identified, instead, both with the first-century Athenian contemporary of St. Paul mentioned in *Acts* 17.34 and, also, with the legendary first bishop of Paris, a martyr victim of the Decian persecution in the mid-third century.[1]

More importantly, he was honoured for the sheer originality of his thought.

This originality is associated with his coinage of two terms. On the one hand: *mustiké theología*, 'mystical theology'. On the other hand: *hierarchía*, 'hierarchy'.

Along with his treatise on *The Divine Names*, Dionysius's little work entitled *The Mystical Theology* represents an injection, so to speak, of pure philosophic shaken-ness into Christian theological tradition. And one might well say that the notion of 'hierarchy' – developed in two treatises, *The Celestial Hierarchy*, an analysis of all that the Bible has to say about angels, and *The Ecclesiastical Hierarchy* – has essentially to do with the divine inspiration for solidarity-building on this basis. Thus, *The Ecclesiastical Hierarchy* discusses the structure of the Church as a dramatic representation of heaven on earth.

§

An elementary formula for the essential truth-potential of Abrahamic religion, generally, is that it consists of the interplay between (a) a formidable capacity to energize solidarity and (b) *two* species of shaken-ness. The first of these two species of shaken-ness, indigenous to Abrahamic tradition right from the outset, is that which gives rise to what I am calling the '*Amos* impulse'. The second species, a subsequent addition, is the shaken-ness deriving from 'philosophy', in a broad sense. The *Amos* impulse lies at the always potentially resurgent origin of the tradition; philosophy supplies supplementary therapeutic critique of the tradition's corruptions.

Both are forms of shaken-ness. However, to adopt Fukuyama's useful terminology, the shaken-ness of the *Amos* impulse, although megalothymotic in expression, is isothymotic in substance: it demands justice in the sense of equal rights for all. By contrast, the shaken-ness at the origins of philosophy is essentially megalothymotic all the way through: it demands justice in the sense of due respect for the right of the individual questioner to raise far-reaching questions. The *Amos* impulse is embattled against the self-defensive prejudices of the privileged; shaken philosophy, against the banal prejudices of the masses as such.

Within the establishment churches of Dionysius's day, the *Amos* impulse appears in fact to have been largely dormant. It had of course been vividly alive in the original Jesus-movement. But the evangelistic impatience of the early Church had effectively subordinated *Amos*-impulse concern for the suffering of the oppressed poor, resultant from their poverty, to concern for the suffering of persecuted Christians, resultant from their profession of faith. And after Christianity had triumphed, to become the official civil religion of the Empire that had previously persecuted it, the inertia of evangelistic impatience grew so entangled with the self-defensive prejudices of the privileged, as such, that it tended to suppress the *Amos* impulse altogether. It is of course true that the counter-cultural heroism of the martyrs was replaced by the counter-cultural asceticism of monks and hermits. But the monasteries needed rich patrons if they were to flourish the way that evangelistic impatience demanded. So, they could not afford to be *overly* counter-cultural in ethos. The remarkable figure of Salvian, presbyter in mid-fifth-century southern Gaul and church chronicler, is the exception that proves the rule. Reflecting on the successive barbarian invasions of the Empire, which had begun in the late fourth century – and on all the consequent turmoil and destruction – Salvian interpreted these disasters, very much after the manner of *Amos*, as an expression of punitive divine judgement on a society in which the rich had viciously exploited the poor. He indeed denounced the very institution of inherited wealth, urging that good Christians were honour-bound, at their death, to bequeath everything to the Church, as an agency of charitable assistance to the destitute. However, it seems that Salvian was very much alone in his views.[2]

In the Byzantine East of that period, it may well be that there was a good deal more *Amos* impulse at work, in the 'heretical' form of Messalianism. Anti-establishment, anti-sacramentalist, ascetic drop-outs or loose-disciplined monks, the Messalians (or Euchites) were also, it seems, fundamentally anti-intellectual. As a result, they have left no literary legacy. We know about them only from the, no doubt, biased testimony of their Orthodox enemies. It is unclear how far they constituted an organized movement; or how far 'Messalian' was just a term of abuse, loosely applied to a general type of non-conformist holy man, unruly enthusiasts, prone to claim direct, physical encounters with God in prayer. In the end, we simply do not know enough about the Messalians to judge them.

But what we *can* say is that Dionysius, for his part, represents the other, philosophical species of shaken-ness, pure and simple. And Alexander Golitzin has argued that we should see him very much – in his monastic context – as a dedicated philosophic *anti*-Messalian.[3] Thus, Golitzin suggests that the prime reason for his adoption of a sub-apostolic pseudonym was precisely to give his work, above all *The Ecclesiastical Hierarchy*, a certain extra heft, by way of contribution to the struggle against these 'heretics'.

At any rate, 'Dionysius' was an Athenian name, a pseudonym chosen to honour the city of Plato. There had of course been a number of Christian Platonists before Dionysius: notably, for instance, Justin Martyr, Clement of Alexandria, Origen, Evagrius, Basil of Caesarea, Gregory of Nyssa, Gregory of Nazianzus, Augustine. However, these thinkers for the most part invoke the authority of Plato either as back-up to their apologetic arguments for the metaphysical truth-as-correctness of Christian faith or else as an aid to their conceptualizing the supposed moral truth-as-correctness of Christian discipleship. The element of Platonist tradition that really counts as a contribution to what I am calling 'philosophic shaken-ness' – its testimony to the rightful sovereignty of truth-as-*openness* – is, by contrast, the *apophatic* doctrine, that systematic de-sacralization of truth-as-correctness in general, which one finds especially in the *Neo*-Platonism stemming from Plotinus. Dionysius is by no means the first Christian thinker to draw on this pre-Christian tradition – Gregory of Nyssa is a notable predecessor in the late fourth century – but he *is* the first to make it absolutely central to his thought. And his work is arguably the real opening of the sluice-gates, to admit the radical challenge that it represents to Christian evangelistic impatience, as such.

Implicitly, as a '*mystical theologian*', his thought is centred on *that* challenge; whilst, as a theoretician of '*hierarchy*', he is at the same time, implicitly, also a critic of the pagan Platonist tradition, for its lack of any adequate solidarity-building strategy.

§

Granted, Dionysius has no actual name for the sickness of evangelistic impatience, no historical account of its development. Nevertheless, he finds in the pagan philosophic tradition initiated by Plotinus – and mediated to him, more immediately, by Proclus – something that is very much a medicine against it.[4] The Neo-Platonist remedy effectively consists in an absolute, generalized refusal to indulge the universal human craving for truth-as-correctness, alike whether dogmatic or sceptical, insofar as it threatens to occlude the proper sacredness of truth-as-openness alone.

Thus, Plotinus's thought, as a whole, echoes the famous – famously enigmatic – teaching which Plato in the *Republic* attributes to Socrates: that, just as

> the sun gives to what is seen … not only its ability to be seen, but also birth, growth and sustenance … [so too with] the things that are known, say not only that their being known comes from the good, but also that they get their existence and their being from it as well – though the good is not being, but something far surpassing being in rank and power.[5]

In the context of Platonist thought – the complete opposite, in this regard, to Heideggerian thought! – I think one might well say that 'being' is whatever belongs to the domain of truth-as-correctness. It is what is shaped by the ideal 'forms', the 'ideas', studied by abstract thought, at its best; the order that abstract thought extracts from the relative chaos of immediate phenomena. The true 'being' of things is just what a correct categorization, a correct analysis, a correct explanation show about them. But 'the good' on the other hand, in the sense of the authentically sacred, is 'beyond being' (*epekeina tés ousias*) inasmuch as the criteria by which it is recognized, in any utterance, are on the contrary the marks of that utterance having been inspired by an impulse towards truth-as-openness. 'The good' indeed relates to 'the things that are known' – that is, to the objects of correct knowledge – as the source of their 'being'. The logic of this is simply that, although it is not '*the* good' in itself, *un-fetishized* truth-as-correctness does indeed mediate 'the good'; as the supreme goodness of 'the good', which is 'beyond being', flows out into the 'being' of things. In other words: to follow the dictates of perfect truth-as-openness is, of course, always *also* to be concerned with, and to honour, truth-as-correctness in all its forms, for its character as truth. The self-revealing truth of sun-like goodness is actively immanent within the truth of 'being', open-mindedly considered; the one channelling the other. And yet, that immanence is equally transcendence. 'The good' that is truth-as-openness is, in Plotinus's phrase, 'being's generator'[6]. It is the cause of 'being', in the sense of putting 'being' in its proper place. It imparts the proper meaning that things have: their meaningfulness to all manner of thought – that is, not only to thought explicitly concerned with the moral demands of truth-as-openness – but to thought more immediately interested in truth-as-correctness, as well. Nevertheless, it sets limits to the status of that latter sort of meaning. 'The good' remains 'beyond being' precisely inasmuch as truth-as-openness is 'beyond' truth-as-correctness – 'in rank and power'.

Plato himself nowhere really develops the Socratic notion that he plays with here. But Plotinus does, at length. Plotinus's work is the rumbling of a great earthquake, which has its epicentre in this original insight.

The pursuit of truth-as-correctness is always in the service of some particular project – of curiosity, or technical mastery, or manipulation. Truth-as-openness, by contrast, is just an unlimited sheer receptivity. Intent on thinking beyond the multiplicity of particular projects associated with truth-as-correctness, and towards the limitless-ness of perfect truth-as-openness, Plotinus speaks of that supreme limitless-ness as 'the one' (*to hen*). The highest wisdom, as he sees it, consists of a contemplative participation in 'the one'; a participation which he calls '*theória*' – although it is not at all a matter of 'theoretical' knowing in the modern English sense!

In neuropsychological terms, *theória* is surely pure right-hemisphere insight. True philosophy, then, consists of an ideal collaboration between the two hemispheres, enshrining the potential for *theória* intrinsic to 'intellectuality' (*nous*). *Theória*, participation in 'the one', arises within the enabling context of philosophic participation in 'intellectuality', just as participation in 'intellectuality' arises within the enabling context of all humanity's potential participation in 'universal soul' (*psukhé*); which in turn is the initial, pre-philosophical impulse towards truth-as-openness, lifting human life beyond mere carnal existence, the level of 'matter'. At each level, the ascent as Plotinus envisages it involves a fresh sort of participation: since truth-as-openness, unlike truth-as-correctness, is truth which by its very nature tends to dissolve one's already given sense of identity, for the sake of some altogether more generous, and troublesome, belonging.

The impatient evangelist proposes one act of conversion – and then peace of mind, in the settled assurance of sacred correctness. Not so Plotinus!

Truth-as-correctness is truth potentially *fixable* in objective propositional form. Again, truth-as-openness is not fixable: in this regard, one and the same proposition may mean a range of different things, all depending on who is speaking, when, where, and to whom. If we are to appreciate truth-as-openness, we have frankly to acknowledge this inevitable slipperiness. As Plotinus puts it:

> Note that the phrase 'transcending being' [*epekeina tés ousias*] assigns no character, makes no assertion, allots no name [in the way that thought oriented towards truth-as-correctness does], [but] carries only the denial of particular being; and in this there is no attempt to circumscribe it: to seek to throw a line about that illimitable nature would be folly, and anyone thinking to do so cuts himself off from any slightest and most momentary approach to its least vestige ... Its definition, in fact, could be only 'the ineffable' ... *We are in agony for a true expression* ... If we are led to think positively of *the one*, name and thing, there would be more truth in silence: the designation, a mere aid to enquiry, was never intended for more than a preliminary affirmation of absolute simplicity to be followed by the rejection of even that statement: it was the best that offered, but remains inadequate to express the nature indicated.[7]

That there is just one ultimate principle of sacredness – this Plotinian '*one*' being truth-as-openness – I hold to be a correct proposition. And yet, even here, the actually intended meaning of the proposition, inevitably, slips and slides. Insofar as the term 'truth-as-openness' itself decays in actual practice, to become a mere item of jargon, all too glibly integrated into arguments, one might be obliged to confess that the one ultimate principle of sacredness is *not* (what is then meant by) 'truth-as-openness'. But, even in that case, since the underlying truth-potential of the original proposition remains, and silence is *not* after all the be-all and end-all of wisdom, it is still better to say that the ultimately sacred is *not not*-truth-as-openness ...

Insofar as the pursuit of truth-as-correctness is cut adrift from the pursuit of truth-as-openness, it is instrumentalized: serving, perhaps, the egoistic desire of the individual to be recognized as an expert; or a corporate enterprise's desire for knowledge useful to its various aims. Truth-as-openness, by contrast, is a commitment to thoughtfulness purely and simply for its own sake. It is an absolute spontaneity of thoughtful attention, undistracted: as Plotinus puts it, a 'thus and no otherwise than thus'.[8] Or rather – he further remarks – when it comes to the spontaneity of 'the one', it is actually truer to say that there is *no* 'thus', *no* 'not thus'; no deliberation about particular purposes whatsoever. He is thinking here of sentences in the form of: 'If you want to achieve this, then you must act thus.'

With regard to 'the one', even to think in such calculative terms at all is misleading. So, he continues:

> The one ... is beyond all things that are 'thus': standing before the indefinable you may name any of these sequents [the whole class of secondary goods, analysable by calculative thought] but you must say, 'This is none of them': at most it is to be conceived as the total power [of the truly divine] towards things, supremely self-concentred, being what it wills to be or rather projecting into existence what it wills, itself higher than all will, will a thing beneath it.⁹

It is 'higher than all will', in the sense of 'all *self-serving* will, all *instrumentalising* will'; 'beyond being', inasmuch as all beings have their own inertia, and all higher beings their own self-serving, and instrumentalizing, will.

Compare the God of evangelistic impatience. Is not *that* God precisely an instrumental projection of His evangelists' self-serving wilfulness, His converts' self-serving wilfulness: the evangelists intent on measurable results; the converts intent on comfortable integration into the herd? 'The one', as evoked by Plotinus, is everything that the resultant God is not. Plotinus himself is not thinking in particular – or, at least, not explicitly – about Christian or Rabbinic Jewish evangelistic impatience. But the *theória* with which he serves 'the one' is just the most radical subversion of such talkative hubris, generally. This *theória* is perfect truth-as-openness, recognized as sacred in itself; and therefore, entirely transcending the particularity of any specific religious tradition, no matter how rich the tradition in question may be in poetic potential to evoke, and to celebrate, it. 'Imagine,' Plotinus thus writes,

> a small luminous mass serving as centre to a transparent sphere, so that the light from within shows upon the entire outer surface, otherwise unlit ... [And] let us then abstract the corporeal mass, retaining the light as power ...

Here we have the act of the Neo-Platonist philosopher, who removes the mass of a particular religious tradition from the sphere of universal wisdom. The mass is luminous with truth-as-openness; but, at the same time, it is lumpish with conventionally agreed notions of sacred truth-as-correctness. So, the philosopher lifts it out, in order to leave behind the pure light of truth-as-openness alone. The result:

> We can no longer speak of the light in any particular spot; it is equally diffused within and throughout the entire sphere. We can no longer even name the spot it occupied so as to say whence it came or how it is present; we can but seek, and wonder as the search shows us the light simultaneously present at each and every point ... ¹⁰

The mass that has been extracted here is, precisely, everything that evangelistic impatience is liable to colonize, and to dim.

§

Dionysius follows Plotinus as far as he can, without ever removing the 'luminous mass' of specifically Christian faith from the 'transparent sphere' of his wisdom.

Or rather, as I have said, he follows Proclus, who in turn follows Plotinus. Proclus takes Plotinus's thought and, somewhat fussily, adorns it with an extensive lace-pattern of conceptual 'threes'. Dionysius develops an alternative, Christian version of such lace-patterning. But Plotinus still remains, in both cases, a dominant inspiration.

And then – at the heart of his little treatise, the *Mystical Theology* – Dionysius also follows Gregory of Nyssa in reading the numinous account, in *Exodus* 19.10-25, 20.18-21, of Moses ascending Mount Sinai to encounter God, as symbolizing the ascent of shaken philosophic thought, in general, towards the ultimate ineffability of the authentically divine.

Plato compares 'the good beyond being' to the sun. *Exodus* 20.21 speaks of Moses approaching 'the thick darkness where God was'. It is Gregory who in his *Life of Moses* first, paradoxically, writes of the highest truth as a '*dazzling dark*'.[11] But in Gregory's work this is just a throwaway remark; made in the context of a lengthy book, covering the whole of the Moses story. Dionysius by contrast picks it out; sets it right at the beginning of his much shorter and more closely focussed work; and then repeats it, so as to establish the whole theme of that work. The dazzling sunlight of the Platonic 'good beyond being' – recognized as pure truth-as-openness valued strictly for its own sake – is, conversely, 'thick darkness' to the intellect still craving some assurance of sacralized truth-as-correctness. To write a book, as Dionysius is doing, is straight away to be prone to that craving. And so, like a recovering addict, he prays

> to become the darkness that cancels [what the devotees of sacralised truth-as-correctness claim as] light. Or [in other words]: through *not*-scanning and *not*-researching, to see and to know – just by virtue of having [thus] *given up on* seeing and knowing – what [forever] *exceeds* all seeing, all knowing; and, in this apophatic fashion, to praise that which is beyond being, and transcends all things – just as sculptors chip away at the marble which encases the image within, and, by that chipping away, reveal its hidden beauty.[12]

Negation ... Negation of negation ... Chip chip chip ... Note that both theism and atheism are, by the same token, equally transcended here. For both alike lay claim to ultimate truth-as-correctness with regard to the sacred; both alike originate as ideologies of evangelistic impatience. Mystical theology breaks free from all such tedious disputatiousness. It seeks, fundamentally, to change the subject.

Evangelistic impatience, seductively, sacralizes what it proclaims to be knowledge of ultimate metaphysical, historiographical and moral truth-as-correctness. But mystical theology says no. However cogent your metaphysical theories, it says, however accurate your stories, or however justified your moral opinions, these are not *in themselves* what is sacred. Only truth-as-openness is.

§

But then – as I have said – if mystical theology represents an implicit challenge, from within the Church, to evangelistic impatience, the Dionysian doctrine of 'hierarchy' at the same time represents an implicit challenge, from within the Platonist tradition of philosophy, to that tradition's, in a sense, quite opposite persisting weakness. Namely: its tendency to *philosophic impatience*. That is, the outlook of proud intellectuals simply too impatient to take part in the observances of catholic belonging, in communion with their non-intellectual neighbours.

Thus, on the one hand 'hierarchy' simply names a fundamental feature common to all Neo-Platonist thought: as the Neo-Platonists set out to rank, and to give an account of, all the various different levels of more or less diluted possible participation in 'the one'. But, on the other hand, it also refers to that aspect of Dionysius's own thinking which most significantly represents an advance over the thinking of his philosophic predecessors.

In order to see this: consider, briefly, the pre-history and history of the Platonist tradition, as a whole, leading up to Dionysius. And, in particular, consider how the Platonists conceive of philosophic solidarity.

The first thinker to speak of 'philosophy' as a discipline is said to have been Pythagoras (*c*. 570–*c*. 490 BCE). Pythagoras evidently identified philosophy with the solidarity of the secretive, quasi-monastic, intellectual community that he founded at Croton, in Calabria. The members of this community, both male and female, are said to have shared their possessions in common. With regard to the wider politics of the city they stood for the defence of aristocratic privilege; and the community was, as a result, violently destroyed by the local advocates of democracy. A century and a half later, Plato similarly saw philosophy as being, by its very nature, an anti-democratic enterprise; for had not the democrats of Athens put his revered teacher Socrates to death? The original community of Platonist philosophers was more diffuse than the Pythagorean community had been; much less sectarian. But Plato's conception of wisdom remains essentially bound up with an ideal political solidarity among philosophers as such; that is to say, the class of those most skilled in sophisticated truth-as-correctness. Both in the *Republic* and in the *Laws* the fundamental assumption is made that the privileged class-interest of philosophers as philosophers will immediately coincide with the highest good for the state as a whole; that a utopian regime involves philosopher-rule.

As Kant however writes, against Plato / Socrates: 'It is not to be expected that kings philosophise or that philosophers become kings, nor is it to be desired, because the possession of power corrupts the free judgment of reason inevitably.'[13] Plato's is a 'hierarchical' ideal in the simple sense of being pyramid-shaped. But it is by no means 'hierarchical' in the Dionysian sense; for its rank-ordering is quite shamelessly manipulative, as the rank-ordering of Dionysian 'hierarchy', at any rate, aspires not to be. Socrates, as Plato portrays him, speaks of the pragmatic need to ground social order in a '*gennaion pseudos*', a 'Big Lie': a myth misrepresenting hierarchical artifice as the law of nature.[14] He is speaking here, with ingratiating frankness, to would-be fellow philosophers. But what provision is made, in his doctrine, to satisfy the *thymos*, the claim to dignity, of the un-philosophic under-classes? The myth merely justifies their subjection. *As addressed to them*, it is nothing but a vindication of servility.

Plotinus, for the most part, quietly abandons Plato's politics. His ideal is

> the life of gods and of the godlike and blessed among men, liberation from the alien that besets us here, a life taking no pleasure in the things of earth, the passing of solitary to solitary.[15]

And Porphyry then, the great pagan Neo-Platonist polemicist against Christianity, follows suit. But the disappearance of the 'Big Lie', along with the whole attitude to politics it enshrines, is not yet followed here with any alternative strategy of more empathetic, patient engagement, on the part of the philosophers, with the masses. Impatiently exclusive solidarity among philosophers just gives way to a kind of wisdom, in effect, abstracted from any serious solidarity-strategy at all.

Iamblichus of Chalcis in Syria, a younger contemporary of Porphyry in the generation following Plotinus, may be seen as making a first attempt to remedy this failing. So, Iamblichus sets out to reconcile the Neo-Platonist tradition with popular religion in the shape of 'theurgy': the conjuring of the gods worshipped in the various cults primarily of Egypt. His treatise *On the Mysteries* is framed as a response to Porphyry, who in his *Letter to Anebo*, had fundamentally rejected theurgy, on the grounds that it falsely involved approaching the gods as if they might, indeed, be influenced by the prayers of their devotees.[16] For Porphyry it was axiomatic that the gods are the epitome of true wisdom at its purest; and that true wisdom involves radical detachment from the sort of emotions, the pitying love, that theurgy seeks to stimulate in them. But Iamblichus radically challenges this conventional notion of wisdom. He is interested in how divine truth is to cascade from the highest reaches of the Neo-Platonist pyramid, where truth is apprehended in purely philosophic terms, all the way down to its lower levels, in which mythic imagination is dominant. And he wants to affirm a type of mythic thinking with which, unlike the Socratic 'Big Lie', the poorer and less sophisticated classes can engage enthusiastically; through which they can channel their most urgent desires. 'Theurgy', then, is his name for such mythic thinking, rendered as transparent as possible to philosophic open-mindedness, whilst crystallizing a certain sort of solidarity also inclusive of non-philosophers.

Another century and a half later, Proclus follows the lead of Iamblichus, rather than Porphyry; as, again, does Dionysius. But now we can see the real benefits of Christian evangelistic ambition – more or less counter-balancing the damage done by evangelistic impatience. It creates an institution which is so much more effective in doing the job which Iamblichus and Proclus had entrusted to pagan theurgy. Namely: creating effective channels of grace right from the very top to the very bottom of the Neo-Platonist pyramid, or 'hierarchy', of 'soul'-life.

For this, after all, is the whole function of 'hierarchy', as Dionysius conceives it. It is a strategy designed to channel divine grace into human society, just as widely and as deeply as possible. By definition, the most successful 'hierarchy' is that which is most catholic in its outreach, drawing people of all sorts together, on the basis of shared respect for genuine moral authority. The Church of Dionysius's day had grown to be a vast, yet remarkably coherent institution aiming, at least, to do just that. Its reach extended over the whole area of the old Roman Empire and beyond; it included people of every class. It also provided a spiritual home for Neo-Platonist philosophers, intent on contemplating the very essence of true divine authority. When Dionysius speaks of 'hierarchy' he is celebrating the organizational structures which had produced that unique range of connectivity.

In *The Celestial Hierarchy* he discusses the cascade of grace, as shaking-power, into human history, symbolically represented by the angels.[17] From the various references to the angels in the Bible, he constructs a pioneering 'hierarchical' classification, three ranks of three. First: seraphim, cherubim and thrones. Second: dominions, virtues and powers. Third: principalities, archangels and simple angels.

In *The Ecclesiastical Hierarchy*, then, the highest level of authority is attributed to the sacraments, considered in themselves: Baptism, the Eucharist and the Consecration of Oils.[18] Next come the ministers, as such: bishops ('hierarchs'), priests and deacons. 'Hierarchs' are charged with 'perfecting': they have supervision, especially, of monks; (countering Messalianism). Priests are charged with 'illuminating' the ordinary laity. And deacons are charged with 'purifying' those not (yet) admitted to the Eucharist, that is, catechumens and public penitents, all manner of sinners and the demon-possessed.

Compare the mystery cults celebrated by Iamblichus and Proclus. Concerned as these were, precisely, to preserve their small-group element of mystery, they lacked the insatiable evangelistic drive of the Church. And, whilst this had the benefit of preserving them from the snares of evangelistic impatience, it will at the same time inevitably have limited their 'hierarchical' down-thrust: that is, their basic potential to communicate divine love even to those self-identified as the lowest of the low.

§

By 'hierarchy', Dionysius means the ideal political dynamic of organized religion, as such. A maximum diffusion of truth-as-openness through the moral authority of a religious institution set up, at any rate in principle, to honour it. Whilst, in his 'mystical theology', he reaffirms Neo-Platonic philosophical shakenness, in his doctrine of 'hierarchy' he balances that with a narrative-rich, catholic solidarity-strategy, to match.

Or, in other words: 'hierarchy', for Dionysius, is strategy for the promotion of truth-as-openness by (correctly) *authoritarian* means.

But then – as soon as one says this – there is an obvious problem! The word 'authoritarian' straight away reminds one of *The Authoritarian Personality*. That great sociological study, conducted shortly after the Second World War, surveyed a large sample of American citizens, with a view to identifying the whole network of attitudes characteristic of 'the potentially fascist individual'.[19] 'Authoritarian' here is thus, in essence, a designation for prejudices liable to render certain categories of people especially liable to manipulation by totalitarian propaganda. And the word 'hierarchy' is, likewise, used with consistently derogatory connotations, of 'potential fascism', in this classic work. Nor is there anything eccentric about such use of the two words. It is of course simply what they have come to mean in standard liberal parlance. Yet, we lack any viable alternative for expressing what, in the primordial thought of Dionysius, 'hierarchy' was meant to designate; no cleaner alternative term, to which we might retreat, for 'authoritarianism', as the set of attitudes bound up with 'hierarchy', in this not at all 'fascistic' sense.

Hannah Arendt, intent on analysing the specificity of totalitarianism as a political disease, insists on proper clarity. So, she writes:

> Since authority always demands obedience, it is commonly mistaken for some form of power or violence.

That is to say, the word is confusingly misused, with reference to different means of getting people to obey; whereas properly speaking, *on the one hand*

> authority precludes the use of external means of coercion; where force is used, authority itself has failed.

And *on the other hand*, authority is no less

> incompatible with persuasion, which presupposes equality and works through a process of argumentation. Where arguments are used, authority is left in abeyance. Against the egalitarian order of persuasion stands the authoritarian order, which is always hierarchical.[20]

To which I would add (a) that 'persuasion', as an alternative to authority, is by no means necessarily to be thought of as a process of pure rationality. In order to achieve results effectively substituting for a culture of authority, a rival culture of persuasion must, for the most part, depend upon manipulative lies, half-lies, appeals to crass unthinking prejudice. And (b): at every level of the Dionysian ecclesiastical hierarchy, in sermons, teaching and counselling, there will of course always be plenty of theologically informed rational argumentation. It is just that the solidarity-building work of the Church as a whole does not *depend* upon persuasion by such means. It depends, rather, upon people's *prior* sheer respect for those who symbolically represent the moral authority of the institution, and of the ideals it stands for.

For the academic contributors to *The Authoritarian Personality* 'authoritarianism' equals latent potential totalitarianism. It remains a fascinating study, but the terminology is surely all wrong. As Arendt argues, there is nothing, in the proper sense, 'authoritarian' or 'hierarchical' about totalitarian regimes.[21] On the contrary, they depend entirely upon manipulation and violence. An authoritarian polity is pyramid-shaped, with everything open to view and subject to legal restraint, but a successful totalitarian one is onion-like, with an uninhibited leadership hidden under layer upon layer of more moderate-seeming front organizations.

Quite unlike an authoritarian regime designed for the preservation of tradition, totalitarian ones are agencies of perpetual revolution. The *truly* totalitarian regimes of post-Christendom, above all in Germany and the Soviet Union, were indeed virulent in their anti-clerical *anti-authoritarianism*.[22]

Moreover, consider *David Graeber's* argument, regarding 'the moral grounds of economic relations'.[23] Graeber compares three such 'moral grounds': (a) an ethos of exchange, giving rise to morality essentially conceived as payment of debts; (b) an ethos of ideal communism based on the principle, 'from each according to their abilities, to each according to their needs'; (c) an ethos of hierarchy, governed by principles of *noblesse oblige*. Strictly speaking, he insists, neither communism nor hierarchy involves debt. Developing Graeber's distinctions (in a way that he may or may not have approved) one might surely say that *das unglückliche Bewußtsein* inclines to a manipulative conception of moral indebtedness, playing upon an exacerbated sense of guilt; and that ideal communism is the pure antithesis to this, mobilizing not so much the guilt of the indebted as the fellow-feeling of the compassionate. And yet, it remains questionable how *politically effective* such communism can be, on a large scale, without at least some authoritative back-up, of the most benignly hierarchic – that is to say, Dionysian – kind.

Our first lessons in morality come from the naturally hierarchic relation of children to their parents. Of course, hierarchy may then be corrupted into an infantilizing regime for adults, perverted by ideologies of caste, or racism. But Dionysian hierarchy really is something else: nothing more or less than a megalothymotic spirit – on the part of those now invested with moral authority, as the licensed representatives of *divine* parenthood – informing an ideally well-structured, and well-ordered, all-pervasive culture of stable isothymia.

The originality of Dionysius, indeed, consists both in the radicalism of his philosophic, 'mystical-theological' testimony to truth-as-openness and in the systematic nature of his moral-authoritarian 'hierarchic' theology. The Church is the 'body of Christ' (*Romans* 12.5; *1 Corinthians* 12.27; *Ephesians* 1.22-23, 5.29-30; *Colossians* 1.18); and Christ, of course, is higher than the angels (*Ephesians* 1.20-23; *Hebrews* 1). The ecclesiastical hierarchy outranks the celestial hierarchy inasmuch as this is the context in which the solidarity-principle of hierarchy encounters the provocations of Christomorphic shaken-ness. But it is in the celestial hierarchy that we see the ideal essence of hierarchy itself, at its very purest, abstractly imagined. Thus, the angels do not need to be coerced, as delinquent humans sometimes do, in order to obey God's basic commands. Nor do they need to be persuaded, by manipulative, debt-invoking argument, as reluctant humans sometimes do. They obey quite simply because they admire; because they adore; because they are amazed.

True, the solidarity that Dionysius celebrates, as a theoretician of ecclesiastical hierarchy, is not yet the solidarity of the shaken, in the full sense. It is simply a well-structured community of shaken fellow-believers, held together by mutual respect. The solidarity of the shaken, in the full sense, requires a much more secular environment in which to grow. And it needs nourishment from the *Amos* impulse, in all the various modern forms which that impulse takes.

Yet, I am arguing, the solidarity of the shaken is properly a sacred ideal. And to vindicate its sacredness, in the most effective fashion, does it not at the same time require to be integrated with the kind of moral bonding, the convivial catholic connectivity, that only a culture of truly open-minded – non-coercive and non-manipulative – authoritarianism, in the most positive sense, can supply? Does it not require a cultivated ethos of respect for the moral authority of those who represent true freedom? That Dionysian hierarchy, as a solidarity-building principle, is eminently compatible with philosophic, or mystical-theological, shaken-ness Dionysius himself demonstrates. Its relationship to the very different shaken-ness of the *Amos* impulse is more problematic. Even so, I see no reason to suppose that the tensions here are altogether un-negotiable. Indeed, to acknowledge Christ the second, greater Amos – Christ the crucified dissident – precisely as the pinnacle of the ecclesiastical hierarchy is already, I think, in itself to set the stage for such negotiations. If Golitzin is right to suggest that Dionysius should be read very much as an anti-'Messalian' thinker – and if I am right in conjecturing that 'Messalianism' may, at least sometimes, have included a genuine upsurge of the *Amos* impulse – then in his particular case the problem is, to that extent, compounded. But the *Amos* impulse *need* not involve the sort of utter disengagement from the church hierarchy that their orthodox critics attributed to the 'Messalians'. Nor, for that matter, *need* theological apologists for the hierarchy insist on honouring only conservative figures as models of faith. And a thinking released from both these species of oversimplification, to the left and to the right, still has plenty of room left for manoeuvre, in between.

Meister Eckhart

Doubt has sometimes been expressed, to what extent Dionysius is 'really' a Christian thinker, as well as a Neo-Platonist. This arises from his apparent complete lack of concern with the problematics of what I am calling 'Second-Person theology'.[24] He is, to be sure, quite orthodox in his acknowledgement of Christ as the Second Person of the Trinity. But the point is just that he does not appear to be at all essentially concerned with spelling out what that means. And hence the radical one-sidedness of his thinking, considered as an expression of shaken-ness: so rich in the implicit megalothymia of shaken philosophy, here reconciled with conservative ecclesiastical isothymia; yet, so devoid of the more *militantly* isothymotic *Amos* impulse. Not all 'Second-Person theology', by any means, is inspired by the *Amos* impulse. But the *Amos* impulse is, I think, always the tremor at the heart of 'Second-Person theology' *at its most authentic*. And the great weakness of the Dionysian notion of 'hierarchy', in particular, is its apparent divorce from this complementary element.

In Trinitarian terms, Dionysius is both a 'First-Person theologian' and a 'Third-Person theologian'. He does not openly debate with the pagans. But the element of truth in his notion of 'hierarchy' consists in the 'First-Person theological' polemical answer it contains, to pagan Neo-Platonism. And what he calls 'mystical theology' is first and foremost a contribution to pure 'Third-Person theology'.

One might compare, for example, the earlier phenomenon of Montanism. This is also primarily a 'Third-Person theological' movement, inasmuch as the Montanist leaders laid megalothymotic claim to an ecclesiastically unlicensed form of authority, deriving from their charism of prophecy. The megalothymia of the Montanists, on the other hand, appears to have been laced with a good deal of anarchic isothymia, as well. And it is the same with the Messalians of Dionysius's own day, with their charismatic asceticism. These were more or less fanatical movements, decidedly inimical to what Dionysius envisaged as good hierarchy. Therefore, he for his part pioneers a movement of spiritual renewal energized by philosophic megalothymia alone: a far more socially conservative alternative.

But then, some eight centuries later, Meister Eckhart brings the tradition of 'mystical theology' to a certain culmination – even whilst seasoning it with a fresh flavour of *Amos*-impulse isothymia. So, Eckhart preaches mystical sermons in the vernacular, to reach the common people, at a time when preaching in the vernacular, of any kind, was not yet usual. He praises 'spiritual poverty' in the most extravagant terms. And he becomes a hero of folk tales, in which he appears not least as a radical dis-respecter of conventional social status. Eckhart by no means repudiates the theory of Dionysian hierarchy. Only, he represents a form of 'Third-Person theology' rendered altogether edgier.

§

As it dissolves complacent notions of metaphysical and moral truth-as-correctness, mystical theology is sometimes described as a 'way of negation'. This, though, is by no means to say that propositions in negative form, saying what God is not, are in any way privileged over propositions in affirmative form, saying what God is. The negativity at issue here is not just a matter of propositional form. Rather, the point is that mystical theology is characterized by a broad tolerance for contradiction: the simultaneous affirming of contradictory propositions, each negating the other. This is a natural consequence of its primary orientation, not towards truth-as-correctness, but towards truth-as-openness. The pursuit of truth-as-correctness is a zero-sum game. Between any two opposing aspects of a topic, it seeks the golden mean: so that the more one aspect is emphasized, the more the other must correspondingly be downplayed. The pursuit of truth-as-openness is different, inasmuch as, in this case, what counts is rather the *shaking-power* of ideas. To attain truth-as-correctness is to arrive at a settled result, quieting the mind; to advance towards perfect truth-as-openness is progressively to be unsettled, by contradictions that can never be resolved. Therefore, the protagonists of mystical theology generally, from Dionysius onwards, have always delighted in hyperbole and paradox.

But Meister Eckhart represents the culmination of the tradition, inasmuch as he is the ultimate master of such provocation, expressed with the very utmost spirited defiance. Not that all his writing is of this kind. His works in Latin, addressed to scholars, are on the whole considerably more conventional than his sermons in German, addressed to a more general audience. And not all of those sermons are equally eccentric. In those which are most 'Eckhartian', however, he defies the banality of evangelistic impatience – its collusion with herd / gang / mob (a) morality, and so with *das unglückliche Bewußtsein* – to a truly extraordinary degree. As a result of which, he has never been canonized.

On the contrary: over the last three years of his life, 1325–8, he was subjected to a series of inquisitorial interrogations. Since he was a Dominican, he was initially required to justify his teachings to Nicolas of Strasbourg, the temporary head of the Dominican Order in Germany; who cleared him. Then, however, the Archbishop of Cologne, Heinrich of Virneburg ordered a further investigation, which led to Eckhart being condemned. When he appealed to Pope John XXII, the case was transferred to the papal court at Avignon, which is where he died. After which, in 1329, the Pope issued a bull, *In agro dominico*, listing twenty-eight statements attributed to Eckhart which had been judged 'heretical' – although clearing him personally of 'heresy', on the grounds that, before his death, he had 'revoked' them. There is, on the other hand, no reason to suppose that he had in fact cracked. The provocations of mystical theology, by definition, can never properly be understood when taken out of context and subjected to pedantic, purely abstract criteria of truth-as-correctness, as opposed to living truth-as-openness; the way the twenty-eight condemned propositions have been. What Eckhart will have rejected, in 'revoking' them, was simply the nonsense that this whole mode of misunderstanding had made of them.

§

The sheer ferocity with which Eckhart appropriates mystical theology is perhaps best illustrated by his famous vernacular Sermon no. 52, *Beati pauperes spiritu*.[25] It is, in fact, quite remarkable that this particular work remained un-condemned by the inquisitors; but, then, they had plenty of other material to consider. And perhaps *Beati pauperes spiritu* was simply too way out. One can only wonder what those who heard it first could have made of it!

The text here is *Matthew* 5.3, 'Blessed are the poor in spirit, for theirs is the kingdom of heaven'. And the basic framework of the argument is summarized in the formula:

A poor man wants nothing, and knows nothing, and has nothing.[26]

These are three aspects of the same.

A poor man *wants* nothing. This is immediately paradoxical! Does not poverty consist in lacking? And the more one lacks, the more, surely – not the less – one wants. But Eckhart, as a member of a religious order bound together by a vow of poverty, is thinking of voluntarily chosen poverty, and then by extension of all other such devout choices, ascetic practices of every kind. The 'wanting' in question is the self-conscious yearning for the kingdom of God which such practices in general express. And what Eckhart is rejecting is precisely the element of self-consciousness involved in this. Evangelistic impatience is forever, either explicitly or implicitly, promising to potential converts, on condition of their being converted – or to the already converted, on condition of their continuing show of loyalty – the complacent pleasure of feeling good about themselves. It is not that Eckhart is rejecting ascetic practices in themselves. Only, his criticism is, in effect, of manipulative preaching which exaggerates the intrinsic value of these practices. Such preaching converts the poverty of the ascetic into a form of seductive spiritual wealth, which then threatens to lapse into the corruption of self-righteousness. Those who are seduced in this fashion, he remarks,

> present an outward picture that gives them the name of saints; but inside they are donkeys, for they cannot distinguish divine truth.[27]

The donkey, of course, is an image of wilfulness. Evangelistic impatience achieves its effects by manipulating people's wilfulness, rendering it devout. But true spiritual poverty, on the contrary, involves the complete abandonment of self-will.

A poor man, secondly, *knows* nothing. Again, preachers in the grip of evangelistic impatience are forever offering, to those they seek to manipulate, the pleasurable sensation of being in possession of definitive moral, metaphysical and historiographical truth-as-correctness. Plotinus and all the other Neo-Platonists after him, not least Dionysius and his Christian followers, set out to frustrate that whole mode of manipulation, by insisting on the *objective* ineffability of 'the one', the divine. Eckhart, however, is primarily concerned here with the *subjective* dynamics of spiritual poverty. He addresses the self-consciousness of the manipulated 'knower': the more or less concealed tingle of self-satisfaction with which impatient evangelists promise to reward compliance. Thus, the manipulated 'knower' is promised the self-satisfaction concomitant to understanding the proper requirements of care for the soul; to having a basic grasp of sacred truth; to having mastered the mystery of God. Eckhart rejects these promises, inasmuch as the self-satisfaction involved immediately, alas, invalidates the supposed knowledge. Indeed, he then doubles down on that rejection:

> Sometimes I have said that a man ought to live so that he did not live for himself or for the truth or for God [sc. in the sense that evangelistic impatience intends]. But now I say something different and something more, that a man who would possess this poverty ought to live as if he does not even *know* that he is not in any way living for himself or for the truth or for God.[28]

The 'poor man', in other words, not only does not pride himself on knowing what it means to care for the soul, to serve the truth or to penetrate the mystery of God; but he does not pride himself on that renunciation, either. Such a one, in short, does not know how to plead his cause, before God, at all.

A poor man, thirdly, *has* nothing. Another paradox; yet further hyperbole:

> I have often said, and great authorities say, that a man should be so free of all things and of all works, both interior and exterior, that he might become a place only for God, in which God could work. Now I say otherwise. If it be the case that ... God may find a place in him in which to work, then I say that so long as that is in man, he is not poor with the most intimate poverty.[29]

Impatient evangelists operate partly with conditional flattery and partly with threats. In this sermon Eckhart is concerned with the flattery. 'Good for you,' the impatient evangelists suggest, 'if you truly *want* to serve God. If you listen attentively, we can give you the necessary *know-how* to do it. And then, look: how much *you have in you*, by way of potential, to offer! How much God needs you, as a "place" in which to work!' Eckhart is working to battle this manipulative impulse of flattery, every step of the way.

Consider the complementarity of these three principles: 'wanting nothing', 'knowing nothing' and 'having nothing'. 'Wanting nothing', here, means sheer *self-forgetful* absorption into the true essence of what we dimly intend when we speak of divine love; just as 'knowing nothing' means sheer *self-forgetful* absorption into the true essence of what we dimly intend when we speak of divine wisdom. And 'having nothing', likewise, means sheer *self-forgetful* absorption into the true essence of what we dimly intend when we speak, more generally, of divine blessedness. In Hegelian terms, again, the primary distortion requiring to be overcome at this level is *das unglückliche Bewußtsein*. 'Having nothing' means retaining no sense of self, either affective or intellectual, into which the boastfully possessive egoism of the Usurper sub-self, there, can insert itself; and through which it can project itself, heaven-wards. Indeed,

> the authorities say that God is a being, and a rational one, and that he knows all things. [But] I say that God is neither being nor rational, and that he does not know this or that.[30]

Here, again, we encounter the old Socratic / Platonist notion of 'the good beyond being'. God is 'not being', if by 'being' one means whatever – 'this or that' – is liable to *representational capture* in terms of truth-as-correctness. And accordingly, God is 'not rational' either – if by 'rational' one means that which has indeed been captured in those terms. But God is what an authentic, impoverished spirit of truth-as-openness *participates in*, instead.

And what is truly startling is the way that Eckhart evokes this ideal by speaking in the retrospective persona of an eternal self, as it were, nostalgic for pre-existence. First: remembering the state of being a potential self, primordially absorbed in God, before Creation. Then: identifying with one's deepest self, as a creature with potential to be reabsorbed into God through proper spiritual impoverishment; or, to use Simone Weil's term, through 'decreation'.[31] On the sixth day of Creation, when all was complete, 'God saw everything that he had made, and indeed, it was very good': *Genesis* 1.31. Of course Eckhart is by no means rejecting that delight in Creation, as such; so essential to good evangelistic proclamation of the gospel.

But here, although preaching a sermon, he is at his most provocatively one-sided, *anti*-evangelistic, sensing the risks of any mere sentimentalizing twist to *Genesis* 1.31. To that end, he elides Creation with the Fall:

> When [prior to Creation] I stood in my original source, I had no [external] God then, and [being one with God] I was my own source. Then I willed not and desired not, since I was a free being and a knower of myself in enjoyment of the truth. Then I willed myself and nothing else. What I willed I was, and what I was, I willed. Here I stood, free of God and of all things. But when I went out from my own free will and I received my created being, then I had a God. Before creatures were, God was not God; he was what he was. But when creatures came to be and received their created being, then God was not God in himself, he was God in the creatures … [32]

Be it noted: in Edmund Colledge's translation five out of the eight appearances of the word 'God' in the above passage have sets of inverted commas around them. I have cited Michael Sells's version, instead, which removes these. Inverted commas were a post-Eckhartian invention of the Renaissance; Eckhart's twentieth-century editor Josef Quint was the first to add them to his text. Translators into English have followed suit, sometimes using them still more extensively; or else have resorted to an upper-case / lower-case distinction between 'God' and 'god'. Sells, as noted above, deplores what he sees as an altogether misguided modern recoiling, here, from apophasis.[33] Thus, Eckhart is surely intent on highlighting the intrinsic ambiguity of the word 'God' in *every* usage: dependent on the moral quality of the one speaking, their poverty of spirit or the lack of it. The punctuation tricks of modern editors and translators simply express a desire, so far as possible, to *minimize* the bewildering ambiguity in which Eckhart for his part *revels*! And this then becomes all the more significant as the passage in question proceeds. In Sells's version:

> Now we say that God, with all that whereby he is God, is not the perfect end of creatures, so great is the richness that the least creature has in God …

On the one hand, there is the false God of impatient evangelism, intent on manipulating human neediness ('behold the perfect end, for all creatures!'); on the other hand, true God, source of the richness which consists in spiritual poverty. *But how can either be told apart from the other?* There is no simple test; truly, we need to be vigilant. Eckhart emphasizes the point, with maximum hyperbole:

> Were it the case that a fly [separated from God] had reason and could rationally seek the eternal abyss of the Godly being from which it came, we say that with all that whereby he is God [as rationally conceived by the still separated creature], he would not be able to fulfil or suffice the fly. Here we pray God that we might be free of God and that we might grasp the truth and enjoy it eternally. There where the highest angel and the fly and the soul are equal [all being equally absorbed within God's infinity], there I stood and willed what I was and was what I willed.[34]

This is said with particular reference to the ideal of 'wanting nothing'; that is, nothing creaturely. And the same anti-evangelistic prayer to God – 'to be made free from God' – along with the same evocation of the soul's pre-existence, also recurs later on in the sermon, this time with reference to the ideal of 'having nothing'.[35]

God does not manipulate. Nor can God, in reality, be manipulated. On the contrary, whatever lies outside the economy of manipulation: just *that* is what belongs to the kingdom of God. But, for animate life, Creation becomes a domain of mutual manipulation at every turn; the Fall of Adam and Eve represents this, in the case of humanity. Cast out of Eden, we survive by manipulating nature, and one another. Impatient evangelism, then, is a bid to manipulate us into serving God. Eckhart's whole counter-project, on the other hand, is to present us with the higher divine truth that constitutes the absolute opposite to manipulation, of any kind; pure truth-as-openness. This truth he here calls the 'breakthrough'.[36] Ideally, it is a breaking right out of Creation – and back – into the indwelling presence of the Creator which persists more or less concealed, as a potential spontaneous energy, somewhere in the deep self of every rational creature.

The sermon concludes, as it were, with a shrug of the shoulders:

> Whoever does not understand what I have said, let him not burden his heart with it; for as long as a man is not equal to this truth, he will not understand these words.[37]

§

Evangelistic impatience operates, on the one hand, with encouraging but manipulative flattery. On the other hand: by deploring the persistent emptiness of our lives, and promising a remedy; even whilst exempting us, however, from the burden of truly having to think, sheltering us from the full shaking-power of difficult moral reality.

Mystical theology, in general, attacks the encouraging flattery. From the beginning it urges believers not to trust evangelistic preaching designed to market faith as a matter of being cheaply, yet flatteringly, 'in the know' about God. And then the notion of 'spiritual poverty' developed in Eckhart's Sermon no. 52 represents the same basic species of mistrust hyperbolically inflated, to an unsurpassable degree.

That, though, is only one aspect of Eckhart's thought. For he also no less vigorously seeks to undermine the defences built by the universal spirit of herd / gang / mob conformism, as such, against difficult moral reality. Indeed, he is not only the consummate mystical theologian. Quite unlike Dionysius he is, as I have said, at the same time a great reviver of the *Amos* impulse, in the context of mystical theology. Thus, in this regard, I am thinking first and foremost of that whole recurrent theme of his preaching: *the birth of God in the soul*. The way in which that theme, in principle, serves rhetorically to equip an Amos-like spirit of resistance against unjust rulers, who seek on the contrary to demean and demoralize those who are under their dominion, in order that they may unquestioningly conform.

The trope of God being 'born' within the soul of each individual true believer is, in one form or another, a commonplace of mediaeval Christian tradition; dating back, at least, to the writing of Gregory of Nyssa, in the later fourth century. Eckhart, however, amplifies it – renders it strange and conspicuous – in three original ways: (a) by the *dramatic* fashion in which he expresses the intimacy between God and the host-soul; (b) by an emphatic insistence on the sheer *necessity* of this gift of grace, if God is to be God at all; and (c) by an insistence on the involvement, in the process, of the Holy Trinity *as a whole*. Let us consider each of these points in turn.

(a) At the great climaxes of his preaching, Eckhart poetically shifts shape. We have already seen how in Sermon 52, when speaking of 'spiritual poverty', he adopts the persona of an eternal soul as such, nostalgic for pre-existence. But when he speaks of the birth of God in the soul, the persona he adopts is that of a mortal individual who is, purely and simply, 'just'; that is, Christ-like. A prime example of this is to be found in the following often-cited passage from Sermon 6, *Justi vivent in aeternum* (*Wisdom* 5: 16):

> The Father gives birth to his Son in eternity, equal to himself. "The Word was with God, and God was the Word." (*John* 1: 1); it was the same in the same nature. Yet I say more: He has given birth to him in my soul. Not only is the soul with him, and he equal with it, but he is in it, and the Father gives his Son birth in the soul in the same way as he gives him birth in eternity, and not otherwise ... The Father gives birth to his Son without ceasing; and I say more: He gives me birth, me, his Son and the same Son.[38]

The preacher began this sermon by talking *about* 'the just'. Now, however, he is speaking *as a representative of* 'the just'. Or, rather: as a representative of every human soul *insofar as* it approximates to Christ-likeness. Amos and his successors, the Hebrew literary prophets, speaking in the persona of God, set out to proclaim the demands of 'justice' with sublime ferocity. The Christian theological notion of the birth of God in the soul reflexively reaffirms the divine authorization of such witness. What Eckhart adds to this reaffirmation is, first of all, fresh drama; freshly *enacted* thought.

(b) In citing that passage from *Justi vivent in aeternum* I omitted one short sentence. Thus: 'the Father,' Eckhart declares,

> gives his Son birth in the soul in the same way as he gives him birth in eternity, and not otherwise. *He must do it whether he likes it or not.*[39]

Setting aside the characteristic tone of provocation here: to be more exact, the point is just that it is impossible God would 'not like' to act in this way. Christian theological tradition has indeed always insisted on the freedom of God's grace, in its character as revelation within history. This is what the gospel adds to pagan Neo-Platonism, as the latter develops an essentially a-historic notion of divine emanation. The dogma of the Trinity gives structure to this Christian openness towards historic contingency, and Eckhart is speaking in Trinitarian terms; he by no means rejects the dogma. However, he is speaking in such terms precisely in order to evoke the divine Unity which transcends the Trinitarian distinctions. And at this depth all contingency falls away. As he also puts it, for example, in Sermon 49 *Beatus venter, qui te portavit, et ubera, quae suxisti*, there is nothing arbitrary about the fundamental divine impulse to be revealed, to speak the Word:

> [God the Father] does not speak this Word by his will, in the sense that when a thing is said or done by the power of the will, by that same power he could refrain if he wished. It is not so with the Father and his eternal Word; [but again] whether he would or not he must speak this Word and beget it unceasingly: for with the Father it is as it were rooted in his nature naturally, as the Father is himself. So you see the Father speaks his Word willingly but not by will, naturally but not by nature [i.e. not according to the sort of wilfulness that is natural to fallen human beings as such]. In this Word the Father speaks my spirit and every individual human being's spirit equally in the same Word. In that speaking you and I are the natural son of God just as the Word itself.[40]

One might, I think, put it like this: that – whereas at the level of Trinitarian distinction there is a great mass of contingent historical truth-as-correctness sucked up (along with much beautiful myth and legend) into the process of divine revelation – at the level of divine unity *what* is being revealed is always, as a matter of strict necessity, pure truth-as-openness alone; how God goes to work in and through *our* being opened up to *one another*, here and now. And Eckhart is talking about that necessity.

(c) As he develops it, the metaphor of divine birth within the soul involves a richly paradoxical interplay between these two levels. Thus, on the one hand, the Christmas story tells of the entry of the Second Person of the Trinity into history, contingently situated in a particular place and at a particular time. But when, on the other hand, this story is transformed into an icon representing the trans-historical *criterion* of divine truth – that is, its necessary nature everywhere and always – then the differentiation between the roles played by the three Persons ceases to apply. If we are talking about the birth of truth-as-openness in the soul, and declaring such truth to be divine – well, each of the three Persons are equally manifestations of *that*. And therefore, it is not only the identity of the 'just' or opened-up soul with the Second Person that we are celebrating. It is the 'just' or opened-up soul's identity with all three divine Persons, alike. Insofar as we are 'just' we participate not only in the work of the Second Person, the one who is born, but also in the work of the First Person, the one who begets, and the work of the Third Person, the one who proceeds from both.[41] For – whereas the doctrine of the Trinity, in the first instance, is the all-encompassing framework for Christian theological truth-as-correctness, that is, the orthodox grammar of the Christian imagination – Eckhart, when he comes to discuss the doctrine, is actually not at all interested in this framework-function. The distinctions which it involves, in effect, fade away here. *All* that Eckhart cares about is (as I would put it) the proper theological subordination of truth-as-correctness, generally, to truth-as-openness.

In the sense that 'metaphysics' is definable as thought aiming at onto-theological truth-as-correctness, he is, essentially, giving *trans*-metaphysical speculation something of a new poetic role, in the preaching of the gospel. 'For He [the Son of God] was made man so that we might be made God': this is Saint Athanasius's classic formulation of a thought that runs right through the post-biblical theological tradition.[42] By deploying the three strategies that I have cited, Eckhart infuses fresh energy into that thought; and furthermore, makes it *the* central theme of his preaching. His aim is evidently to *embolden* the pursuit of truth-as-openness, radically transcending any form of pious herd / gang / mob conformity. And he is doing so in the most forceful, yet thoughtful, fashion. That is what I mean when I say that Eckhart's preaching represents a partial revival of the *Amos* impulse. In Hegelian terms, he is directly confronting '*das unglückliche Bewußtsein*' in Christian form: that is, orthodoxy rigidified, rendered manipulative, the idolatrous worship of a 'God' who is in actual reality little more than a mere projection of one's own servility. As he remarks in *Justi vivent in aeternum*:

> Recently I considered whether there was anything I would take or ask from God. I shall take careful thought about this, because if I were accepting anything from God, I should be subject to him as a servant, and he in giving would be as a master. We shall not be so in life everlasting.[43]

The inquisitors charged with investigating him cited this as one of his worst offending statements.[44] But then they were no doubt anxious because of the way in which people's deference to *themselves* depended upon proper servility towards the God they officially represented; like Amaziah, priest of Bethel, in *Amos* 7.10-17. *Das unglückliche Bewußtsein* is by definition a sacralization of purported truth-as-correctness alone, to the effective exclusion of truth-as-openness; herd / gang / mob existence thus stiffened by self-righteousness. Again, it takes many shapes, by no means all of them theological. But where it is theological, its tendency is always to posit a maximum gulf in nature between the exalted Lord God and the servile individual soul. The whole thrust of Eckhart's preaching is just the opposite of this.

In the Rhineland and the Low Countries, Eckhart, the free-spirited sage, became a figure of folk-legend. Some, at least, of these rather delightful legends were written down and have survived. They appear to have circulated within the more or less antinomian milieu of the so-called 'Brethren of the Free Spirit'; a loosely structured movement of people bonded together in criticism of what to their eyes appeared to be the fundamental betrayal of the gospel by clerical tyranny. That is, the tyranny of clergy altogether lacking in the sort of charisma represented by Eckhart. The first notable written attack on this movement, discussing a specific group investigated by inquisitors in Swabia, is to be found in a treatise by Saint Albert the Great entitled *Compilatio de novo spiritu*. This dates from the 1270s; the days of Eckhart's youth. (Eckhart may in fact have been one of Albert's pupils in the Dominican institute at Cologne.) The Council of Vienne in 1311–12 took measures intended to eradicate the movement – but in vain. It persisted for several generations more; in the fifteenth century developing an increasingly lethal association, in the persecutors' minds, with witchcraft. Marguerite Porete's *Mirror of Simple Souls* was the first great work arguably imbued with its ethos.[45] And then another unequivocal example is the anonymously authored *Sister Catherine Treatise*: a series of exuberant dialogues between 'Sister Catherine' and her confessor, who although unnamed bears a distinct resemblance to the Eckhart of legend. It shows 'Sister Catherine' – in a reversal of roles which suggests the author's desire for ever greater radicalism – becoming her confessor's mentor.[46]

There clearly is a certain sort of kinship between the Brethren of the Free Spirit and the Messalians, a millennium earlier. No doubt any such popular eruption of the *Amos* impulse will be mixed, at times, with elements of narcissism and ignoble resentment, to some extent justifying the hostile reaction of the church hierarchy. And yet, I consider it a quite fundamental principle of ecclesiology that an ideal church should nevertheless be able to give ample space to the awkward truth-potential also inherent in such movements, and to honour it.[47]

Niffarī

So far, in this chapter, I have been talking about Platonism and Christianity – but now, to round it off, let us change tack. As I have said, what fundamentally concerns me here is the role of mystical theology as one of the two prime species of prophylactic strategy not only within Christianity, but within Abrahamic religion generally – against the ever-present temptations of evangelistic impatience; the other species being gnosticism. In the Christian context, to sum up, one might say that Dionysius's original notion of 'mystical theology' represents the coming together of two general themes of reflection:

(a) It emerges as a counter-balance to his thought about 'hierarchy': inasmuch as the latter is concerned with the telos of true evangelism, namely, the establishment of enduringly authoritative solidarity-structures, a civilizing community, within which reflection on the gospel may flourish, and be transmitted, down the generations.

(b) In itself, however, it represents a vigorous critique of evangelistic impatience; an attack on evangelistic impatience's typical over-valuing of mere theological truth-as-correctness, as distinct from truth-as-openness; and consequent hubristic pretensions to a simply impossible fullness of knowledge, with regard to God.

And so too, one might further say that Eckhart's thought, likewise, has two crucial elements:

(a) First, Eckhart's conception of 'spiritual poverty' carries forward that latter aspect of Dionysian mystical theology with astonishing rhetorical energy.

(b) Secondly, Eckhart's preaching of 'the birth of God in the soul' serves as a no less energetic reaffirmation of, and theological support for, the anarchically shaken *Amos* impulse which also lies right at the heart of the primordial gospel proclamation; again, essentially prior to the distorting influence of evangelistic impatience.

However, for the sake of synoptic completeness, let us further consider some non-Christian variants of the same basic critique. In the context of rabbinic Judaism, radical criticism of evangelistic impatience chiefly takes a gnostic form: in the tradition of Kabbalah. I will come back to this in Chapter 5. Islam, on the other hand, is rich in mystical theology; no less radical than the Christian equivalents, but of fascinatingly different aesthetic character.

§

Of course, the overwhelming priority for any ambitious missionary religion, as such, at the time of its launch is simply maximum sheer evangelistic effectiveness. This was the case with Christianity, and it was the same with Islam. Qur'anic evangelism was indeed prodigiously effective from the outset, no doubt in part just because its proclamatory strategy is so straightforward. On the one hand, there is the vivid promise of Paradise; and on the other hand, the no less vivid threat of Hell. This primordial message may, but need not, be interpreted impatiently. As with Christianity, the real importance of spiritual patience, on the part of the Qur'an's interpreters, took some time to emerge. It is however notable how much quicker the mystical recoil from evangelistic impatience took hold in the history of Islam than it had done in the history of the Christian Church. This happened at first quite apart from Neo-Platonist influence. The influence of Neo-Platonism only really started to penetrate Sufi mystical theology in the work of Ibn 'Arabi, who lived from 1165 to 1240 CE. But the beginnings of Sufi recoil are already there long before that. Islamic history is conventionally dated from the *hijrah*, the prophet Muhammad's removal from Mecca to Medina, in 622 CE. And such tendencies are, to some extent, already for example to be found in teachings attributed to Ja'far as-Sádiq, who died in 765, committed to writing by Abu 'Abd ar-Rahmán as-Sulami in the late tenth / early eleventh century; unquestionably, then, in traditions committed to writing by Abu Nasr as-Sarráj in the mid to late tenth century, concerning Abu Yazíd Bistámí, who had died in around 875; also in the vivid, though fragmentary, poetic writing of Abul-Qásim al-Junayd, who died in 910.

In the Islamic context just as in the Christian, evangelistic impatience comes under implicit attack both for the way it typically plays upon people's lust for certainty and for the way it typically seeks to stroke the self-righteous vanity of the human herd.

Thus, as regards the lust for certainty: like Dionysius the Areopagite, and Gregory of Nyssa before him, interpreting the biblical story of Moses' intimate encounters with God, Ja'far, commenting on the Qur'anic portrayal of Moses, also critically insists on the sheer impossibility, for him represented there, of ever conclusively knowing God.[48] And the Bistámí tradition, for example, further develops the theme, in the story of Bistámí's 'heavenly ascent' (*miʿraj*).[49] This text echoes, in particular, the post-Qurʾanic tradition of Muhammad's 'heavenly ascent', which came to be attached to the older story of the prophet's night journey, in the spirit, to Jerusalem. But, at the same time, it also belongs to a larger Near Eastern literature describing other 'heavenly ascents' by such figures as Enoch and Moses. It shows Bistámí travelling through the seven heavens – in each heaven being greeted by a crowd of angels – yet always rejecting the temptation to stop and enjoy the paradisiacal place where he has arrived – always restlessly continuing on towards God – until he is transformed into a magnificent bird. The whole point is just to affirm the utterly incomprehensible sublimity of the divine. In the end, Bistámí is greeted by God – but here words fail him, altogether. Then he is sent back, as a messenger to the Muslim community, charged with transmitting his resultant, all-transformative insight.

Whilst, as regards the conceit of herd / gang / mob (a)morality: right from the earliest beginnings of the tradition, the Sufi answer to that is framed by the ideal notion of *fanáʾ wa baqáʾ*, 'annihilation and abiding'. *Fanáʾ*: the spiritual annihilation, precisely, of the herd-, gang- or mob-member self; Eckhartian 'poverty'. *Baqáʾ*: the abiding of God, hitherto latent as it were within the space thereby vacated; no longer concealed by what has now been annihilated. *Fanáʾ wa baqáʾ* is, in effect, a sort of non-christological equivalent of the Christian notion, brought to its culmination by Eckhart, of 'the birth of God in the soul'.

These concepts are already prominent in the traditions associated with both Jaʿfar and Bistámí. And they are then given dizzying treatment by Junayd. Here, for example, is one of the little essays in his treatise entitled *Some Points on the Affirmation of Divine Unity*:

ANOTHER POINT

Fear grips me. Hope unfolds me. Reality draws me together. The real sets me apart. When he seizes me with fear, he annihilates me from myself through my existence, then preserves me from myself. When he unfolds me in hope, he returns me to myself through my loss, then orders my preservation. When he re-collects me in reality, he makes me present, then calls me. When he sets me apart through the real, he makes me witness the other-than-me, then veils from himself. In all that, he transforms me, rather than making me secure, and desolates me, rather than granting me his intimacy. Through being made present I taste the flavour of my existence. Would that he had annihilated me from myself, then revived me, then in annihilation made me bear witness. My annihilation is my abiding. From the reality of my annihilation, he annihilated me from both my abiding and my annihilation. I was, upon the reality of annihilation, without abiding or annihilation, through my abiding and annihilation, for the existence of annihilation in abiding, for the existence of my other in my annihilation.[50]

In the dervish-dance of Junayd's prose here, first he elaborates upon the basic existential nature of *fanā' wa baqā'*; then prays for it, as a grace only glimpsed, as a future possibility; then, looking back, reflects upon the way that at the moment of crisis – resulting 'from the reality of my annihilation' – all self-conscious reflection on 'my' condition is erased.

§

In the Qur'an, with tremendous lyrical intensity, God declares the urgent necessity, for salvation, of Islamic faith. Writing some two and a half centuries later, Junayd is a loyal Muslim. But with another, quite different sort of lyrical intensity, *his* whole concern is to insist upon the inevitably intense difficulty of true Islamic discipleship, uncorrupted by evangelistic impatience.

Moreover, consider how the Qur'anic voice of God also directly reappears, for example, mutated now however by proto-Sufi concern, in the poetry of Muhammad ibn 'Abd al-Jabbár ibn al-Hasan an-Niffarí (mid-tenth century CE).

Niffarí's great work is his *Kitáb al-Mawáqif*; which A. J. Arberry, its first translator into English, renders as the 'Book of the Spiritual Stayings'.[51] Sells, by way of alternative, has suggested 'Book of Standings'.[52] The three French translations are variously entitled '*Livre des Stations*', '*Livre des Haltes*', '*Livre des Extases*': 'Book of Stations', 'Book of Halts', 'Book of Ecstasies'.[53] But I prefer 'Book of Confrontations'.[54]

Mawáqif is the plural of *mawqif*; each *mawqif* being framed as a report on some event of *waqfa*. The primary sense of the root *w/q/f is* 'stand'. *Waqfa* is an event of being brought to an abrupt stand-still, stopped in one's tracks, by God; urgently alerted to hitherto unobserved aspects of moral reality; and more or less painfully compelled, as a result, to take stock. For Niffarí, *waqfa* is the source of the highest wisdom; connecting to the very deepest truth of faith. One who has been subject to *waqfa* is a *wáqif*; plural *wáqifiyya'*. And note how closely this relates to the concept of 'shaken-ness', as in 'solidarity of the shaken'. *Waqfa*, being stopped in one's tracks, is a confrontational interruption of inertial drift, just as 'shaken-ness' is a confrontational interruption of inertial stasis: both are essentially metaphors for the same.

There are seventy-seven *Mawáqif*, of varying length, in Niffarí's book.[55] Each one tends to follow the same basic pattern: first, an abrupt stopping; then a series of staccato divine utterances.[56] The effect is of a relentless sublimity; the attentive reader is 'confronted', like the speaker, by this hypnotic sequence, as it were, of hammer blows. Consider, for example, *Mawqif* 6:[57]

CONFRONTED BY SEA

Oceanic …
a voice saying

STOP

I saw the ships sink
the planks
floating
I watched the planks sink –

Then I heard the voice say:
*There's no safety
on board* –

say:
*Those who throw themselves in
risk their all
Those who cling to the wreckage
are drowned* –

say:
*Only those who choose risk can survive
The wave surges – it lifts
what's submerged
It runs up the beach* –

say:
*In between
the vast shining confusion above
and the pressures deep down
swim the man-eating sharks* –

say:
*Whilst afloat
you are veiled by the vessel
Abandon your ship
and I'll veil you in brine* –

say:
*On what watery ledge
will you perch?
Can you tackle these waters
like mer-man or -maid?*

say:
*Could I let you rely
on another than me?
It would be a deceit!*

say:
*Beware lest
lost soul
you are drowned
in the other-than-me!*

say:
*Truth which lasts
is my gift to all those
who renounce in their yearning
the gifts of this transitory world –*

This shipwreck in the first instance symbolizes the fate awaiting the usual ethos of the world, in all its various permutations: herd morality, as more or less colluding with gangster codes of honour, or mob rage. Confronted with the spiritually catastrophic consequences of surrender to these phenomena, 'only those who choose risk can survive': the risk, namely, of *fanā'*. God taunts the poet – as representative here of ordinary, dishonest humanity – with the frightfulness of that ideal prospect. (The reference to 'mer-man or -maid' is my elaboration: the original just speaks of the need to 'drown' in the sea, and become like 'one of its creatures'.[58]) In the end, though, the proto-Sufi poet is proposing a counter-intuitive evangelistic strategy, which amounts to a choice between two modes of 'drowning'.

The *Mawāqif* are sacramental poems. For they are enactments of *fanā' wa baqā'*, 'annihilation and abiding', inasmuch as each one begins with the 'stopping', the momentary 'annihilation' of the poet's own everyday voice. The poet's voice melts into the divine Voice. Only this 'abides', in dervish poems that attempt to spell out the preconditions and implications of *fanā' wa baqā'*.

Not all of them are menacing in tone, like 'Confronted by Sea'; although arguably the most interesting are. Niffarī's writing oscillates, with equal conviction, between divine menace and divine compassion. But always there is the same element of shocked amazement, framing it; the same excitement; the same general prodding, in maxims and parables, at the poet's conscience; as God, playfully, speaks to him through his own talking to himself, his anguish. *Mawqif* 8, 'Confronted with Confrontation', is the nearest he comes to systematic theory. It consists of a lengthy series of formulations reflecting upon contrasted levels of devout relationship to God. The most elementary level is *'ilm*: truth-as-correctness in the knowledge of sacred scripture and tradition. The expert in *'ilm*, the *'ālim*, is concerned with the basic theological and juridical structure of their community's religious belief-system; the defining and refining, so to speak, of its grammar, its orthodoxy. Then, the next level up is *ma'rifa*: gifts of poetic eloquence, and pastoral wisdom, deepening one's actual ability to apply the data of *'ilm* to specific circumstances. The expert in *ma'rifa*, the *'ārif* is thus a skilled preacher, an evangelist. Operating within the bounds of orthodoxy defined by *'ilm*, the truth of true *ma'rifa*, on the other hand, is spiritual know-how, or insight, in the sense of a certain quality of will, a settled orientation towards truth-as-openness. The third and highest level, however, is *waqfa*. For here we have the sheer *infinitude* of perfect truth-as-openness breaking in upon the scene, with an abrupt jolt; no longer confined, as *ma 'rifa* still is, by the immediate requirements of evangelistic populism; but, precisely, presenting a confrontational challenge to evangelistic impatience. So, Niffarí posits these three descending categories: the *wáqif* / 'the *'árif* / 'the *'álim*.[59]

As literary works, Niffarí's poems belong to the level of *ma'rifa*. And yet, the point is that this is *ma'rifa* absolutely dedicated to the task of paying homage to *waqfa*; a species of event the deep reality of which forever transcends it. In his distinctive, un-philosophic way, Niffarí is thus a radically apophatic thinker. The chanting quality of his verse serves, hopefully, to numb the argumentative part of the brain, the part belonging to *'ilm* and *ma'rifa*, which *waqfa* transcends, but which is always itching to reassert its lost hegemony. Indeed, one might well say that the only argument in the *Mawáqif* is argument against over-valued argument. That is to say: against argument as the armoury of the resistant ego, under assault from God's essentially non-argumentative sheer authority, invested in openness. For example, consider *Mawqif* 44:

CONFRONTED WITH THE QUESTION:
'WHO ARE *YOU* WHO AM *I*?'

The voice stopped me and asked:
Who are YOU who am I?

Then the sun and the moon and the stars
all the lights danced
their dance
and I heard the voice say:
There's no glint
anywhere
in my ocean-expanse
that you haven't now seen –

And then everything came up close –
nothing remained that did not –
kissed my brow
wished me well
slipped aside in the shadows –

And then: *Do you think*
that you know
who I am?
I by no means
know you!

I saw one holding tight to my robe
not to me –
The voice said: *Let me show you
the meaning of Love* –
And my robe bellied out
although I was
unmoved –

Once again
the voice spoke:
Who am I?

And the sun was eclipsed
And the moon was eclipsed
And the heavens were emptied
No light was left other than God's
And my eye did not see
And my ear did not hear
All familiar perception had ceased
And everything spoke
It declared the vast splendour of God
O and everything came up close –
lance in hand!

Flee! the voice said
I – distraught – cried out:
'Where?'

Plunge! the voice said –
Then I saw myself
plunge –

And again the voice said:
*See in this
your eternal self
fallen and trapped
in the darkness
without any exit
apparent* –

*But when I release you
I'll show you my truth –
You will find yourself right
at the back of the crowd
breathing easy
at last* –

God gently tugs at the poet's robe. The poet here initially represents the limitations of *ma'rifa* alone, not yet sublated by *waqfa*. So, the tug is ineffective. By itself, it does not produce the existential transformation intrinsic to the fullness of truth: being fully 'known' by, in the sense of being fully at one with, God. That requires more drastic measures.

Many readers will no doubt recoil from the abrasiveness of Niffarí's theology. Repudiating evangelistic impatience, this God is not in any way ingratiating! But then what else is to be expected of authentic sacred truth, decisively interrupting the ordinary kitsch-projection of *das unglückliche Bewußtsein*?

§

We know very little about Niffarí the man. The conventional dating of his death as occurring in 965 CE comes from the seventeenth-century Ottoman scholar Hájji Khalífa; and is dubious.[60] His name indicates that he had been born in Mesopotamia. The thirteenth-century poet Tilimsání wrote a commentary on the *Mawáqif*, in which he remarks that Niffarí lived a vagrant life; and that he is said to have died 'in one of the villages of Egypt'.[61] Tilimsání also reports a tradition that Niffarí himself only ever wrote his poetry down on scraps of paper (by the mid-tenth century quite a plentiful commodity in the Arab world, unlike in Europe); and that it was his son, or perhaps his grandson, who assembled the *Mawáqif* as an ordered collection. Ibn al-'Arabí discusses his work with respect.[62] However, his historic influence was not great.

This obscurity contrasts markedly with the fame of the great showmen amongst his predecessors in the proto-Sufi tradition: for example, Husayn ibn Mansúr al-Halláj (died 922) or Bistámí. Halláj derives his fame above all from his career as a religiously inspired dissident, climaxing in spectacular martyrdom. Bistámí's life was less dramatic, but he became a sort of symbol for proto-Sufi tradition as a whole. Both Halláj and Bistámí had a reputation for startling, risqué ecstatic utterances, framed as an expression of intense religious devotion, yet nevertheless wilfully offensive to conventional Muslim propriety as such.

Halláj will thus forever be associated with his reputed saying, *aná 'l-haqq*, 'I am the [divine] Truth'. Whether he ever actually uttered these words is uncertain. But the belief that he did has come to encapsulate his mystique. One may, at one level, understand the saying as a general affirmation concerning the essence of divine Truth: its being, first and foremost, the perfection of truth-as-openness, rather than any form of truth-as-correctness; or, in other words, a truth in which one *participates*, rather than a truth in which one believes as a mere matter of opinion. ('Divine Truth is the way of one's being who one truly is.') In terms of *faná' wa baqá'*, it may be understood as expressing Halláj's own personal identification, at the deepest level, with what alone will 'abide' when, at the Last Judgement, his surface-ego is 'annihilated'. ('My true self is who I am when I am most transparent to God.') However, in the light of his martyrdom, it also becomes a thrilling assertion of the dissident moral authority-claim with which he confronted the oppressive rulers of his world. As such, it is comparable with the saying of Jesus, 'I am the way, and the truth, and the life' (*John* 14.6).[63]

The earlier, direct equivalent in the Bistámí tradition is Bistámí's reported cry of *subhání subhání*, 'Glory to me! Glory to me!' Or rather, since *subhán* is a term which is ordinarily only ever addressed to God: more exactly, 'Hosanna to me! Hosanna to me!' Bistámí here is glorifying God. But, again, the point of course lies in the equivocal nature of the affirmation; inasmuch as this is God considered as indwelling his own soul.

Sufi tradition has long contrasted the 'drunken' form of Godfriendship, exemplified by Halláj and Bistámí, with the relative 'sobriety' exemplified by Junayd. Certainly, Junayd's reported comments on Bistámí do indicate some ambivalence: expressing, as they do, both fulsome praise and yet also a distinct undertow of reservation. Although, as Junayd sees it, Bistámí came very close to the highest level of insight, nevertheless, just because of his 'drunken' excess, he fell short.[64] And as for the younger Halláj: whereas he was at one stage a disciple of Junayd's, eventually it seems that they also fell out.

At all events, it is clear that Niffarí, the obscure, belongs with Junayd on the 'sober' side of this disjunction. In fact, *Mawqif* 43 is implicitly framed as a nuanced response to Bistámí's *subhání*, in particular:

CONFRONTED BY A GRIPPING PRESENCE

I was stopped by a presence
which gripped me
and said:

Never mind what you are
Never mind what you have

Hosanna to you!

But observe:
it's for me to give glory to you
not for you to give glory to me
Indeed, I'll take the lead
over you
How could you take the lead over me?

As I gazed
all the lights were extinguished
forgiveness was strife
and the Way a dead-end –

Then a challenge:
Assert your own glory

your own holy glamour
your power –
and hide!
For you'd better not lay yourself
open to me –
I would set you ablaze
I would leave you
amazed –

No – don't hide!

Rather lay yourself open –
If not
I will tear your concealment away
I will leave you exposed
anyway –

First, I hid and held back
Then repented and ceased to resist
as, bewildered, I saw
what before was condemned
now approved –
what before was approved
now condemned –

And again the voice said:
Whilst the doubter
is faithful to Truth
all too often
the self-professed
fervent believer
lacks genuine faith –

I saw God
I knew God
saw myself
knew myself

In the end the voice said:
You're embarked
And yet when you arrive
before me
all this will be gone
For then you can know neither me
nor yourself –

'It's for me to give glory to you / not for you to give glory to me': the *Mawáqif* consistently follow this rule. Evangelistic impatience is of course always 'glorifying' God; often, alas, in quite manipulative fashion. But in the *Mawáqif* the glory of God is established by the simple event of *waqfa*, the first effect of which is to strike the poet dumb. Any sacralized manipulation is straight away precluded. And God then 'glorifies' Niffarí, as representative *wáqif*, just by the act of addressing him.

§

Niffarí does not explicitly name evangelistic impatience as such, any more than Dionysius does; or Meister Eckhart. The evangelistic impulse, in general, is so deeply ingrained in both Christian and Muslim tradition as to have rendered direct criticism of its deformation by impatience scarcely admissible, prior to the rise of modern secular humanism. Yet, Niffarí certainly does come close. In *Mawqif* 38, for instance, he puts it as follows:

CONFRONTED BY DIVINE REALITY

Reality
stopped me
and said:

Picture all as a sea
and you'll fancy you're sailing –
Where to? You can't say
Just away (as you hope) from the shores
of illusion –
Know though that your commonplace notion
of all as a 'sea'
still belongs to those shores
So – the metaphor fails

 Then the shimmer was gone
 and the waters were rock –

First – by way of restraint –
(said the voice)
there is needed
mistrust of appearance
and after that also
mistrust of self-will –
All creation's elaborately veiled –

> Then the whole of reality
> passed in review –
> A prodigious display … !

The voice said:
Let the stuff of decay just decay –

> Then my vision gave way
> to eternal Ideas
> Nothing moved nothing spoke –

The voice said:
Now consider the everyday world
What is there?
I replied:
There's mere tumult and noise –
The voice said:
You must closely attend to the difference
that you may be saved!

> I returned to the tumult and noise
> and I saw it was void –

The voice said:
I have given you all sorts of knowledge
With knowledge goes power
But from knowledge and power
springs
temptation –

And then:
You must know that
my Truth can have nothing to do
with your trifling ambition –

'I have given you all sorts of knowledge / With knowledge goes power / But from knowledge and power / springs / temptation' – Arberry renders this passage, more literally: 'Thou seest everything, and everything obeys thee, and thy vision of everything is a trial, and the obedience of everything to thee is a trial.'[65] What else, though, is the knowledge- and power-conferring 'vision' that Niffarí chiefly has in mind here if not that which is bound up with devout orthodoxy? And what else is the associated trial, or temptation, if not that of evangelistic impatience; as it descends all too quickly into the everyday world of tumult and clamour, and so becomes bound up with the mere egotism of the evangelist?

Chapter 4

DECADENCE OF 'MYSTICISM'

By 'mystical theology' I mean what Dionysius the Areopagite, Meister Eckhart and Niffari for instance, those three very different figures, nevertheless all have in common.

But now: to forestall all-too-prevalent confusion, some further distinctions may perhaps be in order. Consider in particular what it means when the mediaeval phenomenon of '*mystical theology*' morphs into the post-mediaeval phenomenon of '*mysticism*'.

Essentially, I think it signifies a deflection from the original recoil from evangelistic impatience – and the replacement of that impulse by a sort of 'mystical' *boasting*, instead. To the extent that this is so, 'mysticism' is just the morbid decomposition of 'mystical theology' proper. Whereas, in grand-narrative terms, 'mystical theology' is a discipline unequivocally helping prepare catholic religious traditions to appropriate the solidarity of the shaken, 'mysticism' by contrast is a much more equivocal phenomenon.

There are two basic species of 'mysticism' in this sense.

(a) One species is a plundering of 'mystical theology' for incidental items of embellishment, edifying mementoes, precisely to decorate the propaganda-ideology of an evangelistically impatient church, or sect. Here, 'mystical theology's' critique of herd-and-gang religion mutates, in effect, to become a matter of competitive corporate self-assertion, against rival outsider-groups as such. So, the great 'mystics' of the past are honoured, as a vital contribution to the boasting of the group. 'Look at our great saints! Ours, all of them ours!'

(b) The other species of 'mysticism' converts 'mystical theology's' critique of herd-and-gang religion into justification for wholesale withdrawal from the ethos of (small 'c') catholicity. In other words: it abandons that depth of conversational openness across the boundaries dividing different social classes, different ethnic groups or different secular cultures in general, which only religious institutions, at their best, can facilitate. This second species of 'mysticism' thus gives legitimacy to a boastfully evangelistic pride in spiritual deracination. It expresses an impatient desire to be innocent of contaminating religious loyalties. Such a craving for innocence is, however, already in itself a corruption.

'Mysticism' of Church and sect

The mainstream twentieth-century Christian theological notion of 'mysticism' – as found, for example, in the work of Evelyn Underhill – is basically an amalgam of three quite diverse elements.[1] It still does include something of the recoil from evangelistic impatience classically encoded in Dionysian mystical theology. But that is more or less diluted here by the addition of two other, very different elements. Namely: (a) the rhetoric of impassioned love for God deriving from exegesis of the *Song of Songs*, and (b) the testimony of women visionaries.

The secular love poetry of the *Song of Songs* (or *Song of Solomon*) was included in the Bible, notwithstanding that it lacks any overt reference to God, originally as a supposed allegory of the love between God and the people of Israel. In the Jewish context the first century CE rabbi Aqiba played a key role in its final acceptance as canonical, on that basis. Hippolytus of Rome wrote the first Christian commentary, in the early third century, reading it as an allegory of the love between God and the Church, supplanting Israel. Origen, a younger contemporary of Hippolytus, was the first to interpret it as referring to the love both between God and the Church, and between God and the individual Christian. And Gregory of Nyssa also wrote a notable commentary. But it was Bernard of Clairvaux (1090–1153) with his eighty-six sermons on the first two chapters of the *Song of Songs* who really launched the mediaeval tradition in this regard.[2]

As a Cistercian, Bernard was at the forefront of the most dynamic monastic reform movement of his day. And there was in twelfth-century literature, also, a general tendency to experiment with fresh rhetoric of heightened affective intensity; of which Bernard is a prime example. Bernard was, in particular, the first to develop the highly influential notion of the 'spiritual marriage': an ideal *covenantal* relationship between God, as bridegroom, and the individual soul, as bride; licensing, for monks, much sweet, homo-erotic metaphor.

Bernard pre-dates the great surge of later-mediaeval Dionysian mystical theology. (Dionysius, for his part, does not actually appear to have been much interested in the *Song of Songs*, other than as a potential source of embarrassment if, as he puts it, 'those passionate longings fit only for prostitutes', of which on the surface it consists, are not properly allegorized!'[3]) And yet, there is very considerable subsequent overlap between the 'Dionysian' and what one might term the 'Bernardine' tradition. Many of those most notably influenced by Bernard, his successors in the interpretation of the *Song of Songs*, are also leading exponents of Dionysian thought: Gallus, Grosseteste, Suso, Ruysbroeck (whose masterpiece is entitled *The Spiritual Espousals*), Gerson, Denis the Carthusian, John of the Cross.

Bernard was a theologian of exemplary orthodoxy, undoubted passionate sincerity and exceptional creative flair. He is also, just by virtue of his genius, a prime symbol of the insufficiency of those qualities, insofar as they are merely coupled with closed-minded ideology. For, alas, he lived in an age when the church ideology deriving from the Gregorian Reform, to which Bernard was loyal, was turning horribly septic.

As never before, intellectuals within twelfth-century Western Christendom were keen to promote their own prestige by representing themselves as the guardians of orthodoxy against all manner of threat from 'heresy'. Bernard himself enjoyed tremendous prestige as a battler against 'heresy': in 1141 he saw to it that Peter Abelard was condemned at the Council of Sens; and alongside Abelard, also the (somewhat Amos-like) church reformer Arnold of Brescia; in 1145 he set out on a preaching campaign through the south of France, dedicated to the suppression of the Petrobrusian and Henrician 'heresies', and of Catharism; in 1148 he prosecuted Gilbert of Poitiers. These were very different opponents, but in each case, Bernard was invoking the use of coercive power to close down debate within the Church, in a way that was still quite new, and that in retrospect surely represents a most depressing upsurge of clerical *libido dominandi*. This was also a period of recurrently murderous Christian antisemitism. Bernard was swift to respond when the mobilization of the Second Crusade in 1146, which he had energetically promoted, immediately led, just as in the case of the First Crusade fifty years earlier, to pogroms in the Rhineland. He went straight there, to stop the slaughter. But whilst he deplored the murder of Jews, it may be noted that he still remained quite conventional in his theological antisemitism: there it is, for instance, in number 14 of his *Sermons on the 'Song of Songs'*. And one might also note the casual misogyny that surfaces in sermon 38. Such misogyny was, likewise, entirely conventional in his monastic world; Bernard merely endorses it in passing. But, all the same, it does not exactly show him as a great champion of truth-as-openness.

As for the women visionaries of the mediaeval Church, in the West, some are clearly influenced by Bernard: notably, the women 'bridal mystics' of the thirteenth century, Hadewijch of Antwerp, Mechtild of Magdeburg, Mechtild of Hackeborn and Gertrude of Helfta.[4] But, in general, these women – and the others like them – were driven to boast of their visionary experiences just because that was the only way the Church of their day could be persuaded to let them participate at all, as writers, in the public domain. Such boasts are clearly, thus, symptomatic of a basic deficiency in the Church; a lack of properly inclusive Catholicism.

Teresa of Ávila (1515–83) represents both the culmination of this mediaeval visionary tradition and the beginning of something new. For she not only reports a variety of God-given visions and locutions, 'favours' as she calls them. She also develops, with unprecedented precision, a schema of different stages in a developing capacity for contemplative prayer in general; distinguishing 'prayer of recollection', 'prayer of quiet', 'prayer of union'; and systematically tracing the ascent of the soul through seven sets of 'mansions', within the 'interior castle'.[5] In other words, she represents a whole new intensity of analytical self-consciousness. Underneath all her protestations of humility and submission to her ecclesiastical superiors, there is an unprecedented sophistication in her thought, informing the insurgent authority-claims she is effectively making. And note further, her sheer success: officially beatified in 1614 and canonized in 1622, just forty years after her death, at a time moreover of very few fresh canonizations. She had faced militant opposition in her own lifetime, and her cause also faced fierce opposition after her death. Yet, it prevailed.[6] How is this to be explained? At least to some extent, it must have been due to the way her work dovetailed so well with the propaganda needs of the Roman Catholic Church, at that time, in the context of its great struggle against Protestantism. It was, absolutely, a matter of corporate boasting: 'Look at our great saints, in the contemplative religious orders which Protestantism has abolished! See the wisdom which the Protestants have forfeited as a result!' Teresa, *par excellence*, came to represent that. The legacy of her free-spirited individuality was unfortunately, in the end, more or less swallowed up by this very different impulse.

Teresa was declared a 'Doctor of the Church' in 1970. And this simply served to confirm the already well-established authority of her writings. Indeed, the first quarter of the twentieth century saw the development of a veritable scholastic industry, chiefly in France, in which her analytic account of the stages in the development of mystical prayer was pored over; compared especially to that of her colleague and friend, John of the Cross; and systematically integrated into the prevailing Thomist systematic theology of the day. Dom Cuthbert Butler gives an account of this thought-world in the 'Afterthought' appended to the second edition of his book on *Western Mysticism*: reviewing the various contributions of the Abbé Auguste Saudreau, Père Augustin Poulain S.J., Monsignor Albert Farges, Père Reginald Garrigou-Lagrange O.P., Père Ferdinand Joret O.P., Père Ludovic de Besse O.F.M. Cap., Père Ambroise Gardeil O.P., Père Joseph Maréchal S.J. and others.[7] (Butler's own contribution is to advocate a systematic extension of the debate to consider the 'mystical' element in the thought of Augustine, Gregory the Great and Bernard.)

'Though there has been a progress in the formulation of mystical theology as a science,' Butler writes, 'the mystical experience itself has not progressed'.[8] The 'progress' of 'mystical theology as a science' which he has in mind is evidently the development of theologically orthodox 'mysticism' out of Dionysian 'mystical theology'. I would describe this far rather as *retrogression*: away from a bid to render theology more transparent to truth-as-openness – and towards an essentially regrettable preoccupation, instead, with a certain sort of truth-as-correctness, in the description of 'the mystical experience'. In relation to the institutional Church as a whole, this is a tamed mode of thought. And, alas, it is recruited to a spirit of corporate boasting: the boasting of a Church, in France, freshly embattled against a surge of militant secularism.

Compare St. Paul's self-confessed 'boasting' in his *Second Letter to the Corinthians*, Chapters 10–13. Note how different *this* is, in tone! The general scholarly view is that these Chapters were originally a separate letter, which has then been conflated with the rest of *2 Corinthians*: a rather bitter letter, reasserting Paul's authority over the Christian congregation he had founded at Corinth perhaps four or five years earlier. Since the founding of that congregation, he has been back just once. Now he intends to return again; but before he does so he is writing to help prepare for what threatens to be an awkward encounter, due to the recent arrival in Corinth of other Christian missionaries, who have in the meantime set themselves up as his rivals.

Paul refers to these would-be rivals, with heavy irony, as 'Superlative Apostles' (11.5, 12.11); but also, as 'Pseudo-Apostles', servants of Satan (11.13-15). It is not clear whether the 'Superlative Apostles' have any significantly different teaching from Paul's. But the basic problem appears just to be a spirit of competitiveness, informing their claims to authority. How, then, is Paul to respond? He despises precisely their competitiveness (10. 12). But if he does not himself compete against them, he will be handing them victory, on their own terms. This he refuses to do. And therefore, he is driven, very much against his will, also to boast, on his own behalf, reasserting his claims to authority. Yet, even as he boasts, he repeatedly confesses the foolishness of such boasting (11.1, 16-19, 21; 12.11).

Paul boasts first, here, of his credentials as a zealous practitioner of Jewish piety, according to the discipline of Pharisaism (11.22); then, of the hardships he has undergone, and the risks he has taken, as a missionary of Christ (11.23-33). And finally:

> It is necessary to boast; nothing is to be gained by it, but I will go on to visions and revelations of the Lord. I know a person in Christ who fourteen years ago was caught up to the third heaven – whether in the body or out of the body I do not know; God knows. And I know that such a person – whether in the body or out of the body I do not know; God knows – was caught up into Paradise and heard things that are not to be told, that no mortal is permitted to repeat.
>
> (12.1-4)

So, how much weight does Paul actually intend to set upon this account of his own ecstatic vision of Paradise? The whole polemical thrust of the passage is to deplore the foolishness of such boasting; even as Paul seeks to show that, if he deplores it, this is not because he is himself incapable of it. He deplores such boasting with all the authority of one who might well boast – yes, and who does indeed boast, in order to demonstrate that authority – but only in order to deplore the state of affairs that has driven him to do so. Thus, he boasts of his ecstasy in the same spirit that he also, in the same passage, boasts of his credentials as a pious Jew, according to the special discipline of the Pharisees. But, of course, in *Romans* and *Galatians* he is determined, above all, to downgrade the proper significance of the latter sort of boasting among Christians. It is, for him, a fundamental principle that, *in the end*, true Christian faith excludes religious boasting (*Romans* 3.27). And this surely applies just as much to boasting about ecstasies as it does to boasting about how rigorously one has fulfilled the works of the Law. Both cases alike involve great gifts of God – which are, however, corrupted just as soon as they become sources of boasting. The clear suggestion is that this is what has happened with the 'Superlative Apostles': that these were, much like Paul himself, Jewish Christian missionaries with an impressive background of Jewish piety, as well as their own stories to tell of ecstatic 'experience', perhaps; and that they sought to ground their rival authority on that basis. Why indeed does Paul write of his own ecstasy in the third person? The self-distancing is surely meant, still further, to reinforce the basic point that it is sheer foolishness to boast of such blessings, as if it was their proper purpose to be invoked as a source of personal authority. For Paul, on the contrary, his true authority simply inheres in his proven effectiveness as an evangelist for Christ. What he heard whilst in ecstasy were, as he puts it, 'things that are not to be told': they therefore had nothing whatever to do with the authority of an evangelist, whose whole life's work is, of course, absolutely a matter of 'telling'. And he refers to the 'elation' he felt (12: 7) following his ecstasy, essentially, as a temptation; a potential distraction from his true calling.

The scholastic protagonists of 'mystical theology as a science' have traditionally always claimed Paul as a pioneer 'mystic'. And yet, the whole point of his thought in this regard lies in its all-boasts-dissolving irony, a quality of which their intellectual discipline seems to be largely devoid.

§

Meanwhile another, sectarian mode of un-ironic 'mystical boasting' appeals to anti-'modern' esotericist notions of 'perennial philosophy'.[9] By which I mean: that whole movement of thought which its major founder, René Guénon (1886–1951) termed 'Traditionalism'.[10] (I prefer to call it 'anti-modern esotericism', out of resistance to the imperialistic claim intrinsic to Guénon's terminology.) Guénon is intent on systematically identifying authentic religious 'Tradition', as a whole, with whatever, in any particular tradition, is most polemically hostile to 'modernity'. An ideal, strictly charismatic contemplative-elite 'mystical' communion: cutting across every sort of institutionalized division between distinct religious cultures.

Thus, Guénon's thinking is effectively founded on his identification of the highest wisdom with the experience of undergoing a valid discipline of initiation, and subsequent ascetic / contemplative training. To Guénon, it did not in fact matter which tradition the discipline of initiation and training might belong to – just so long as it had some capacity to cut people decisively free from the spiritual inertia of 'modern' life. For him, it was simply a matter of rescuing at least a few exceptional individuals from the general shipwreck, as he sees it, of 'modernity'. At first, he thought to find the necessary disciplines in the lively world of early twentieth-century French Freemasonry. Increasingly, however, he felt the need for older, deeper-rooted 'mystical' traditions; ones capable of more effectively reconnecting the initiate with older, less corrupted strata of human history. Yet he found nothing in the institutionalized world of Roman Catholic Christianity, in which he had been raised, that would do the job. Rather, he turned towards the rather less regulated Sufi traditions of Islam. In 1930 he moved to Cairo, and joined a Sufi order there. It should, though, be noted that Guénon's 'Traditionalist' notion of Sufism introduced elements which are in fact quite alien to actual Sufi tradition: he advocated a novel form of Sufism systematically cut off from the (in his view) deeply corrupted wider world of 'modern' Islam, behind veils of secrecy. This veiling was crucial to Guénon. It was, one may suspect, partly connected with a certain element of paranoia in his personality. Yet, at the same time, it was meant to conceal, from his fellow Muslims, a commitment to the notion of perennial philosophy, as such, largely without precedent in any previous Sufi self-understanding. For Guénon found 'Tradition' not only in Sufi Islam; but also,

4. Decadence of 'Mysticism'

with more or less equal authority, especially in Hindu Vedantism. His esoteric perennialism really did produce a very idiosyncratic version of Islam!

Guénon is, as I have said, generally acknowledged as the major founder of 'Traditionalism'. Another key factor in its inception, on the other hand, was the alliance he developed with the prolific British / Sri Lankan scholar of Asian art, *Ananda Coomaraswamy* (1877–1947). In fact, Coomaraswamy already a perennialist by conviction a decade or more before, in the late 1920s, he entered into correspondence with Guénon. And, by contrast to Guénon, he represents a generally less polemical, more academic approach.[11]

But then some of the more extravagant possibilities of anti-'modern' 'mystical' esotericism are represented by two other figures. First: *Frithjof Schuon* (1907–98). Second: *Julius Evola* (1898–1974).

Unlike Guénon, the Swiss-born Schuon was not only a gifted writer, with many admirers, but also an organizer.[12] He followed Guénon into Sufism, as did a number of others; eventually, there were four separate 'Traditionalist' Sufi orders. Schuon, having adopted the name Isa Nur al-Din, was, to Guénon's own growing dismay, the founder of the most innovative of these.[13] It was at first simply the European branch of a new Algerian order, the Alawiyya. But later, in the 1960s, as it became more independent, Schuon renamed it the 'Maryamiyya'.

As the shaykh of this order, right from the outset, Schuon adopted a remarkably lax attitude to the non-obligatory *sunna* prayers of mainstream Muslim piety; a laxity later, for instance, also extended to the observance of Ramadan. And, in the name of the freedom supposedly conferred upon him by his 'Traditionalist' expertise in perennial philosophy, he added a number of, in the Muslim context, quite un-traditional *extra* practices. The new name of the Maryamiyya reflected his innovatory devotion to the Blessed Virgin Mary: closely associated in his own mind with particular memories of a frustrated romantic love affair; reinforced by a series of visions; and, later on, expressed in his devotional paintings of her, sometimes nude. Meanwhile, he developed an intense interest in Native American religion. Having moved his community in 1981 to Indiana, he began to enact newly invented rituals which involved him dressing up in Native American garb, great feather head-dresses and all. As a guru, Schuon increasingly allowed his followers to develop a cult of his own personality. This created a context in which he also started to allow himself a considerable degree of sexual licence. He started to stage naturist 'primordial gatherings'. In 1991 he was indicted by a grand jury on allegations of child molestation and sexual battery. The case never came to trial; Schuon was exonerated. But, clearly, by conventional Sufi standards something had gone rather wrong in that community.

Whilst, as for Evola: he never became a Sufi. His thinking was, far rather, an attempt to integrate Guénon's militantly anti-'modern' and initiatory version of perennial philosophy into more overtly political strategies.[14] Arguing with Guénon, Evola saw himself as seeking to reverse the Vedantist spiritual subordination of the *kshatriya*, or warrior, caste to the *brahmin*, or priestly, caste; a subordination which Guénon absolutely upheld. So Evola sought to develop a *kshatriya* ethos: just as 'mystically' turned against 'modernity' in all its forms as Guénon's Sufi-inflected *Brahmin* ethos, but much more a this-worldly waging of war. Having seen himself, to begin with, as a campaigning pagan, under Guénon's influence Evola moved towards an altogether more broadly 'Traditionalist' stance. This, however, was a form of 'Traditionalism' eagerly flirting with Fascism. Of course, Evola abominated the modern, democratic element in Fascism: the vulgarity of its nationalist propaganda; its attempts to appeal to the mere class-interests of the bourgeoisie. Nevertheless, in the 1930s he presented himself as the advocate – against all that – of 'a more radical, more intrepid Fascism, a really absolute fascism, made of pure force, inaccessible to compromise'.[15] Evola also made forays into Germany, at one point in 1938 actually attempting to win a role for himself as an ideologist of the SS. His racism, though, was deemed inadequate by the Nazis. (He advocated a 'spiritual', as opposed to biological, racism.) In Vienna, right at the end of the War, he was caught in an explosion, and spent the rest of his life in a wheelchair. Yet then, undaunted, he embarked on a new career: achieving notoriety, in the 1970s, as the prime ideologist indirectly behind the murderous terror campaigns of the Italian Far Right.

What has happened here? Both these later streams of 'Traditionalism', represented by Schuon and Evola, in their contrasting ways evidently represent, at least to some extent, a fundamental diversion of authentic religious critique into an ethos of mere *contempt*: the contempt felt by a self-certified, self-congratulatory 'mystical' sect for their neighbours at large. Religious resistance to the *libido dominandi* has mutated into a generalized rejection of 'modernity'; the grand put-down notion of 'modernity' being rendered as vague and capacious as possible, basically it seems so as to channel every possible impulse of bitter superiority. 'Traditionalism', in effect, exalts secrecy as a pre-emptive gesture of self-satisfied contempt for all those from whom the 'secrets' are to be kept. To this extent, its celebration of perennial philosophy is, after all, nothing more than a pooling-together of the capacity for such contempt regrettably present within all religious cultures alike.

Evola in particular, be it noted, celebrates a certain sort of 'hierarchy'. But this is by no means 'hierarchy' in the catholic sense that Dionysius understands it; namely, as a strategy for maximally inclusive community life. He makes no acknowledgement of Dionysius. And his militant advocacy of 'Ghibelline' anti-clericalism clearly sets him on a quite opposite course. Indeed, the contrast is instructive. Evola's esotericism represents a fundamental rejection of 'modernity' in the sense of a levelling ethos: values determined solely by utilitarian considerations; politics subordinated to the demands of market forces; government in accordance with party-political propaganda-ideology; the rule of kitsch. All well and good! But what he opposes to the element of corruption in all that is the lost 'Traditional' ideal romantically symbolized by the figure of a sacralized *warrior-king*, a Charlemagne for instance. This, it seems to me, straight away intrudes an element of impatient violence into the critique, which fundamentally vitiates it. 'If on the hand', he writes, the original synthesis of the two powers [religious and military] is re-established in the person of the consecrated king, on the other hand, the nature of the hierarchical relationships existing in every normal social order between royalty and priestly caste (or church), which is merely the mediator of supernatural influences, is very clearly defined: regality enjoys primacy over priesthood, just as, symbolically speaking, the sun has primacy over the moon and the man over the woman.[16]

But how is *such* a 'hierarchy' more than just a glorified pecking-order? The warrior-king represents an ethos of coercive power; the catholic clergy of the Dionysian ideal, at any rate in principle, represent the opposite, a community built on non-coercive, liturgically articulated consensus. Evola is an admirer of Nietzsche: his 'revolt against modernity' involves radical repudiation of any ideology infected with a spirit of servile resentment. Yet, what he sets against servile resentment looks very much like mere self-flattery of the privileged, as such; a no less ideological phenomenon.

Today, Evola's politicized version of 'Traditionalism' lives on chiefly as a prime inspiration for the all-too-influential far-right 'Neo-Eurasianism' of Aleksandr Dugin in Russia.[17] In a bid to fill the ideological gap left by the disappearance of Soviet Communism, Dugin has hitched 'Traditionalism' onto a wild, sabre-rattling affirmation of the Russian Orthodox Church, as a focus for a renewed aggressive nationalism. And the resultant, intoxicating brew is truly ugly stuff.

'Mysticism' deracinated

Meanwhile, the prime philosophical advocacy of the second, radically individualistic species of 'mysticism' is that of *Walter T. Stace*. A British-born professor of philosophy at Princeton University, Stace – towards the end of his life, in the early 1960s – published two works: a systematic survey entitled *Mysticism and Philosophy*, and an anthology with a running commentary, *The Teachings of the Mystics*.[18]

Stace defines his notion of 'mysticism' as follows:

> By the word 'mystic' I shall always mean a person who himself has had mystical experience. Often the word is used in a much wider and looser way. Anyone who is sympathetic to mysticism is apt to be labelled a mystic. But I shall use the word always in a stricter sense. However sympathetic toward mysticism a man may be, however deeply interested, involved, enthusiastic, or learned in the subject, he will not be called a mystic unless he has, or has had, mystical experience.[19]

He is interested, as a philosopher, in the proper truth-claims of 'mystical experience'; his claim is that such 'experience' offers its own, uniquely *direct* access to a level of sacred reality lying altogether beyond every kind of cultural or confessional difference. Therefore, his focus is on '*pure* mystical experience': ecstasy, uncomplicated by supernatural-seeming visions, or voices; decisively abstracted from any imagery originating in a culturally specific context.

Supernatural-seeming visions and voices naturally tend to bear the marks of their cultural context; but Stace is a cosmopolitan thinker, concerned with so-called 'mystical experience' as the potential basis for a truly cosmopolitan, overarching, new religious culture. He does not purport to be a 'mystic' himself, according to his own definition; and indeed R. C. Zaehner, for instance, dismisses Stace's work as if it were automatically invalidated as a result.[20] Stace however defends the right of a philosopher like himself to examine the truth-claims of 'mystical' testimony from the outside. For he is simply writing as a systematic mediator between religious traditions: proposing an ideal basis for consensus. As he himself formulates his project in *Mysticism and Philosophy*:

> Two questions are here raised. First, is it a fact that mystical experiences are basically the same, or similar, all over the world, or at any rate that they all have important common characteristics? Secondly, if this is true, does it constitute a good argument for believing in their objectivity? I maintain that the whole argument has never been properly probed, analysed, and impartially evaluated by any previous writer. And this is the task which I propose to undertake.[21]

His answer to both questions is yes. Thus, when he speaks of the 'objectivity' of 'mystical experience', he intends to draw an analogy to the 'objectivity' of ordinary perceptual experience: his claim is that there is something here which exceeds all differences of cultural conditioning, just as surely as the most basic human access to the objective reality of sense-perception does.

But now compare Plotinus, Dionysius, Eckhart or Niffarí, for example. None of these appear to be at all interested in claiming what Stace calls 'mystical experience' for themselves! Stace has in mind a type of event occurring in certain quite exceptional individuals' private life, as such; the basis for a form of polemically asserted individualistic prestige. These thinkers, however, are each of them affirming a spiritual discipline, a mental orientation, an ethics of thinking, ideally valid for all. And to that end, they are committed to certain literary roles, behind which their individual identities disappear. Plotinus adopts the role of impersonal philosophic observer, evoking the adventures of two primordial energies, to some extent universal features of all human life – *psukhé* and *nous* – as they engage in the practice of contemplation. Dionysius, as he writes his *Mystical Theology*, is in the role of a character from the *Acts of the Apostles*, who is commenting on the Bible; specifically, on the story of Moses ascending Mount Sinai. Eckhart, in Sermon 52, for instance, adopts the dramatic persona of an eternal soul nostalgic for pre-existence; or in sermon 6, the dramatic persona of an ideally just man. Niffarí, throughout the *Mawaaqif*, plays the part of the prototypical *waaqif*.

These are key figures in the pre-history and history of 'mystical theology'. And yet, none is exactly concerned with what Stace declares to be *the* defining feature of 'mysticism'; none is actually claiming to be a 'mystic' in that sense. They may well have been. Stace assumes that they, and others like them, were; and reads them in that light. Only, that is not how they themselves present things. They clearly do not share Stace's sense of priorities.

Plotinus does not in fact say, 'I, Plotinus experienced such and such'; as a properly Stacean 'mystic' would have done. He does not seek to boast in this fashion. On the contrary: he is advocating a discipline that aims at contemplation, and inasmuch as authentic contemplation is a suspension of self-consciousness, one might well argue that the notion of 'contemplative experience' is, strictly speaking, a contradiction in terms.[22] For, after all, 'experience', in the normal usage of the word, immediately implies self-consciousness. It is what constitutes our self-conscious selves; it is the content of the stories that we tell about ourselves, in order to establish who we are. In a professional context, 'experience' is what qualifies one for promotion. It is also what a guru is liable to invoke, as a basis for claiming competitive spiritual authority. That this story-telling then immediately gets caught up into boastful egoistic projects of *libido dominandi* belongs to the very essence of 'original sin'. But at certain moments of self-forgetfulness, of the kind that Plotinus seeks to celebrate, all *experience* as such drops away. And then, for the time being, one is released from the self-conscious mind; one swims, quite tranquilly awake, in the sea of the deep mind, instead. One's only 'experience' of such a moment is in its afterglow. Plotinus, however, is looking for truth precisely in the *supra*-experiential immediacy; the extinction of self-consciousness in the oneness of 'the one'.

Nor does Dionysius say, 'I, Dionysius experienced such and such'. He does not boast. We know nothing about him, not even his real name. How then can we really speculate about his so-called 'mystical experience'?

And even though both Eckhart and Niffarí do indeed recount events in the first person, these narratives are not Stacean boasts, either. The poetic utterance of Eckhart's wilder sermons scarcely relates to his quotidian ego. Niffarí's work stems from proto-Sufi tradition, with its core notion of *faná' wa baqá'*: the 'annihilation' of the surface self, the 'abiding' of God-within, deep down, alone. And what else is the surface self ideally 'annihilated' here if not the self-conscious ego of boasted 'experience'?

In general, these thinkers are developing various imaginative devices for upholding what I would call the proper sacredness of perfect truth-as-openness, in recoil from the dire consequences of evangelistic impatience. This is surely what matters to *them*; far rather than any approximation to Stace's 'experiential' criterion, which appears to be so much more a mere invitation to boast.

§

As an advocate of deracinated 'mysticism', Stace also represents a larger academic movement, flourishing not least in the United States. Thus: amongst the pioneers of such thinking was *Richard Bucke*. On the basis of a single, brief, but intense, remembered moment of ecstasy in his own life, Bucke developed an evolutionary theory, according to which, just as human self-consciousness has arisen out of animal consciousness, so ordinary human self-consciousness in general is eventually destined to give way to 'cosmic consciousness'; that is, life governed by 'mystical experience', understood as a purely natural, trans-cultural phenomenon. In his *magnum opus* published in 1901, Bucke backed up this theory with a series of case histories, spanning many centuries and a wide range of religious cultures; some of them famous, others not.[23] Stace, for his part, is wary of Bucke's somewhat extravagant enthusiasm; but nevertheless, acknowledges him as a direct predecessor.[24]

Another rather more sober pioneer of the same ideology, contemporaneous with Bucke, was *William James*, whose famous Gifford Lectures of 1901–2 on *The Varieties of Religious Experience* Stace in fact rates very highly.[25] James's approach to 'mysticism', and to 'religious experience' generally, is radically privatizing in character. He presents this in the first instance as a methodological option, simply narrowing down the field of study in order to make it manageable.[26] However, there is no mistaking the polemical thrust that accompanies this methodological option: James's radical *hostility* to any form of institutionalized religion as such.[27]

Subsequent notable figures such as *Carl Jung* and *Roberto Assagioli* more or less replicate this strictly individualistic notion of authentic spirituality. As does *Gordon Allport*; whose distinction between 'mature' and 'immature' religion correlates to the more general concern of American scholars in the immediate aftermath of the Second World War to identify malign latent energies lurking within their own liberal society, as a threat to its liberalism; the concern also represented by the study of *The Authoritarian Personality*. 'Immature' here essentially means illiberal.[28] And *Abraham Maslow* is another key exponent of such spiritual individualism. As the co-founder (with Stanislav Grof and Anthony Sutich) of the *Journal of Transpersonal Psychology*, in 1969, Maslow moreover launched whole new academic industry, dedicated to the cause.[29] *Ken Wilber* for instance is a prominent product of the resultant milieu; although he has actually come to reject 'transpersonal psychology' as a label, preferring 'integral philosophy'.

However, it is Stace who, to my mind, develops this general tendency in the *philosophically* most interesting way. He does so, above all, by virtue of his argument in Chapter Six of *Mysticism and Philosophy*, regarding the general relationship of 'mystical experience' to language.

Thus: already in Chapter 2, when he comes to listing the typical characteristics of 'mystical experience', Stace very pointedly refers to it as something '*alleged* by mystics to be ineffable, incapable of being described in words, etc.'[30] – Only 'alleged to be' … ! He himself highlights his 'reservations' about this; and the crucial departure that these 'reservations' represent, even from the theory of William James, whom he otherwise reveres. Chapter 6 spells out the reasoning behind them. As he puts it:

> James and other writers have listed "ineffability" as one of the common characteristics of mysticism everywhere and in all cultures. But this word "ineffability" is only the name of a problem, not something the meaning of which we understand at once. The problem which we have to face can be put in

a number of interconnected questions. What is this difficulty about the use of language which the mystic feels? *Why* can he not express himself in words? And how is it that, if he cannot describe what he experiences, he nevertheless does write and speak about it often with great eloquence and force? ... How do his words function?[31]

The answer to these questions seems to me, in fact, to be quite straightforward. The difficulty in question is, as I have argued, essentially a *moral* one, consequent upon the elementary taboo against boasting at the root of the older traditions of mystical theology. It is the difficulty of keeping one's own ego out of one's testimony to the divine; disowning any claim to special knowledge, such as might be hijacked by a spirit of boasting. So, in describing a moment of sublime revelatory inwardness, the discipline of mystical theology requires that one also immediately half-retract what one has said; lest it be misunderstood in such terms. Like Saint Paul, one retracts one's testimony, even as one presents it. One retracts it, as a futile attempt to communicate the incommunicable, just at the point where it might be mistaken for an un-ironic boast.

But Stace cannot see this. How could he, when he himself is, in effect, advocating a certain form of 'mystical' boasting? He values 'mystical experience' – considered in decisive abstraction from any particular cultural context – precisely for its boasting-potential, as source for an alternative form of spiritual authority, opposed to that claimed by institutionalized religion. Indeed, this is the whole thrust of the privatized conception of 'mysticism' proposed by the modern academic tradition stemming from Bucke and James, in general. But Stace is uniquely, and I think quite admirably, frank in his consequent attack on the classical conception of divine 'ineffability'.

'The mystic,' he writes, 'in saying that no language can express his experience *is making a mistake*'[!][32]

This talk of 'ineffability' is, he thinks, 'mistaken' inasmuch as it represents an unnecessary loss of nerve. In his view, it expresses an altogether exaggerated humility; one might say, a loss of properly pugnacious self-confidence. The remembered 'experience' *ought*, in his view, to have served as grounds for an exhilarating insurgent authority-claim counter-posed to, and decisively outbidding, the established authority of institutionalized religion in general. 'Look,' the 'mystic' *should* have said, 'I have encountered the divine, without any need for the mediation supposedly represented by those benighted institutions!' But no. Instead – alas – he or she retreats, saying, 'Now, indeed, I know that I know nothing ... ' Here are two voices at war within the 'mystic's' mind. And Stace simply laments the inhibiting power of the second voice, in relation to the first. He is one who seeks to oppose the church-ideological boasting bound up with evangelistic impatience by countering it with another rival form of boastfulness: 'mystical' boasting of the individualistic kind. In so doing, he departs quite radically from the Dionysian and Sufi traditions, which by contrast represent a systematic rejection of *all* boastful ideology; alike whether the boasting is corporate or individualistic.

Classical apophaticism, which Stace considers a 'mistake', is very much an expression of sacralized shaken-ness. Moreover, the traditions of Dionysian mystical theology and of Sufism integrate this into catholic solidarity-structures of great durability; which Stace, alas, also tends to devalue. Albeit still within the constraints of confessional religious monoculture, they are pioneering anticipations of the solidarity of the shaken. Stace, however, rejects *both* the confessional monoculture and, in effect, the nascent solidarity of the shaken that it harbours.

§

Of late, the modern privatizing, or experientialist, notion of 'mysticism' developed by Bucke, James, Stace and the others has in fact come under sustained scholarly attack. Leading the charge here, from a 'Religious Studies' point of view, has been *Steven T. Katz*: in a series of volumes which he has edited, and to each of which he has contributed a substantial essay; the first of which appeared in 1978.[33] Katz's argument is methodological: that the basic procedure of this tradition – in positing a primary layer of 'mystical experience', differently reported of course according to cultural context but nevertheless supposed to be *essentially* identical in all contexts alike – is, after all, nothing but a recipe for trans-cultural misunderstanding. The 'experience' in itself, he contends, is surely just as much shaped by its context as is the subsequent reporting of it. To abstract it, as this tradition does, is straight away to run the risk of imposing a set of modern scholarly prejudices onto texts which are, in actual fact, quite innocent of them. That is to say: it is, right from the outset, an imperialistic mode of hermeneutics.[34]

Nor has there been any lack of theologians to highlight the actualization of that general risk, in specific relation to Dionysian mystical theology. For example: *Nicholas Lash's* 1986 book *Easter in Ordinary* features a fierce polemic against William James, especially.[35] And other theologians have sought to revive the classical critique of (what I have called) 'mystical boasting' in all its forms; also including the church-ideological kind. *Rowan Williams* for instance has discussed this with reference to Dom Cuthbert Butler's representative work.[36] *Denys Turner's* book *The Darkness of God* is a history of the Dionysian tradition, as it interacts with Augustinianism, polemically celebrating its combination of catholic belonging with a truly radical apophaticism; the exact opposite to Stace's approach in both regards.[37] *Bernard McGinn* is the great historian of 'Christian mysticism' as a whole.[38] He does not go quite as far as Turner would like.[39] But he, too, is keen to insist just how alien the abstract concept of 'mystical experience' is to classical Dionysianism. *Grace Jantzen* has resituated the same basic argument in a feminist context.[40] And *Maggie Ross* has developed it further, with admirable acerbity.[41]

One might perhaps be tempted to cite Jean Gerson, in the early fifteenth century, as a significant exception: a self-professed mystical theologian who already anticipates later 'mysticism'. Gerson, a late representative of classic Dionysianism, thus famously ventures the following formula:

Theologia mystica est cognitio experimentalis habita de Deo per amoris unitivi complexum.[42]

Which William Harmless translates into modern English as:

Mystical theology is an experiential knowledge of God that comes through the embrace of unitive love.[43]

But Ross – I think, quite rightly – protests.[44] 'Experiential' is not the right English word at all. For, as she puts it, this way of speaking straight away tends to bring mystical theology down to the level of someone who says: "'Of course it's true I was abducted by aliens: *I experienced it.*'"[45] And look, the original Latin immediately suggests the proper alternative! Dionysian mystical theology is an *experimental* knowledge of God. It is essentially a matter of experimentation, in poetically evoking the infinite demands of perfect truth-as-openness; which, not least, surely does entail a strict discipline of intellectual humility.

Chapter 5

'GNOSTICISM'

The question regarding divine 'almightiness'

I have suggested that 'mystical theology' – but not 'mysticism' – is one of two basic therapies for the disease of evangelistic impatience, internal to Abrahamic religious tradition.

And 'gnosticism' then ('gnosticism' at its non-sectarian best) is the other. Thus, mystical theology and gnosticism are surely to be understood as two quite different, but nevertheless complementary modes of thought.

The difference indeed goes deep. It reaches right to the primordial origins of the two disciplines. Whereas mystical theology derives from an encounter of Abrahamic faith with Platonist philosophy, gnosticism by contrast is an essentially *un*-philosophic, mythopoetic development out of biblical tradition.

'*Wonder* is the only beginning of philosophy', declares Socrates, as Plato depicts him.[1] And Aristotle says the same; adding that 'the myth-lover [*philomythos*] is [also] in a sense a philosopher [*philosophos*], since myths are composed of wonders'.[2] But what does Abrahamic faith, equivalently, *begin from*? Surely one has to say that it begins from *transfigured grief*. Or rather: from sheer moral urgency, intensified to anguish, refusing to be dulled by resignation. In historical terms, it begins from the anguished, raging, sympathetic openness towards the suffering of others which is so momentously sacralized in the breakthrough-book of *Amos*. And every fresh renewal of authentic Abrahamic faith, in its *core* distinctiveness as a trans-philosophic (sometimes pre-philosophic) approach to truth-as-openness, is again a channelling, a managing, a working-though – but, also, a resurgence – of something like the same. True faith begins as participation in that infinite restlessness which we call God; a being opened up by that restlessness.

Both philosophic / philomythic wonder and faith-transfigured grief involve intense discomfort with the common-sense prejudices of the herd, the gang, the mob. In this sense, they are two basic modes of what I am calling 'shaken-ness', rendered articulate. Hence their complementarity. Ordinary polemical atheism, seeking to mobilize philosophy against faith – and so to turn the *philosophos* against the Abrahamic *philomythos* – systematically fails to see this. It fails to see the true beginning of faith *in* grief. Instead, it assumes that, on the contrary, faith begins as consolatory flight *from* grief. So, it attacks not faith in itself, but faith as distorted by the disease of evangelistic impatience. Typically, atheism confuses the two. The basic imperative of true faith, that one stay with the grief of others, can scarcely be rendered widely attractive to the herd, the gang, the mob; therefore, evangelistic impatience turns aside from it. But then so does ordinary atheism, which is a no less impatient form of ideology, quick to flatter its 'enlightened' adherents, and soothe them with superficiality; forever converting its own outrage into polemical self-satisfaction. Both evangelistically impatient theism and ordinary impatient atheism, alike, traffic in ideological heroin. Evangelistic impatience projects an idolatrous counterfeit-notion of God; ordinary atheism projects a blank in God's too troubling place. These are just two alternative ways of evading the real difficulties that are in fact the heart of the matter.

Joachim of Fiore, in the twelfth century, set out to construct a Trinitarian grand narrative, positing three ages to correspond to the three divine Persons. I do not want to do that. Rather, as I have said, I am interested in the correspondence of the three Trinitarian Persons to three elementary theological problem-clusters, the contexts in which each Person is encountered; and, then, in the historically evolving inter-relationship of these three clusters. Thus: First-Person theology, which originated with the process by which biblical thinking came to terms with the 'God of philosophy', may in general be defined as the *primordial encounter* between shaken-ness-as-grief and shaken-ness-as-wonder, as rival-but-complementary principles. Second-Person theology may be defined as that which logically follows on from this, by way of specifically Christian solidarity-building; and hence, evangelism. The proper role of Third-Person theology however, as I see it, is to mediate between the other two – it 'proceeds' from both – by way of corrective, especially to the effects of evangelistic impatience. So, it looks, above all, to remedy the way in which such impatience, unfortunately, tends to generate a form of solidarity which, yes, achieves popular traction – but only at the cost of obscuring the actual truth inherent in shaken-ness. Third-Person theology, at its truest, is *essentially* a matter of rendering of Christian confessional solidarity transparent to the solidarity of the shaken.

The appearance of the Third Person of the Trinity, the Holy Spirit, in the New Testament narrative of the first Pentecost, the birth of the Church, is proleptic: inasmuch as this is the divine Person who reappears in every fresh ecclesiastical beginning; every genuine movement of renewal, inspired by corporate repentance. The need for corporate repentance is often diagnosed as a simple matter of inertial drift: typified by lack of deep feeling; even widespread scandalous insincerity. Yet, to my mind, the theologically most important movements of this kind are just those that represent the most radical critique of evangelistic impatience, with its concomitant impassioned closed-mindedness, indeed its over-reliance on mere orthodox sincerity to bring about salvation. Evangelistic impatience, after all, may be altogether sincere, truly invested in the supposed correctness of all that it says; but still at a deeper level be dishonest, in the sense of precluding any real openness towards the other. The Holy Spirit is the true 'Comforter', precisely by virtue of excluding the *false* 'comfort' proffered by evangelistic impatience. Mystical theology and gnosticism, then, belong side by side as the two primary forms of Third-Person theology at its most authentic.

Mystical theology is philosophic therapy addressing the impact of the disease on faith as a whole: as evangelistic impatience eclipses faith's testimony to the demands of existential truth-as-openness, in general, behind an idolatry of supposed doctrinal truth-as-correctness.

But gnosticism, by contrast, springs direct from un-philosophic, faith-transfigured grief. And it tackles the same disease with reference to one particular theological concept. Namely: *divine almightiness*. Where evangelistic impatience seeks to wriggle free from grief, gnosticism, insisting on shaken-ness, systematically refuses to allow it to do so.

§

So: what does it mean to affirm that God is 'almighty'? There are at least four distinct potential levels of meaning here.

In the first place, there is the simple sense in which, *for faith*, 'God' primordially means: the ultimate source of all authentic meaning in life. By definition, in other words, there exists no other power with capacity to render our lives truly meaningful. No essentially egoistic drive, be the egoism individual or corporate: no addictive pleasure of any kind whatever, no hungering for glamour, for material wealth, for coercive control of others; and no essentially servile form of self-abnegation, absorption into the collective, either. Only that which, in one way or another, reflects the glory of God – understood as the absolute antithesis to human egoism or servility of every kind – properly has this sort of power.

Second, there is the sense in which affirming God's 'almightiness' is equivalent to the moral imperative: '*no resting in, no moralising of, resentment!*' So, we are invited to receive all that happens to us in life, even the very worst of it, as coming from the Almighty's hands; that is to say, as occurring at any rate by divine permission. Where people are then driven – like Job – to argue with God over the multiple injustices of the world, natural and man-made, of which they are made victim, there, in this regard, we see the doctrine fulfilling its proper, inhibitory purpose.

Third, there is the sense in which the affirmation of divine 'almightiness' is intended as a prophylactic against despair. When, during the twelfth of the sixteen 'shewings' reported by Julian of Norwich, Jesus assures her that 'All shall be well, and all shall be well, and all manner of thing shall be well', it is not because she has been complaining, as Job does, about her own sufferings.[3] Rather, it is a response to her more general, anguished awareness of the effects of sin in the world; her being tempted, consequently, to lose the *moral energy* that depends on hope.

The truth of true faith in 'almighty' God consists in the sacralization of perfect truth-as-openness, which alone gives authentic meaning to life, drives out resentment and hopes against hope. But then there remains yet a further, fourth possible notion of divine 'almightiness': one that has, in essence, been corrupted by evangelistic impatience, and, as a result, no longer has anything to do with truth-as-openness. Indeed: *it precisely tends to do away with the truth of true faith, inasmuch as that truth is truth-as-openness revealed through transfigured grief.* For this corrupted notion is, in essence, a source of *moral anaesthesia*. The reassurance that God is in control, and all must therefore end well, comes to serve precisely as licence for *not*, after all, unduly grieving when one's neighbours suffer. It provides just the sort of comfort that polemical atheism, mistakenly, tends to see as the chief seductive attraction of faith, right from the outset. Indeed, its attractiveness to the impatient evangelist is obvious.

There is nothing anaesthetic about the hope that Julian of Norwich, say, represents. On the contrary! But the anaesthetic notion of divine almightiness, by contrast, is either a source of seductively soothing resignation, to the convert, or else – insofar as it is wedded to the ambition of the impatient evangelist – a quietening of potential scruples. So, it becomes, in effect, a metaphysical projection of the impatient evangelists' own bully-nature. Here, in other words, *das unglückliche Bewußtsein* prevails: objective deep unhappiness, prohibited from recognizing itself as such. The calming promise of eventual victory for the Almighty is twisted around, to become an extension of that prohibition. The victory in question no longer belongs to truth-as-openness; but, again, is the triumph of an idolatrously exalted partisan claim to ultimate metaphysical, historiographical and moral truth-as-correctness, instead. The egoistic self-assertion of the impatient evangelist as such is thereby dressed up as piety. Resentment is in effect readmitted, and eschatologically re-channelled. The deepest existential difficulties of true faith, its proper demands, those *necessary obstacles* to conversion, are dissolved. Potential converts are lured by the delightful prospect of placing themselves under the patronage of a thunderously 'almighty' warrior god; the most thunderous, the 'almightiest' of them all, celestial boss of bosses. And the already converted are also drilled in ever greater enthusiasm for such a Master.

In short: God by definition both is, and is not, 'almighty'. It all depends on how 'almightiness' is, in practice, understood. And I would argue that gnostic doctrine, at its best, is first and foremost a variety of attempts to capture that ambiguity, in the narrative form from which theology in general derives its imaginative potency.

With a basic intention to probe at the perennial ambiguity of 'almightiness', gnostics tell stories. (a) They develop critical theogony: mythic narratives in which different aspects of the divine are configured as belonging to so many distinct stages, or layers, in the process of God *becoming* God. And (b) they follow this up with critical cosmogony: mythic narratives in which Creation is represented as a spin-off from that logically prior theogonic process. Gnostic theogony pictures eternity in temporal terms; it serves to distinguish authentic divine almightiness from merely arbitrary power, as an eternally opposing principle. Gnostic cosmogony then shows these principles, embattled against each other, in the context of Creation.

In short: whereas evangelistic impatience tends to market faith as a source of consolation, in the sense of moral anaesthetic, gnostic myth does the opposite. Working against the briskly simplistic notion of divine almightiness typical of evangelistic impatience, gnostic myth sets out, in systematic fashion, to complicate matters. So, it situates the energy of authentic divine almightiness in the midst of a maelstrom: an equi-primordial turbulence of other, competing energies, with which it is in constant danger of being idolatrously confused. It highlights the essential vulnerability of divine almightiness.

§

Accordingly, the typical underlying pattern of classical gnostic myth consists of a sixfold narrative:

1. The story begins with God, in eternity before created time. Or, rather: with *potential* God, as it were preparing to engage, in intimate and therefore necessarily complex fashion, with the other-than-God. Here we have nothing more than a purely abstract, not yet realized, germ of divine almightiness.
2. The initial engagement of this potential with the other-than-God becomes more or less conflictual, as the heavenly realm fragments, and coalesces, at its worst, into a wilful resistance, to God, of evil defiantly laying claim to divine authority on its own behalf: the Usurpation, represented in mythic terms.
3. Out of this struggle, then, in one way or another there emerges the Creation, first of the cosmos, then of humanity: a battlefield for the struggle of true God against the equiprimordial Usurper.
4. Celestial evil replicates itself in the Fall of Adam.
5. By way of response, celestial goodness eventually appears upon earth in the person of the Messiah, initiating a new epoch in salvation history.
6. In the end, that history culminates in the Last Judgement: the full truth of divine almightiness only now revealed – its meaning clarified by having passed through all the trouble of the interim.[4]

Moments 4–6 of this narrative coincide with more popular forms of Christian and Jewish theology. It is moments 1–3 that really mark it out, as something altogether distinct.

Such thinking – expressive of a mixed, *yes-but-no* response to the God of Rabbinic, or Catholic Christian orthodoxy – is a mythopoetic critique of evangelistic impatience, systematically complicating the biblical notion of divine almightiness. As such, however, it needs to be distinguished from a variety of other unbiblical notions of almightiness, which are altogether murkier. I am thinking here, in the first instance, of *Marcionism*; springing up alongside early gnosticism in the second century CE.

Thus, for Marcion the God of *Genesis* is straightforwardly evil; the enemy which the God of true Pauline Christianity has overthrown. Marcion's thinking is not a challenge to evangelistic impatience. On the contrary, it is surely just a rival form of evangelistic impatience to that of the mainstream Catholic church; only more bitter, more boastful, and laced with a large dose of antisemitism. Evangelistic impatience, after all, does rather thrive on the most simplistic polarizations, corresponding to a sanctified 'us' / a demonized 'them'. A proper critique needs to recognize, and so dissolve, the endless *ambiguity* that such impatience generates. Yet, Marcionite dogma excludes all ambiguity in this regard.

And the same also goes for those other, later, militantly other-worldly movements, *Mandaeism, Manicheanism, Paulicianism, Bogomilism, Catharism*. To what extent, indeed, did that great evangelist, the prophet Mani truly resemble the figure portrayed by Amin Maalouf in his novel *The Gardens of Light*: an ideal third-century precursor of the most enlightened twentieth-century religious liberalism?[5] It seems improbable!

At any event, what I would call 'early gnosticism' does not include these sects at all.[6] Instead, it is confined quite specifically to the teaching of the *Sethians* (also variously known as *Barbeloites* or *Ophites* etc.); the teaching of *Basilides* and his followers; the teaching of *Valentinus* and his followers. These groups repudiated the fanatical Catholic cult of martyrdom associated with evangelistic impatience; the heresy-hunting drive to intellectual conformity; the emergent hierarchical discipline of the Catholic Church. Together, in recoil from that, they constituted a thriving free market in guru-led alternative spirituality. The distinctive, mysterious names which each group gave the various cosmic principles they posited, in the ensemble (the *pléróma*) of the more-or-less divine, may well, to modern readers, look like mere mumbo-jumbo; but they are surely to be understood as a branding device, necessary for competitive purposes. Their competitiveness in that market, however, by no means necessarily rendered them complete outsiders from the wider Church. Or, at least, not of their own choice; not until they were thrown out. The greatest of all the early gnostic leaders, Valentinus himself (*c.* 100–*c.* 60) had actually been a prominent member of the Church in Rome. In fact, according to Tertullian, he had even at one point had quite realistic ambitions to become pope![7]

Kabbalah

Gnosticism in the strict form, then, originated in the hyper-evangelistic Judaeo-Christian world of the first and second centuries CE. It has never taken root in Islamic culture.[8] The most spectacular flowering of such thought was in late-mediaeval / early modern Judaism. And then it has also had a bit of a later Christian history.

§

We cannot really judge to what extent the bitterness of early Catholic anti-gnostic polemicists such as Bishop Irenaeus of Lyons was in fact justified by prior bitter / boastful sectarian aggression on the part of those they were denouncing.[9] But note: it is, at any rate, in principle quite possible for whole gnostic sub-cultures to flourish in friendly partnership with larger popular-religious traditions. That is, if they are allowed to. To see this, one has only to consider the phenomenon of Kabbalah, in its relation to the wider world of Rabbinic Judaism.

Kabbalah first emerges into the historical light of day in Provence, around the year 1200, with the appearance of the book *Bahir*. In the early thirteenth century there was a thriving Kabbalist culture in Catalonia. The great Kabbalist classic, the *Zohar* was written towards the end of that century, in Castile, probably by Rabbi Moses de Leon. And then the second great spike in Kabbalist creativity occurred in the mid-sixteenth century; above all, in the little Upper Galilean town of Safed (Zfat), where Moses Cordovero taught, popularizing the *Zohar*; and, after him, Isaac Luria, the great innovator. There is no surviving evidence of any actual oral tradition spanning the millennium that separates Kabbalah from the early gnosticism of the Sethians, the Basilideans, the Valentinians and their like. Yet, notwithstanding the natural differences in literary and exegetic style, the affinity of the two cultures, in terms of basic doctrine, is uncanny. They share the same taste for extravagant theogonic, and cosmogonic myth. And yes, they do also share the same fundamental anxiety about discordant manifestations of the divine; the same unease about the effects of evangelistic impatience, about distorted notions of divine almightiness.

The fact that, apart from Sabbatian convulsion of 1665–6, all the prime actual examples of evangelistic impatience in the world of the classical Kabbalists belonged to the surrounding Christian culture, rather than to Judaism itself, no doubt explains why the wider Jewish community as a whole never turned against the gnostics in its midst. In that context, Kabbalah was, not least, a vindication of persecuted Jewish spiritual integrity, as contrasted with the corruption of persecutory Christendom. To be sure, there were Jewish critics of Kabbalah right from the outset.[10] And in the nineteenth century the modernist scholars of the *Wissenschaft des Judentums* movement, such as Heinrich Graetz, tended to be hostile. (The altogether more sympathetic secular-scholarly approach *Gershom Scholem* has to be seen against this background.[11]) But, as a rule, wherever Kabbalism has flourished, its adepts have participated in synagogue liturgy alongside their non-Kabbalist neighbours without any serious conflict erupting.

The contrast with early Christianity, in this regard, really is striking.

§

In the beginning, according to the logic of gnosticism, God is not yet, in the full sense, God. Latent divinity is, so to speak, held within an absolute, abstract plenitude of, therefore, arbitrary almightiness; but still lacks the defined character of true God, which can only come by virtue of a certain restraint on that arbitrariness.

In the Sethian *Apocryphon of John*, for instance, this original latency is called 'the Monad'.[12] But the 'Monad' breaks up into a series of emanations, notably including 'Sophia', that is, 'Wisdom'. And 'Wisdom', unwisely, then seeks to bring forth a further being on her own initiative – a projection, here, of the arrogance all too typical of intellectuals! – which is eventually to feed into evangelistic impatience. The immediate result is the birth of the corrupt, usurpatory creator god Yaltabaoth. This demiurge lapses into ignorant blasphemy and madness. Having created humanity, Yaltabaoth demands worship from these creatures of his. He demands it, precisely, in a spirit of evangelistic impatience. However, his creative power derives from his mother Sophia, that is, Wisdom. The birth of Yaltabaoth represents an innocent mistake on the part of Wisdom. She swiftly repents and, invoking the higher powers, toils to counteract her progeny's mischief. True God is revealed through this struggle.

The Valentinian *Tripartite Tractate*, by contrast, begins from a form of Trinitarian doctrine.[13] First comes 'the Father', arbitrary almightiness. Next, the first benign checks on that arbitrariness: the emanation of two co-eternal heavenly beings: 'the Son' and 'the Church'. And, after that: a great flowing-out of further emanations from the third principle. This, to be sure, is still in eternity, 'before' Creation. However, one of these emanations is 'the Logos'. And it is the fall of the Logos which brings Creation about. The Logos sincerely loves the Father and is eager to honour Him. But (as with Wisdom in the *Apocryphon of John*) the trouble is just that he is over-eager; impatient. That impatience is what generates the problem which the Logos then penitently recognizes. His solution: the creation of the Saviour; and of the world, as an arena for the Saviour's remedial work.

Kabbalist literature, for its part, speaks of the first principle as '*En Sof*, that is, 'the Limitless'.[14] There is no real possibility of human understanding or prayerful connection with the absolute impersonal remoteness of *En Sof*. But the possibility of authentic human spiritual life derives from a procession of divine emanations (the ten '*Sefiroth*'; contracted, in Lurianic Kabbalah, into the five '*Partsufim*') carefully qualifying the almightiness of *En-Sof*. In Isaac Luria's thought particularly, the initial dynamic that climaxes in the creation of the universe begins in an act of divine self-limitation, '*tsimtsum*'; a renunciation of total control, leaving space for the *Sefiroth* / *Partsufim*. This is, on the one hand, a rendering-possible of enrichment: the possibility ultimately expressed as the intimate in-dwelling of the last emanation – the divine-feminine element or '*Shekhinah*' (for Luria, '*Rachel*') – within the people of Israel. But, alas, the more deeply the divine enters into the spiritual domain of the human the more it is also inevitably exposed to the risk of distortion. Luria pictures this risk in cartoonish fashion, as an outpouring of divine light from the eyes, mouth, ears and nose of *Adam Kadmon*, the 'primordial man', into a series of bowls; some of which however break, and spill their sacred content. And the result is a certain dimming of the divine light, especially in the figure of the fourth *Partsuf*, which, together with the fifth (*Rachel*, or the *Shekhinah*), constitutes the God of impassioned popular religion. This fourth *Partsuf* is called '*Zeir Anpin*', 'the Impatient One'.[15] He is indeed, surely, none other than the God of popular religion both transcending and yet tragically obscured by evangelistic impatience.

The Creation of the world is not the work of a malign demiurge in Kabbalist thought, as it is in the *Apocryphon of John*. Nor is it the work of a foolish demiurge, as it is in *The Tripartite Tractate*. The Creator is unequivocally true God. But the point is, simply, that God's almightiness remains qualified: necessarily hampered by the limitations of the possible, the logic of *tsimtsum*.

Böhme

Around the turn of the fifteenth and sixteenth centuries a number of Christian scholars (notably Pico della Mirandola, Johannes Reuchlin and Francesco Giorgi) began to integrate elements of Kabbalah (in this context generally written as 'Cabbalah') into their own thinking. And, whilst this was, at first, chiefly just for purposes of Christian evangelism among Jews – and therefore only quite a shallow appropriation – the resultant reintroduction of originally gnostic themes into the thought-world of Christendom was, at length, to bear altogether more substantial fruit in the work of *Jakob Böhme* (1575–1624).

Böhme is often ranked among Christian 'mystics'. But in his case the term 'mystic' is a misnomer. He was not a mystic; he was a gnostic.

Indeed, he represents a new form of Christian gnosticism, quite unlike that of the second century 'heretics', inasmuch as he does not appear to have had any divisive sectarian intent at all. Subsequently, it is true, various sectarian thinkers laid claim to Böhme as an inspiration. But he himself simply professed to be a good, if eccentric, Lutheran.[16] Amongst Böhme's later admirers, moreover, William Law (1686–1761) attempted to integrate his thought into mainstream Anglicanism.[17] Whilst Louis-Claude de Saint-Martin (1743–1803) and Franz von Baader (1765–1841) – linking Böhme to the not at all gnostic but similarly imaginative Paracelsus – attempted to integrate his thought into mainstream Roman Catholicism.

An inspired autodidact, in the last six years of his life, 1618–24, Böhme was writing at great speed, the words pouring pell-mell from his pen: a great eruption of speculative prose-poetry, Paracelsan jargon, fanciful exegesis of biblical texts, pietistic edification; all in a German still as fresh as Shakespearean English. He is indeed a notable thinker in several ways: a leading Lutheran Pietist;[18] a polemicist against predestinarianism;[19] a theological proto-feminist(?), affirming the mythic androgyny of both the First and the Second Adam.[20] First and foremost, however, he is quite simply *the* great post-Reformation renewer of gnostic thought, within Christendom. And, as such, he has had a number of distinguished later admirers.

Hegel, for instance, gives him an honoured place in his Berlin *Lectures on the History of Philosophy* as 'the first German philosopher'.[21] *Schelling*, in his 1809 *Philosophical Investigations into the Essence of Human Freedom*, attempts a translation, as it were, of elements drawn from Böhme's imagistic thought, into more abstract, disciplined philosophical language.[22] Contrariwise, *William Blake* hails the inspiration of Boehme (anglicizing his name as 'Behmen') with an extravagant poetic flourish. So, in an autobiographical fragment of verse, part of a letter dated 12 September 1800 to John Flaxman, describing the original sources of his prophetic vision, Blake writes:

Paracelsus & Behmen appear'd to me, terrors appear'd in the Heavens above
And in Hell beneath, & a mighty & awful change threatened the Earth.
The American War began … [23]

Not that Blake was by any means a doctrinaire 'Behmenist'. But, still, he salutes Böhme as a fellow free spirit.

Whilst, as for the secular-scholarly study of Böhme's thought as a historical phenomenon: this – having been initiated by Hegel in his *Lectures on the History of Philosophy* – was then sympathetically taken up the great founder of the Tübingen School of theology, F. C. Baur.[24] And subsequent admirers, following Baur, include Kierkegaard's *bête noire*, the Hegelianizing Bishop of Zealand and primate of the Danish Lutheran Church, *Hans Lassen Martensen* who, in 1881, published a notable study of Böhme's thought.[25] Also: that great theological maverick, *Nikolai Berdyaev*.[26] And later: the still more maverick *Thomas Altizer*.[27] All these are writers who have wanted to argue that Böhme still has important things to teach the Church.

§

Böhme, like all other classic gnostic thinkers, thinks of God as being in process of evolution: away from sheer shapeless potency, towards the enrichment that can only come from intimate engagement with creatures.[28] Thus, he presents us with a mythic depiction of divinity's intrinsic drive to self-expression. One might say: the drive of truth-as-openness to be expressed in terms of truth-as-correctness – which it precedes and transcends, and which is a species of truth forever liable to corruption, distorting the relationship – but which, where all goes well, simply enriches the openness it communicates.

His narrative begins with divinity enveloped in the '*Unground*'. This is equivalent to the Kabbalist notion of *En Sof*. The 'Unground' (in German, *der Ungrund*) is pure, abstract, potential divinity. However, it is impersonal, because inchoate, void of self-expressive capacity, and in that sense deficient, not yet properly almighty. 'When it comes to describing [the primordial nature of] God', Böhme writes at the beginning of his commentary on *Genesis*,

> I say: He is the One; in relation to creatures, an eternal Nothing. He has neither foundation, beginning, nor home ... He is the Will of the Unground ...
> (*Mysterium Magnum* 1: 2)[29]

The Unground is the original divine condition of being 'Nothing' to creatures; that is to say, having simply no *reciprocal* relationship to anything external. About the Unground in itself, indeed, nothing more can be said; it is a metaphysical black hole. One can only speak of what escapes from it. Namely: the '*Will* of the Unground', which drives God's progressive break-out from this confinement; the Will, in other words, to become creative, a Ground for otherness.

Again: what does faith in God *do*? At the most primitive level – that is to say, universally, across all theological cultures – it simply intensifies *urgency* of moral concern. The shaping and reshaping of that concern is secondary to faith's intensification effect – its transfiguring intensification of grief, anguish, longing, everything restless. Böhme's German term for divine sheer urgency is '*Lust*'.[30] In itself quite inarticulate, yet forever restlessly seeking to become articulate, this is the break-out energy of the 'Will of the Unground'. He abstracts the truth of *Lust* from the various forms it assumes in historic human life – abstracts it entirely, bracketing those forms – and then sets it right at the beginning of his theogonic narrative.

He has two distinct but complementary ways of presenting this first moment of his narrative. On the one hand, he represents it in Trinitarian terms:

> [God] generates himself in himself, from eternity to eternity … [And] in this eternal generation we have to acknowledge these three:
> 1. An eternal Will
> 2. An eternal Mind, corresponding to the Will
> 3. That which issues from both, the spirit of Will and Mind.
> (Mysterium Magnum, 1: 2-3)[31]

With this notion of the immanent Trinity, he is reaching out (albeit in highly abstract, reductionist fashion!) towards mainstream Church tradition.

But, on the other hand, he also represents the break-out of divine truth, from the Unground, as beginning with the generation of a single divine other: *Wisdom*. The traditionally assumed femininity of Wisdom serves as balance to the masculinity of orthodox Trinitarianism. And, at the same time, Wisdom is associated, in Böhme's thinking, with a lingering, retrospective focus on the primary moment of divine truth: its essential sublation of urgent yearning. Thus, he writes:

> What initially issues forth [from the Unground] may be called the urgency of the divine. *Or*: eternal Wisdom. She is the primordial source of all powers, colours and virtues. In her the threefold spirit [of the immanent Trinity] becomes an urgent desiring … And that desiring is a shaping process. It is a development of self-awareness.
> (Mysterium Magnum, 1: 6)

There is at this stage no created world yet in existence. But, through the mediation of Wisdom, the Will of the Unground grows aware of its own creative potential. For Wisdom is none other than an urgent contemplation of all the beautiful possibilities that stand ready to be deployed in Creation. And so Böhme goes on:

> The Will conceives Wisdom in the Mind, and what is conceived is the eternal Word, comprising all colours, powers and virtues. This utterance is the self-expression of the eternal Will, by the Spirit, via the understanding of the Mind.
>
> It is the motion or life of the divine: the optics of the eternal seeing, where each power, colour and virtue is perceived in distinction from the rest, and all of them in correct proportion, albeit [as yet] without actual weight, limit or measure [which only Creation will confer] to divide them. All the powers, colours and

virtues lie together, in well-tuned, pregnant harmony; and this then is, as it were, captured by an eloquent Word; in which Word, all words – all powers, colours and virtues – are contained. And as they are spoken, they unfold themselves, in a pageant of meaning.

(*Mysterium Magnum*, 1: 6-7)

Here he is attempting to evoke the colourful, powerful and virtuous urgency with which the divine bursts out of the Unground: both before time, archetypally; and also historically, within the dawning consciousness of each individual person of faith insofar as they are opened up to the imperatives of true Wisdom.

§

In *Mysterium Magnum*, Chapters 3–7 Böhme then goes on to analyse what he calls 'Eternal Nature': a series of fundamental value-determining energies. 'Eternal Nature' as a whole, for him, has seven '*forms*' or '*properties*' in all. The first three correspond to the three-foldness of the still developing immanent Trinity – or let us rather say the 'proto-Trinity'.[32] This proto-Trinity has all the urgent intensity of divine truth emergent from the Unground whilst nevertheless falling short of authentic divinity, inasmuch as it corresponds to the false Trinitarian 'God' of *absolute* evangelistic impatience – indeed, impatience of every kind – a 'God' without any real capacity for forgiveness or love at all. It is, in effect, the basic structure of an *abortively* Trinitarian dialectic, *flawed* Wisdom.

The fourth 'form' of 'Eternal Nature', on the other hand, involves the breakthrough emergence to *true* Wisdom, accomplished by way of a patient openness to actual reality.

Böhme is a maestro of mixed metaphors, applied in thick impasto. Running right through this whole discussion of 'Eternal Nature' there is a good deal of Paracelsan pseudo-science: the proto-Trinitarian energies are described partly in astrological terms, as Saturn / Mercury / Mars; partly in alchemical terms, as Salt / Mercury / Sulphur; the three then conjoining to produce a single Oil, to represent their out-flowing oneness. But the infinite ideal dynamism of the process is further represented in a mass of other terms. Proto-God the Father is the nascent will of God envisaged as an impatiently domineering sovereign wilfulness, resisting deflection. Böhme describes the proto-Father's will as 'astringent', 'rough', 'harsh', 'hard', 'thick', 'cold', 'keen', 'sharp' (*Mysterium Magnum* 3: 9). Proto-God the Son is the nascent mind of God, in the sense of an impatiently all-questioning insurgent attitude to established power. So Böhme understands the work of the proto-Son to be a matter of 'stinging', 'pricking', 'stirring', 'setting in motion', 'enlivening', 'restlessness', 'rage' (3: 10). God at this stage, before the Creation of the world, not yet being fully God, the relationship between proto-Father and proto-Son, still only just emerged from the Unground, is tense. The proto-Father seeks to 'hold, restrain and keep under the disobedient Son' (3: 11)! And proto-God the Holy Spirit, then, is the registering of the resultant conflict. The prime characteristic of the proto-Spirit is, accordingly, sulphurous (!) 'anguish', or 'distress'; even 'madness'; a tormented despair of ever being able to heal the breach between the other two persons of the proto-Trinity (3: 12, 14-16). In order for such healing actually to be possible, the process – of God becoming God – has to continue; fresh contexts have to be found, for the praxis of discernment, distinguishing true intensity (heaven) from false intensity (hell), which in the proto-Trinity are muddled together. And the fourth 'form' of 'Eternal Nature', then, represents the totality of these fresh contexts, considered in the most comprehensive terms.

The fifth, sixth and seventh 'forms', following on from this, are discussed in *Mysterium Magnum* Chapters 5–6. As I understand the admittedly turbulent argument here, these constitute the value-determining energies of authentic inspiration, transfiguring the mutually conflictual, and therefore chaotic, impatience of the first three 'forms', the proto-Trinity. Thus, the impatient sheer wilfulness of proto-God the Father is transfigured to become the essentially patient 'love-desire' of the fifth 'form'. The impatient critical negativity of proto-God the Son is transfigured to become the essentially patient universal will-to-negotiate constitutive of the sixth 'form': the divine Word – the 'understanding, voice, sound, speech' of God – echoing throughout Creation. The impatient despair of proto-God the Holy Spirit is transfigured to become the essentially patient spirit of hope, in the practical realization of the kingdom of God, which constitutes the seventh 'form'.

However, the *fourth* 'form' is pivotal here, as the initial all-encompassing negation of flawed proto-divinity, clearing the way for divine truth to emerge. Böhme envisages it to be an eternal *Kindling* of divine truth.[33] How are we to understand this?

Alongside his distinction between the seven 'forms' of 'Eternal Nature', Böhme also distinguishes three '*Principles*'. Right at the start, before all beginnings – before time, before the existence of anything actual – there was just possibility. Of course, however, as soon as any possibility is realized, certain other possibilities logically cease to be possible. Nor does divine almightiness, by any means, do away with such limits. The First Principle, then, is the sheer impatient frustration, wrath and despair of the proto-Trinity ('forms' 1–3) provoked by reality as determined by the logical rules of mutual exclusion. The Second Principle, on the other hand, ('form' 4 in itself) is the primordial Fire: true God revelling in the vast expanse of creative possibility, now however ready patiently to accept the inevitable constraints that so enrage the proto-divinity of the First Principle; burning away that impatience. And the Third Principle (the outworking of 'forms' 5–7) is the eternal conflict of the First and Second Principles brought down to earth, and fought out within human history; God more or less reflected in the thinking of redeemed humanity.[34]

But the crucial twist in the argument at this point is Böhme's insistence on the fundamental *co-dependence* of the First and Second Principles: primordial intensity of chaotic *Lust* and clear-sighted patience. As he puts it, here

> two Kingdoms are split apart, even though they still remain one. They divide in their essence, their [acknowledged] source, their governing will; they lose sight of one another; the one fails to see its original conjunction with the other.

Yet, they share the same coming to be; they each depend on the other; the one without the other would be nothing.

(*Mysterium Magnum* 4: 1)

Two 'Kingdoms': one, the Kingdom of sheer intensity, truth-element of the First Principle; the other, the Kingdom of rationality, patient sober realism in coming to terms with inevitable constraints, all that the Second Principle brings to the First in the process of their fiery coming-together. Revelation is twofold, as true God in the Second Principle both shares in the intensity of the proto-divine in the First Principle, yet also rises above the initial expression of that intensity; above its expression in sheer, impatient frustration, wrath and despair. Again, true Wisdom is, first of all, intensification of care. And certainly, there are many reasons for intensified care to issue in frustration, wrath and despair, given all the unrealized delightful future possibilities that any actual choice, once made, must take away; the impossibility of excluding potential evil, alongside the primarily intended good; the perhaps grim collateral risks involved in any initiative. Yet divine frustration, however justifiable it may be, is not to be misunderstood as vindication of a radical polarization, setting the two dialectically related Kingdoms altogether at war. Divine truth is *eternal* Fire: both the fuel (maximum-intensity sheer urgent care) and the flames (the work of patient realism) are always necessary. *The flames will never consume the fuel; the fuel must never be withheld.*

Hence, implicitly, we have a mythic representation of two basic forms of religion gone wrong. First there is the error of fanaticism – alike, whether it be the fanaticism of the evangelistically impatient orthodox, or that of their no less impatiently embittered sectarian-gnostic opponents. Both impatient evangelists and embittered gnostics supply the fuel of the First Principle, all that grief-stricken intensity, in plenty. Yet, in each case, the chimney is blocked. There is not enough air-flow for the Second Principle, so the 'flaring-up' is more or less stifled. *Their grief is not properly transfigured.* And then there is the counter-balancing error of ethical sentimentalists. In their case, the problem is just lack of fuel. The fire of their thought, therefore, remains all too meagre. *Their grief is deficient.* Against both errors alike, Böhme insists:

> Get this straight. Out of the fieriness there proceeds the breath of life, which in its character as free urgency is holy and joyous, but in relation to the realm of darkness is painful and full of wrath. The wrath and source of pain is the root of the realm of joy. And the realm of joy is the root of the enmity of the dark wrath. So, there is a *contrarium*, by which the good is revealed as the good that it is.
>
> (*Mysterium Magnum* 4: 19)

Here the metaphor of Fire mutates into the metaphor of mutual rootedness. 'The wrath and source of pain is the root of the realm of joy': in the sense that the flourishing of joyous divine revelation depends upon the primal grieving urgency which it transfigures. And 'the realm of joy is the root of the enmity of the dark wrath': in the sense that the transfiguration in question is, indeed, radically provocative. In other words:

> The darkness [consequent upon the First Principle] is the great enemy of the light [the Second Principle], and yet it is the reason why the light is apparent. For if there were no black, then white could not show up. If there were no sorrow, then joy would never know itself.
>
> (*Mysterium Magnum* 5: 7)

First, the Fire requires its fiercely combustible fuel: the, to begin with, discordant passions of the proto-Trinity. Then, the best possible ventilation for its flames: the discipline of true Wisdom, blazing up, feeding on those passions, preserving yet transfiguring their original anarchy.

§

And so, we come to the event of Creation. By contrast to the early Christian gnostics, Böhme gives us a gnostic account of Creation without the figure of a corrupted demiurge. Where the early gnostics attribute Creation to the fall of a demiurge, Böhme's features the supreme angelic figure of Lucifer, who is similarly fallen, but who is *not* the world's Creator. In *Mysterium Magnum*, Lucifer, the narcissistic would-be Usurper, assumes all three 'forms' constitutive of (what I have called) the proto-Trinity, but above all the first:

You ask: what was it about him that brought [Lucifer's rebellion] about?

> It was his great beauty. For his free will looked into the fiery mirror. And there, seeing what he was, he glimpsed a lustre which so moved him, that he eagerly reached out to lay hold upon the properties [of proto-divinity] there at the *centre* of his own self, with immediate effect. For astringent, austere desire [that is, the first 'form' or 'property' of 'Eternal Nature'] went to work, awakening sting [the second 'form'] and anxiety [the third 'form']. And then this beautiful star darkened itself; its essence grew altogether astringent, rigorous, harsh; its proper angelic humility was transformed into a being entirely austere, harsh, rigorous, and sombre [the disposition of proto-God the Father]. The bright Morning Star was undone; and, with him, all his legions. And this was his Fall.
>
> (*Mysterium Magnum* 9: 10)

Meanwhile, Böhme's first work, *The Aurora*, primarily deals with the Luciferian appropriation of the second proto-Trinitarian moment.[35] Thus, here the primordial struggle, leading to Creation, is between Christ and Lucifer as two rival brothers (*Aurora* 12: 134; 13: 36; 13: 47–8; 13: 61; 13: 115; 13: 164). Lucifer, the older Son, is to be understood as celestial prototype of all the false God-concepts historically evoked by evangelistic impatience. And Christ then, the Second Person of the fully divine Trinity, *replaces* the fallen Lucifer.

The three 'forms' of the proto-Trinity represent the inspiration of evangelistic impatience envisaged as a self-enclosed primal confusion. Lucifer is the same; only, now instead envisaged as a spirit explicitly embattled against true God.

Compare Lucifer's Fall in Böhme's narrative, for instance, to the fall of the demiurge Yaltabaoth in the Sethian *Apocryphon of John*; or – in the Valentinian scheme of the *Tripartite Tractate* – to the more qualified fall of the demiurgic Logos. As Böhme envisages it:

> Foolishly King Lucifer aspired to be an artist and absolute lord like the Creator.
> (*Mysterium Magnum* 9: 17)

His ambition is 'foolish' inasmuch as, unlike those other, demiurgic figures, he lacks the necessary 'artistic' ability to be a Creator. In terms of what has gone before in the story, he represents a quite unqualified return to the wilful sheer incoherence of the First Principle. As with the demiurgic figures of earlier gnosticism, his downfall is precisely an outcome of hubristic impatience; the catastrophic impatience by which the First Principle is distinguished from the moderating Second. On earth Lucifer, masked as the God of evangelistic impatience, typically boasts of his imaginary almightiness: seducing humankind with such boasts, and with the delightful promises that they are supposed to justify. Yet, for Böhme, the moment of Creation has also to be seen as the very moment of his fundamental discrediting and defeat. It is none other than the moment when the powers of true God

> confiscate the disobedient child's inheritance from his Father, and cast him out, as a perjured wretch, from his childhood home, into an eternal prison, a house of darkness and anger: the one who had sought to be master over the essence of God's love, and to rule as an illusionist, mixing the holy with the unholy, performing his tricks, swaggering about.
> (*Mysterium Magnum* 10: 14)

Lucifer's Fall leaves all dark. Whereupon, God's primal creative word, 'Let there be light' is a simultaneous *answer* to that Fall.

Vainly boasting of his impossible supposed almightiness, Lucifer is imprisoned in the falsehood of his bragadoccio. Indeed, he *is* the spirit of that impatient boasting, that imprisonment. True God, on the contrary, does not boast like this; but patiently accepts the limitations of what is possible, and works within them. Thus, Böhme back-projects critique of evangelistic impatience right to the moment of Creation – thereby developing his prior account of the fiery struggle between the First and Second Principles 'of the divine essence' within eternity. This constitutes the basis for a gnosticism radically free of bitterness and boastful scorn: as the Second Principle sublates the First.

Only at the Last Judgement will a *full* revelation of true divine almightiness – dispelling Luciferian delusion, and so vindicating Creation – eventually have become possible. And, finally, Böhme also goes on to discuss this emergent revelation, the unfolding of the Third Principle through Christian salvation history, in a series of other, rather more conventional works ... [36]

'Gnostic return in modernity?'

How are we to understand the grand-narrative significance of gnosticism?

Baur, in his seminal 1835 book *Die christliche Gnosis*, attributes a key role to Böhme, as a link between early gnosticism and those major intellectual figures of the then recent past and present: Hegel, Schelling and Schleiermacher. Not that Böhme had had any direct contact with early gnostic literature. And, really, the notion of 'gnosticism' with which Baur is working is very fuzzy. Hegel and Schelling admire Böhme, but they are not myth-making thinkers in Böhme's manner; or in the manner of his gnostic predecessors. And I am all the more bemused by the inclusion of Schleiermacher in Baur's list.

§

Baur, in general, admires what he calls 'gnosticism'. Eric Voegelin, writing in the mid-twentieth century, takes up the idea of a return of 'gnosticism' in modernity, but transforms it into a preposterous nightmare.

All honour to Voegelin for his boldness as a scholarly provocateur! Even though he seems to me quite misguided, he was, after all, a major grand-narrative advocate of truth-as-openness, in philosophic form. He celebrates Plato and Aristotle as ideal models of constant philosophic *zétéma*, purely open-ended enquiry. And he sets out, in the context of modern scholarship, as it were to re-enact the early Christian project of reconciling Platonist philosophy with the heritage of Hebrew prophecy.[37] Moreover, Voegelin systematically opposes true philosophy in this sense to 'philodoxy': thinking, of any kind, which lays hubristic claim to final dogmatic truth-as-correctness. He repudiates both, on the one hand, the philodoxy of established religion, or conservative political ideology; and on the other hand – still more urgently – the philodoxy of counter-cultural movements, preying upon people's alienation. It is the latter which, in the context of Judaeo-Christian cultural tradition as a whole, he calls 'Gnosticism'. Thus, 'Gnosticism' is, for him, a sickness which originates from a corrupting 'metastasis' of Hebrew prophetic thought. At first, in antiquity, the result is an altogether other-worldly mode of ideological hubris. But then, as he sees it, beginning with Joachim of Fiore in the twelfth century the 'metastatic' outcome turns this-worldly. In consequence, it goes from bad to worse; and eventually, issues in the secular totalitarian ideologies of Voegelin's own life-time.

For my part, I have three basic objections to this Voegelinian grand narrative. (i) His admiration for Plato appears to be unbounded. But, as I have said, Plato can by no means be regarded as an unequivocal early champion of the solidarity of the shaken.[38] What Plato stands for is, far rather, solidarity among philosophers as such: in other words, shaken thinkers who are *also* gifted with great learning, products of a superior education; individuals, therefore, with a strong natural bias towards defending the educational privilege which they and their ilk enjoy, along with all that helps preserve it. Leo Strauss is an admirably self-aware upholder of Platonist 'philosophic politics', so defined – and I will come back to Strauss. But Voegelin's thought is I think already symptomatic of the inevitable, strong tendency towards (to use his own terminology) conservative philodoxy in such an outlook. He sees no problem in Plato's explicit licensing of the 'Big Lie' (*gennaion pseudos*); sacred myth designed to pacify the masses and manipulate them into a willing acceptance of being governed by their betters. For him, this is just satiric playfulness.[39] In my view, Voegelin's Platonism is all too un-critical.

(ii) Conversely, his understanding of Hegel is, as Thomas Altizer justly remarks, quite 'absurd and grotesque' in its sheer hostility.[40] Thus Voegelin, in effect, swallows Kojève's flamboyant caricature of 'Hegel' – only, without any of Kojève's mischievous admiration for this fictional 'Hegel's' outrageous self-promotional flamboyance.[41] Hegel, for Voegelin, is indeed the most formidable representative of modern 'Gnosticism', pitched to its ultimate 'egophanic', as opposed to authentically theophanic, extreme. As Altizer puts it, 'Hegel is the great villain of [Voegelin's] *The Ecumenic Age*. He looms so large in these pages as to be a virtual Anti-christ.'[42] Considering the actual resemblance, in scope, of Voegelin's grand-narrative enterprise to that of Hegel, before him, Altizer even wonders whether one might not say that 'Voegelin's hatred of Hegel is an attempted *Oedipal murder of his father*?'![43] It is true that Hegel, more perhaps than any other philosopher in history, has suffered repeated malicious mis-reading, by a whole range of commentators. But Voegelin really is an extreme case.

(iii) More generally, as well, what does it add to our understanding of Joachim of Fiore, for instance, to call him, as Voegelin does, a 'Gnostic'? The conventional usage of the term originates in the literature of early Christian theology, the work of thinkers such as Irenaeus, attacking those they regard as heretical teachers. There is a veritable gulf, though, between the thought-world of Irenaeus, back in the second century, and the thought-world of Joachim, a millennium later! Or, likewise, how does it help to categorize such diverse, and altogether secular, modern figures as Comte, Marx, Nietzsche or Heidegger as yet further 'Gnostics'? Voegelin, in so doing, surely stretches the term to breaking point![44] And then he largely overlooks Kabbalah, and Böhme, in his narrative. Whilst his discussion of early Gnosticism remains quite sketchy.

§

Another grand bogeyman-concept, closely related to Voegelin's extended notion of 'gnosticism', is to be seen in *Glenn Alexander Magee's* discussion of what he calls the 'Hermetic Tradition'.[45] For this too is a fierce polemic, primarily attempting to discredit Hegel, and Hegelians – in which however Böhme features as a key co-accused. The 'Hermetic Tradition' is Magee's name for a rag-bag of esoteric teachings, with origins in the Renaissance, crucially including, amongst other things

– (speculative astrology, alchemy, a whole riot of superstitious ideas) – Christian appropriation of Kabbalah.[46] As he sees it, Böhme is a major representative of the 'Hermetic Tradition', intent, so far as possible, on reconciling it with Christianity.

Magee argues that true philosophy is fundamentally incompatible with the Hermetic Tradition. For: 'Hermeticism replaces the love of wisdom with the lust for power.'[47] And therefore Hegel – infected, like Böhme, with Hermeticism – 'is not a philosopher'![48] But one may well wonder, in that case, how many true philosophers there actually are. Is Plato – dreaming of a utopian social order in which philosophers (deploying the Big Lie) are rulers – a true philosopher, altogether free from the 'lust for power'? Is the subsequent tradition in general, identified by Leo Strauss, of Platonist 'philosophic politics' truly philosophic? Or should philosophers, simply, steer clear of any serious attempt whatsoever to translate philosophic theory into political practice, lest their philosophic purity, perhaps, be thereby compromised? Not only does Magee's *ad hominem* attempt to impugn the basic motivation for Hegel's thought, here, seem to me altogether misguided. He is also, I think, being radically unfair to Böhme. I will be coming back to Hegel in Chapter 8. With regard to Böhme, however: if I am right in my interpretation of his basic fellowship with other 'gnostic' thinkers, then – quite contrary to what Magee is arguing – his poetic creativity may well be said to be, precisely, a *strategy of resistance* to 'lust for power', insofar as such lust is antithetical to 'love of wisdom'. For it resists the theological workings of 'lust for power' at the heart of evangelistic impatience.

Granted, there are (in Magee's sense) other 'Hermetic' elements in Böhme's somewhat chaotic thought; largely deriving from his reading of Paracelsus. And Paracelsus – Renaissance magician, faith-healer, intellectual con-man, iconoclast, genius self-publicist, brilliant obscurantist – is indeed, morally, a very much more questionable thinker. (He became something of a cult-figure among German academics of the Third Reich.) Böhme is fascinated by the poetic potential of Paracelsus's 'bombastic' philosophy of nature. In particular: the Paracelsian theory of 'signatures' in the outward look of things, indicating their inner constitution; which is license for all manner of pseudo-scientific nonsense, but also a celebration of metaphor.[49] Magee's diagnosis of 'Hermeticism' as an expression of 'lust for power' makes at least some sense in relation to Paracelsus. It makes no sense at all however in relation to Böhme, whose borrowings from Paracelsus, although extensive, are surely in fact quite superficial; more formal than substantive.

§

Undoubtedly, however, the leading present-day academic authority on Böhme, and his place in the history of philosophy, is *Cyril O'Regan*. In 1994 O'Regan published a major study of *The Heterodox Hegel*, in which the particular influence of Böhme on Hegel is a major theme.[50] Then, in 2001: *Gnostic Return in Modernity*, in which he introduces his systematic multi-volume project of 'redeeming and reconstructing' Baur's model of 'gnostic return in modernity' in the light of twenty-first century scholarship.[51] O'Regan's historical account of this return, like Baur's, naturally begins with Böhme, whose thought is the subject of the next book in the series.[52] And, after an interval in which he has been working, amongst other things, on two substantial works conceived in homage to Hans Urs von Balthasar – one on Balthasar and Hegel, the other on Balthasar and Heidegger – he now proposes to complete his discussion of 'gnostic return' with volumes first on 'gnostic' echoes in German Idealism (Fichte / Hegel / Schelling), and then on 'gnostic' echoes in English and German Romanticism (Blake / Hölderlin / Novalis).[53]

O'Regan is a formidably indefatigable scrutineer of metaphysical narrative; a systematic taxonomist of ideas. Thus, in general, he sets out to analyse the complex interweave of different elements in the plot-constructs of great sacred-story-tellers such as Hegel or Böhme. That is to say: he studies their narratives as the outcome of inner debate between the various voices, or spirits, which they are channelling, and which they seek to reconcile. He picks those voices, or spirits, apart from one another: comparing their various distinct contributions to the end-result. To this end, he deploys a rich, distinctive jargon – to read him is to hack one's way through dense scholarly undergrowth, with a great wealth of endnotes, but notably little direct quotation to ease one on one's way. His primary interpretative concern is with the patterning of the whole body of thought with which he is concerned, in its wholeness. Typically, in analysing such patterns he adopts the role of referee, adjudicating between rival 'ascriptions': different suggestions regarding the categorization of the work in question, each with their own particular 'advantages' or 'disadvantages', as they compete for taxonomic pre-eminence. So, in Böhme's case, there is his belonging to the tradition of 'Spiritual Reform' (Franck, Schwenkfeld, Weigel); his use of alchemical and astrological metaphors, largely derived from Paracelsus; his distinctive form of apocalyptic thought; his appropriation and transmutation of originally Neo-Platonist ideas; his echoing, perhaps, of Kabbalah. And above all, O'Regan concludes: his (it seems spontaneous) Neo-Valentinianism.[54]

O'Regan's conception of 'gnostic return in modernity' is immeasurably more substantial and coherent than Voegelin's. It also represents a clear advance over Baur's conception. However, when it comes to his *evaluation* of Böhme (and of Hegel) I must confess to having some misgivings. For, alas, he is all too faithful a disciple of the great Hans Urs von Balthasar! Which means that, for him, the dominant ideal will, after all, always be scholarly faithfulness to orthodox Roman Catholic tradition, as grounded in Scripture, *pure and simple*. His project is accordingly a prophylactic one. He is alerting us to the pathology of what he calls 'metalepsis' in the systems of thought that he studies: that is, the 'swerving' of these thinkers from the scriptural straight and narrow, their 'vicious torquing of central aspects of Christianity'.[55]

But what if even the New Testament itself is already infected by the growing disease of evangelistic impatience? As, indeed, at least to a certain extent, some parts of it surely are. (The most spectacular example, to my mind, being the fanaticism that pervades the whole *Book of Revelation* …) I have looked hard, but nowhere in O'Regan's copious discussion do I find any adequate acknowledgement of *why* the thinkers he considers, and others like them, are drawn to 'gnostic' heterodoxy.

I mean: a proper recognition of *what they may, perhaps after all quite justifiably, have been reacting against, in the mainstream Church*. It seems to me that in this regard he somewhat fails to see the wood for the trees.

O'Regan is an altogether more temperate thinker than either Voegelin or Magee; and he devotes far more attention to Böhme than they do. But for him, as well, Hegel's admiration for Böhme is very much a black mark against him. What is it, though, that really comes to light in this admiration? Let us go back to Hegel's analysis, in the *Phenomenology of Spirit*, of '*das unglückliche Bewußtsein*'.[56] Drawing on his own formulations and extending them a little further, one might in summary say that *das unglückliche Bewußtsein* is the culturally universal phenomenon of self-imposed unfreedom; mental servitude; wilful perverse submission to the mindlessness of herd / gang / mob – reinforced by the ideological self-projection of the inner despot sub-self onto notions of the sacred; which, in the context of Abrahamic religion is then disastrously entangled with evangelistic impatience.

Böhme's telling of the mythopoetic tale of Lucifer – the Luciferian delusion of misconceived divine almightiness – is, I would argue, a specifically Christian *picture* of what Hegel is thinking about in purely *conceptual* terms, trans-confessionally.

For Hegel, *das unglückliche Bewußtsein* is the primordial crystallization of the most basic moral blockage to *Geist*, Spirit, in the context of each individual human life. That is, blockage to the imperatives of truth-as-openness; which he then goes on to track in all their multi-layered historic unfolding. Böhme, on the other hand, develops a symbolic primal myth: the Usurper, Lucifer versus true God, in Christ – the emergence of that conflict and its telos. Yet, this myth represents the self-same elementary species of ideological struggle, considered in macrocosmic terms, the origins of which Hegel's account of *das unglückliche Bewußtsein* presents, in pluralistic microcosm, as arising from the inner turmoil of historically embodied single minds.

Macrocosm and microcosm: the framing of these two intellectual enterprises could scarcely be more different. But the underlying critical energies at work in each case are, surely, in essence complementary. As Hegel, himself, clearly sees.

§

As regards its aesthetic flavour, mystical theology, with its origins in the Neo-Platonist philosophy of Plotinus and his successors, is infused with a serenity – pure shaken-ness-as-wonder – which gnostic thought, far rather a form of shaken-ness-as-grief, repudiates. As Plotinus envisages it, the ultimate, ineffable plenitude of 'the one' is a process of untroubled overflow. 'Intellectuality' (*nous*), the highest domain of actually articulated truth, is an impersonal object of tranquil contemplation to participants in 'universal soul' (*psukhé*). The *quieter* the human mind, the greater its capacity for truth: for Plotinus, that correlation is absolute. Of course, Christian Neo-Platonism modifies the Plotinian doctrine, inasmuch as it has to allow for a personal relationship between God and believer. But, still, it does its utmost to soften the original element of turbulence intrinsic to the Hebrew prophetic notion of God. Not so, gnostic theogony / cosmogony. On the contrary, gnostic narrative is a baroque churn of embattled principles, layer upon layer of struggle; truly, very far from serene.

Both mystical theology and gnosticism are essentially megalothymotic challenges to evangelistic impatience. But there is a disarming, self-deprecating mildness to the mystical theologian's rebuke to the impatient evangelist: 'Look, you don't really *know* God, the way you think you do. But then neither do I. The fact is, we none of us mere mortals do.' This is very different from the brash, insurgent self-confidence of the gnostic, declaring to the impatient evangelist: 'You may rest assured, I *know* the necessity of honesty and open-mindedness in faith. And I won't be bullied out of my conviction, by your distorted dogmatism!' Far more directly than any form of mystical theology, gnosticism is by its very nature a mutation of the primordial *Amos* impulse; a dissident mythopoetic cry for 'justice and righteousness', as opposed to mere sacralized herd / gang / mob (a)morality. Thus, the gnostic imagination, at its truest, is fiercely embattled against all forms of fanaticism: the fanaticism of a martyr-church in the second century; the fanaticism, primarily, of persecutory Christendom, for Kabbalah; the Luciferian fanaticism manifest in inter-Christian Wars of Religion, for Böhme.

Plotinus, for his part, wrote a polemic (the ninth tractate of the Second *Ennead*) against what seems to have been a school of Sethian gnosticism. It appears that this school was active in Rome, where he also taught, and that he was moved to write because some of his own pupils, or potential pupils, were being drawn away, towards it (II. 9: 10). He mis-perceives gnosticism, in essence, as a form of Platonist philosophy gone wrong (II. 9: 6). These gnostics offend him with what he sees as their arrogance (II. 9: 5, 9); the bitterness of their complaints against the injustice of the social order (II. 9: 9); their lack of cultivated serenity in general (passim). They are, it seems to him, lamentably blind to the true *beauty* of reality as a whole, even as reflected in the material world (II. 9: 17). Unsurprisingly, he shows no sympathy for that element in gnostic thinking which derives from the essential *sublimity* of the Hebrew prophetic tradition: the gnostic transformation of that sublimity into theogony / cosmogony. For Plotinus, true Platonist philosophy is irreconcilable with 'gnostic' speculation. And if the highest truth to which both of these species of thought aspire were a form of *truth-as-correctness*, then yes, one would have to agree. It would indeed be either-or.

But, since the primary truth of true faith is *not* a form of truth-as-correctness – since it is, in fact, a form of truth-as-*openness* – the matter is much less clear-cut. Whereas perfect truth-as-correctness is allergic to contradictions, truth-as-openness on the contrary potentially thrives on them. After all, it requires input from a multitude of different voices, with different styles of expression, representing different intellectual cultures and different existential perspectives; the more the merrier. It holds together purely and simply as a quality of will. All it excludes is ill-will: a will to mere thoughtlessness, or a malicious will. Mystical theology and gnosticism may well be regarded as complementary enterprises, for they are two therapeutic projects, each addressing different aspects of one and the same basic soul-sickness. Their apparent contradictions to one another are, in principle surely, just what enable us to see the basic problem, at issue for the two of them alike, in the round.

In tracing both mystical theology and gnosticism back to a fundamental recoil from evangelistic impatience, I am placing them, together, within a grand-narrative account of what I consider to be the prime source of theological resistance to authentic truth-as-openness. Admittedly, however, neither species of thought is *in itself* especially notable for grand-narrative creativity! At most, mystical theology borrows elements of biblical and qur'anic grand narrative in order to allegorize them. Its real originality, however, derives from the impact of essentially a-historic Neo-Platonism, entering the bloodstream of Abrahamic religion. And neither do the purely mythic narratives of gnostic thought really count, either. Here, the historic witness as such of scripture is, on the contrary, very much in the process of evaporating.

This general lack of historic self-awareness is certainly I think, in both cases alike, a major deficiency. But grand narrative is by nature a rich sort of stew, within which all sorts of intellectual and spiritual tradition may be stirred together as ingredients; some of them earlier essays in the genre; others, though, quite different in original form. It is the art of grand narrative to find out what flavours – perhaps at first somewhat surprisingly, as here – go together. The apparent conflict between mystical theology and gnosticism dissolves in the grand narrative stew.

Again: in the context of Christianity, my grand-narrative contention is that mystical theology and gnosticism are the two most truly radical cultures emergent within the larger domain of Third-Person theology; where the word 'domain' means an enduring species of problem-cluster, determining a context of prayerful encounter with God. [57] Of course, the three Trinitarian domains to a very large extent overlap, as regards topics requiring to be addressed, and influences to be absorbed. But each has its own distinctive centre of gravity. 'Third-Person theology' – the domain, in the first instance, of church-historically informed projects aiming at institutional reform – at one level, yes, addresses the corruption deriving from simple lukewarm-ness and insincerity. But let me repeat my objection, that this is a relatively superficial form of self-critique.[58] Deeper down, it is surely called to be a reckoning not just with insincerity, for all sorts of dishonesty may be perfectly sincere – but rather with dishonesty in the sense of sheer closed-mindedness; the effect above all, in this context, of evangelistic impatience. 'Third-Person theology' differs from 'Second-Person theology' in that it develops beyond the systematic Bible-centred-ness of the latter. Less tied to the needs of regular preaching, it is in principle more fully enabled to step back from the immediate demands of maximum evangelistic effectiveness, which remain primary for 'Second-Person theology'.[59] This is by no means to suggest that 'Third-Person theology' in any way supersedes 'Second-Person theology'; only, that its deepest calling is to serve as a corrective to distortions all too readily originating in the other domain. 'Second-Person theology' channels the basic self-assertion of Christian faith as a distinctive phenomenon. 'Third-Person theology' is an opening to critical voices intent on modifying that initial impulse in the light of its actual out-working in church-practice.

By contrast to 'First-Person theology', on the other hand, 'Third-Person theology' remains *essentially* a domain of intra-ecclesiastical debate. Some of its incidental inspiration may be pre-Christian – the prime example being the influence of Plotinus and his successors on mystical theology. But even here, this is not mediated in the form of explicit debate with pagans in question. 'First-Person theology' differs, inasmuch as its *whole* concern is with working through the dialogic relationship of gospel truth to non-Christian religious cultures; and to post-Enlightenment secular philosophy, as well.

What is required, in order to open up theology to the full, trans-confessional challenge of the solidarity of the shaken? In mystical theology and gnosticism we have two very different 'Third-Person theological' therapeutic contributions to that altogether desirable prospect. But ultimately, it can only be consummated by way of a further 'First-Person theological' appropriation of certain crucial, later developments in the emergent philosophic discipline of *ethical phenomenology*.

And so it is to these later developments that I now turn.

Part III

PHILOSOPHY AND CATHOLICITY:
ETHICAL PHENOMENOLOGY

Chapter 6

PHILOSOPHIC MEDITATION ON THE 'PATHOS OF SHAKEN-NESS'

I have distinguished three great species of religion originating in the Axial Age. They differ in terms of their relationship to politics in the narrow sense of matters pertaining to secular governance: (a) intra-political religion; (b) pre-political religion and (c) anti-political religion.[1] But, as I would see it, all three, *at their best*, have one thing fundamentally in common. They are each, in their various different ways, stratagems for the sacralization of perfect truth-as-openness. And each is therefore, ideally, engaged in constant struggle against the temptations, instead, wrapped up in diversionary, and divisive, sacralized claims to ultimate historiographical, metaphysical and moral truth-as-correctness.

The sacralization of perfect truth-as-openness involves two moments, negation and negation of negation. First: negation of all established social norms, insofar as they are associated with mere closed-mindedness, the inertia of unquestioned prejudice. This is what (following Patočka) I mean by 'shaken-ness'. And second: negation of that negation, insofar as, in itself, it might appear altogether to invalidate every kind of real, 'catholic' community life. Scylla and Charybdis: evangelistic impatience inhibits the first negation; philosophic impatience inhibits the second. We need to steer between the two. And here the argument of this book shifts from a primary emphasis on the necessity for evangelistic patience to a primary emphasis on the necessity for philosophic patience. True religion, in all its many possible metaphysical and moral variations, must surely still remain a vivid communitarian affair; only, suffused with the solidarity of the shaken.

There is indeed a clear tension intrinsic to any at all aggressive project of religious solidarity-building, just because of the sheer difficulty of combining the solidarity of the shaken with immediate evangelistic success. Hence, the primordial problem already identified in Chapter 2: the problem opened up by the earthquake in the book of *Amos*. After all, perfect truth-as-openness will always be too demanding to be popular. And, since Abrahamic monotheism has tended to be so ferocious in its evangelistic ambition, the resultant difficulty has, historically, been at its most intense within that anti-political religious context. Which is also, on the other hand, why the Abrahamic family of traditions has, in mystical theology and gnosticism, generated the most urgent modes of moderating, self-critical response.

My argument as a whole, however, is developing towards an ever-fuller appreciation of the essentially *trans-confessional* solidarity of the shaken, as a sacred ideal. The kingdom of God = the solidarity of the shaken. And vice versa.

In Part Two we have been dealing with the high-intensity *pathos of pure shaken-ness*, not yet as a basis in itself for solidarity, but in confessional religious form. And, now, the next step is – by no means to reject the particularism of that confessional form – but nevertheless to transcend any merely hampering dependence upon it. As the prime initial solvents of evangelistic impatience *within* Abrahamic religion, mystical theology and gnosticism may well be seen as, at any rate, starting to clear a potential space in which the solidarity of the shaken may come to flourish, as a sacred ideal. Yet, the fully explicit sealing of trans-confessional alliances to this end, that is, solidarity of the shaken *purely and simply as such*, not just solidarity among shaken people of Abrahamic faith, requires more. It requires the matrix of a secular intellectual culture. In essence a secular phenomenon, although implicitly infusing religious traditions at their best, the solidarity of the shaken further requires to be thought through in secularized philosophic terms; a possibility that only, in actual fact, begins, step by step, to emerge in the post-Enlightenment era.

Accordingly, in this chapter I want to consider three closely inter-related post-Enlightenment pioneers – ethical phenomenologists – whose prime originality, one might say, consists precisely in their contrasting approaches to high-intensity pathos of pure shaken-ness considered in philosophic terms. Namely: *Søren Kierkegaard* (1813–55), *Emmanuel Levinas* (1906–95) and *Knud Løgstrup* (1905–81).[2]

Kierkegaard

Where I prefer to speak of the sacralization of 'truth-as-*openness*', Kierkegaard, for his part, focuses on the truth intrinsic to the most intense '*subjectivity*', radical '*inwardness*'.

Here we have two essential aspects of authentic thoughtfulness. Yet, observe how the difference between them plays out. Both Levinas and Løgstrup are, in their different ways, critical of Kierkegaard's thought in this fundamental aspect.

Openness or subjectivity / inwardness: which should ultimately be ranked higher?

The crucial Janus-faced slogan '*truth is subjectivity / subjectivity is truth*' is to be found at the heart of the *Concluding Unscientific Postscript*, which Kierkegaard brought out in 1846 under the pseudonym 'Johannes Climacus'.[3] His decision to half-conceal his authorship with this, and other, pseudonyms is already, in itself, a gesture of commitment to radical inwardness: a shrinking back from full public exposure. He is a megalothymotically individualistic religious writer, who however does not want to boast of his faith. And when, at the end of his life, he dropped the pseudonyms, the upshot was a furore. Then his aggressive, Amos-like contempt for what he considered to be the prevailing superficiality of the Danish Lutheran Church, of which he was a member, burst forth in a witty – but, at the same time, frantically embittered – pamphlet-campaign. In retrospect, the playfulness of his earlier pseudonymous writings appears to have been a device for staving off this eventual, rather shocking denouement.

'Johannes Climacus' first appears as the hero of the unfinished and only posthumously published narrative entitled *Johannes Climacus, or De Omnibus Dubitandum Est* (1842–3): the tale of a young man who sets out to be a truly serious sceptic, that is, one who doubts all claims to authoritative moral or metaphysical truth-as-correctness, without exception. Then, he is named as the author of *Philosophical Fragments* (1844): a text contrasting the rationale of Socratic 'recollection', as one mode of teaching, with that of Christian revelation, as another.[4] Both methods, he argues here, in principle drive the individual learner inwards. But Christian revelation, where it is authentically appropriated, does so with far greater intensity of passion. To the ordinary human herd animal, content with his or her superficiality, such intensity of shaken passion for truth must appear quite absurd; a monstrous offence against common sense; indeed, an incomprehensibly paradoxical option for anyone ever to have chosen. However, for Climacus – recoiling now from his previous radical scepticism – everything depends upon grasping the character of authentic Christian faith as an appropriation of what he calls the 'Absolute Paradox'.

Philosophical Fragments is a short book; with an abstract core argument quite tersely presented. Its companion piece, the *Concluding Unscientific Postscript* is by contrast a verbose, rambling work, of much greater length. In it, Climacus portrays himself as a perpetual student, a flaneur; indolent; facetious; a devotee of ironical detachment. One day, he tells us, he was seated at an out-of-doors café in the Frederiksberg Gardens, Copenhagen, smoking a cigar, when he began to think:

> "You are going on," I said to myself, "to become an old man, without being anything, and without really undertaking to do anything. On the other hand, wherever you look about you, in literature and in life, you see the celebrated names and figures, the precious and much heralded men who are coming into prominence and are much talked about, the many benefactors of the age who know how to benefit mankind by making life easier and easier, some by railways, others by omnibuses and short recitals of everything worth knowing, and finally the true benefactors of the age who make spiritual existence in virtue of thought easier and easier, yet more and more significant. And what are you doing?" Here my soliloquy was interrupted, for my cigar was smoked out and a new one had to be lit. So I smoked again, and then suddenly this thought flashed through my mind: "You must do something, but inasmuch as with your limited capacities it will be impossible to make anything easier than it has become, you must, with the same humanitarian enthusiasm as the others, undertake to make something harder."[5]

For, after all, do not people also enjoy an occasional challenge? And so, he conceives it as his fundamental task, as a writer, 'to create difficulties everywhere': as far as possible, bringing out the difficulties in *everything*.

Compare the vocation of the mystical theologian. In sharp contradiction to impatient evangelism, which always wants to make faith easier, the mystical theologian is another whose whole work is a matter of making things, existentially, more difficult. And yet, Climacus is no mystical theologian. None of Kierkegaard's various *alter egos* are. Kierkegaard is far rather (as I have said) a prophet, in the guise of a philosopher; here, *qua* Climacus, in the further guise of a comedian. Prophets are at one with mystical theologians in radicality of shaken-ness; but the essential difference between the two categories has to do with the *polemical tone* in which that shaken-ness is then expressed. It is the difference between contemplative thinkers, wary of aggression, and dissident activists, whose aggression is allowed to spill out. Mystical theologians are always anxious not inadvertently to threaten the catholic unity of the liturgical community they belong to; the art of mystical theology is thus a constant negotiation between the shaken-ness of the individual and the solidarity bonding their community together. (And neither were the pagan Neo-Platonists, before them, by any means public trouble-makers.) One does not, therefore, find mystical theologians, as such, *mocking* their intellectual opponents. Nor, however much they may be at odds with the prevailing thoughtlessness of the human herd around them, do they vent their resultant frustration in rhetoric of open *scorn*. Kierkegaard however, intent – above all in the persona of Johannes Climacus – on attacking Hegelian philosophy, constructs a grotesque caricature, which he then assails with relentless mockery. And, intent on attacking the complacencies of what he calls 'Christendom' (that is, herd-Christianity) scornfully taunts his neighbours, without any apparent concern, at all, for the catholic unity of the Church.

The comedic persona of Johannes Climacus may give him some recognizable licence to do so: the licence of a jester. But when Kierkegaard finally drops all pseudonyms, in the pamphlets of his final whirlwind 'Attack upon Christendom', his prophetic scorn, as spokesman for the unappreciated claims of inwardness, or true subjectivity, is unbounded.

§

'Truth is subjectivity / subjectivity is truth.' In what sense is this so? Climacus expounds his slogan, perhaps a little clumsily, as follows.

> *When the question of truth is raised in an objective manner, reflection is directed objectively to the truth, as an object to which the knower is related. Reflection is not focussed upon the relationship, however, but upon the question of whether it is the truth to which the knower is related. If only the object to which he is related is the truth, the subject is accounted to be in the truth. [But] when the question of the truth is raised subjectively, reflection is directed subjectively to the nature of the individual's relationship; if only the mode of this relationship is in the truth, the individual is in the truth even if he should happen to be related to what is not true.*[6]

To which, in a footnote, he adds: 'The reader will observe that the question here is about essential truth, or about the truth which is essentially related to existence.'

Or, in other words, it is the truth of that which, in principle, matters most. Above all, Climacus is concerned to analyse the claim of Christian faith to elucidate that which matters most: namely, the rationale governing its notion of an 'eternal happiness'.

In this regard, as he also puts it,

> *The objective accent falls on WHAT is said, the subjective accent falls on HOW it is said.*[7]

The true promise of Christian faith, he wants to argue, does not so much depend upon the objective correctness of WHAT is affirmed – with regard to exegesis of scripture, formulation of orthodox dogma, logical cogency of apologetic argument or understanding of world-history – but, far rather, upon HOW that belief-content is subjectively appropriated. Theological truth is, as he puts it,

> *an objective uncertainty held fast in an appropriation-process of the most passionate inwardness.*[8]

Let the inescapable uncertainty of the objective element in faith (its claims to truth-as-correctness) be quite un-defensively acknowledged, Climacus urges. But, at the same time, let us also be quite clear about the relative insignificance of that element, compared with the real, existential challenge of the gospel, considered as a stimulus to inwardness.

§

Writing under two other pseudonyms, 'Vigilius Haufniensis' ('Watchman of Copenhagen') and 'Anti-Climacus', Kierkegaard further proceeds to develop a systematic phenomenological analysis of the pathos of shaken-ness. (My term, not his.) 'Vigilius Haufniensis' is the supposed author of *The Concept of Anxiety* (1844).[9] 'Anti-Climacus' – set over against Johannes Climacus inasmuch as he has a much less playful, more earnestly Christian persona – is credited with *The Sickness unto Death* (1849) and *Practice in Christianity* (1850).[10]

The arguments of Vigilius Haufniensis and of Anti-Climacus dovetail together. They track the potential development of herd-dissolving inwardness towards maximum intensity of encounter with the eternal; with Anti-Climacus, especially, focussing on the psychological resistances that this development runs up against.

Vigilius Haufniensis, for his part, begins develops a demythologizing psychological reading of *Genesis* 3, the story of Adam and Eve. Their original condition of innocence in the Garden of Eden is a form of animal existence, in which there is no real individuality. Without individuality, there can be no inwardness. But then they fall. By virtue of the fall, human life is infused with 'anxiety' – the initial growth-pangs of inwardness, confronting our resistance to its demands – which, from the mildest of beginnings, steadily escalates. In *The Concept of Anxiety* two aspects of that escalation are analysed. First, anxiety over matters of sexuality: the phenomena of sexual modesty; erotic love; and the suspension of the erotic in ascetic discipline. Second, anxiety channelled by religion: the spirit of fatalism; the dynamics of guilt; and the leap of faith. Fatalism is discussed as the supposed essence of 'paganism', although also as the mentality of a Napoleon, say. Guilt is considered with regard to the inspiration of the 'religious genius'; a category in which Kierkegaard privately included himself. Vigilius Haufniensis is likewise a 'religious genius', whilst the concept is further associated by him with a notably abstract and unrealistic notion of 'Judaism'. However, it is argued that only a Christian leap of faith – appropriating the gospel of divine forgiveness – can, in the end, deliver us from the limitations of mere anxiety.

Then, following on from this, Anti-Climacus in *The Sickness unto Death* analyses 'despair': anxiety's last stand against true faith. By contrast to Vigilius Haufniensis, who is concerned with the challenge of the eternal as mediated by various different cultural environments, Anti-Climacus's concern is with the challenge of the eternal as *a presence indwelling the self*.

There is some overlap here. Vigilius Haufniensis already distinguishes between 'anxiety over the evil', rendering one unable to acknowledge one's guilt before God, and 'anxiety over the good', leading to a 'demonic' rejection of God's love. Anti-Climacus, however, recasts this distinction in terms of two ways in which one may resist God-within:

> Sin is: *before God, or with the conception of God, in despair not wanting to be oneself, or wanting in despair to be oneself.*[11]

'In despair not wanting to oneself' is the despair of weakness. It means more or less lapsing back into mere conformity to the herd or the gang. 'Wanting in despair to be oneself' is the despair of strength: defiantly cultivating a nonconformist persona, but in quite unethical fashion. Either way, despair is a basic failure to recognize who one truly is, in the light of God's forgiving love; occluding the deep self, through which God might shine. And this failure, also, escalates. So, one despairs over one's sin; allows it to become fixed habit. One despairs of the forgiveness of sins, to the point of taking offence at the gospel. This attitude of offence grows fiercer. In the end, it tips over into explicit polemic: indignantly repudiating critical prophetic testimony of the sort represented, for example, by Anti-Climacus's other work, *Practice in Christianity*.

In short, the writings attributed to Vigilius Haufniensis and to Anti-Climacus may well be said to constitute a prophetic vindication of specifically Christian pathos of shaken-ness.

Yet, note on the other hand Kierkegaard's complete lack of interest in any form of freshly organized *solidarity*-building, any actual (anti-)political alliances. And hence: his fundamental closure (alas!) towards the solidarity of the shaken, after all.

Indeed, he sets up a road-block here, distinguishing as he does between two levels of Christian therapeutic response to the problematics of anxiety and despair; one of which is a form of Christian shaken-ness not yet, as he sees it, adequately set apart from other, non-Christian forms. Writing in the persona of Johannes Climacus he calls this phenomenon 'religiousness A' and contrasts it with what he sees as the more fully Christian form of shaken-ness that he calls 'religiousness B'.[12] 'Religiousness A' is already an authentic form of religion, decisively emancipated from herd or gang morality. It serves to liberate the individual and cultivate a spirit of real inwardness. Climacus regards it as a necessary first stage, on the journey towards the higher level of 'religiousness B'.[13] Only, the difference is that, unlike 'religiousness B', it may also exist in 'paganism'.[14]

Climacus does not say *which* 'pagans', if any, he has in mind. Rather, he says: 'even if it [viz. "religiousness A"] has not been exemplified in paganism, it could have been, because it has only human nature in general as its assumption', whereas 'religiousness B' presupposes the specific provocation intrinsic to Christian revelation.[15] As for Christian examples, 'religiousness A' would seem to relate, in Climacus's mind, primarily to the Middle Ages: the mediaeval ethos of monasticism, and pre-Reformation penitential practice.[16] No doubt Climacus would judge mystical theology to be a form of Christianity still largely confined to 'religiousness A'. And then in the non-Christian world generally, although he speaks of 'paganism', would not Sufism and Hasidism provide examples? Pagan Neo-Platonism surely would. In fact, all the more shaken modes of pre-political religion, or intra-political religion, must in principle be included under this heading.

For Kierkegaard, 'religiousness A' has at least something of the 'existential pathos' proper to the highest truth. What however he sees it as lacking, which only 'religiousness B' can provide, is the ideal, 'paradoxically dialectic' theological expression for that pathos.[17] *And here I would suggest that, after all, he fails fully to follow through on his own basic principle that 'truth is subjectivity'!* For he is still, it seems to me, according altogether too much to the objective specificity of Christian faith; and not enough to Christ's ability also to work anonymously, through other objective channels, quite regardless of their objective otherness.

Granted, Christianity has unique imaginative resources for expressing 'existential pathos', that is, the pathos of shaken-ness. But then so do other religious traditions; each has at least some potential to attempt the same, in its own unique fashion. Intent on affirming the truth that is 'subjectivity', Kierkegaard chips away at traditional Christian idolatry of supposedly 'objective' truth-as-correctness. He theoretically excises all that he deems inimical to 'subjectivity' understood as synonymous with 'inwardness'. But since his concern is with 'inwardness' rather than 'openness', he nevertheless remains caught within the traditional competitive *closure* of Christian theology towards other religions; even though this closure is, in itself, also part of the same idolatry. For religions are only rivals, after all, in the domain of 'objectivity'. It is only in their claims to 'objective' historiographical, metaphysical and moral truth-as-correctness that they are necessarily doomed to clash. Considered, on the contrary, as so many openings towards the sacred ideal of perfect truth-as-openness, they are allies. Notwithstanding his general attack on objectifying notions of ultimate truth, Kierkegaard does not yet see this.

True 'inwardness', for him, remains exclusively an ideal appropriation of the Christian gospel. And so, he cannot think the trans-confessional solidarity of the shaken.

In the *Concluding Unscientific Postscript* 'religiousness A' is essentially differentiated from 'religiousness B' as being a lesser religious affirmation of inwardness. But now let us follow Merold Westphal, who with reference to this passage proposes a supplementary notion of '*religiousness C*'.[18] Westphal defines the movement from 'B' to 'C' in terms of the difference between Christ purely and simply approached as 'the Paradox to be believed' and Christ, at the same time, as 'the Paradigm or Pattern or Prototype to be imitated'; Christ the Paradox being the incarnate imperative of perfect inwardness; and Christ the Paradigm being the ideal inspiration of organized solidarity.[19] Up to a point, I mean the same. But I would go further. I would propose using the term 'religiousness C' to designate, precisely, religion grounded in explicit dedication to the trans-confessional solidarity of the shaken: so transcending Johannes Climacus's schema of 'religiousness A' / 'religiousness B', inasmuch as it refutes Climacus's dogmatic, and surely unwarranted, assumption that maximum intensity of true inwardness must necessarily correlate to strict confessional exclusivism.

'Religiousness A', in Kierkegaard's scheme, achieves a significant degree of inwardness; yet cannot adequately express it. In 'religiousness B' intense inwardness begins to attain what Kierkegaard regards as ideal Christian expression. But this still remains a close ring-fenced form of exclusively Christian faith. The truth of what I am calling 'religiousness C', by contrast, supplements intense inwardness with a highly articulate overcoming of inter-religious rivalry.

Both Levinas and Løgstrup are, in effect, celebrants of 'religiousness C', so defined.

§

I have described Kierkegaard as an 'Amos-like' prophetic thinker. This resemblance is clearest of all in the satirical pamphlets of his late 'Attack upon Christendom'. Thus, I repeat, before Amos (so far as we can see) all gods resembled one another, inasmuch as what they were known to love most of all was liturgical praise from their devotees. In this regard, Yahweh the god of Israel had been just the same as the others, the gods of the neighbouring peoples. Shockingly, however, in *Amos* 5: 21–4 *Yahweh says no*. After all, he declares that he loathes the festivals with which his own people seek to flatter him – that he rejects their sacrifices and their hymns – that nothing of the kind will ever please him, until they learn to practice, far more seriously than hitherto, 'justice and righteousness'! How then to please a divinity with such a perversely ambivalent attitude to being worshipped? This is the root-problem that comes to haunt the Hebrew people, and to set them spiritually apart from their neighbours. The book of *Amos* represents the historic moment when one of the gods begins to be true God.

Approximately 2,615 years after the prophet's original dramatic appearance on the public scene something similar occurs. Like Amos, Kierkegaard urges his people to boycott the official liturgy of their God – until the leaders of the Danish Lutheran Church publicly confess that Church's betrayal of the essential truth with which it has been entrusted. Amos, in pursuit of his calling, had (we are told) gone to the national shrine at Bethel, to remonstrate with the high priest there, Amaziah; and the bitter words of their confrontation echo down the ages in *Amos* 7.10-17. The trigger for Kierkegaard's final campaign was the death of Bishop Mynster, the head of the Danish Church. Previously he had been restrained by his respect for Mynster; a man whom his father in particular had revered. But Mynster represented, with singular gravitas, just that ethos of religiously adorned mere bourgeois respectability that Kierkegaard called 'Christendom', and that he abhorred. (Hence, Mynster had for instance been very dismissive of the book *Training in Christianity*.) Professor Martensen, who was to be Mynster's successor, gave the funeral address, praising the dead man as 'a genuine witness to the truth'. Kierkegaard, who himself liked to use the same phrase, but always with reference to the suffering of those whose faith led to their being persecuted, was enraged above all by this sermon of Martensen's.

Now, though, consider the basic difference between Kierkegaard and Amos.

Again, this has to do with the contrast between the two forms of spiritedness, *megalothymia* and *isothymia*.[20] (Megalothymia: spirited insistence on being respected for who one uniquely is, one's particular calling, one's gifts. Isothymia: spirited insistence on the properly equal rights of all.) Amos is both a megalothymotic figure – demanding to be respected as one who had been directly commissioned by Yahweh, even though without formal status – and also an isothymotic one, hammering home the duty of the rich and powerful to respect their fellow citizens in general. However, Kierkegaard's stand differs in that the *fury* informing it is exclusively megalothymotic.

Thus, the truth-potential of megalothymia consists in spirited resistance to the thoughtlessness of the human herd. The high value that Kierkegaard accords to the inwardness that generates authentic individuality is a prime philosophic expression of megalothymia. Take his discussion of the biblical injunction to love one's neighbour, in *Works of Love* (1847).[21] He interprets this as an ideal of the most radical self-renunciation. But the 'self' to be renounced here is none other than who one is as a banal herd-animal. Not all megalothymia, after all, is an affair of naïve egoism. Kierkegaard's is, far rather, an aspiration to be transparent to God; as in the Sufi notion of *fana' wa baqa'*, 'annihilation [of the banal ego] and abiding [of God indwelling the deep self thereby uncovered]'.

The truth-potential of isothymia, however, consists in spirited resistance, not so much to the thoughtlessness of the herd, as to the manipulativeness of gangs, and to the violence of mobs; the gang and the mob being the two chief modes of enforcement, serving to reinforce the illegitimate subordination of one social group to another. Kierkegaard, as a rich man's son, was never compelled by his own life-experience to confront the problematics of social inequality. And, in fact, he shows little or no interest in the matter. Of course, he acknowledges the egalitarian nature of neighbour-love, inasmuch as this is inescapable.[22] But the acknowledgement nevertheless remains quite abstract; it does not seem to lead anywhere, beyond the immediately obvious. There is no real opening towards 'political' or 'liberation theology' in Kierkegaard's work.

Truth-as-openness, however, surely does in principle demand both megalothymotic inwardness and isothymotic compassion, working together. 'Religiousness C' – as the sacralization of such truth in its well-balanced wholeness – is a more comprehensive ideal than either 'religiousness A' or 'religiousness B', as conceived by Kierkegaard / Climacus. It by no means signifies a rejection of Kierkegaardian inwardness. Only, it subsumes inwardness into the phenomenologically *prior* category of openness; not least, *also* including openness towards the affliction of the afflicted poor as such.

Levinas

In sharp contrast to Kierkegaard, both Levinas and Løgstrup may be seen as pioneering philosophic celebrants of a purely trans-confessional, trans-cultural ideal of truth-as-openness.

Or, to put it in Levinas's terminology, they are concerned to draw a strict distinction between truth in *'the saying'* and truth in *'the said'*; with the former given decisive moral priority. Always, beneath and beyond the culturally framed claims of 'the said': 'the saying'. That is, the primordial possibility of being opened up to the other person, with all consideration of confessional or class identity completely dissolved.

§

Westphal has persuasively argued the case for acknowledging a basic affinity between Kierkegaard and Levinas.[23] Their historical contexts are of course very different. And, two great philosophical stylists as they are, each one writes in an altogether different style from the other. Whereas Kierkegaard wraps the explosive charge of his fury in rhetoric of humorous mockery, there is by contrast nothing humorous about Levinas's writing. It is haunted by the trauma of the Shoah; from which Levinas himself had only escaped with his life by virtue of being captured as a French soldier, and held as a prisoner of war. However, they are at one in their being militant phenomenologist-celebrants of the pathos of shaken-ness, for whom the *prime* task of philosophy has become the mounting of a hyperbolic rhetorical assault on the ideologies of clever complacency.

Again: Kierkegaard, in the persona of Johannes Climacus, opposes his philosophic method to that of Socrates. These are indeed two alternative strategies for combating the moral complacency of the unthinking herd. But, unlike Socrates who approaches that task indirectly – by highlighting the collusion of moral complacency with muddled thinking, and seeking to remedy muddles as such – Kierkegaard / Climacus by contrast approaches it altogether more directly by confronting complacency with the shock of the ideal Christian demand for inwardness, presented with maximum brutality. And Levinas, albeit in more secular fashion, is likewise absolutely direct, and brutal. Other forms of philosophy, following the Socratic model, represent themselves as disciplines of Reason. Levinas, like Kierkegaard / Climacus, presents his thinking, in this sense, as a move 'beyond Reason'.[24] Philosophical Reason may well be persuasively justified to unphilosophical common sense as a form of systematic pedagogy and problem-solving expertise. Kierkegaardian or Levinasian thinking 'beyond Reason', however, cannot. From the point of view of common sense, it *must* appear quite absurd; perverse; even crazy. Nor can it ever make much headway in an environment governed by the un-common sense of great empire-building academics. As Kierkegaard mocks that great would-be academic empire-builder Hegel, so Levinas distances himself from those other great would-be academic empire-builders Husserl and Heidegger: for he and Kierkegaard entirely agree that you cannot hope to build an academic empire without compromising the actual 'madness' of true wisdom.

Where Kierkegaard affirms the proper absurdity of the Christian 'leap of faith', Levinas for his part affirms the madness of what he calls the ethical 'epiphany of the face'. In his parlance, 'the face' of the Other is synecdoche for the most primordial ethical challenge: prior to all external justification, and just for that reason without limit, utterly exorbitant. This is not ethics justified in terms of an enlightened pursuit of happiness; or freedom; or logical consistency, in observing the Categorical Imperative; or, politically, with reference to the social contract. Nor is there any appeal made to a sacred communal tradition. Rather, a thought-world is evoked in which the very possibility of egoism is excluded: individualistic egoism and corporate egoism, both alike. At this stratum of ethics there is nothing to charm the ego, no element of beauty allowed to suffuse the ideal. The ethical imperative here is, purely and simply, sublime: appalling, yet compelling, in its 'madness'. Thus, Levinas converts the raw *Amos* impulse into philosophic rhetoric. His work is, in effect, a phenomenology of that stimulus. But, as his phenomenological method involves bracketing every historical reference, his actual name for it is simply 'the face of the Other'.

Relics of historical context intrude into this phenomenological enterprise only faintly, or marginally. And yet, the context is surely crucial. Levinas's two great works are *Totality and Infinity* (1961) and *Otherwise than Being or beyond Essence* (1974).[25] The title of the former hints at its context in the aftermath, especially, of Nazi totalitarianism. And the latter bears an epigraph:

> To the memory of those who were closest among the six million assassinated by the National Socialists, and of the millions on millions of all confessions and all nations, victims of the same hatred of the other man, the same anti-semitism.

By 'the epiphany of the face' Levinas means the prick of conscience that might for instance inspire a gentile in Nazi-occupied Europe to shelter Jews, on the run; or anyone, in any sort of comparable circumstances, to do something similar. The most basic considerations of self-preservation militate against doing so. Nor is it only the state authorities who are intent on deterring such acts of rescue; few, if any, among the rescuer's neighbours can be trusted with the secret. Informers are everywhere. Say, moreover, that the rescuer scarcely knows the rescued, so they are not bound together by any particular, pre-existing ties of friendship. Say, even, that they lack a common language. Say, in short, that everything possible counts against the rescuer taking this initiative. And yet – it happens! Levinas is intent on evoking *that* level of ethical driven-ness; immune even to the very worst that a persecutory totalitarian regime can do to inhibit it.

'The epiphany of the face' is a condition of being opened up to the needs of the other person, quite independent of any actual demands that the other person may make; regardless of what the other person may, or may not, feel entitled to, and of likely gratitude, or otherwise, in response. Here is pathos of ethical shaken-ness entirely prior to negotiation; free of calculation; without any possibility at all of diminution by compromise.

Ethical medicine, not least, against totalitarian terror, the intransigence of this epiphany is, in quite opposite fashion, terrifying.

§

Levinas does not discuss Kierkegaard at any great length, or with any at all detailed reference to any of Kierkegaard's writings. However, he does make some interesting general remarks about Kierkegaard. On the one hand, he celebrates the way that Kierkegaard sets himself against any actual or would-be moral consensus as such. On the other hand, he repudiates the manner of this confrontation.

As he himself puts it:

> There is, in Kierkegaard, an opposition not between faith and knowledge, in which the uncertain would be set in opposition to the certain, but between truth triumphant and truth persecuted. Persecuted truth is not simply a truth wrongly approached. Persecution and, by the same token, humility are modalities of the true. The grandeur of transcendent truth – its very transcendence – is linked to its humility.[26]

'Persecution and, by the same token, humility are modalities of the true': truth-in-persecution, as discovered by the prophet Amos, in his oracular warnings of divine wrath; truth-in-humility, as discovered by the author of *Deutero-Isaiah*, in his portrayal of the suffering servant (*Isaiah* 52.13–53.12). The intransigent summons of the highest truth, at its ultimate extreme, feels like 'persecution' to the unregenerate ego. This is not Kierkegaard's own terminology; but the 'persecution' in question includes every provocation to anxiety and despair as analysed by 'Vigilius Haufniensis' and 'Anti-Climacus'; as the ego wriggles to escape.[27] So Levinas salutes the sheer sublimity of Kierkegaard's rhetoric. However, proper surrender to this 'persecution' straight away entails a radical 'humility'; which, in turn, means honest acceptance that the truth in question can never become hegemonic in society at large; could never, without self-betrayal, become the teaching of a well-established institution. In this sense, he writes:

Here with Kierkegaard something is manifested, yet one may wonder whether there was any manifestation. Someone began to say something – but no! He said nothing. Truth is played out on a double register: at the same time the essential has been said, and, if you like, nothing has been said. This is the new situation – a permanent rending, an ending that is no ending. Revelation – then looking back on it, nothing.[28]

'Nothing' – that is to say – in terms of would-be hegemonic authority. Or, as Kierkegaard would put it: nothing 'objective'. For the governing principle in this domain is that 'truth is subjectivity'.

And yet, whilst Kierkegaard 'rehabilitated subjectivity – the unique, the singular – with incomparable strength', the problem, as Levinas sees it, is that 'he bequeathed to the history of philosophy an exhibitionistic, immodest subjectivity.'[29] Kierkegaard bears witness to 'humility'. But, alas, the way he expresses it, this is such an 'exhibitionistic, immodest' humility! 'It is Kierkegaard's violence that shocks me,' writes Levinas. He means, precisely, the scornful megalothymia of Kierkegaard's style.

The manner of the strong and the violent, who fear neither scandal nor destruction, has become, since Kierkegaard and before Nietzsche, a manner of philosophy. One philosophizes with a hammer.[30]

In particular, he objects to Kierkegaard's downgrading of 'ethics' in the name of 'faith'. Obviously, what Kierkegaard means by 'ethics' is not what Levinas means; in counterposing 'ethics' to 'faith' Kierkegaard is talking about herd or gang morality. But it is the brutal megalothymia of Kierkegaard's notion of 'faith' – as represented by the great figure of father Abraham, as he conscientiously sets out to sacrifice his beloved son Isaac – that Levinas finds troubling. Kierkegaard, in the persona of 'Johannes de Silentio', celebrates Abraham's shocking transgression of conventional herd-values, as a great symbol of faith-inspired inwardness.[31] For Levinas, however, the point of the story lies far rather in Abraham's final return to 'the ethical order'; as the sacrifice is averted.[32]

Unlike Kierkegaard, Levinas is indeed a profoundly isothymotic thinker, affirming the majesty – even, or especially, in abjection – of the Other: that is to say, of every Other alike, just by virtue of their equal otherness. Hence, he is faithful to that essential aspect of the *Amos* impulse; as Kierkegaard, even whilst repeating the prophet's rebellion against herd-piety, is not.

§

And then Levinas (as I have said) further differs from Kierkegaard not only by virtue of his allegiance to Rabbinic Judaism, rather than Christianity; but also, in what one might well say is his much more secular, or trans-confessional approach to philosophy. Thus, whereas Kierkegaard's whole concern is to evoke the pathos of shaken Christian faith as such, Levinas by contrast is first and foremost intent on evoking pathos of shaken-ness in itself – and only quite separately goes on, in addition, to illustrate the possibility of its incorporation into particular confessional cultures, by taking his own Jewish religious tradition as an example. So, at one level, he writes purely secular works of phenomenology, without any explicit reference to Jewishness; at another level, he writes essays in religious Zionism, plus readings of Talmudic texts. There is a strict division between these two categories of his writing – a division without equivalent in Kierkegaard's oeuvre.

But the division is problematic! Approaching it from the side of his trans-confessional ethics, one cannot help but feel a bit surprised by the general tenor of his political thought. His purely philosophic writings promise an *Amos*-like ferocity of critique directed just as much against the state of Israel as against the gentile world – which, however, does not materialize.[33] He criticizes Martin Buber (I think unfairly) for not being radical enough, in abstract theoretic terms, as a prophet-ethicist. Yet, in actual practice, Buber illustrates just what one might have expected from Levinas in this regard; just what is missing.[34]

Meanwhile, comparing his religious writings to his philosophical ones, note the fineness with which, by contrast to what we find in the former, the concept of God has in the latter been *sieved*. The Talmud readings and the essays on Judaism are clearly conceived in a basic spirit of loyalty to all the dead of the Shoah, all the martyred Jewish dead down the centuries – inasmuch as they honour the God of Jewish religious tradition as a whole. But when it comes to his phenomenological texts, he writes far rather as a translator of the primordial *Amos* impulse: an altogether more discriminating ambition, allowing much less of that tradition through.

His first philosophic name for divinity is 'the Infinite'. His second: the curious fresh coinage, '*illeity*'.[35] This derives from the Latin, '*ille*', 'he'; as in 'he the primordial law-giver', 'he the judge of judges'. And there is a particular thrust here against Buber. Thus, Buber's philosophical thought combines lyrical anti-utilitarianism with largely *un-sieved* faith in the God of the Bible; there is much less tension here than in Levinas's thought. Buber's anti-utilitarian argument takes shape as a radical opposition between two attitudes of thought, 'I – You' and 'I – It'; two possible attitudes of the 'I' to other individuals, or to human community at large, or to things, or to God; 'I – You' transcending utilitarianism, 'I – It' surrendered to utilitarianism.[36] So Buber speaks of true God as 'the eternal You'. This is quite unproblematically the God of the Bible, as a whole. Levinas's thought is, also, lyrically anti-utilitarian; to that extent, he is at one with Buber. But, unlike Buber, he combines anti-utilitarianism with sieved philosophic faith in the God of the pure *Amos* impulse alone. And, indeed, the sieving has eliminated even the residual 'I – You' back-and-forth of *Amos* 7.1-9; where the prophet pleads (ultimately in vain) for his people. There is no *conversation* possible with divine 'illeity', as distinct from the God of the Bible. All that remains is a flood of imperatives: one is forever being directed to the 'epiphany of the face', and hence to an all-absorbing urgent immediacy of 'obsessive' ethical concern for one's neighbour. One meditates upon those imperatives, reported as commands of God in the third person. And that is all that matters!

One may presumably pray as a token of one's loyal participation in the worshipping community. Only, one must do so always with the strictest of mental reservations, to exclude the banal intrusion of egoism. The whole purpose of Levinasian philosophy, in relation to religion, is to insist on these reservations; this strict grading of intention, when it comes to worship.

Abrahamic religion, in general, is an endlessly variable mix of the prophetic-sublime and the beautiful. Buber, for his part, revels in the mix. Levinas, however, is the more *interesting* religious thinker, above all by virtue of the profoundly problematic way in which, as a philosopher, he replicates the sublime puritanism of *Amos* 5.21-24, YHWH / *illeity*'s drastic repudiation of everything most beautiful in his people's worship of him. YHWH / *illeity* here rejects the liturgical practices prescribed in the *Torah* not because some other sort of beautiful liturgy would be better, but just because of the difference between beautiful liturgy, in itself, and surrender to the sheer sublime urgency of '*mishpat wa tsedaqah*', 'justice and righteousness'; or the 'epiphany of the face'. 'Take away from me the noise of your songs', YHWH / *illeity* says here; rejecting the beauty of the book of *Psalms*. The psalmist's beautiful intimacy with 'the eternal You' is rejected; along with the psalmist's celebratory mirroring, in liturgical beauty, of natural, divinely created beauty at large. In this gesture everything that the psalmist represents – everything that Levinas himself implicitly accepts in his non-philosophical writing – is called into question.

'*Illeity*', in short, is the sacred sublime at its very purest, radically transcending the God-concept of popular religion. In *Otherwise than Being* Levinas defines this transcendence as

> the detachment of the Infinite from the thought that seeks to thematise it and the language that tries to hold it in the said.[37]

As noted above, a fundamental 'theme' of *Otherwise than Being* as a whole is the subordination of the truth-potential of 'the said' to that of 'the saying'. This is Levinas's formula for the difference between truth-as-correctness, abstractly containable within propositions, whether of observation, science, or belief – and truth-as-openness, contained in character, and therefore altogether dependent on who is speaking and in what context. By '*illeity*' – it might be said – he essentially means all that is engaged in the effective sacralization of *perfect* truth-as-openness. But nothing, after all, could be more elusive! Here, in his words,

> The subject is inspired by the Infinite, which, as *illeity*, does not appear, is not present, has always already passed, is neither theme, telos nor interlocutor.[38]

All the energies of popular religion, in its deployment of beauty, are so many attempts to make God appear; to awaken a sense of God's presence in the here and now; to render God readily intelligible as a theme of theological exposition; to spin stories in which the revelation of God is the telos; to inspire prayer like the psalmist's. But all the energies of Levinasian prophetic philosophy, as such, are devoted to frustrating this enterprise, in the name of '*illeity*'.

Westphal, for instance, gently recoils from Levinas's extremism. Kierkegaard seems to him a better-balanced thinker: 'Levinas and Kierkegaard', he writes, 'agree in emphasizing that neighbour-love runs counter … to our *conatus essendi*'. Counter, that is, to the whole momentum / inertia / self-preservative and self-assertive rationale intrinsic to our natural being. 'But how [then], if at all, is [neighbour-love] possible, even imperfectly?' What does *psychological realism* require in this regard?

> Only by being loved do we develop the capacity to love, and Kierkegaard's God is fully personal enough for his answer to be "We love because he first loved us" (*1 John* 4.19). He gives us a moral transcription of God as *mysterium tremendum et fascinans*.

('Mystery both terrifying and alluring': Rudolf Otto's formula for the 'numinous'.)

> God is *mysterium* by remaining hidden even within the piety of hidden inwardness, *tremendum* by commanding the subordination of self-love to neighbour-love, and *fascinans* by being the fountain of forgiving love that gives us both our own sense of worth and our capacity to love others. Levinas's God is the *mysterium tremendum*; but where is the *fascinans* in the Good that gives no goods but only compels to goodness? When the command to love is unaccompanied by the love that enables obedience to the command, is this not a recipe for despair and even cynicism?[39]

Despair and cynicism: nature's response to fanatical excess.

Westphal indeed remains respectful. But compare *David Bentley Hart*'s quite violently allergic reaction to Levinas! Hart is a great Christian apologist; a theological adherent specifically of Eastern Orthodox tradition; erudite, brilliant, and waspish, not only in this instance. He is however a particular admirer of Hans Urs von Balthasar. And, along with other Balthasarians, he mistrusts the whole general tendency to favour the sublime over the beautiful, typical of French self-professedly postmodern thought.[40] The very distinction seems fraught with danger to him. Far better, in his view, a thought-world like that of Byzantium, in which it played no role; where the affinity of beauty to truth was simply acknowledged as axiomatic.

Whilst Hart criticizes every variant of the postmodern sublime, he thinks that Levinas represents its absolute nadir. He is infuriated by Levinas's prestige:

> The good opinion that Levinas's work at present enjoys is so great,

he complains,

> that it may seem somewhat coarse to observe that it is poor philosophy – the banal tortured into counterfeit profundity, the obviously false propounded

as irresistibly true, other forms of thought caricatured and condemned with a vehemence frequently vicious, and a fulminant tone of mystical authority assumed wherever principled argument proves impossible – but even so this is my contention; as is the no doubt even coarser assertion that Levinas advances a view of the world that is perhaps a little depraved [!][41]

Well, I am simply puzzled by the charge of 'banality'. And 'depravity'? Here, Hart is doing just what he, quite unjustly, accuses Levinas of doing. But yes, tone down the reciprocal hyperbole on both sides – just enough to allow for some real debate between them – and there is I think a real issue to be pondered. Still more forcibly than Westphal, Hart sees Levinas's rhetorical intransigence as self-defeating:

Could there really be ethics devoid of the will to be, the *conatus essendi*?

he asks. That is what Levinas sets out to evoke. Yet,

after all, the desire to be is always in some part a desire to be *with others*, and but for the wish to persist in being and enjoy its goodness – even when one must give it up – one has nothing to extend to another and no reason to desire being *for another*. Levinas's ethics is perhaps for this very reason stringently minimalist; it proscribes murder and callousness but says nothing about increasing another's joy.[42]

Levinas speaks of 'solidarity'. However, he does so only in a sense utterly devoid both of eros and of strategic organization, two elements crucial to the development and sustaining of the solidarity proper to any viable catholic community as such; which is what, above all, concerns Hart. 'Obviously', Hart writes,

Levinas's concern is to safeguard the purity of ethical intention – but this always means only *my* purity. Does this not perhaps serve a somewhat self-aggrandizing moral heroism, a selflessness so hyperbolic that it must ultimately erase everything distinct, desirable, and genuinely *other* in the other in order to preserve itself from the contamination of need, dependency, or hope?[43]

The 'depravity' that he (so wildly) suspects in the Levinasian worldview is in that sense a perverse, inverted narcissism; yet another, latter-day version of philosophy's age-old arrogance; notwithstanding Levinas's Jewish loyalties, a wilful, individualistic turning aside from true whole-heartedness of catholic belonging. Wisdom, for Levinas, essentially consists in hyper-sensitivity to the latency of crass narcissism, somewhere in the background to pretty well all that one thinks and does; it involves detecting and repudiating the resultant standard-issue corruption, everywhere. But the question surely does have to be asked: what is the value of such hyper-sensitivity if – as Hart suspects – all it generates, in practice, is this other, more refined, and tortured mode of narcissism?

It is a question not altogether inapplicable to Kierkegaard's thought, as well.

§

Hart criticizes Levinas in the name of all the beauty in the catholic traditions which the latter, in the spirit of *Amos* 5.18-24, implicitly disrespects, with his invocation of the ethical sublime. A partisan advocate of Levinas might well riposte by pointing to the corporate narcissism forever liable to infect catholic communities; the ubiquitous effect of evangelistic impatience. And there is I think much truth on both sides of this fundamental debate.

- On Levinas's side, we encounter the very purest pathos of shaken-ness. And I certainly do want to honour Levinas as a great mixer of the sublime shaken-ness intrinsic to the *Amos* impulse with the shaken-ness informing existentialist philosophy.
- On his theological critics' side, appeal is made to that deepest form of potential solidarity between people of all kinds, all ethnic backgrounds, all social classes, all different levels of intellectual sophistication, which only religion, precisely at its most beautiful, can inspire. This is what I mean by 'catholicity'. And I, for my part, fully share Hart's commitment to it.

The great justification for (patient!) evangelism on behalf of Abrahamic religion is the proven capacity of such religion, at any rate from time to time, to become a matrix for truly catholic community, porous to pathos of shaken-ness and, hence, opening towards the solidarity of the shaken. This solidarity, the very essence of the authentically sacred, is a secular phenomenon, in the sense of being altogether trans-confessional in its openness. Yet it requires incorporation, ideally, into every living form of religion – and the more catholic they are the better – in order to provide the most vivid context for its sacralization. As it is, in its purest form, the most valuable, but also the most difficult form of solidarity to organize, and by its very nature therefore the most ephemeral, it requires in principle whatever religious backing it can be given; so far as possible, to fix it in place. To this end, the two embattled sides here require reconciliation, the absolute one-sidedness of both alike being overcome.

– Perhaps Løgstrup may help?

Løgstrup

Løgstrup was not only an almost exact contemporary of Levinas. As a young man he also belonged to the same general intellectual milieu: the world of post-Husserlian phenomenology, chiefly flourishing in German and French universities. Both, for example wrote notable works on Heidegger.[44] Yet there is no unequivocal evidence that either was ever aware of the other.[45] Levinas's work only really became famous in the 1980s, too late to compel Løgstrup's attention. And Løgstrup, as a Dane, wrote in a language Levinas did not speak. Indeed, despite being 'world-famous in Denmark' as the saying goes, Løgstrup has only in the last few years come to be at all widely discussed outside Scandinavia.[46] The two, also, inhabited quite different religious cultures. For Løgstrup was a minister of the Danish Lutheran Church. Before being appointed Professor of Ethics and Philosophy of Religion at Aarhus University in 1943, he was for some seven years the pastor of a rural parish, in the west of the island of Funen.

Nevertheless, as philosophers, there clearly is good reason to compare these two ethical phenomenologists; each, alike, intent on exploring the ethical implications of purely pre-reflective pathos of shaken-ness, in all its potential subversiveness.

Again, 'pathos of shaken-ness' is my term, not Løgstrup's. He talks instead, quite simply, of 'the ethical demand'; which is also the title of his first major work, published in 1956.[47] Here, Løgstrup analyses 'the ethical demand' as being (a) 'silent', (b) 'radical', (c) 'one-sided' and (d) 'unfulfillable'.[48] The demand is, *firstly*, 'silent' in the sense that, whilst it is in essence a matter of scrupulous attention to the other person's needs, it is quite independent of the other person's own voiced perception of those needs. It by no means has to coincide with what the other person requests; nor does it manifest itself in the form of argument, from that or any other quarter, seeking to secure compliance through persuasion. An immediate sheer shaken impulse of conscience, its impact precedes any prescriptive teaching, or any calculation of what is prudent. *Secondly*, the ethical demand is 'radical' by virtue of the absoluteness with which, in principle, it trumps any other authority-claim. It is an anarchistic principle, in the sense that – whilst it may be quite compatible with all sorts of authoritative social norms, as such, serving to uphold civilized co-existence – by its very nature, it is nevertheless forever pointing beyond the limitations of such norms, towards a more generous ideal. *Thirdly*, it is 'one-sided' in that it allows one's conscience no room for bargaining on the basis of what one may suppose is one's due. Belonging as it does to pathos of shaken-ness – as distinct from the solidarity of the shaken – it is trans-political. That is to say, it operates on quite another level from any talk of rights. Moreover, Løgstrup insists that, at this level, life is properly regarded as a gift. Thus, the shaken-ness in question originates from a great upsurge of gratitude. The ethical demand, then, is just the compulsion to live out that gratitude. And *finally*: the reasons for gratitude being in fact inexhaustible, the concomitant demand is also – by definition – forever 'unfulfillable'. It is, after all, an infinite *demand*, defined by the pathos from which it emerges, not a set of finite *commands*, only intelligible with reference to specific goals that have to be fulfilled. (Again, one might illustrate the point here with reference to the contrast between *Amos* and *Hosea*.) Indeed, the whole truth intrinsic to pathos of shaken-ness lies in the condition of moral restlessness it inspires. The closer one comes to fulfilling what such pathos is seen to demand, the further away the possibility of truly *satisfactory* fulfilment will therefore always appear.

That Løgstrup's work is substantially akin, in each of these respects, to Levinas's is clear enough. Only, its tone is nevertheless quite different. Indeed, the tone of Løgstrup's writing is in sharp contrast to both that of Levinas's and that of

Kierkegaard's. For, whereas Levinas's rhetoric is hyperbole heaped upon hyperbole – and Kierkegaard's is so rich in rollicking megalothymotic sarcasm – Løgstrup by contrast is a very much quieter writer. And, just by virtue of that relative quietness of tone, his thinking is, I would venture to suggest, much more readily reconcilable with (in his case a Lutheran form of) catholicity.

§

There are three main places where Løgstrup discusses Kierkegaard. The 1950 lecture series he delivered in Berlin on the Kierkegaardian and the Heideggerian 'analyses of existence' is the first.[49] Then, at the end of *The Ethical Demand* there is a 'Polemic Epilogue' in which he criticizes Kierkegaard's great ethical treatise *Works of Love*. And in 1968 he published a book entitled *Controverting Kierkegaard*.[50]

During his time as a pastor on Funen he had been part of the circle around the theological journal *Tidehverv* ('Turn of an Era'). In more recent times *Tidehverv* has, as it happens, become a significant force very much on the right of Danish politics; but back then its readership covered a wider span, and within that context Løgstrup was very much a moderate. At any rate, here was a world in which, amongst historic Danish thinkers, Kierkegaard (and emphatically not Grundtvig!) tended to be seen as a prime authority.[51] After the war, however, Løgstrup turned away from the *Tidehverv* circle, and also, increasingly, away from Kierkegaard. During the German occupation of Denmark, he had been active in the Resistance. But how, one might well ask, does Kierkegaard's thought – hemmed in, as it is, by purely *ecclesiocentric* critical concerns – relate to the memory of such a struggle, against secular evil, requiring secular alliance-building?

I think one has to distinguish three essential respects in which Løgstrup's thought diverges from Kierkegaard's, as a philosophic channel for pathos of shaken-ness. And the first is just this: that he is a Christian thinker whose project in *The Ethical Demand* is an

> attempt to give a definition *in strictly human terms* of the relationship to the other person which is contained within the religious proclamation of Jesus of Nazareth.[52]

That is to say, his primary interest is in the universal, secular element here. Whereas Kierkegaard is forever intent on interpreting Christian uniqueness – all that, as he sees it, the particular character of uniquely Christian faith implies – Løgstrup is, in effect, exploring the trans-political basis for Christian participation in the solidarity of the shaken; secular humanity at its ethical fullest. He is not yet indeed a political, or anti-political, strategist for the solidarity of the shaken. He lacks any equivalent to that actual concept; and, unlike Patočka, does not develop the sort of open-ended grand narrative which is philosophy's proper contribution to such strategy. However, his ethical thinking surely does belong in the immediate antechamber to this species of grand narrative. And, in general, it seems to me that he represents trans-political philosophic pathos of shaken-ness much more amenable to direct translation into political, or anti-political, terms than is the case with either Levinas or Kierkegaard.

When the Barthian theologian N. H. Søe protested against his split-level understanding of gospel truth, dividing the confessional from the 'strictly human', Løgstrup responded with a basic statement of what he sees as basic Christian principle:

> I regard it as a Christian claim that the ethical demand is not a specifically Christian demand. Thus, Christians should not fight their own battle in situations where Christians and non-Christians have a common battle to fight, for if they do, then in the eyes of Christian faith the Christians thereby deny that the ethical demand is universal.[53]

Indeed, does not the gospel itself require that Christians have split loyalties, both to each other as fellow-Christians and to their neighbours, simply as such?

Other critics, on the other hand, have questioned the authenticity of Løgstrup's seculariszng intent.[54] For, when he represents the ethical demand as springing from a basic sense of having received one's life as a gift, the obvious question is, who then is the giver? And how, after all, such critics may ask, is this other than just a rather coy way of doing what Kierkegaard does more brashly: rendering faith in God an essential *presupposition* for authentic ethical concern?

Well, yes – one might reply – it is of course true that Løgstrup himself, being a Lutheran pastor, regards the giver as God. But the point is surely that, unlike Kierkegaard, he does not, when arguing as an ethicist, by any means require others to follow suit. The crucial point with regard to the ethical demand still remains, just the same, if for instance one opts to speak, altogether more abstractly, of one's life as a gift from 'Nature'. *Deus sive Natura* ... Talk about God, wrapped as it is in ages-old liturgy, is poetically far richer than talk about 'Nature' alone. And in general, one may well regard atheism, when all is said and done, as a perverse, mistaken option for imaginative impoverishment. But *in this context* never mind! To take to heart the givenness of the gift of life is simply to be *shaken*, into a reciprocal generosity of spirit. Never mind the name of the giver; whether God is invoked by name, or remains anonymous in the giving.

In the first eleven chapters of *The Ethical Demand* Løgstrup is arguing strictly as a phenomenologist, with questions of theology bracketed. Only in the final, brief chapter, before the 'Polemical Epilogue' – that is, only in Chapter 12 – does he revert to theology: identifying his secular conception of the ethical demand with what Jesus teaches, about the divine commandment to love one's neighbour. But the point here is: it is not that the authority of the ethical demand, as proclaimed by Jesus, *derives from* our acknowledgement of his divine status. Instead, for Løgstrup, it is the other way round. He is interested in the way that recognition of Jesus's divine status may be seen as initially deriving from the manner of his ethical proclamation. For, what first opened the eyes of Jesus's disciples to his being the 'Christ', already before the events of Easter? Løgstrup suggests that it was the unique combination, in his teaching, of the ethical demand, presented in all its stringency, with what alone can render that demand at all widely tolerable: the assurance of ultimate (astonishing!) forgiveness, for those who repent their actual failure, no matter how grievous, to fulfil it.

§

Løgstrup's second turning away from Kierkegaard – besides the secularity of his thought, just discussed – consists in a militant isothymia. And here too he is at one with Levinas. The *locus classicus* for this is, in fact, his critique of Kierkegaard's treatise *Works of Love* in the 'Polemical Epilogue' to *The Ethical Demand*. Thus, *Works of Love* consists of a series of 'discourses' on what Kierkegaard conceives to be the uniqueness of Christian ethics. But Løgstrup argues: just look how Kierkegaard's ethical teaching differs from that of Jesus himself!

The very familiar gospel passage in question is *Luke* 10.25-37. Jesus is in conversation with a lawyer. 'Teacher', the lawyer says, 'by what deeds may I inherit life in the Age?'[55] In reply Jesus cites *Deuteronomy* 6.5 and *Leviticus* 19.18, as a pair: 'You shall love the Lord your God out of the whole of your heart and in the whole of your soul, and in the whole of your strength, and in the whole of your mind and your neighbour as yourself.' But then the lawyer asks, 'Who is my neighbour?' To which Jesus responds with the parable of the Good Samaritan. A man has been robbed by gangsters and left half dead in a ditch by the roadside. A priest passes by on the other side, averting his eyes. A devout Levite likewise passes by. (Perhaps they were both constrained by concern for ritual purity; supposing the man was actually dead.) But then a Samaritan arrives, an outsider in the orthodox Jewish world. He salves and bandages the man's wounds; hoists the man on his donkey; brings the man to an inn; pays for the man's lodging, and promises to pay more when next he is around, in case there are any further costs. 'Who of these three,' Jesus asks – the priest, the Levite, or the Samaritan – 'does it seem to you became a neighbour to the man'?

For Jesus, in short, the criterion for true love of God is the essentially isothymotic principle of 'loving one's neighbour as oneself': as the concept of 'neighbour' encompasses all human beings equally, with regard to the ethical demand. At this level, all have an equal claim upon one's generosity, quite regardless of their particular deserts; strangers equally with family and friends, as the man in the ditch is a complete stranger to the Samaritan; enemies equally with allies, as orthodox Jews in general were traditional enemies to Samaritans in general.

Kierkegaard however, whilst of course he acknowledges all this, immediately *races on further*. Indeed, he does not dwell on Jesus's own teaching at all. But whereas Jesus's argument simply moves from love of God to love of neighbour, the logic of Kierkegaard's thought in *Works of Love* may well be said to move from love of God to love of neighbour *and then back to love of God again*; with this last transition being very much the one most emphasized. For him, true love of neighbour is defined in terms of true love of God, interpreted in radically megalothymotic fashion. Thus, here as always in his work, true love of God is identified with the defiant, assertive 'inwardness' of the purely selfless individual, the outsider from the human herd, the embattled prophet. *And, for him, true love of neighbour is, in essence, a matter of helping one's neighbour also love God, in this self-same sense.*

> For the Christian view means this: truly to love oneself is to love God; truly to love another person is with every sacrifice (even to become hated) to help the other person love God or in loving God.[56]

'With every sacrifice': here speaks the neurotic man who, after all, could not bring himself to marry Regine Olsen. 'Even to become hated': he means, in general, to become hated by the very neighbour whom one loves. After all, if love of God means constant megalothymotic battle against the human herd as such – and if, as is usually the case, one's neighbour is a more or less contented participant in that human herd – then, certainly, one's pesky desire to 'help the other person love God or in loving God', recruiting them to that battle, is scarcely calculated to elicit much real gratitude. But so much the better, from Kierkegaard's point of view: the truth of true love of one's neighbour consists in utter selflessness, unsullied by any desire for reward, such as the other's gratitude would provide.

Indeed, his argument is quite ruthless, even with regard to the most beautiful love:

> If there were a relationship of love between two or more people, a relationship so happy, so perfect, that the poet must needs exult over it – yes, so blissful that one who was not a poet would become one from wonder and joy over this sight – the matter is by no means ended. For now Christianity steps in and asks about the God-relationship, asks whether each individual is related to God, and then whether the love-relationship is related to God. If this is not the case, then Christianity, which still is the defender of love, or precisely because it is that, will in God's name have no scruples about splitting this relationship until the lovers understand it ... And if only one [of them] understands it, then shall Christianity, which still is the defender of love, have no scruples about leading him out into the horror of a conflict such as no poet ever dreams about or has ever dared to portray. For the poet can have no more to do with the Christian demand *to love one's enemy* ... than he can have anything to do with the Christian demand to *hate the beloved* out of love and in love. Yet Christianity does not hesitate in God's name to strain the relationship so tensely.[57]

This anguished, self-destructive conception of Christian neighbour-love has come a long, long way from the parable of the Good Samaritan! And Løgstrup, for his part, wants to go back.

A theological defender of Kierkegaard might well respond that he is only drawing out the moral of the Passion story. Jesus embodies the ideal of neighbour-love – and look what that then leads to! Yes, but what Løgstrup is criticizing is the way in which Kierkegaard appears positively to *devalue* any form of neighbour-love which falls short of Christ-like martyrdom. It is Kierkegaard's rhapsodic *impatience*, in this regard, that so troubles him. What Løgstrup finds problematic is Kierkegaard's definition, no less, of true Christian neighbour-love: as the task of 'helping the other person love God'. For, might this not be taken, in actual practice, as a formula to license *moralistic bullying*? It is all too ambiguous. I mean: did the Good Samaritan give much thought to the other, stricken man's relationship with God; or to how the other might be edified? *Was he that controlling and manipulative*? The story does not say so. And I hope he was not. I hope that, as the story suggests, the help he gave was given without any strings attached, at all.

Nor was Christ's Passion the fate of a moralistic bully. It was the fate of one who proclaimed the ethical demand, but with the assurance of divine forgiveness; and who thereby gave offence both to the complacent herd and also, precisely, to the moralistic gangster-bullies of his world. In skipping so fast beyond the ethical teaching contained in the gospels themselves, the trouble is, Kierkegaard obliterates the clear guarantee, there, that Christian faith is not just another mode of moralistic bullying. But attention to that guarantee is a key *negative* requirement of authentic Christian catholicity. The threat of moralistic bullying immediately tends to destroy the atmosphere of trust upon which all healthy catholic community life depends.

Unfortunately, Kierkegaard's doctrine represents a sublimely megalothymotic blockage to full catholicity just as dire as the sublimely isothymotic blockage in Levinas's doctrine. These are two expressions of the *Amos* impulse at its most problematic: *pathos of shaken-ness impatiently resisting incorporation into organized solidarity*. Therefore, more or less irreconcilable, it would appear, with the actual religious belonging of the two thinkers in question.

§

As for Løgstrup's third major divergence from Kierkegaard: this is in his discussion of what he calls '*the sovereign* [or the *spontaneous*] *expressions of life*'. And, unlike the other two divergences, this one involves him parting company from Levinas, too.

For these 'expressions of life' are none other than the most basic *positive* preconditions for catholicity.

Thus, catholicity thrives above all on its co-option of beauty, through sacred narrative and liturgy. But by 'the sovereign expressions of life', one might well say, Løgstrup means the primary elements of ethical beauty; just those beautiful impulses, in other words, which are most importantly to be co-opted in this way. In itself, the ethical demand is not beautiful. Rather, it is a sublime principle. However, the sovereign expressions of life are, so to speak its beautiful outriders.

He in fact first introduces the concept in *Controverting Kierkegaard*. And then he develops it in various subsequent writings. Several of his texts on the topic are available in English, in the volume entitled *Beyond the Ethical Demand*.[58]

The sovereign expressions of life constitute a spectrum of sociable attitudes, *a priori* dispositions to warm-hearted benevolence: ranging (in terms of the power-relationships involved) from trust to mercy; or (in terms of emotional intensity) from love to simple kindliness, or authentic courtesy. What Løgstrup has in mind are the underlying habits or drives at work; not any definitive rules of behaviour. So, for instance, at the beginning of his 1972 book *Norm og spontaneitet* (Norm and Spontaneity) he illustrates the concept with a true story.[59]

The story is set in Denmark under Nazi occupation. At four o'clock in the morning a woman (unnamed in the text but in actual fact Løgstrup's own wife Rosemarie) hears the insistent ringing of the doorbell. She goes down and opens the door. It is the secret police, two of them, heavily armed. They want to know where her husband is. She says he is away on business. In reality, because of his involvement in the Resistance, he has been obliged to go into hiding. One of the men starts to search the house, whilst the other one 'possessed of an engaging manner, all amiability and courtesy', engages the woman in conversation. But what interests Løgstrup is her response. Of course, she is very well aware that the policeman's courtesy is fake; that he is just trying to trick her into revealing secrets she would be better advised to conceal. So, she fends him off. Yet, at the same time, she finds herself constantly obliged to suppress a natural inclination to open up, and respond to his fake courtesy with genuine, that is, warm and incautious courtesy of her own. Why? Løgstrup asks.

> What manifests itself in that inclination? Nothing other than the elemental and definitive peculiarity attaching to all speech *qua* spontaneous expression of life: its openness. To speak is to speak openly.

(Or, in other words: to speak openly is to speak with proper *loyalty* to the spirit from which speech in the first place derives.)

> This is not something which the individual does with speech; it is there beforehand, as it were, *qua* anonymous expression of life. We yield to its sovereignty at the very moment in which we begin to speak. Even in a situation where hoodwinking the other is a matter of life or death, where the other's destructive intent is patently obvious and his strategy wholly transparent – even there, it makes itself felt, so that not speaking openly is palpably felt to be contrary to nature. The sovereign expression of life pre-empts us; we are seized by it. Therein lies its spontaneity.[60]

And thank God that this is so! For – whilst, yes, there are circumstances such as this story illustrates in which life-'expressing' spontaneity has to be suppressed – still, it remains the original germ of fully developed truth-as-openness. It is just the most primitive precondition for the possibility of true catholicity; which then has the potential to open further, and merge with the solidarity of the shaken.

The sovereign expressions of life express life inasmuch as they are vivifying, generous, creative impulses. I have said that they are beautiful: the beauty lies in their sheer magnanimity. There is no rancour in them: Løgstrup, for his part, opposes them to what he calls the 'obsessive movements of self-enclosedness': namely, taking offence, jealousy, envy.[61] The obsessive self is essentially reactive;

self-enclosed because self-defensive. But the expressions of life are 'sovereign', in the sense that they represent a higher authority (divine or natural) which on the contrary demands self-surrender. These are not phenomena that I am free to judge, in terms of criteria that I have sovereignly chosen for myself. Rather, their goodness is intrinsic.

> They make me their own before I make them my own. They have intimated to me what is good and bad before I consider the matter myself and evaluate it.[62]

Thus, at this level we are not talking about the rightness or wrongness of specific acts. We are talking about motivation: the motivation that is involved in one's becoming one's true self, or in one's soul being liberated. That the expressions of life are 'spontaneous' means, in the first place, that – just as in the case of the ethical demand – we are talking about sheer pre-reflective purity of motivation, not yet complicated by any calculation of consequences, or application of theoretic principle. And, like the ethical demand, they are trans-culturally universal phenomena; given more encouragement, of course, in some cultural contexts than in others, but never not there; primordial aspects of being-human.

However, the sovereign expressions of life are *not only* pre-reflective and trans-culturally universal in character, *but also*, as Løgstrup himself puts it, 'pre-moral'.[63] In other words: his phenomenological conception of them comes from yet a further act of bracketing, over and above that which he has earlier accomplished with regard to the ethical demand. In his analysis of the ethical demand, he has bracketed all that belongs to the theoretic regulation and application of ethical principles: utilitarian, deontological, moral-theological or other-religious. In his analysis of the sovereign expressions of life, however, *he has additionally bracketed what belongs to the ethical demand itself*: the inchoate, restless upsurge of gratitude; the consequent nagging of conscience; the pangs of guilt, inevitable for anyone who takes the demand at all seriously, it being forever unfulfillable. And the sovereign expressions of life are what then remain, as the front-line of humanity's trans-political defence against the fallenness of herd, gang and mob.

Indeed, there are surely three distinct such lines of trans-political defence. The first line of defence is made up of the sovereign expressions of life. In some happy contexts that first line of defence may be sufficient in itself. To the extent, though, that the sovereign expressions of life fail, they need to be reinforced by the second line, consisting of the ethical demand. Two barriers, then: one ranged behind the other. And still these pre-reflective, universal remedies are not enough to subdue the overflowing evil of the herd, the gang, the mob! It is because they sometimes fail that we also then need the third line: the supplementary protection provided by various culturally specific modes of moral argumentation – whatever of that kind helps serve the same essential purpose. That is, the diverse prescriptive attitudes enshrined in particular intellectual cultures, particular liturgical and artistic cultures, all sorts of particular cultural identity, insofar as they are genuine bulwarks against barbarism. *But these culturally specific defences can, after all, only really be at all effective to the extent that the first force of the onslaught has already been broken, and diminished; to begin with by the sovereign expressions of life; and then by the ethical demand.*

Løgstrup complains of Kierkegaard, whose gaze remains so firmly fixed upon the Christian sector of the third line of defence, that he 'never spared the sovereign expressions of life so much as a thought'.[64] Ultra-intellectual as he is, Kierkegaard identifies the core truth of true Christian faith with a hyper-intensification of austere *self-consciousness*, 'dying away from immediacy' as he puts it in the *Concluding Unscientific Postscript*.[65] Løgstrup, of course, emphatically disagrees:

> Kierkegaard is mistaken in thinking that the escape from desire and pleasure's immediate attachment to the world calls for an effort of reflection in which the individual recalls to mind the infinite and eternal in himself, and becomes an abstract and negative self. The immediacy with which the individual is bound to the world through desire and pleasure is matched by the immediacy with which he is bound to the world through such sovereign expressions of life as trust, mercy, and the openness of speech …
>
> Kierkegaard is mistaken in thinking that the infinite movement of resignation is needed for the individual to apprehend himself in his eternal truth. He is mistaken in thinking that the ethical task consists in concerning oneself at every moment of one's earthly life with the winning of one's identity and becoming a self by using every instant of time to relate oneself to eternity. That concern is one of which the human person is free. Winning one's identity and becoming a self is something the individual should let happen unawares, by leaving it to the sovereign expressions of life.[66]

The truth of true Christian faith, for Løgstrup, begins in fulsome appreciation of *un*-self-conscious goodness.

Levinas, also, ignores the sovereign expressions of life. *He* does so because his whole attention, as a phenomenologist, is fixed instead upon the second line of defence, alone. Levinas's ethical doctrine in effect presupposes an apocalyptic, calamitous suppression of the sovereign expressions of life – he turns to the 'epiphany of the face' precisely by way of response to the consequences of such suppression. And yes, clearly, both Nazi and Soviet totalitarianism were systems pretty much dedicated to suppressing the sovereign expressions of life, minimizing the scope for action of those catholic communities in which the expressions of life were still being cultivated. But, outside that sort of totalitarian context, what reason is there, still, to *despair* of their potential? In this aspect, Levinasian ethics surely does remain incomplete.

Løgstrup is not as wildly eloquent as either Kierkegaard or Levinas. Nevertheless, he is I think an interesting thinker not least because of the way in which, unlike them, he seeks to do proper justice to *all three* lines of defence against barbarism. First, in the role of Christian theologian, he represents faith quite admirably untainted by evangelistic impatience. And then, in the role of phenomenologist, he is remarkable for the judicious balance in his thought between the ethical demand

and the sovereign expressions of life, considered as two entirely complementary sorts of impulse. On the one side, the ethical demand: in my terms, sublime pathos of shaken-ness; spiking in the primordial *Amos* impulse. On the other side, the sovereign expressions of life: in my terms, beautiful pathos of shaken-ness; the primordial basis for catholicity. To an exemplary extent, as I see it, Løgstrup seeks to give both sides their phenomenological due.

§

Three lines of *trans-political* defence: Løgstrup surveys all three. And now we just need a *political*, or *anti-political*, policy for maintaining them, reinforcing them, extending them. Going beyond Kierkegaard, Levinas and Løgstrup – in other words – we surely do require appropriate philosophic grand narrative, as a basis for further cosmopolitan solidarity-building, among the shaken.

What such narrative might look like is, then, the topic of the next chapter.

Chapter 7

SHAKEN-NESS, MINUS CATHOLICITY

Heidegger

To think through the solidarity of the shaken, straight away, requires grand narrative. For, after all, every form of solidarity-building initiative, to a large extent, depends upon the sharing of narratives; but, in this instance, the relevant memories include the whole history contributing to the possibility of a proper appreciation for the imperatives of perfect truth-as-openness. Again, the 'grand narrative' in question will not lay claim to authority on the basis of supposed predictive truth-as-correctness. And so, it belongs to quite a different *genre* of thought from Marxist grand narrative; or from Enlightenment grand narrative as represented by Condorcet, Fichte, Comte; or from gloomy prophet-of-doom grand narrative of the type exemplified, say, by Spengler. What I am fumbling towards here is simply a retrospective account of how it has as a matter of fact (look!) now at last become possible to appreciate the imperatives of perfect truth-as-openness in terms of the equation, the kingdom of God = the solidarity of the shaken.

Or, to take the matter one stage further, it is a grand narrative of the emergent equation: *the kingdom of God = the solidarity of the shaken = the ideal confluence of 'pathos of shaken-ness' with authentic (small 'c') 'catholicity'*.

The kingdom of God / solidarity of the shaken has essentially to do with the political – and, still more, the anti-political, or prophetic – drawing-together of those latter two, in themselves, *trans*-political elements.[1]

In Chapter 6 I illustrated the concept 'pathos of shaken-ness' with particular reference to the philosophical arguments of Kierkegaard, Levinas and Løgstrup. Elsewhere, I have discussed the more immediately poetic expression of such pathos in the work of William Blake, Friedrich Hölderlin and Nelly Sachs.[2] In this chapter I am concerned with how 'pathos of shaken-ness' interacts with the ideal of 'catholicity', in a grand-narrative context.

I am, admittedly, using the term 'catholic' in somewhat idiosyncratic fashion. (And yet – what better term is there, for my purpose?) By it, I mean in the first place: as applied to communities, *a maximum possible coherent, because liturgically focussed, egalitarian inclusiveness*. And then, secondly: *the corresponding virtue, in participant individuals.* Thus, it is the sacred ideal given classic Christian theological expression by St. Paul in *Galatians* 3: 27–8:

> For as many of you as were baptised into the Anointed have clothed yourselves in the Anointed. There can be neither Judaean nor Greek, there can be neither slave nor freeman, there cannot be male and female, for you are all one in the Anointed One Jesus.[3]

In the Christian-confessional context, one might compare the Russian concept of *sobornost*. But for my part, I am by no means thinking of an exclusively Christian ideal. For I am also keen to speak of potential Jewish 'catholicity', potential Muslim 'catholicity', potential Buddhist 'catholicity'; even potential Hindu 'catholicity', where the caste system is truly transcended; and so forth. And, for me, the key point is: 'catholicity', on the part of intellectuals, is also just that quality of truth which is most radically opposed to *philosophic impatience*. For it involves a patient readiness to work hard at egalitarian relationships with folk belonging to other social classes from one's own. Thus consider, for instance, Paul's ironic celebration of the 'folly' of 'the word of the cross', as opposed to the (impatient) 'wisdom' of 'the dialectician of this age' in *1 Corinthians* 1.18-31! 'Catholicity', the way I am using the term, is, above all, that which differentiates authentic solidarity of the shaken from a more restricted, elitist solidarity among philosophers, or more broadly among intellectuals, *alone*.[4]

And so, in order to explore what that might mean, let us begin by considering the grand-narrative thought of those two great twentieth-century celebrants, and strategists, of an ideal solidarity among philosophers: *Martin Heidegger* (1889–1976) and *Leo Strauss* (1899–1973). Heidegger and Strauss are the two modern thinkers who to my mind, above all, share something of the same ambivalent greatness as Plato, in the classical world. Specifically, that is to say: as sophisticated philosophical solidarity-strategists, for the cause of Truth at its most open – *only, with the key qualifying proviso that the openness in question fundamentally excludes any element of catholicity.*

§

Thus, take *Being and Time* for example, the work – first published in 1927 – that decisively established Heidegger's status as *the* leading German philosopher of his day.[5] How does *Being and Time* relate to the problematics involved in conceptualizing the solidarity of the shaken? As I say, these are not exactly the problematics with which Heidegger himself is concerned. And we will I think need to deploy some non-Heideggerian terms to bring out the difference in question; in that sense, laying rough hands on his argument. I make this apology in view of the unique intellectual beauty, and apparent self-sufficiency, of *Being and Time*. Yet, only by introducing fresh terminology can the distinctions I want to draw, in fact, be drawn.

Being and Time is what Heidegger himself calls a work of 'fundamental ontology'. It has to do with 'the question of Being', where 'Being' refers to the whole of what is, apprehended as a source of wonder. Philosophy begins in wonder, and Heidegger is intent on going back to that beginning; finding a way to begin as a philosopher all over again.[6] He is a pioneer post-Husserlian phenomenologist, and this is a systematic phenomenology of *Dasein*: literally, 'being-there' – colloquially, just 'existence' – but, more exactly in this context, the universal features of human existence, considered in the light of philosophic wonder. A study of the universal possibility of wonder, as such, involves the bracketing of all that is culturally specific; all worldviews, religious or irreligious; all ethical norms; all political ideologies. None of these are allowed to distract from the essential topic. And what then remains, as the pathway to 'authenticity' for *Dasein*, is nothing but pathos of shaken-ness – or, rather, a certain variant mode of such pathos: 'Being-towards-death' awakening a fundamental truth-laden 'anxiety', which in turn is worked through as a deepening of 'care'. The argument, as a whole, pivots around these concepts.[7]

What Heidegger presents us with in *Being and Time* is, however, pathos of shaken-ness in one particular mode. For, there is nothing isothymotic about this pathos of shaken-ness. Compare Levinas, or Løgstrup. (Or indeed compare Buber, before them.) Heidegger's conception of 'authenticity' in this work has nothing immediately to do with any very challenging encounter with one's neighbour, isothymotically encountered as neighbour. He not only brackets culturally specific ethical norms, but also brackets 'ethics' in the altogether broader sense that these other thinkers explore.

In the essentially megalothymotic dynamic of his thinking, he is indeed more akin to Kierkegaard. But of course, he differs from Kierkegaard in having bracketed the culturally specific claims of Christian faith. Already in 1921–2 he declares: 'Philosophy, in its radical, self-posing questionability, must be *a-theistic* in principle.'[8] And in the distinctive, non-ideological sense of 'atheism' he intends, this remains an elementary presupposition of his thought to the end. As George Kovacs puts it:

> Heidegger's definition of the very nature and task of philosophical thinking may be described as a methodological atheism; it is neither "for" nor "against" but rather "without" God (as the last and first explanation of beings and thinking); it comes from and returns to Being (and not from and to God, who cannot be forced into the categories or concepts of philosophical reflection). This quality of being "godless" (that is, not being closed by a narrow philosophical, metaphysical notion of God as a principle of explanation), according to the "final word" of Heidegger on the question of God, can also be understood as a new and liberated, genuine (philosophical) thinking becoming free for God, for a larger (more transcendent) and more profound idea of God.[9]

But in *Being and Time* the ultimate stimulus envisaged to pathos of shaken-ness is Being-towards-death; not, as for Kierkegaard, divine grace.

And then another basic difference from Kierkegaard: Heidegger's ideal of 'authenticity' in *Being and Time* is *beautiful*, rather than *sublime*. In his later thinking, about 'releasement' (*Gelassenheit*), the distinction is somewhat less clear-cut. However, there is no real equivalent, in either *Being and Time* or his later work, to the Kierkegaardian identification of sacred truth with sublime prophetic self-sacrifice; the scalding terror evoked by Kierkegaard's rhetoric; the sublimely confrontational *Amos* impulse driving Kierkegaard's attack upon 'Christendom'. Heidegger's writing, by contrast, is always beautifully serene in tone, even when tinged with apocalyptic melancholy.

Nevertheless, consider the freshly minted concept of 'the they' (*das Man*) in *Being and Time*. This is very much the same as what Kierkegaard calls 'the crowd'. It is precisely the human herd, which, in Christian form, becomes 'Christendom'. Heidegger for his part analyses it as the 'everyday' state of *Dasein's* 'fallenness' into 'inauthenticity'; a 'fallenness' expressing itself in 'idle talk'; 'curiosity' leading to constant distraction; moral thinking forever mired in complacent 'ambiguity'. Concerned to preserve the (beautiful) serenity of his stance as a detached philosophic observer, he tries to reassure his readers that he by no means intends to harangue them. As he uses the term, 'fallenness' (*Verfallenheit*) 'does not express any negative evaluation'.[10] Nor is the term 'idle talk' (*Gerede*), in particular, meant here 'in a disparaging signification'.[11] But how can 'fallenness' escape the lingering influence of its theological connotations? And, as the translators remark in a footnote, the German '*Gerede*' is after all just as intrinsically disparaging a term as 'idle talk' is in English! The prose of *Being and Time* is as coolly and as intricately academic as Heidegger can make it. Yet, there is at its heart a megalothymotic contempt for 'the they' just as deep ingrained as Kierkegaard's contempt for 'the crowd'.

The pathos of shaken-ness in *Being and Time* differs from that in Kierkegaard's writing by virtue of its beautifully systematic, phenomenological character; and hence also its 'methodological atheism'. It differs from the pathos of shaken-ness in the writing of Buber, Levinas or Løgstrup by virtue of its imbalance towards megalothymia, rather than isothymia. And it differs also, this time from the pathos of shaken-ness informing all four of those others' work, inasmuch as *Being and Time*, its two 'Divisions' taken together, was in turn originally conceived as the First 'Part' of a two-Part magnum opus, the second Part of which would be a grand-narrative history of philosophy.[12] And although the second Part was never written, this merely meant that the grand narrative, already gestating here, subsequently appeared in more fragmentary form.

Heidegger's oeuvre, as a whole, is indeed a prime case of grand narrative engaging with pathos of shaken-ness alone – pathos of shaken-ness as delineated by the categories of *Being and Time* – decisively cut loose from any form of catholicity.

Hence, his is a grand narrative governed by a certain ideal version of solidarity among philosophers, in a broad sense: *shaken thinkers who are, crucially, also the product of an elite education.* In his thinking of the early 1930s this fatefully crystallizes into a dream of philosopher-rule, in effect a modernized equivalent to

Plato's Republic: philosopher-solidarity rippling out into ideal *völkisch* solidarity, under philosophic guidance. And yet, it is a version of such solidarity which diverges right from the outset, to a marked degree, from Plato's original version.

Thus, for Heidegger of course the trouble with Plato is that he is the father of '*metaphysics*'. At one level, in Heidegger's lexicon, 'metaphysics' is just what I would call the idolatry of propositional truth-as-correctness; as opposed – not yet, perhaps, to fully fledged truth-as-openness – but, at any rate, to attitudinal truth-as-'authenticity'. Heidegger himself distinguishes the two species of truth as corresponding to the Greek terms, '*orthotés*' and '*alétheia*'; translating '*alétheia*', according to its etymology, as '*Unverborgenheit*', that is, 'unhidden-ness'. '*Alétheia*', the truth of authentic *Dasein* thoughtfully appropriating the revealed wonder of Being, is he argues a prime concern of Pre-Socratic philosophy. (He discusses in particular Anaximandros, Herakleitos and Parmenides.) But Plato introduces the sacralization of 'Ideas', instead. By which he means: ideal perceptions of truth-as-correctness, inviting definitive capture in philosophic propositions. Although Plato writes about '*alétheia*', Heidegger argues, all too often what he means in actual practice is '*orthotés*'. And, following Plato, philosophy has sunk into a lamentable ages-long state of forgetfulness; forgetting the proper sacredness of *alétheia*.

How fair is this as a reading of Plato, and of Platonism? It should be noted that Heidegger's interpretation of Plato varies over time. He published just one work on Plato in his lifetime: the essay *Platons Lehre von der Wahrheit*, completed in its final form in 1940.[13] There he simply insists on the 'metaphysical' nature of Plato's thought, and leaves it at that. In earlier lecture series, however (on the *Sophist* in 1924–5, on the *Theaetetus* and the *Republic*, the cave allegory, in 1931–2) he is rather more indulgent: finding a deep ambivalence, concerning the two species of truth, right at the heart of Plato's thought.[14] And it should also be noted that he nowhere, in his mature work, devotes any close attention to *Neo*-Platonism; the apophatic thrust of which seems to me to be, absolutely, a transcendence of 'metaphysics' in his sense of the word.[15] But what really interests Heidegger is the line that runs from Plato to Aristotle; and then on from Aristotle to mediaeval scholastic philosophy and theology. The very word 'metaphysics' derives, of course, from its use by the editors of Aristotle's work, as a book title. As for the higgledy-piggledy collection of Aristotelian texts which go under that title, these hang together inasmuch as they all deal with the nature of truth-as-correctness, systematically considered. And in Book XII explanatory truth-as-correctness is sacralized in the notion of God as the 'unmoved mover'; in essence, the impassive ultimate cause of all correctly explained causality. In Heidegger's terminology, 'metaphysics' is thus 'onto-theology' as opposed to 'fundamental ontology', which is what, by contrast, he is undertaking.

The Aristotelian notion of God is *the* classic paradigm example of 'theology' in that sense; eventually reconciled with Abrahamic faith by mediaeval scholasticism. But the new beginnings in philosophy pioneered first by Descartes and then by Kant are no less onto-theological in remit, as they insist on the question: what is the bare minimum that is certainly correct? Finally, in the nineteenth and twentieth centuries, sundry yet more aggressively irreverent forms of 'metaphysics' start to flourish: ideological projects seeking to vindicate and interpret the supposed truth-as-correctness of dogmatic unbelief, vis-á-vis religion in general. Heidegger professes to break free from the constraints of 'metaphysics' in all of these forms, alike. And, for my part, I am quite happy to go along with Heidegger in this, to the extent that 'metaphysics' may indeed be strictly defined as: any exclusive concern with truth-as-correctness, as regards what is sacred, resulting in sheer distraction from the prior claims of truth-as-'authenticity' or, better still, truth-as-openness.

Unfortunately, however, that is *not* all that he means by the word. Or put it this way: the problem is that he nowhere considers how the boundary-definition of 'metaphysics' may, after all, require to be qualified by the legitimate demands of catholic community-life.

For (again) catholicity, in itself, is a vital practice of truth-as-openness. It is a solidarity-building work of truth-as-openness in breaking down the barriers to free-spirited conversation between people of different social class, gender or ethnic identity, in general; and, not least, the barriers dividing people on the basis of different educational attainment. Therefore, it necessarily challenges any elevation of solidarity among philosophers, as such, to the status of supreme ideal. But how does catholic community hold together? Typically, it does so by means of shared liturgy; which then becomes the matrix for a whole shared sacred-artistic culture. Liturgy, on the other hand, further requires a certain basis in shared doctrine, in order to define the grammatical structure of its symbolism. To be sure, there is always an ineradicable risk that the resultant shared doctrine may be corrupted into 'metaphysics', distracting from truth-as-openness and, just to that extent, losing its true catholic character. Yet, this is by no means inevitable. For there is always also the possibility which I am attempting to explore: of catholicity being rendered transparent to the solidarity of the shaken. In which case, whilst the orthodox doctrine remains as sort of social glue, it has more or less ceased to distract from truth-as-openness. Heidegger, though, does not discriminate: he automatically counts *any* sophisticated worldview-defining orthodoxy as 'metaphysics'. And so, his critique lapses into overkill.

Under the influence of Hölderlin (although ignoring Hölderlin's own enduring, if eccentric, Christian faith) Heidegger in his later writings starts to contrast 'the god of philosophy', meaning philosophy reduced to 'metaphysics', with 'the divine God', or 'gods' in the plural, as accessed in poetry. Borrowing Spinoza's Latin terminology, he designates the former as the '*causa sui*'. In his little 1957 essay on *Identity and Difference* (which he once called the most important thing he had published since *Being and Time*) he remarks that

> man can neither pray nor sacrifice to this god. Before the *causa sui*, man can neither fall to his knees in awe nor can he play music and dance before this god.

> The god-less thinking which must abandon the god of philosophy, god as *causa sui*, is thus perhaps closer to the divine God. Here this means only: god-less thinking is perhaps more open to Him than onto-theo-logic would like to admit.[16]

However, that reference to kneeling in prayer, and so forth, scarcely seems to be more than a poetic turn of phrase. It does not, for instance, mean that he had started attending church! There is in fact no indication of his ever wondering about the possibility, for him, of proper catholic belonging. He nowhere broaches the question of how such belonging might be reconciled with the vocation of a philosopher, as he had now come to understand it.

Heidegger's later thought is suffused with dreamy longing for a re-enchanted world. In his 1966 interview with journalists from *Der Spiegel* – which was held over until his death ten years later, and was intended by him as a sort of final testament, part apologia, part apocalyptic prophecy, addressed to the general public – he famously declares that, given the present plight of humanity, 'only a(nother) god' (*nur noch ein Gott*) 'can save us'.[17] A god, yes – but only *another* god: not the God of Abrahamic faith, in any of its more or less catholic traditions, Jewish, Christian or Muslim. Heidegger is indeed the great philosophic champion of those who profess to be 'spiritual but not (Abrahamically) religious'. And he is also a great symbol of the potential dangers intrinsic to the *rigidification* of such an attitude, even at its philosophically most articulate; the distorted sense of priorities to which it may contribute.

§

So, in the end, it is clear that Heidegger's notion of *alétheia* excludes both too much and too little. Too much: because of its identification with a rigidified anti-catholicism. And too little: as the events of 1933–4, in his life, and their aftermath, so dramatically demonstrate. When, as it were, Mephistopheles appeared to him, Heidegger agreed to sell his soul not because he had always been a latent Nazi, but just because he was, implicitly, so committed to the cause of solidarity among philosophers, or the intellectual elite more generally, as a class – and because, all of a sudden, such a fantastic opportunity seemed to have arrived, in the turmoil of revolution, for the advancement of that very cause.[18] Afterwards, once the Third Reich was history, he liked to present his motives for having let himself be put forward, under the auspices of the new Nazi regime, as a candidate for the Rectorship of Freiburg University very much as a matter of him wanting to do his bit for the defence of an endangered institution. But it was surely rather more than that; as the programmatic address he delivered on receiving the appointment makes clear.[19] What that somewhat bombastic speech, entitled 'The Self-Assertion of the German University', really seeks to express is the self-assertion of Heideggerian philosopher-poets, laying claim to a role as the leading guardians of their natural habitat. And, moreover, it is at the same time a bid so far as possible to elevate the self-definition of the now-ruling Nazi movement, in philosophic terms. Nazism, before 1933, differed from Marxism, for instance, in that it simply lacked any real philosophic substance. (Bäumler and Rosenberg scarcely count! Carl Schmitt joined the Party the same day as Heidegger himself, 1st May 1933.) The sheer innate stupidity of the movement meant that there was a void, crying out to be filled. And, in filling it, might not a brand-new super-authoritative class of phenomenologist philosophers be brought into alliance with the brand-new revolutionary government, in an attempt gradually to transform the ethos of German universities, and thereby also that of the whole *Volksgemeinschaft*, the whole nation-community? Might not the raging torrent of German nationalism be channelled, by this means, into a renewed sense of pride, above all, in Germany as 'a land of poets and thinkers' (*Land der Dichter und Denker*)? Might not Heidegger's own distinctive style of poeticized philosophy, perhaps, emerge as a dominant expression of such intellectual-elitist pride, for ages to come? This is what the voice of Mephistopheles whispered in his ear.[20]

Well, *we* enjoy the wisdom of hindsight, as Heidegger in 1933 did not. Disillusioned, he resigned from the Rectorate after just one year, in April 1934; although retaining his Nazi Party membership. Then, after his resignation, he engaged in a curious form of veiled dissident resistance: never, indeed, unequivocally disowning 'Nazism' as he had formerly idealized it; but attacking what he deplored as its prevailing actual vulgarization. This resistance came to expression in his lectures on Hölderlin, and on Nietzsche. In 1934-5 he delivered his first lecture series on the former; in 1936-7, his first lecture series on the latter. And he continued lecturing on both throughout the immediately following years. In these lectures he obliquely retracts the revolutionary enthusiasm of his early days as Rector. On the one hand, he confronts the Nazi version of German national sentiment with the very different, not at all racist or militaristic, but poignantly wistful German patriotism of Hölderlin. By implication, thus, opposing to the Führer – as symbolic embodiment of the nation at its noblest – the solitary mad poet! Whilst, on the other hand, the subtext of his Nietzsche lectures is precisely anguished self-critique. He is criticizing none other than the excessive impulse that had (as he now sees it) misled himself: pure megalothymotic pathos of shaken-ness – cut loose from all due restraint. So, Nietzsche comes to symbolize for him the inner potential for truth, in that regard, which actually existing Nazism betrays. In Nietzsche, he sees a sort of proxy for his own folly. As he criticizes Nietzsche's celebration of Dionysian 'will to power' – that uncanny mix of controlling ruthlessness and creativity which Nietzsche represents incarnate in the mythic figure of the *Übermensch* – Heidegger is recoiling from his own, all too historical, past fantasies of political glamour. And when he speaks (as he somewhat oddly does) of Nietzschean 'nihilism' colluding with the 'nihilistic' reality of runaway technology, he is I guess thinking, first and foremost, of the overlap between the two in the nihilism of the Nazi war machine: its (sub-)'Nietzschean' heroic ethos and its *Blitzkrieg* weaponry.[21]

In a little samizdat essay of 1976, entitled 'Heroes of our Time', Patočka, whose own moral authority as an anti-totalitarian dissident is unimpeachable, generously salutes Heidegger's 'spiritual resistance'.[22]

Whether he would still have wanted to do so had he known all that has subsequently emerged, or by muckrakers been alleged, about Heidegger's conduct during his time as Rector – or if he were aware, for instance, of the rarefied elements of antisemitism that have since been dug up in Heidegger's *Black Notebooks* – may perhaps be doubted. But it is clear that he was grateful for what he had learnt from Heidegger. And so, who knows?

§

What, though, of Heidegger's notorious inability, after the War, to incorporate the Holocaust into his increasingly melancholy grand narrative? In view of his stature as a thinker, and close proximity to the catastrophe, this inability surely does raise fundamental questions. For, at our historic distance, it seems clear that the Holocaust was, truly, a supreme climax of what might be termed 'negative revelation'. By which I mean: *an event of such extreme evil that – in the light of it – whatever most effectively, and unequivocally, contributes to combating any repetition of its essential elements is, just by virtue of that combativeness, to be accounted sacred.*

That the solidarity of the shaken is the highest of sacred ideals is, I would argue, negatively revealed to us today, above all, by the whole history of twentieth-century totalitarianism; but within that history, with unique power by the horror of the Holocaust. Heidegger, however, did not see this. – Why not? I think it was basically because he still remained so fixed in his commitment to solidarity among philosophers, as a rival ideal; which for him was always, really, the highest. Whilst the genocide was underway, any public expression of the solidarity of the shaken, in Nazi-ruled Europe, meant martyrdom. But the work of philosophy, by contrast, was *not* mortally endangered: Professor Heidegger was still allowed to teach.[23] There were still some students attending his lectures. A community of philosophers still survived; the fellowship within which he thrived. In the end, it seems to me, the problem is that he overvalued this superficial continuation of normality.[24] He was so preoccupied with philosophy that he had no eyes for even the most obtrusive other reality. And, therefore, his philosophy failed.

As noted above, Patočka, the philosopher who actually coined the phrase 'solidarity of the shaken', was much influenced by Heidegger. Patočka's eventual political activism was quite un-Heideggerian; the contrast could scarcely be starker. Yet, it emerges out of a phenomenologically cultivated pathos of shaken-ness which remains close kin to Heidegger's evolving equivalent. The Czech's personal acquaintance with Heidegger was rather slight. He spent the summer semester of 1933 at the University of Freiburg, whilst Heidegger was Rector; but did so primarily as a student of Husserl. Still, no student of Husserl could avoid engagement with the related, yet more or less rival thinking of Heidegger, as well. And Heidegger remains an abiding major presence in Patočka's writing thereafter. (In some of his later writings he simply refers to Heidegger as 'the Philosopher' *par excellence*.) Patočka's conception of the solidarity of the shaken thus presupposes – in the sense that it reworks – the Heideggerian polemical subordination of *orthotés* to *alétheia*; and the consequent Heideggerian bracketing of, or step back from, metaphysics. Not only was Patočka a close contemporary of Levinas and Løgstrup. His thinking was shaped by very much the same philosophical environment as theirs; a context in which Heidegger loomed large.

But then it was also shaped by the negative revelation intrinsic to the trauma of life under totalitarianism regarded from the point of view of one who, unlike Heidegger, never suffered the slightest temptation to collude. Patočka was a university lecturer who for most of his career was banned, by the totalitarian regime in his homeland, from lecturing in the university; and was subject to drastic censorship.[25] The idea of the solidarity of the shaken first emerges as an explicit ideal in the mind of a Neo-Heideggerian philosopher decisively exposed, by his life-experience as a perennial dissident, to the negative revelation which Heidegger never could fully recognize as such.

Strauss

By contrast, the moral that Heidegger himself drew from his misadventure of 1933–4 remained the one that he had arrived at in the course of his Nietzsche lectures. In effect, it is that, although philosophy springs from an intrinsically megalothymotic will-to-question, megalothymia must nevertheless never be allowed to degenerate into intemperate nihilism – either in the way it had done in the case of Nietzsche or in the quite different way it had in his own case. Rather, true philosophy also involves a restraining, contemplative will-not-to-will. For which he adopts the term, also prominent in the sermons of Meister Eckhart: '*Gelassenheit*'; in English, 'releasement'. By way of critical response to a mainstream culture governed by the all-conquering 'progressive' drive of rampant technology, philosophy must simply seek a space apart; a space where it may practice releasement – meditative rather than calculative, or controlling, thoughtfulness – so far as possible, released from any involvement in that mainstream.[26]

This is a highly abstract argument! Compare, however, *Leo Strauss*'s variant.

Strauss develops another, altogether more concrete thesis, regarding the essential vocation of philosophy in relation to politics, which (whilst indeed it still falls well short of Patočka's position) seems to me to be a natural amplification and revision of the later Heideggerian standpoint – even if it is not, perhaps, one that Heidegger would have wanted to acknowledge.[27]

Thus: Strauss is a political philosopher who is both a believer in the proper primacy of solidarity among true philosophers, as a class, and also one who values political realism. As a political realist, what he abhors above all else is the intrusion of extravagant revolutionary 'visions' into politics. His being a political philosopher sets him apart from Heidegger. Thus, in Strauss's own words:

> There is no room for political philosophy in Heidegger's work, and this may well be due to the fact that the room in question is occupied by gods or the gods … [28]

But then he goes on to contrast Heidegger with Marx and Nietzsche. All three entertain revolutionary visions. In Marx's thought, the vision intrudes into politics with disastrous effect. Nietzsche's revolutionary vision, by contrast, remains more poetic than immediately practical. However, it is the later Heidegger who 'severs the connection of the vision with politics' in the most decisive fashion; with a view to keeping the vision fixed in its proper place.

Strauss approves of this. He comments:

> One is inclined to say that Heidegger has learned the lesson of 1933 more thoroughly than any other man.[29]

And yet, he wants to translate what he sees as the vital element of truth in chastened Heideggerian reticence into the quite un-Heideggerian form of revitalized political philosophy.

Strauss's overall assessment of Heidegger is indeed a mixture of the highest praise, plus a degree of exasperation. At the end his life, he writes in a letter to Gershom Scholem:

> To me it is now clear after many years what is actually wrong in Heidegger: a phenomenal intellect inside a kitsch-soul.[30]

And yes, the 'kitsch-soul' is, without doubt, a key element in Heidegger's vulnerability to Mephistophelean temptation. But, in a 1956 lecture, Strauss also declares Heidegger to be 'the only great thinker of our time'.[31] In a lecture delivered in 1940, just three years after he had settled in the United States, he acknowledges that he himself is indebted, above all, to Nietzsche and Heidegger.[32] In 1959, he reminisces about the impression made upon him when attending some of Heidegger's early lectures in Freiburg, way back in 1922:

> Certain it is that no one questioned the premise of philosophy as radically as Heidegger. ... [B]y uprooting and not merely rejecting the tradition of philosophy, he made it possible for the first time after many centuries – one hesitates to say how many – to see the roots of the tradition as they are. ... Above all, his intention was to uproot Aristotle: he thus was compelled to disinter the roots, to bring them to light, to look at them with wonder.[33]

His correspondence, as well, bears repeated testimony to a lifelong subsequent wrestling with Heidegger's legacy.[34]

Strauss differs from Heidegger, not least, in his take on Plato. Not that he has any direct quarrel with Heidegger's critique of Plato's inclination to 'metaphysics'. He loves Plato; but not especially the Platonist 'doctrine of ideas'.[35] Rather, he focuses on another aspect of Plato's thought altogether. What interests Strauss is Plato's systematic political rendering, in the *Republic* and the *Laws*, of solidarity among philosophers – not only, first, into the impossible ideal dream of a city actually ruled by philosophers – but also (so Strauss argues) by implication, into general negotiative strategy for philosophers to pursue in other, less favourable contexts. And he celebrates what he sees as the whole tradition stemming from Plato's *esotericist* politics.

Thus, Strauss's reading of the *Republic* focuses notably on Socrates' evolving relationship with Thrasymachus, irritable sophist advocate of the most ruthless megalothymia. Much of Book One consists of dialogue between the two.[36] The given topic is the nature of '*diké*', 'justice'. Thrasymachus, resolutely hostile to any hint of plaintive moralizing, argues that true justice, in essence, equates to the interest of the stronger party, that is, the ruling classes as such. Socrates, playfully, objects: suppose the rulers fail to understand what is in their own true interest? Thrasymachus seeks to brush the objection aside. After all, even if the rulers are sometimes foolish, the basic principle of ruthless megalothymia still holds good: let those who can, truly *rule*! Nor does Socrates, in fact, challenge this. For he is interested, far rather, in the question, what it takes for a ruling class to be in the truest possible sense enlightened as to what is best for them; to acquire the corresponding technical skills; to unite as a class; to fulfil, thereby, their highest potential. And in the rest of the work, he will go on to try and spell out the ideal role of philosophy in the training of rulers. At the end of Book One, Thrasymachus abruptly departs; yet, not to be altogether forgotten. In Book Six his name crops up again, when Adeimantus challenges Socrates' counter-cultural contention that philosophy is more a proper concern for old men than for the young. You will find most people disagree, Adeimantus remarks, and especially Thrasymachus. To which Socrates replies:

> Now don't start a quarrel between me and Thrasymachus, when we've just become friends – not that we were ever really enemies.[37]

They were never enemies because for Socrates the spirit of true philosophy is just the most thoughtful and enlightened form of what Thrasymachus represents. Namely: the self-same ruthless megalothymia – only driven deeper.

Again, the prime example of such ruthlessness is Socrates' playful advocacy of the '*gennaion pseudos*', the 'Big Lie': a myth designed to inculcate a strict spirit of deference, amongst the rest of the population in his ideal city, for the philosophically trained upper caste; a fiction in which the upper caste itself (or at any rate its elders) perhaps only pretend to believe.[38] The main text of what is to be taught, as Plato has Socrates present it, runs as follows:

> You are, all of you in this land, brothers. But when God fashioned you, he added gold in the composition of those who are qualified to be Rulers (which is why their prestige is the greatest); he put silver in the Auxiliaries [their agents] and iron and bronze in the farmers and the rest. Now since you are all of the same stock, though children will commonly resemble their parents, occasionally a silver child will be born of golden parents, or a golden child of silver parents, and so on. Therefore, the first and most important of God's commandments to the Rulers is that they must exercise their function as Guardians with particular care in watching the mixture of metals in the characters of the children ... For they know that there is a prophecy that the State will be ruined when it has Guardians of silver or bronze.[39]

As a narrative, there is not much to this myth. However, in licensing the 'lie' here, Socrates is by implication licensing a whole genre of other such sacred deceptions – also where philosophers are not rulers – serving in the same general fashion to mask the intrinsic potential subversiveness of philosophic questioning, behind a soothing show of support, so far as possible, for public order, social stability, national security. – And God forbid that I should be too pious about such trickery! (I do not want to be Karl Popper-ish, in relation to Plato; or Shadia Drury-ish, in relation to Strauss …) But being a priest – a believer in catholicity – I for my part can by no means agree to the glorified conceit involved.

Strauss was no more a believer in catholicity than Heidegger was. He was, in the end, loyal to philosophy alone. However, in view of the dangers to which philosophy is by nature exposed, by virtue of its deeper-seated irreverence for established sacred norms, he is fundamentally supportive of any strategy helping disguise that irreverence from non-philosophers in power, who are liable to be infuriated by it; even whilst preserving the integrity of philosophy, for those few who are capable of appreciating it. In other words: he is ready to back any strategy for the transmission of true philosophy which, hopefully, avoids exposing the philosophers to anything resembling the fate of Socrates himself. Still, he thinks, it is essential that philosophy should remain true to its all-questioning vocation, even whilst finding ways to remain safe. In mediaeval Christendom, where orthodoxy was largely a matter of correctness in the formulation of metaphysical belief, philosophy was protected, insofar as it had become embedded within the study of those orthodox formulations. In the worlds of mediaeval Judaism and Islam, where the emphasis was so much more on sacred jurisprudence, this was less the case. However, Strauss argues,

> The precarious status of philosophy in Judaism as well as in Islam was not in every respect a misfortune for philosophy. The official recognition of philosophy in the Christian world made philosophy subject to ecclesiastical supervision. The precarious position of philosophy in the Islamic-Jewish world guaranteed its private character and therewith its inner freedom from supervision.[40]

In the period 1930–7 he devoted himself to the study of mediaeval Islamic traditions of philosophy, and their echo in the Jewish world. Of particular importance to him was the work of that great pioneer, Abú Naṣr Al-Fárábí (a contemporary of Niffarí, c. 872–950 / 951 CE). Amongst Fárábí's works is a short *Summary of Plato's Laws*. As a summary of the Platonic text, it is a curious, inaccurate and incomplete work; but Fárábí's preface is interesting. In it, he tells a little story: of how, once upon a time, there was a pious ascetic who had made an enemy of the ruler of his city. Needing to flee, but conscious that the guards at the city gates would have received instructions to arrest him, this pious ascetic put on gaudy clothes, and pretended to be drunk; clashing a pair of cymbals, he sang a raucous song; and so, presented himself to the guards. 'Halt, and identify yourself,' they ordered. 'I am that pious ascetic you are looking for,' he answered, with a foolish grin. The guards, supposing that this was mere mockery, let him through. That is how it is with Plato, Fárábí comments. In the end, he is always committed to the truth, but he is a trickster.

It is the same with Fárábí himself, Strauss suggests. He too is a trickster: concealing his true thoughts from those unfit to appreciate them; but, to his proper audience, signalling his procedure. In the first part of his three-part treatise *The Philosophy of Plato and Aristotle*, entitled *The Attainment of Happiness*, he indicates that his prime loyalty will always be to philosophy. And, as Strauss puts it, in the second part

> We may say that Fárábí's Plato … replaces the philosopher-king who rules openly in the virtuous city, by the secret kingship of the philosopher who, being "a perfect man" precisely because he is an "investigator", lives privately as a member of an imperfect society which he tries to humanize within the limits of the possible.[41]

In these circumstances, the true philosopher does not pick unnecessary fights, which he cannot win. But in Fárábí's own words,

> He should have sound conviction about the opinions of the religion in which he is reared, [and] hold fast to the virtuous acts in his religion … Furthermore, he should hold fast to the generally accepted virtues and not forsake the generally accepted noble acts.[42]

From this point of view, it does not matter which religion is involved. Nor does it matter how truly catholic its ethos may or may not be. Loyal in the first instance to philosophy alone, the philosopher will simply accommodate himself to whatever is the religious orthodoxy of his world. He will assent to that orthodoxy in just the same way that Socrates advocates assent to the Big Lie. Thus, Fárábí will dress himself in gaudy garments of Islamic ideology; he will feign drunkenness, clash his cymbals and sing his song; he will proclaim the Prophet Mohammed to have been the greatest of all philosopher-rulers. But what Strauss sees here is another Socrates; that is, another ultra-elitist friend of Thrasymachus. And Strauss agrees with Fárábí that this is in fact the proper philosophic way: effectively excluding not only religious fanaticism, but also any possibility of open-minded catholicity, those two quite opposite species of phenomena, both at once.

Fárábí's most radical follower within Islamic tradition was Averroes (Ibn Rushd, 1126–98). And, in the Jewish context, he was also much admired by Maimonides (Moses ben Maimon, 1135/8–1204). These thinkers address themselves to those for whom the authority of sacred Scripture is already well established. They then seek to vindicate the legitimacy of philosophy, as a method for probing the secrets which they consider to be hidden within Scripture. And they also prescribe, for philosophers, how to deal with apparent conflicts between the thinking-style of Scripture and that of Platonist / Aristotelian philosophy: the way that Scripture pictures God as being subject to fierce passion, whereas Platonist / Aristotelian philosophy associates divinity with perfect serenity; or the way that Scripture pictures eternal life in terms of physical resurrection, whereas Platonist / Aristotelian philosophy sees it essentially as a release of the soul from the body. For the philosophers: the pure truth. For the others: whatever will work for them, in order to produce moral, and political, results in harmony with those that the philosophers have arrived at through philosophy.[43]

§

Strauss not only affirms the general strategy of these mediaeval thinkers but also seeks to carry it forward, now in relation to the urgent challenge of secular modernity. A key text in this regard is his 1953 book *Natural Right and History*; largely based on a series of lectures delivered at the University of Chicago in 1949. And it is there that he develops perhaps his most direct riposte to Heidegger.[44] Not that Heidegger is anywhere referred to by name in *Natural Right and History*. But the book begins by evoking a threat, which Strauss refers to as the threat of 'historicism':

> Historicism emerged in the nineteenth century under the protection of the belief that knowledge, or at least divination, of the eternal is possible. But it gradually undermined the belief which had sheltered it in its infancy. It suddenly appeared within our lifetime in its mature form.[45]

The 'infancy' of 'historicism' appears to be identifiable with the work of Hegel.[46] But its 'mature form' is surely that which Heidegger gives it.[47] Never mind that 'historicism' is not a positive term in Heidegger's own lexicon. What Strauss has in mind is presumably Heidegger's meditation on 'authentic historicity' in *Being and Time*.

He calls Heidegger's position 'radical historicism' or 'existentialist historicism'. At one level, 'historicism' in general is just the perennial negativity of philosophy towards all unquestioned norms, as such; only, now amplified by the new historically informed self-awareness made possible by the advances of modern scholarship. Seeing how contingent norms are upon historical circumstance helps call them in question. The Heideggerian critique of 'metaphysics', however, radicalizes this, inasmuch as it dissolves any legitimation of sacred norms, whatsoever, grounded in the supposed truth-as-correctness of dogma relating to eternal nature, or divine revelation. No other basis for the sacred survives the Heideggerian 'radical historicist' treatment except pure pathos of shaken-ness, maximum exposure to *alétheia*. 'Authentic historicity' is, then, the pathos of shaken-ness analysed in *Being and Time: Dasein*'s shaken 'Being-towards-death', issuing in comprehensive irreverence towards all that *das Man*, the unshaken non-philosophic world, reveres as sacred. It is the philosopher's sense of 'fate', or personal destiny; as a singular calling, to be fulfilled in principled defiance of the conformist world.[48] Again, deep down Strauss absolutely shares the megalothymia of this attitude. But, he remarks, 'historicism culminated in nihilism'.[49] All good philosophy, insofar as it breaks free from ideology, tears down norms; and the best, most of all. But good philosophy,

Strauss thinks, at the same time also rebuilds. The trouble with 'radical historicism' is just its failure in that latter regard.

For Strauss, the basis on which good philosophy is to rebuild must be a shrewd solidarity among philosophers. Heidegger's failure is that he is not shrewd enough. Because the philosopher-class, in actuality, lacks the necessary strength, on its own, to seize and retain power as in the fantasy-world of the *Republic*, everything in the end comes down to a shrewd choice of allies, a shrewd negotiation of alliances.[50] So, what does the philosopher-class, as such, need in political terms? Above all, surely, it needs two things:

(a) a safe environment, for its educational institutions to put down roots and establish themselves, as transmitters of the tradition; and
(b) a maximum possible freedom from censorship within those institutions, to keep the tradition truly creative and adventurous.

And what allies are likely to be most helpful in this regard? 'According to the classics,' as Strauss puts it – which is his way of saying, 'from the point of view that (*mutatis mutandis*) I, Leo Strauss, am advocating' – the small class of true philosophers basically needs to seal a strategic alliance with a much larger ruling class of 'gentlemen'. Thus:

> The gentleman is not identical with the wise man [i. e. the philosopher]. He is the political reflection, or imitation, of the wise man. Gentlemen have this in common with the wise man, that they "look down" on many things that are highly esteemed by the vulgar or that they are experienced in things noble and beautiful. They differ from the wise because they have a noble contempt for precision, because they refuse to take cognizance of certain aspects of life [i. e. realities tending to call their own instinctive prejudices into question], and because, in order to live as gentlemen, they must be well off.[51]

On the other hand, they will not generally be inheritors of immense wealth: philosophy should be wary of associating itself with people the spectacular luxury of whose lives is liable to generate destabilizing envy and resentment. But rather, to be still more specific: 'according to the classics', the ideal gentleman

> will be an urban patrician who derives his income from agriculture. The best regime will then be a republic in which the landed gentry, which is at the same time the urban patriciate, well-bred and public spirited, obeying the laws and completing them, ruling and being ruled in turn, predominates and gives society its character.[52]

Or, translating this into the very different terms of class-structure in an industrial / post-industrial society: the ideal allies of philosophy will surely be the professional bourgeoisie. It is not just that that is the class from which most philosophers are likely to be recruited. As Strauss remarks:

> We need not take issue with the contention that, in studying a political doctrine, we must consider ... the class bias of its originator. It suffices to demand that the class to which the thinker in question belongs be correctly identified. In the common view the fact is overlooked that there is a class interest of the philosophers qua philosophers.[53]

And the 'class interest of philosophers qua philosophers', today, essentially calls for a rapprochement to the more conservative, and liberal, elements in the professional bourgeoisie: indulging their natural pieties, therefore – both religious and secular – just as Fárábí advocates indulging the piety of the Muslim gentry, in his world.

As Strauss sees it, Heidegger the 'radical historicist' went off the rails in 1933 for the simple reason that he had not properly considered such matters beforehand. Nobody could be less properly conservative than the Nazis; nobody could be less properly liberal; nor was their support, in the first instance, drawn from the professional bourgeoisie. To say the very least, they were not 'gentlemen'! Nor did Heidegger really remedy matters afterwards, inasmuch as his later thought is 'nihilistic', in the sense of a sheer tearing down of norms which leaves no basis for rebuilding. It provides no such basis, since it is a form of all-too-pure philosophy, which has finally given up on sealing any strategic alliances at all.

§

My own fundamental objection, however, is to what Strauss and Heidegger continue to have in common.

So, once again, compare the two solidarity-principles: solidarity of the shaken and solidarity among philosophers as such. All genuine philosophers, as distinct from mere ideologists, are by definition amongst the 'shaken'. But the solidarity of the shaken is an altogether broader category than solidarity among philosophers. For, unlike solidarity among philosophers, the solidarity of the shaken does not presuppose any particular degree of argumentative articulacy. Pure solidarity among philosophers is solidarity restricted exclusively to the, in argumentative terms, most articulate among those who are 'shaken' by the imperatives of perfect truth-as-openness. But, as a result, it is a form of solidarity with split loyalties. *One criterion for mutual loyalty here: shared dedication to truth-as-openness. Another criterion: shared expertise in the exploration and articulation of philosophic truth-as-correctness.*

And the trouble is that, *when it comes to evaluation of catholicity*, these two criteria become conflicting energies. They tend to go to war with each other. For true catholicity brings shaken philosophers into systematic communion with shaken non-philosophers, as equals in their primordial, intuitive, shared sense of what is sacred, their shared prayerful approach to the sacred. It rightly over-rules exclusive solidarity among philosophers, in the sense of those most expert in argument about first principles, just as it also over-rules any other exclusive solidarity – based on social class, ethnic identity, age, gender, sexuality – within the catholic community. But philosophic impatience is just an excessive upsurge of megalothymia, refusing to be over-ruled in this way.

(To my mind, the Blessed Virgin Mary is the proper patron saint of catholic theology, as such, precisely by virtue of her presumable illiteracy. For, after all, the ability to pray is not an intellectual gift.)

Against both Heidegger and Strauss, philosophy with a proper dedication to truth-as-openness will want to affirm the ideal of catholicity; just as by the same token it also affirms trans-confessional solidarity between members of different catholic communities. To my mind, this is the crucial point. There is a fundamental ambiguity about Heidegger's bracketing of 'God' in *Being and Time*. It not only signals a withdrawal from traditional, idolatrously overloaded, inquisitorial debate regarding onto-theological truth-as-correctness. But it also signifies his withdrawal from any thought of participation in what are after all – at their not at all inquisitorial best – the chief actual nursemaids of catholicity in Western civilization, namely, the various institutions of Abrahamic religion. The Heideggerian 'step back' from 'metaphysics' is, at the same time, a side-step; indeed, an evasive soft shoe shuffle, to escape the proper challenge of catholicity. And his post-'metaphysical' invocation of 'the gods', in his later writings, has the same basic function. Whilst, as for Strauss: he may advocate indulging the religious prejudices of the conservative 'gentry'. But why is the Straussian philosopher obliged to be a trickster? It comes of his just not seeing the quite different truth-potential of *real* catholicity, in itself. That is to say, its ideal character as a tributary, flowing directly into the solidarity of the shaken.

Adorno

Let me stress at this point that I am interested, here, in Heidegger and Strauss as two ultra-sophisticated cases of what, *in itself*, most often appears in much cruder forms. 'Philosophic impatience', in the basic sense of an intellectual deficit in catholicity, is by no means confined to *their* learned admirers. They are, moreover, both of them politically right-wing thinkers. But ultra-sophisticated philosophic impatience may just as well appear in left-wing form.

To take just one example: their contemporary *Theodor Adorno* (1903–69) is a classic exponent of left-wing philosophic impatience. I have chosen to begin my argument in this chapter by discussing Heidegger, basically because of the relationship of Heidegger's thought to Patočka's. But I could in fact almost equally well have begun by discussing Adorno.

Indeed, the contrast between Adorno and Strauss is, I think, especially revealing: in that, whereas Strauss represents disguised philosophic impatience at its *frankest* – frankly acknowledging the need he sees for the class of true philosophers to be, on occasion, strategically hypocritical, and self-aware about it – Adorno, on the contrary, may be said to represent philosophic impatience, likewise hypocritically disguised, but also in the most remarkable state of no doubt *perfectly sincere denial*, as to its hypocrisy! Here, philosophic impatience is in denial, by virtue of the Marxist self-presentation of the philosopher-class's power-hungry corporate egoism: as selfless revolutionary service rendered to quite another class, the oppressed proletariat. So, to put it crudely, Adorno is a bourgeois philosopher who – thanks not least to his immersion in avant-garde music (about which he wrote at great length) and truly highbrow literature – feels, in all sincerity, that urgent revolutionary contempt for the established order which, he thinks, the proletarian masses, in principle, *ought* to feel; but which all too often they do not, due now not only to old-time anaesthetic religion, but also to the new-fangled 'opium of the people' served up by the secular 'culture industry'. Adorno's writing is witty, relentlessly epigrammatic, full of sarcasm. It ranges far and wide, often tangled in expression and seemingly disordered.[54] However, what above all holds his thought together, as a whole, is just its predominant underlying tone of moral contempt: in the first instance, entirely justified contempt for the world that generated Auschwitz; but also, then – spilling over from that – Marxist-inflected, exhilarating contempt for a wide range of others.

Adorno does not actually engage with Strauss. He is, on the other hand, full of particular contempt for Heidegger.[55] And yet, observe how much he nevertheless still does have in common, deep down, with the later, trans-political Heidegger, precisely as another devotee of the most demanding truth-as-openness, whose thought however remains, as I would see it, fundamentally distorted by philosophic impatience. As Martin Jay remarks, 'What [Adorno] once complained about in Heidegger could ... be extended to him as well: "He lays around himself the taboo that any understanding of him would simultaneously be falsification".'[56] To be sure, being-misunderstood is inevitable when one is engaged in the sort of ultra-ambitious enterprise that both these two thinkers were undertaking. But *catholicity* demands a simple, Eckhartian shrug of the shoulders, by way of response. Adorno was vain in quite a different philosophic style from Heidegger. Nevertheless, he was scarcely any humbler.

His thought originates as an offshoot from the Western Marxist tradition, stemming from the work of György Lukács and Karl Korsch, in the immediate aftermath of the First World War. The philosophic adherents of this tradition, and their artist-comrades, were none of them comfortable with the crudities, and lies, of Stalinist propaganda-ideology. Some – Lukács above all, but also Ernst Bloch and Bertolt Brecht – nevertheless steered quite close to positive collusion with it. Adorno did not. Critique of the Soviet Union is not a prominent theme of his writing. Yet his major work, *Negative Dialectics*, does begin with the striking statement:

> Philosophy, which once seemed obsolete, lives on because the moment to realize it was missed. The summary judgment that it had merely interpreted the world, that resignation in the face of reality had crippled it in itself, becomes a defeatism of reason after the attempt to change the world miscarried ...[57]

The question indeed arises to what extent Adorno's thought remains meaningfully Marxist at all in the light of this disillusion. Very little, of substance, seems to me to remain of his Marxism, in practice, *apart from* (a) his unacknowledged concern (as I have said) to conceal the actual class-interests driving his thought, and (b) the traditional Marxist banally prejudicial rejection of catholic religious faith.

The title of *Negative Dialectics* bespeaks a commitment to infinitely restless, shaken thought. However, Adorno shows no interest in any negative-dialectical confrontation with the quite *un-shaken* 'no' which is traditional Marxism's response to the challenge of a shaken catholicity. Compare Heidegger. 'Being', for Heidegger, is surely nothing other than an elusive residue left behind by 'negative dialectics', in Adorno's sense. A sacred residue: a residual source of wonder – albeit with all attendant catholicity cut away. By contrast to Heidegger however, Adorno, nihilistically, turns his back on even that last, attenuated element of reverence. His friend Ernst Bloch, for his part, wrote a vast work entitled *The Principle of Hope*.[58] This 'principle' comprises all forms of energized isothymia. In Bloch's view, it achieves ultimate fulfilment in Marxist form; but, amongst other things, also provides a basis for sustained, critical but nevertheless potentially friendly, engagement with Christianity, inasmuch as Christian tradition is also suffused with isothymotic hope. Adorno's 'negative dialectics', though, provides no such basis for engagement. There is no 'principle of hope' here; no grand narrative round which to rally effective, cosmopolitan solidarity, extending beyond the confines of academia. Any such possibility, it seems, has been dogmatically negated, *a priori*. But what good does that do, besides the pleasure it, perhaps, gives the 'negative dialectician', as a vindication of his, or her, impatient intellectual contempt for their neighbours?

Arendt

One may, I think, distinguish two aspects to a proper critique of philosophic impatience. On the one hand, there is a primarily isothymotic aspect, a bid to reconcile shaken philosophy with the principle of catholicity. This will be the ongoing theme of the following chapter. On the other hand, there is also another, primarily megalothymotic aspect; which is represented, above all, by *Hannah Arendt* (1906–75).

A thinker of the same generation as Patočka, Strauss, Levinas and Løgstrup, and like them also emergent from the Heideggerian milieu, Arendt was, by contrast to Patočka in particular – alongside whom she stands – altogether freer, by virtue of having made her escape and being based in the United States, openly to investigate the element of negative revelation in the nightmare-experience of twentieth-century totalitarianism.

Arendt has indeed been much criticized, by thinkers both of the left and of the right, for her abiding association with Heidegger.[59] Prominent among those critics, for example, is that notable Straussian, Thomas Pangle.[60] Nevertheless, in one sense at least, Arendt's critique of Heidegger is really far more radical than Strauss's. For, like Patočka, she too breaks decisively free from 'philosophic politics'.

Her ultimate view of Heidegger's political blunders may perhaps be criticized for being over-indulgent; but this is because she considers his error, not so much as his alone, but rather as reflecting a fundamental weakness endemic to the very discipline of philosophy. To some extent or other in all of its traditional forms, she argues, philosophy over-privileges the sort of insight only possible to those who enjoy contemplative quiet. It therefore tends, by its very nature, to under-value the virtue of the thoughtful citizen-activist. Yet, life under totalitarianism is precisely the most vivid possible negative revelation of the need for this latter species of virtue. The philosopher, under totalitarian rule, may retreat; or may even, in hope of patronage, collude. By contrast, the thoughtful citizen-activist is *obliged* to resist. Heidegger's misadventure, as Arendt sees it, is a tragedy of philosophical innocence, way out of its depth; but, as such, also a demonstration of the limits constraining even the most thoughtful *mere philosophy*.

In effect, Arendt sublates the systematic Heideggerian disentangling of *alétheia* from *orthotés*, transferring it to the quite un-Heideggerian context of the contrast between contemplative philosophy and thoughtful citizen-activism. Traditional political philosophy, from Plato onwards, has seen itself essentially as a matter of contemplative thinkers prescribing for rulers or would-be rulers; working towards an ideal programme for good rule. That is to say: a programme for implementing the dictates of ultimate metaphysical and moral *orthotés* / truth-as-correctness. What Arendt, however, is engaged in, as a political thinker, is first and foremost a celebratory discussion of thoughtful citizen-activism. Fresh initiatives from below: public testimony to *alétheia* / truth-as-openness. Her critics have charged her with what is typically called 'decisionism': meaning that she leaves too much scope for arbitrary decision-making by rulers, does not properly hem them in with specific criteria for their action. It seems to me, however, that the criticism misses the point. For it judges her as if she were still a political philosopher in the traditional sense; or at any rate ought to be. But, again like Patočka, she is attempting something much bolder: she too is, to all intents and purposes, a thinker of the solidarity of the shaken. She steps back from traditional political philosophy. In short: her concern is much less with what is expedient for rulers, than with what ought to be, in political terms, held sacred.

Movements embodying the solidarity of the shaken, unlike political parties, will not aspire to rule; they will not have whole programmes for government. Their ambition will simply be to try and change the moral context with which government has to reckon. As Patočka remarks, at most they will speak 'like Socrates' *daimonion*, in warnings and prohibitions' … [61]

§

The Origins of Totalitarianism, which Arendt wrote in the immediate aftermath of the Second World War, is an urgent and gripping book.[62] As Samantha Powers comments, it 'might have been better titled "The Originality of Totalitarianism"'; a less euphonious title, but a more accurate one.[63] For it is not so much an attempt to explain the causes of twentieth-century totalitarianism, but rather to show the scope and context of all that is new about it.

In Parts One and Two Arendt is concerned with the originality of Nazi totalitarianism in particular, as its antisemitic ideology outstripped all precedent. Accordingly, she traces the evolution of organized secular antisemitism over the nineteenth century, leading to the formation of the first populist anti-Semitic political parties, in Germany, Austria and France, from the 1870s and 1880s onward; also, the incorporation of antisemitism into more generalized racialist doctrine, as pioneered by Gobineau and Chamberlain; and its developing relationship with ideologies of imperialism. That is to say: all that directly anticipated the eventual explosion of the Nazi phenomenon. Then, in Part Three, she goes on to discuss the organizational originality of both the Nazi and the Stalinist forms of totalitarianism, as twin phenomena, both equally characterized by

- their conversion of the state into a terrorist enterprise, with a plethora of concentration camps for the isolation of dissent;
- the limitless mendacity of their propaganda, and the complete secretiveness in each case framing the messianic leader's cult of personality;
- the onion structure, layer enclosing layer, of their bureaucracy, and their systematic concealment of actual power behind a multiplicity of front-organizations;
- their deliberate promotion of chaotic internecine power struggles, crisis after crisis, so as to prevent any build-up of a stable administrative hierarchy capable of resisting the arbitrary will of the leadership;
- their proneness to spectacular self-harming irrationality: for instance, rendering large parts of the economy dependant on the inefficient slave labour of half-starved prisoners; or rooting out competent officials and military officers as 'traitors' whilst promoting the incompetent on grounds of mere ideological loyalty; or, in the Stalinist case, brutally collectivizing agriculture, at the cost of vast famine.
- their insane, murderous targeting of whole population categories at a time, quite regardless of anyone's actual 'guilt' or 'innocence', as an individual.

Granted, twentieth-century totalitarianism was not entirely original. It may well be argued that Jacobin France in 1793–4 was already totalitarian, in essence. But, for the first time, during the twentieth century totalitarianism appeared in multiple guises, and over sustained periods. The element of potential negative revelation here is latent in the monstrous originality of that spectacle, as the kernel in a nut.

Arendt cracks the nut open, inasmuch as she pursues, with unrivalled determination, the basic question: How had such a thing become possible? Or, more precisely: *What was lacking, in the various host cultures, by way of a spiritual immune system, that should have guarded against it?* And to this, one might say, she has an essentially twofold answer. One part of her answer is very well developed, above all in *The Human Condition* (1958) and *On Revolution* (1963). The other part is just lightly sketched, in the essay 'What Is Authority?' (1961).

§

An initial formulation of the first answer: totalitarianism was rendered possible by the lack of a well-rooted *ethos of isonomy*.

The Greek term here is *isonomía*; a compound of *ísos* ('equal') and *nómos* ('custom', 'law'). It is sometimes translated 'equality of rights' or 'equality before the law'. But this is to miss the crucial, concomitant element of *invitation* in the original concept.

Thus, isonomy may be defined as the political ideal of a society with procedures the prime purpose of which is to try and maximize the participation of all its recognized members, as equal partners, in public debate and decision-making. Or, in other words: precisely, a culture to the greatest possible extent *encouraging* free-spirited citizen-activism.

Other Greek terms for types of political environment focus on the business of ruling; in the sense of the right to issue governmental orders, and enforce them. So, the classic terms 'monarchy' and 'oligarchy' derive from the root noun *arché*, 'rule', as does Dionysius's later coinage 'hierarchy'. 'Aristocracy' and 'democracy' derive from the root noun *krátos*, 'power'; which is then taken up into Polybius's term 'ochlocracy' (second century BCE); Josephus's term 'theocracy' (first century CE); and such modern coinages as 'plutocracy', 'bureaucracy', 'kleptocracy' and 'meritocracy'.[64] 'Isonomy', however, differs from all of these, in that it immediately shifts attention – away from the business of ruling – to ideal processes of solidarity-building, instead.

Herodotus tells of a debate among the seven original conspirators at the outset of the rebellion in the Achaemenid Empire that was eventually, in 522 BCE, to establish Darius 1 on the throne.[65] What are they fighting for? Three views are canvassed. In the end, Darius prevails, arguing for a continuation of the previous monarchical system – but not before Megabyzus has argued for oligarchy, and Otanes for isonomy. Arendt remarks:

> The [Athenian] *polis* was supposed to be an isonomy, not a democracy. The word 'democracy', expressing even then majority rule, the rule of the many, was originally coined by those who were opposed to isonomy and who meant to say: What you say is 'no-rule' is in fact only another kind of rulership; it is the worst form of government, rule by the demos [the mob].[66]

Indeed, this is just what Megabyzus, in Herodotus's tale, argues, against Otanes. And one finds a similar mistrust of ruthless demagogues, manipulatively representing themselves as upholders of isonomy, in Thucydides for instance.[67] Not that Megabyzus attacks Otanes personally, as being such a demagogue. On the contrary, Otanes is clearly meant to represent the spirit of isonomy in the truest sense. So, at the end of the debate, when it remains to be decided which of the seven should be the prospective monarch, he straight away withdraws his own candidacy, declaring: 'I want neither to rule nor to be ruled.'

Arendt, then, is another advocate of isonomy in the truest sense. Her discussion of the actual term itself in *On Revolution* is quite brief; and in *The Human Condition* is confined to a single footnote on Otanes.[68] Yet, it nevertheless remains a pervasive ideal underlying the argument of both works. In *The Human Condition* her narrative starting point is the political culture of ancient Athens. The classical school of Platonism turned against Athenian isonomy in reaction to the fate of Socrates. But was not the thought of Socrates itself a product of the intellectual ferment which that isonomy facilitated? In any case, the alleged crime for which he was in the end condemned to death, of blaspheming against the city's gods, would have been a grave offence under any regime. Platonism, rejecting the citizen-activist ethos of isonomy, decisively elevates the *vita contemplativa* over the *vita activa* in any form. And Strauss, for instance, rejuvenates the original prejudice of philosophy, in this regard, as a systematic basis for 'philosophic politics'. Arendt, however, seeks to reaffirm the *thymos* of isonomy at its un-demagogic best, as representing an altogether more radical opposite to totalitarianism. Of course, the ethos of the Athenian *polis* as a whole was anything but *catholic*, inasmuch as the isonomous activism of the citizens rested on a complete exclusion, from public affairs, of the slaves and of the women. Like the practice of philosophy, it depended on the freedom from drudgery of the privileged few. But, in defending such activism against the traditionally hostile prejudice of philosophy, Arendt's point is just that it constitutes another species of opening towards the highest truth, complementary to that of philosophy; and in the light of twentieth-century negative revelation, moreover, a yet more urgently needed one.

She constructs a grand-narrative account of how that opening has, as she sees it, over the centuries been mis-remembered, its proper significance forgotten. Christianity, for her, plays a major role in this forgetfulness. For isonomy, after all, expresses the most intense love of the world, that is, the world of the *res publica*, public affairs.[69] But, as the Church Father Tertullian put it, 'No matter is more alien to us [Christians] than what matters publicly'![70] Arendt's doctoral dissertation, originally completed in 1929, was on *Love and Saint Augustine*.[71] It discusses in particular Augustine's distinction between the two opposing forms of *appetitus* (craving desire): *caritas*, love focused on eternity, and *cupiditas*, love focused on the world. As a Christian, Augustine is not, as the Stoics or Epicureans are, against all intensity of *appetitus* as such; it just depends which form it takes. However, from the later Arendtian point of view, his conception of *cupiditas* is all too undiscriminating. Inasmuch as its political essence appears in the *City of God* as 'lust for domination', the very different possibility of *isonomous* this-worldliness is simply occluded in his thought; as in classical Christian theology as a whole.[72] And *caritas*, love of God flowing out to become charitable love of neighbour, is consequently reduced to the basic business of sustaining life – rather than sustaining the world, as a potential arena for isonomy. In *The Human Condition* she cites Augustine's remark that 'even robbers have between them what they call charity'; and remarks:

> This surprising illustration of the Christian political principle is in fact very well chosen, because the bond of charity between people, while it is incapable of founding a political realm of its own, is quite adequate to the main Christian principle of worldlessness and is admirably fit to carry a group of essentially worldless people through the world, a group of saints or a group of criminals, provided only it is understood that the world itself is doomed and that every activity in it is undertaken with the proviso *quamdiu mundus durat* ("as long as the world lasts"). The unpolitical, non-public [i. e. non-isonomous] character of the Christian community was early defined in the demand that it should form a *corpus*, a "body," whose members were to be related to each other like brothers of the same family. The structure of communal life was modelled on the relationships between the members of a family because these were known to be non-political.[73]

On the one hand, Christian theology inherits the Platonist prejudice exalting the *vita contemplativa* over the *vita activa* generally; on the other hand, it further intensifies that prejudice with an injection of eschatological urgency.

Eventually, as Arendt tells the tale, from the Enlightenment onwards there begin to appear a whole succession of metaphysical and moral challenges to the hitherto prevailing hegemony of Platonist prejudice – yet still no vindication of isonomy. Thus, the argument of *The Human Condition* is built around a threefold conceptual sub-division of the *vita activa*: between

- 'action', in the sense of a more or less isonomous engagement in public affairs;
- 'work', in the sense of what a skilled maker of things does, or a scientist making experiments; and
- 'labour', in the sense of relatively unskilled productivity.

To these three elementary categories there further correspond, in her thinking, three human types. Action, as distinct from work or labour, generates the citizen-activist. Work, as distinct from action or labour, generates *homo faber*. Labour, as distinct from action or work, generates the *animal laborans*. And each of these types is by nature predisposed to a different sense of what is sacred.

The initial Enlightenment rehabilitation of the *vita activa*, in the Arendtian story, is the work of thinkers representing the worldview of *homo faber*. Galileo is a key symbolic figure here; as are his younger contemporaries and admirers, Descartes and Hobbes, both seeking to revolutionize philosophy as Galileo had revolutionized science. It is Hobbes, above all, who represents the revolutionary moment of this turning point in relation to political theory. So it is that he presents his argument as a craftsman's blueprint, for the fabrication of a *golem*-Leviathan:

> Nature (the art whereby God hath made and governes the world) is by the art of man, as in many other things, so in this also imitated, that it can make an Artificial Animal. For seeing life is but a motion of Limbs, the beginning whereof is in some principall part within; why may we not say, that all Automata (Engines that move themselves by springs and wheeles as doth a watch) have an artificial life?

That he feels the need to justify his key metaphor in this way indicates his sense of the daring intellectual breakthrough it represents. But it encapsulates the natural worldview of *homo faber* perfectly.

> For what is the Heart, but a Spring; and the Nerves, but so many Strings; and the Joynts, but so many Wheeles, giving motion to the whole Body, such as was intended by the Artificer? Art goes yet further, imitating that Rationall and most excellent worke of Nature, Man. For by Art is created that great LEVIATHAN called a COMMON-WEALTH, or STATE, (in latine CIVITAS) which is but an Artificial Man; though of greater stature and strength than the Naturall, for whose protection and defence it was intended.[74]

For *homo faber*, the prime criteria for judging the success or failure of a political regime are: how durable and comfortably adaptable its governmental architecture is; how much like clockwork, its processes; how well constructed it is, precisely, to guarantee 'protection and defence', in the sense of stability, to the society in its charge. Hobbes sets out in systematic fashion to sacralize these criteria, invoking, for that purpose, the same deist 'God' as Descartes also believed in, the 'God' of *homo faber*.

Yet then (so the story proceeds) the Industrial Revolution progressively ushers in quite another sort of political thinking, now responding far rather to the aspirations of the *animal laborans*. What the *animal laborans*, as such, wants is not so much the stability so prized by *homo faber*, but far rather – on the contrary – social fluidity, in the form of opportunities to escape the hardships into which one was born. The best regime, from this point of view, is that which is most effective in delivering affluence, and never mind if the pursuit of affluence involves a bit of turbulence, or even a whole lot of turbulence, along the way. There is no scope for isonomy in the political worldview of the *animal laborans*. If he, or she, has any sacralized political passion, it is for that very different thing, liberal democracy – with its expensive propaganda-saturated elections, in which 'it's the economy, stupid,' that matters – or else, perhaps, the altogether more dangerous dream of violent socialist revolution.

Immediately following the publication in 1951 of *The Origins of Totalitarianism*, where she had analysed the nineteenth-century antecedents of Nazism, but not those of Stalinism, Arendt embarked on a project to remedy that imbalance, with a study of 'Totalitarian Elements in Marxism'. It was never completed, because she became side-tracked instead into writing *The Human Condition*. Nevertheless, the tragic figure of Marx, as the great revolutionary champion of the *animal laborans*, still haunts the latter work.[75]

§

To the extent that the attitudes of the *animal laborans* prevail, or the lingering prejudices of *homo faber*, there can be no proper recognition of the truth-claims of isonomy. Still, the hegemony of these two types is by no means absolute. And in *On Revolution* Arendt is, not least, searching for examples of recrudescent isonomous thought and practice in the post-Enlightenment world. She thinks to find it above all in the 'lost treasure of the revolutionary tradition', namely, the spontaneous efflorescence of insurgent grassroots councils, debating clubs, and campaigning federations in the early stages of the great revolutions, or attempted revolutions, up to the time she was writing. So, she cites the New England townships at the time of the American War of Independence; the Paris Commune, and its forty-eight local Sections, from 1789 to 1793, as well as the *sociétés révolutionaires* of those years, all over France; the Paris Commune of 1871; the *soviets*, or workers' councils, that sprang up in 1905, and then again in 1917; the similar *Räte*, centred in Berlin and Munich, in 1918–19; and the workers' councils of the Hungarian Revolution in 1956.

Arendt applauds Thomas Jefferson, in particular, for his retrospective appreciation of this 'lost treasure'; first of all, in a series of letters written in 1816. Seven years after his retirement from the Presidency of the United States, Jefferson thus comes to advocate a new constitutional order, designed to facilitate maximum popular participation in politics, with the creation of little local 'ward republics'. She quotes him, near the end of his life: 'As Cato concluded every speech with the words, *Carthago delenda est*, so do I every opinion, with the injunction, "divide the counties into wards."'[76]

But in vain! The insight was too radical to gain any widespread acceptance in Jefferson's day. And it was also largely alien to the 'professional revolutionists' of the later nineteenth century, and the twentieth.[77] Marx, in 1871, may briefly have been excited by the element of isonomy in the revolutionary Paris Commune; but only as a transitional phenomenon, on the way to that very different ideal, the 'dictatorship of the proletariat'. Lenin, likewise, responded to the events of 1905 by hailing 'the revolutionary creativity of the people' as manifested in the *soviets*; and went on to launch the October Revolution in 1917 with the slogan: 'All power to the *soviets*!' Yet, he for his part still valued the *soviets* only as a field of operations for the Bolshevik Party, not as forms of organization possessing an intrinsic value of their own. And when, in 1921, the Kronstadt mutineers sought to uphold the *soviet* ethos *against* the party dictatorship, he was ruthless in suppressing the rebellion.[78] Political parties, as agencies essentially dedicated to the pursuit of governmental power, tend by their very nature to be mistrustful of isonomy; and well-disciplined revolutionary parties, most of all.

§

Meanwhile, Arendt's quite different second answer to the question, how – in the most fundamental terms – totalitarianism was possible appears at the beginning of her essay, 'What Is Authority?' (already referred to in Chapter 3) where she writes:

> The development of a new totalitarian form of government ... took place against a background of more or less general, more or less dramatic breakdown of all traditional authorities. Nowhere was this breakdown the direct result of the [totalitarian] regimes or movements themselves; it rather seemed as though totalitarianism, in the form of movements as well as of regimes, was best fitted to take advantage of a general political and social atmosphere in which ... the government's authority was no longer recognized.[79]

The predominant *modus operandi* of totalitarianism, after all, is violence. But again, by definition, insofar as genuine authority still prevails, social order subsists without violence. And, conversely, any use of violence necessarily tends to diminish genuine authority.

Totalitarianism is, therefore, just as antipathetic to genuine authority as it is to the sort of power generated by isonomy.

With a grand gesture, however, Arendt announces *the downfall of authority* in general: 'Authority,' she declares, 'has vanished from the modern world.'[80] I am not sure about this. The last time I looked, there were still at any rate some children who seemed to respect the authority of their parents; still at any rate some students who seemed to respect the authority of their teachers; still at any rate some sick people who seemed to respect the authority of medical experts. In fact, though, Arendt makes clear that she is speaking, not about 'authority in general', but about 'a very specific form which had been valid throughout the Western world over a long period of time'.[81] She is speaking about *sacred* authority; and, moreover about sacred authority that is valued above all for its *services to 'law and order'*.[82]

There is, though, another type of sacred authority, with a much closer relationship of complementarity to the ethos of isonomy, which unfortunately Arendt ignores. Precisely: sacred authority valued for its *megalothymotic services to isothymia*. The authority that Arendt, in such sweeping fashion, declares to have 'vanished from the modern world' is, as she herself makes clear, sacred authority of *the Roman type*. The alternative she ignores is sacred authority of *the catholic type*.

Thus, the Roman type is typically established in the aftermath of conquest; helping render the immediacy of violence no longer quite so necessary for ruling. Such was, for example, the sacred authority classically enjoyed by the Roman Senate; or, subsequently, in the Constantinian world, the sacred authority claimed by Christian councils of bishops, and the lower clergy representing them; in mediaeval Western Europe, it was the sacred authority radiating out of the Vatican; the sacred authority, also, of Christian emperors, and of Christian kings, ruling 'by divine right'. Within the world of Christendom this formally institutionalized type of sacred authority flourished by allying itself with the Church's endemic evangelistic impatience. Insofar as it has now, as Arendt argues, 'vanished', the reason is partly that modern rulers have found other sources of legitimacy for themselves, notably involving democratic elections and the achievement of economic growth; partly also that they have so many new instruments of coercion available to them, as alternative methods of ensuring law and order.

By contrast, however, the catholic type of sacred authority represents the aftermath, and the continuation, of prophetic witness to truth-as-openness. It is the moral, rather than institutionalized, authority of those recognized as notable advocates of justice and peace, seeking to achieve their goals through a principled choice of non-violent strategy. This type of authority quite clearly has *not* vanished. And its being honoured, in the widest possible catholic context, surely remains a key ingredient in any moral vaccine against totalitarianism.

I have said that the solidarity of the shaken comes of grand narrative governed by, and seeking to reinforce, both pathos of shaken-ness and catholicity; that it is the political, or anti-political, drawing-together of these two, in themselves, trans-political elements. And now I would add: the solidarity of the shaken comes of grand narrative sealing an alliance precisely between *traditions of isonomy*, informed by pathos of shaken-ness, and *traditions of sacred authority*, informed by an authentic spirit of catholicity.

For the solidarity of the shaken to be at all widely *recognized* as a supremely sacred-authoritative ideal surely requires that, so far as possible, it be incorporated into already existing catholic traditions of sacred authority, capable of endorsing it. For this to happen, those already existing traditions must be purged of evangelistic impatience, and thereby opened up to pathos of shaken-ness; in other words, transfigured by the recurrent-earthquake holy anarchy of the *Amos* impulse. But equally, a matching philosophical response is also required. Philosophic pathos of shaken-ness has to be purged of philosophy's traditional tendency to privileged self-enclosure, its ideological capture by the corporate egoism of well-educated, the corporate egoism of their various factions. And this, I would argue, in two ideal respects: on the one hand, as regards philosophers' proper isonomous engagement with their fellow-citizens as such (so that elite solidarity among philosophers truly grows transparent to solidarity of the shaken in general); on the other hand, as regards philosophy finally overcoming its hitherto alternate servility or scorn *vis-à-vis* organized catholic religion, so as to arrive at a proper partnership with theology.

Arendt represents the break-out of pathos of shaken-ness from self-enclosed philosophy, in relation to civic solidarity. The question, then, remains: how shall we further co-ordinate that first, 'Arendtian' break-out with the second, in relation to the solidarity-building potential of religion?

Chapter 8

SHAKEN-NESS, PLUS CATHOLICITY: HEGEL, AND BEYOND

Desegregated 'Sittlichkeit'

The solidarity of the shaken is a response to the imperatives of truth-as-openness, the truth of an ideal, open-minded empathy. By contrast, both religion governed by evangelistic impatience and self-enclosed, impatient philosophy, alike, idolatrously sacralize propositional truth-as-correctness: the former, a certain conception of truth-as-correctness belonging to orthodox metaphysical / historiographical belief and sacred law, as a datum of divine revelation; the latter, the capacity for truth-as-correctness dependent upon a trained expertise in cogent argument.

Set catholic religion free, however, from evangelistic impatience, and set philosophy free from the impatience bound up with the self-enclosure of a privileged class. The result will be the equilibrium of, to put it in Hegelian terminology: two complementary 'forms' for one single 'content'. Philosophy here will not be a mere apologia for the presumed truth-as-correctness of religious faith. Nor, on the other hand, will religion either be rejected as failing in philosophic truth-as-correctness or reduced to a mere instrument of manipulation strategically licensed by 'Platonic political philosophy', in the Straussian sense. Rather, religion and philosophy will collaborate as autonomous partner disciplines – each with very different roles, of quite incommensurable status – both now dedicated purely and simply to the channelling of their shared 'content': '*Geist*', 'Spirit', the energy of truth-as-openness.

Hegel, indeed, is the great philosophic negotiator of this 'two forms for one content' alliance, in grand-narrative terms. And the multiple criticisms to which his work has commonly been subjected throw a harsh light on the intrinsic difficulty of such diplomacy!

§

I would argue that Hegel is very much a prophet of the solidarity of the shaken *avant la lettre*. Thus, his greatest work, the *Phenomenology of Spirit*, culminates in a chapter entitled 'Absolute Knowing'. And what does 'absolute knowing' know? *In effect*, I think, it is precisely the know-how of this solidarity's enactment; and the acknowledgement of its sacredness – as key to the element of revelation gradually developing through the whole of history.

But now here are five different angles from which Hegel has been subject to fundamental attack.

1. One sort of attack is that directed against him by philosopher-maestros of pathos of shaken-ness, shrinking back from the *political realism* with which Hegel for his part seeks to integrate such pathos into the potential inspiration of truly potent solidarity-strategy. Kierkegaard and Levinas are both notable examples of this species of hostility. But another more recent variant of the same, paying much closer attention to Hegel's actual texts, is to be found for example in the work of *William Desmond*.

Desmond surely is one of the great thinkers of our day. To read his trilogy, *Being and the Between*, *Ethics and the Between* and *God and the Between* is to be caught up into a wonderful, relentless flood of thought; scholarly, witty, absolutely illustrating what I would call pathos of shaken-ness.[1] Yet, his critique of Hegel is savage.[2]

Desmond's ideal is not the solidarity of the shaken. It is 'the community of agapeic service'. What is the difference here? The solidarity of the shaken, as the fulfilment of *Geist*, is an ideal crying out for the sort of self-awareness, on the part of its participants as such, which only grand narrative can provide; the more comprehensive, yet also the more specific, the better. 'Community of agapeic service' on the other hand, as Desmond conceives it, appears to be an ideal almost completely outside history, too pure for any actual instantiation.

Reading Desmond, I find myself continually responding: 'Yes, this is sublime! But what does it mean in actual down-to-earth practice?' Hegel gives us a down-to-earth discussion of the state: as a more or less adequate legal framework for *Geist*, in effect depending on the potential space afforded to the solidarity of the shaken. And he gives us an equally down-to-earth comparative history of religions, as so many more or less adequate potential sacralizers of *Geist*. Desmond does neither of these things. Instead, *he* gives us a metaphysical argument designed, it seems, merely to close down such – to my mind, rather important – areas of questioning, in the name of a forever more transcendent, more celestial ideal. In the course of his polemic against Hegel, he gives just one historic example of what he means by 'agapeic service': namely, Francis of Assisi.[3] And yes, I would certainly agree that Francis is an inspiring figure. But the history of the Franciscan Order is also a vivid illustration of the problems involved in translating this model of 'agapeic service' into an enduring rule of actual *community* life. Does Desmond also side with the Spiritual Franciscans against their more moderate brethren within the order? He does not say. For here matters start to become political; and, in stark contrast to Hegel, he seems to be allergic to down-to-earth politics.

Desmond's ideal is 'community of agapeic service'. The solidarity of the shaken – by contrast – is a rich mixture of *agapé* and *eros*: the former primarily as (divine) source of, and (human) participative response to, the shaken-ness;

the latter primarily as a driver of the solidarity. In the context of trans-political religion, Desmond does indeed assign a certain value to *eros*; albeit a strictly subordinate one. But he shows no interest in political *eros*. In this sense, what he calls 'community of service' looks to me very much like charity without its necessary complement of solidarity in struggle. (One might well, I think, compare Arendt's critique of Saint Augustine; as, in her view, Augustine's notion of *caritas* suffers from the same deficiency.)

Consider Hegel's discussion of the three modes of conscientiousness, reviewed at the end of Chapter 6 / Section C. BB in the *Phenomenology of Spirit*.[4]: Hegel himself gives them fluctuating names, but let us call them the 'beautiful soul', the 'pragmatic compromiser' and the 'moralistic judge'. That all three are modes of *conscientiousness* means that in each case alike pathos of shaken-ness is very much at work. But the 'beautiful soul' (paragraphs 654–8), precisely, represents pathos of shaken-ness shrinking back from any form of down-to-earth political, or anti-political, struggle for justice. In its inhibition, Hegel remarks, this mentality still remains prey to the inner servitude of *das unglückliche Bewußtsein*; it is just *das unglückliche Bewußtsein* at its most shaken. What will a community of 'beautiful souls' look like? Hegel is, in fact, quite caustic:

> The spirit and the substance of their union is … the mutual assurance of their conscientiousness, of good intentions, the rejoicing over this reciprocal purity, and their basking in the splendour of knowing and declaring, of the care they lavish on such excellence.
>
> (paragraph 656)[5]

Their community is all talk – eloquent talk perhaps but, in the end, nothing more. The 'pragmatic compromiser' (paragraph 659) differs in just this regard. Confident in his or her good intentions, such a one plunges into the fray, with no compunction about offending those whose moral horizons remain bounded by conventional notions of 'duty', or, in other words, the official proprieties prescribed by herd morality. 'Let's get things done!' says the 'pragmatic compromiser'. 'Even if at times this may require tactical alliances with some quite dubious, gangster-ish types – or placating some quite un-idealistic interests – never mind: just keep the ultimate goal in view!' The 'moralistic judge' (paragraphs 660–1), on the other hand, reacts with horror: insisting that such readiness to make moral compromises is surely nothing but a recipe for being corrupted oneself, and that such invocation of the ultimate moral goal, by way of justification, is nothing but hypocrisy. Deadlock then ensues between these two types (paragraphs 662–5). A mere stand-off, to begin with – until at last the 'pragmatic compromiser' gives way (paragraph 666), at any rate to the extent of confessing the partial validity of the other's suspicions. The 'pragmatic compromiser's' confession is an appeal for forgiveness, and for the other to respond with equal, un-defensive generosity, acknowledging that there is truth on both sides; which, for Hegel, is just what the forward movement of *Geist* at this point requires. But when the 'moralistic judge' is challenged in this way, it is at first (paragraph 667) to no avail. We find ourselves back at the beginning: the 'hard-hearted', unforgiving moralist is simply the obverse side of the sweet-tempered 'beautiful soul' (paragraph 668).

Note that Hegel sets the interplay of the 'beautiful soul', the 'pragmatic compromiser' and the 'moralistic judge' right at the threshold of his chapter on 'Religion'. In so doing he is signalling that, as he sees it, the essential truth-claim of religion, in general, derives from its potential to host a properly chastened, yet also highly effective, engagement with the (anti)-politics of *Geist*. Thus, in the *Phenomenology*, the breakthrough comes when, at the end of the day, the hardened heart of the 'moralistic judge' breaks. He, or she, forgives the other their otherness, acknowledging the need for mutual respect between them, after all. And for the onlooker, now, it is apparent:

> the breaking of the hard heart ... is the same movement which was expressed in the consciousness that made confession of itself.

The conflict dissolves.

> The wounds of the spirit heal, and leave no scars behind ...
>
> (paragraph 669)

Here is the ideal: one healing movement, ricocheting back and forth; a determined maintenance of the balance between the two inter-dependent impulses in question, a well-balanced tension of sustained thoughtfulness. This, in short – for Hegel – is the very definition of the sacred.

The trouble is, though, that such balance is entirely absent from the thinking of Kierkegaard, Levinas, Desmond and their anti-Hegelian ilk. They, on the contrary, are eloquent spokesmen for unbroken hard-heartedness ...

2. There is of course, also, the Marxist critique: the charge that Hegel has fundamentally mis-identified the true nature of morally significant historical inevitability.
3. And, on the other hand, the post-modernist critique, already anticipated by Arendt: rejecting Hegel as a prime example of grand-narrative *hubris*. That is to say, the danger – of lethal descent into propagandist ideology – inherent in *any* claim to diagnose historical inevitability as a basis for political hope; alike whether the hope in question be revolutionary, as in Marx's case, or reformist, as in Hegel's.

It seems to me that both these critiques are rooted in one and the same essential mistake. They take it that Hegel must be claiming to diagnose historical inevitability. Which I continue to deny.

I am indeed inclined to side with Arendt, and with the postmodernists, in their generalized mistrust of any grand narrative belonging to the same species as the Marxist one. Yet they are, I think, quite wrong to assume that Hegel's grand narrative is of that species. The mistake is readily understandable in the historical circumstances of the Cold War, when Marx's thinking loomed so large; and when therefore it seemed only natural to approach Hegel, in the first instance, as a predecessor of Marx. And it has to be admitted that Hegel himself, not foreseeing the possibility of this misinterpretation, does not take any great precautions to rule it out in advance. Why, however, would Hegel *need* a grand narrative of the same species as the Marxist one?

The purpose of any grand narrative is to found a form of trans-culturally universal solidarity. But what Hegel is intent on founding is (in effect) solidarity on a basis of shared shaken-ness *alone*: in his terminology, shared participation in the dynamics of *Geist*, quite regardless of future expectations. Hegel, unlike Marx, refrains from making any predictions regarding the future, not just because he was by temperament more cautious or more conservative in his hopes. Rather, it is because predictions of the future would quite simply have no relevance to his real concern. Hegelian grand narrative is purely retrospective: it originates as an attempted explication of the freshness of the fresh orientation towards 'absolute knowing' achieved in the *Phenomenology of Spirit* by systematically considering its various antecedents.

Hegel addresses the basic question he asks – the question, how had his fresh turn of thought historically become possible? – in encyclopaedic fashion. The story he tells reaches right back into antiquity, and spans the globe, insofar as the scholarly sources available to him allowed. But, as regards the three immediately preceding centuries, he identifies the Lutheran Reformation as a key religious factor. In the field of philosophy, meanwhile: the work of Descartes, Spinoza, Kant, Fichte, Schelling. And politically: the cataclysm of the French Revolution. He had been just eighteen at the time of the storming of the Bastille, on 14 July 1789; for the rest of his life, it remained his custom to drink a toast on the 14th July in remembrance of that event, as having been, for him, a great symbolic calling into question of all hitherto unquestioned norms. But then he had been twenty-three at the time of the first great eruption of totalitarianism, in the Jacobin Terror. His subsequent commitment to political realism is very largely a response to the shock, the trauma, of that moment of negative revelation; his looking for the most realistic possible bulwarks against any repetition of the same.

These are the prime historic developments identified by Hegel as helping equip him for his role as negotiator of 'two forms for one content'. It is not that any of them were, *in themselves*, necessary, in the sense of being inevitable; just that, as a matter of contingent fact, they each played a vital part in the shaping of his intellectual world. They were the necessary preconditions for him being who he was; contingently necessary to his own arrival at the standpoint of his mature thought. Contrast Nietzsche, say. Hegel's grand narrative is an intellectual self-portrait in which his own ego quite modestly dwindles away, dwarfed by the vast background of influences conjured up. There is, after all, no *hubris* here …

4. Hegel's anti-religious critics, beginning with Feuerbach, have often wanted to argue that he was 'really' an atheist in disguise. As noted above, Alexandre Kojève takes this line. So does Robert C. Solomon for instance.

5. His theological critics, beginning with Tholuck among the Protestants and Rosmini among the Catholics, have wanted to argue that he is a more or less 'pantheist' heretic. This remains the general verdict of Barthians and Balthasarians, in particular, today.

But I think that both these sets of critics go wrong in the same way. For they fail fully to appreciate the sense in which Hegel is seeking to point beyond the criteria of truth-as-correctness in this context – that is, beyond what he himself calls the fulfilment of '*die Idee*' ('the Idea', in this technical sense) – towards the higher criteria of truth-as-openness, the concern of *Geist*. They miss the true radicality of the contrast here.

Thus, there are three levels on which one may consider Hegel's thought about religion. First: one may approach it as a set of metaphysical, or ontological, opinions, more or less persuasively argued for. Hegel professes to be a Christian, a loyal Lutheran. Certainly, he is an eccentric one. However, I am inclined to take him at his word on this – if only because viewing him as a covert proto-Feuerbach renders him, in the end, so much less coherent a thinker. Indeed, his theological eccentricity surely has a good deal more to do with his enthusiasms for Böhme, and for Meister Eckhart, than it does with any veiled atheism.[6] As I have indicated, I share these enthusiasms. I have no sympathy, on the other hand, with the element of cultural imperialism in his Christianity: his designating it the 'consummate religion', the uniquely 'revealed religion'. Here, early nineteenth-century prejudice unfortunately still stifles the proper universalism of 'absolute *Geist*'.

Second: one may focus on the micro-logic of his thought; its pervasive methodological rationale. This is the approach that *Nicholas Adams* polemically advocates – and nicely demonstrates by example – in close readings of various particular passages.[7] Adams focuses on Hegel's negotiative practice in general: his characteristic use of a 'logic of distinction in inseparable relation', or 'logic of participation'; the way he works to overcome rigid abstraction, by taking pairs of, at first, apparently quite opposed concepts and then, by looking closer, trying so far as possible to break down any over-simplified oppositions between them. So, he shows how Hegel's mediation between philosophy and religion emerges out of, and involves, an all-encompassing mediatory practice; sustained logical repair-work on the relevant vocabulary. How did Hegel originally arrive at the idea of this logic? Adams suggests that it likely originated from reflection on the Chalcedonian dogma regarding the union, in Christ, of two 'natures', human and divine, in one 'person'; which then becomes the model, in his thinking, for a whole assortment of other two-in-ones, including 'two forms for one content'.[8]

Third: besides the micro-logic governing the flow of argument throughout the Hegelian system, there is also the macro-logic to be considered, structuring the system as a whole. And here the crucial feature is the contrast between the *Science of Logic*, dealing with the intellectual instrumentation of *die Idee* – that is, truth-as-correctness considered as a whole – and the *Phenomenology of Spirit*, mapping a path towards the ultimate sacralization of truth-as-openness, in 'absolute knowing'. The argument of the *Science of Logic* is a steadily progressive zooming-in: all the while deploying the 'logic of distinction in inseparable relation' – beginning with reference to the vaguest and most generalized categories, 'being' and 'nothingness' – and ending with a classification of explanatory processes involving quite precise, detailed analysis. The argument of the *Phenomenology* is a somewhat jerkier zooming-out: beginning with the first, simple learning-experiences of a newborn infant, and then progressively adding complexity, in ever more filled-in adult social contexts, as *Geist* generates a more and more sophisticated opening-up to moral reality. Inasmuch as the *Science of Logic* works through the vocabulary of metaphysics, setting that vocabulary in order, Hegel himself calls it a metaphysical work. But, as regards the negotiation between philosophy and religion, what is striking is just how extraordinarily *reticent* this metaphysics is! The existence of God is presupposed; but in stark contrast to other theistic metaphysical systems, Hegel's includes very little discussion of God.[9] In the Introduction he grandiloquently describes it as 'the exposition of God as he is in his eternal essence before the creation of nature and of a finite spirit'.[10] Inasmuch as it deals with truth, it has to do with God, since the being of God includes all truth. But the point is that the God in question is not, in the first instance, the God of *everyday religion* at all – since the God of everyday religion is, absolutely, the God of revelation in nature and history, which this God expressly is not. Inasmuch as metaphysics aims at ultimate onto-theological truth-as-correctness, Hegel's philosophic engagement with religion is indeed, at its heart, quite *un*-metaphysical in nature. It is enacted, not in the *Logic*, but above all in that radically trans-metaphysical work, the *Phenomenology*, instead; with the *Lectures on the Philosophy of Religion* a fascinatingly erudite but altogether less-well-focused work by way of follow-up.

The trouble, however, with the Feuerbachians, the Barthians, the Balthasarians and others like them is that they tend to remain fixated on the *first* of these three levels. That is to say, they judge Hegel according to the criteria of their own already given metaphysical orthodoxies, their own ontologies: atheistic in the case of the Feuerbachians; Christian in the case of the Barthians and Balthasarians. And to that extent I think they, straight away, largely miss the point.

For I agree with Adams: what is challenging in Hegel's work here does not so much consist in the various (actually quite marginal) scraps of more or less idiosyncratic onto-theological opinion attributable to him. But, far rather, it is the radicalism with which he develops – as it were from scratch – fresh criteria to regulate the negotiation between philosophy and religion. It is the whole negotiating *methodology* he pioneers; the systematic way in which he places himself plumb in the middle, between the two parties …

§

What then, in Hegelian terms, does philosophy bring to the negotiation?

One answer (with particular reference to sections 79–82 of the *Encyclopaedia Logic*[11]) is that ideally it brings

(a) the challenge of uncorrupted *Verstand* ('Understanding'), with its fierce mistrust of 'mere' poetic self-indulgence, its bracing fresh-air assault upon sacralized superstition as such, its sheer hatred of 'hocus-pocus', or 'obscurantism'; plus
(b) the work of Dialectic, with its cultivated sensitivity to the ineradicable ambiguity of dogma – all dogma, alike whether religious or anti-religious – highlighting the constant slipping and sliding, according to context, of what the affirmation of a dogma *really* means, that is, its *existential* significance; plus
(c) the culminating contribution of Speculative Reason, with its programmatic offer of a fully explicit partnership, 'two forms for one content', the reconciliation of philosophy and religion presented within a truly comprehensive philosophic account of that one 'content', *Geist* in grand-narrative terms.

In the first place, uncorrupted *Verstand* is break-out thinking, beyond the confines of conventional edifying thoughtlessness, which it negates. But then, on the one hand, Dialectic therapeutically negates the subsequent corruption of one-sided *Verstand*, insofar as it still remains trapped within the 'unhappiness' of *das unglückliche Bewußtsein*; merely rationalizing that unhappiness. And, on the other hand, Speculative Reason negates the nihilistic scepticism of overblown, all-negating Dialectic; which would otherwise be altogether disabling of any serious cultural matrix for the solidarity of the shaken.

The passage on *das unglückliche Bewußtsein* is indeed quite crucial in establishing the basis for philosophic negotiation with religion, as a potential such matrix, in the *Phenomenology*. Again, the ideal of 'absolute knowing' – towards which the whole argument of the *Phenomenology* builds up – is, in effect, the sacralizing of perfect truth-as-openness. But *das unglückliche Bewußtsein* is, on the contrary, the underlying impulse behind the sacralizing of purported truth-as-correctness, instead. In other words, it is the very essence of idolatry. *Das unglückliche Bewußtsein* is the normal condition of humanity; the banal state of mind proper to herd / gang existence, in general. Hegel analyses it as the interaction between the two parts of a split self: the dominant sub-self, 'unchangeable' in the sense of being rigidly attached to moral prejudice; the other sub-self 'changeable', in the sense of being potentially opened up to fresh moral insight, but servile, being as it were bullied into submission, and therefore unable to fulfil its potential. The intellectual energy of the 'unchangeable' sub-self surely belongs to corrupted *Verstand*. That is to say: *Verstand* polemicizing, no longer just against superstition; but, now, against any intellectual deviation from herd / gang conformity, as such. *Das unglückliche Bewußtsein* can in principle take all sorts of religious, or anti-religious, ideological shape. The 'unchangeable' self may equally project its prejudices onto God, or onto the Buddha, or onto Humanity, or onto any other sacred principle. That in the *Phenomenology* Hegel illustrates it by a series of veiled allusions to the history of Christianity is by no means the expression of an especial animus against Christianity, on his part. Rather (I repeat) it is just because he is himself a devout Christian; and because this is a category that comes alive in corporate self-critique.[12]

The prime role of Dialectic with regard to philosophy's negotiation with religion is, then, its combating of corrupted *Verstand*, as content-supplier to *das unglückliche Bewußtsein*. As I have said, the 'unhappiness' of *das unglückliche Bewußtsein* (literally 'the Unhappy Consciousness') is an objective unhappiness, but not necessarily an unhappiness that is subjectively felt; insofar as it successfully evades challenge, it remains *sub*-conscious. (Hegel calls it a form of 'consciousness'; but this is not 'consciousness' as distinct from the 'sub-conscious'. That distinction had not yet become commonplace in his day.) *Das unglückliche Bewußtsein* depends, for its efficacy, on disguise. No religious or secular expression of piety is beyond being co-opted by it, converted into a form of such disguise; not even those with the very profoundest genuine truth-potential. Hence the need here for Dialectic: in the form of a relentless hermeneutic of suspicion, for which no provocative question is taboo. Always, with regard to any expression of piety, one has to probe and ask, to what extent *in this particular case* it either transcends *das unglückliche Bewußtsein* or fails to do so. This is the basic task allocated by Hegel to Dialectic, in relation to the sacred: negating simple reliance on propositional 'correctness'; dissolving ideological self-certainty.

And yet, Dialectic alone will not suffice. Dialectic alone is the principle of 'scepticism', the mentality which Hegel briefly discusses just before he comes to *das unglückliche Bewußtsein*.[13] 'Scepticism', in Hegel's argument, is paired with 'stoicism'.[14] These are two modes of thinking both, one might say, fundamentally devoid of Speculative Reason; lacking any grand-narrative basis for solidarity-building; and demonstrating, by not having it, the need for that further level of thought.

In terms of the tripartite schema *Verstand* / Dialectic / Speculative Reason, 'stoicism' may thus be said to constitute a simple identification of the sacred with philosophic *Verstand* more or less mixed with Dialectic. 'Scepticism' then transcends it, by jettisoning the element of *Verstand* as a matrix for the sacred, to leave Dialectic alone; resulting in a wholesale, nihilistic dissolution of the sacred. *Das unglückliche Bewußtsein* – insofar as the outlook of the dominant 'unchangeable' sub-self sacralizes sheer resistance to Dialectic – in the first instance represents a regression from both of these purely philosophic positions. However, at the same time, the latent, suppressed potential of the 'changeable' sub-self for pathos of shaken-ness points beyond: towards the ultimate reconciliation of philosophy with catholic religion, to be accomplished by Speculative Reason. Insofar as the objective unhappiness of *das unglückliche Bewußtsein* comes to be registered, also, as subjective unhappiness – insofar as it is felt as a restless, inchoate discontent – there is, after all, some hope of eventual release. Both 'stoicism' and 'scepticism', on the other hand, presuppose an equation of wisdom with ataraxy, that is, serene detachment from any sort of pathos; including even the very purest pathos of shaken-ness. 'Stoicism', by virtue of its withdrawal from pathos, is left with only the most abstractly cerebral notion of the sacred. 'Scepticism', as Hegel portrays it, tends to degenerate into mere childish frivolity. (Adorno's 'negative dialectics' represents a more serious version of the same …) To contemplate these two phenomena is, for Hegel, very much a lesson in appreciation of philosophy's perennial need of supplementation from the deep resources of pathos stored up in grand narrative.

The *Phenomenology* as a whole is a great work of Speculative Reason. In it, we are shown the evolution of the philosophic 'form', namely, the form of true 'conceptual thought' (*Begriff*), systematically readying itself to receive and express the 'content' which it shares with religion: the dynamics of *Geist*. But note in particular the prehistory of the concept of *das unglückliche Bewußtsein*, leading up to its emergence here. Hegel's early writings, unpublished in his lifetime, were pre-philosophical; in form, they are what, later, he calls works of religious 'representational thought' (*Vorstellung*). In consequence their polemic is not yet exactly targeted on *das unglückliche Bewußtsein*. For the concept of *das unglückliche Bewußtsein* is, in the end, only properly intelligible to philosophical Dialectic, moderated by Speculative Reason. But these early writings are so to speak initial range-finders. So, in the essay entitled 'The Positivity of the Christian Religion' he represents Jesus as a great proto-Kantian critic of the mental servitude of his people; an 'enlightened' twist on traditional Lutheran theological antisemitism.[15] Then, in the subsequent essay on 'The Spirit of Christianity and Its Fate' he turns against Kant; and a similar portrayal of Jesus attacking Jewish mental servitude is coupled with a more or less equivalent attack on mental servitude dressed up in terms of the Kantian notion of moral duty.[16] This coupling of ancient Judaism with modern Kantianism draws closer to the philosophic concept of *das unglückliche Bewußtsein*, mental servitude as a universal possibility in all manner of different cultural contexts. However, in order finally to arrive at that concept he has, by definition, to step beyond 'representational' thought, which lacks the necessary theoretic 'self-consciousness' to deal with it. Hegel's transition from 'representational' to 'conceptual' thought is precisely the advance in 'self-consciousness' which allows him to conceive of *das unglückliche Bewußtsein* in all of its universality: thereby escaping his earlier, inherited religious antisemitism. And it is this advance which, then, renders the *Phenomenology* possible.

Yet, it is by no means an abandonment of the truth-potential intrinsic to religious pathos of shaken-ness.

§

Desmond complains that in Hegel's thought

> the dialogue of religion and philosophy is primarily orchestrated from the side of a philosophy claiming the more absolute absoluteness.

This will not do, he argues. On the contrary:

> We need a new poverty of philosophy, and a new porosity of philosophy to religion.[17]

I agree absolutely: to the extent that religion is infused with pathos of shaken-ness, the greater the porosity of philosophy to religion, the better! And yes, one may well I think regret, from this point of view, that Hegel nowhere follows up his programmatic opening-up, as a philosopher, towards religion, by engaging more closely with the actual development of Christian theological tradition. He always remains, himself, so very much a philosopher, as opposed to being a theologian. There is little or nothing in his work to aid preachers in their task; his allergic reaction to his own training as a preacher, at the Tübingen Stift, abides.

Nevertheless, consider Hegel as a philosophical advocate of catholicity; and hence of religion, as soil in which catholicity grows. I am using the term 'catholicity' in a more extended sense than is usual. Granted: this is not Hegel's terminology. But, whilst he has no actual name for this ideal, in a sense the whole drift of the argument in Chapters 6 and 7 (or sections C. BB and C. CC) of the *Phenomenology*, as a whole, actually tends towards an implicit coupling together of pathos of shaken-ness with catholicity. Thus, in Hegelian terms, one might, again, define what I am calling 'catholicity' as the conjunction of two distinct religious elements:

(a) abundant *Sittlichkeit* ('ethical life' or 'ethical order'); that is, the most intensely felt sort of well-rooted moral belonging to a community; in relative freedom however from *das unglückliche Bewußtsein*; and
(b) a strict taboo on class segregation; grounded in vigorous affirmation of *divine indwelling within human individuality*, purely and simply as such.

Chapter 6 / Section C. BB of the *Phenomenology*, entitled '*Geist*', evokes a range of diverse cultural phenomena, with just one thing in common. Precisely: that they belong on a spectrum of lamentable failure with regard to *Sittlichkeit*, so defined.

And contrariwise, Chapter 7 / Section C. CC, entitled 'Religion', is largely focussed on the possibility of progressive de-segregation within *Sittlichkeit*; as illustrated by the contrast between Ancient Greek paganism and Christianity, at its best.

Thus, let us consider these two chapters.

§

As for Chapter 6, this opens with Hegel's portrayal of a damaged mode of pre-modern *Sittlichkeit*.[18] The main focus of the discussion here is on Sophoklés' drama *Antigoné*. But Hegel's lumbering, hyper-abstract style is not just a result of authorial incompetence, or malice. It is a device for keeping the careful reader's attention hooked into the larger argument, about the nature of *Geist*. So, this section is *not* in fact about *Antigoné*! Rather, it is about *Geist* astir in cultures of the same general type as that which is the context for *Antigoné*: cultures of intense *Sittlichkeit*; drastically weakened however by a great, slicing – un-catholic – divide between the elite of privileged men, the political decision-makers represented here by king Kreón, and all the rest of the population, liable in this case to sympathize with Antigoné's rebellion, since she is upholding the basic values of family loyalty and almost everyone has a family.

Sophoklés' drama shows the pathos of that weakening in the simplest, and therefore the starkest, fashion. Antigoné's two brothers, Eteoklés and Polyneikés, following their father Oedipus's departure from Thebes, have quarrelled over who should take over the rule of the city. Eteoklés, with the backing of their uncle Kreón, has made himself sole king; Polyneikés has raised a rebel army; and the ensuing battle has left both brothers dead upon the field. Kreón, the new king, decrees that the 'rebel' Polyneikés should be denied the elementary honour of a proper burial. When Antigoné defies him, and buries her brother herself – at any rate under a light covering of dust, and with funerary rites – Kreón orders that she should die a gruesome death, immured in a cave. He is no mere moral monster; but remains a man of *Sittlichkeit*. Before long, he is persuaded by the intervention of the prophet Teiresias to relent – but too late! The play ends with three successive suicides: that of Antigoné herself; of Kreón's son, Antigoné's betrothed, Haimón; of Eurydiké, Haimón's mother. And *we*, contemplating the tragic devastation, are left with the fundamental, Rousseauan question: *how, in general, might* Sittlichkeit *be better structured, to mediate the general will, rather than just the particular will of the autocrat, and his advisors?* In other words: what would a mended, that is, a truly catholic *Sittlichkeit* look like?

Then, as the discussion proceeds – having shown us *Sittlichkeit* damaged – Hegel invites us to consider *Sittlichkeit* in a much more advanced state of decay; even dying and dead. The allusions in the central chunk of the chapter are all to seventeenth- and eighteenth-century France; the phenomena in question being retrospectively chosen for the purpose, inasmuch as they may be seen as precursors to the catastrophic total eclipse of *Sittlichkeit* in the French Revolutionary Terror.[19] First, we are shown *Sittlichkeit* dwindling away amongst a sophisticated, but progressively demoralized aristocracy; as an original *sittlich* notion of 'good breeding' mutates, into an altogether more alienated, cynical, and hence un-*sittlich* ethos.[20] And next: pietist 'faith' embattled against secularist 'pure insight'; two ideologies equally devoid of real *Sittlichkeit*, and therefore of catholicity.[21]

In his discussion of 'good breeding' (*Bildung*) Hegel impressionistically conjures up the decadent form of that ideal: the spirit of an elegant, high-society culture, governed by essentially amoral individualism. Here, to be 'well bred' is to do what one's vanity requires one to do, and to do it with panache; but no longer with any real belief in higher values. Hegel points back to what once was: a world in which 'good breeding' *had been* a form of *Sittlichkeit*: an ethos of '*noblesse oblige*'; moral loyalty to one's high-ranking class; gladly fulfilling the duties understood to derive from the privilege of wealth, and proximity to State-power. But that *sittlich* feudal ethos had demanded a high level of self-respect, entirely excluding any servility in relation to one's overlord, or despotism in relation to one's subordinates. It had upheld an ideal 'heroism of service'.[22] In the story Hegel tells, its corruption is sealed when State-power falls into the hands of a despotic sovereign (like Louis XIV) who positively demands an attitude of servility from the aristocrats at his court, and makes their continued enjoyment of wealth and privilege dependent upon it. Now 'heroism of service' is supplanted by, in Hegel's caustic phrase, 'heroism of flattery'![23] Loyalty extorted by such manipulation is not at all the sort of loyalty proper to *Sittlichkeit*. Manipulation by the sovereign, of the nobility, elicits reciprocal manipulation by the nobility, of the sovereign. The true noble-mindedness of the older ethos degenerates into mere greed. Even acts of charity are typically rendered manipulative in this context. And the dishonesty of a decadent aristocracy comes to irradiate the wider intellectual world. As Hegel tells the tale, the artifice of 'good breeding' degenerates into a whole culture of shameless deceit and pretence; the true nature of which, in pre-revolutionary Paris for example, is exposed for example by the impudent 'sniggering' mockery of that wild man, Rameau's nephew.[24]

But note once again that the basic, general *question* that Hegel wants to pose at this stage of his argument remains fundamentally independent of its particular illustration in his text. The question is: *what will, ideally, replace a class-based ethos of* Sittlichkeit, *when that ethos has, for one reason or another, lost its moral grip?* One might equally I think illustrate it, say, with reference to recent developments in UK politics. Thus, consider the fading away both of the older, patrician sort of Toryism, which came to a crisis in the Thatcher years, and also of the older, proud working-class ethos of the Labour Party, more or less deflated by the rise of 'New Labour' in the 1990s. Hegel, for his part, presents us with a situation in which an older high-morale class-identity is uprooted, and mutates into something else. And here are two other opposing modes of high-morale class-identity also increasingly uprooted and starting to disappear. Of course, the specific social mechanisms involved in this case are quite different from those that Hegel has illustratively in mind. Nevertheless, there surely is at least a certain sense in which the more recent example serves to highlight much the same basic issue as Hegel's does.

And likewise with the ensuing discussion of 'faith' and 'pure insight': does not that have clear parallels with the twenty-first-century culture wars between 'religious fundamentalism' and the 'new atheism'? For, let us focus on the underlying question being raised here. Namely: *how to restore the proper element of* Sittlichkeit *to a religious tradition, as such, which has lost it?* 'Faith', in this passage, is a derogatory term – precisely, for religious belief emptied of true *Sittlichkeit*, inasmuch as it has been hollowed out by *das unglückliche Bewußtsein*. 'Pure insight' is a polemical attack on mere 'faith' in this sense, which however just compounds the problem, inasmuch as its initial inspiration is (in Hegelian terms) essentially 'stoic' or 'sceptic' in character; that is to say, equally devoid of true *Sittlichkeit*. In Chapter 4 / Section B of the *Phenomenology* 'stoicism', 'scepticism' and *das unglückliche Bewußtsein* are considered as separate phenomena, serially juxtaposed, in purely trans-cultural abstraction. But in Chapter 6 / Section C. BB, by contrast, we are shown the struggle between them: on the one side, *das unglückliche Bewußtsein* in the particular context of pietistic 'faith'; on the other side, a mix of 'stoicism' and 'scepticism' translated into Enlightenment ideology.[25]

However, these categories are fluid; reflecting the fluidity of actual existence. And the more partisan, or even obsessional, 'pure insight' becomes, the more it, too, takes on the characteristics of *das unglückliche Bewußtsein*; now, in militant anti-religious mode. Then, un-self-critical group-think confronts un-self-critical group-think; one rigidified notion of the sacred confronts another; two ideological gangs face off, each far more interested in point-scoring than in truly appreciating the other's point of view. 'Faith' and 'pure insight' become twin phenomena; warring twins. The interaction between the one and the other takes shape as outright warfare between the two 'forms' of religious and philosophic thought; warfare in which their proper shared 'content' has become altogether invisible to both sides. 'Faith', in this context, is 'pure consciousness': 'pure' in the sense of priding itself on its sincerity, in a world of deceit.[26] And 'pure insight' is 'pure' in the same sense. Both are equally impatient, in the alienated, anxious sincerity of their propaganda. 'Pure insight', as the aggressor, caricatures what it supposes to be the inherently superstitious nature of 'faith'. It mocks the ascetic disciplines prized by 'faith'; and proposes a fresh, deist notion of 'God', a 'God' of utilitarian Reason, the sacralization of 'pure utility itself'.[27] Of course, there are elements of truth in 'pure insight's' critique of 'faith'. Indeed, where it is at its most benign, Hegel remarks,

> the communication of pure insight is comparable to a calm expansion or to the *diffusion*, say, of a perfume in the unresisting atmosphere.

And he ironically borrows from Diderot's description of Jesuit evangelization in China and India, to provide a picture of what happens next: the new deity, having once been installed in the shrine, and having made itself at home there,

> *one fine morning* it gives its comrade a shove with the elbow, and bang! crash! the idol lies upon the ground.[28]

Yet, insofar as 'pure insight' grows fanatical, its previous gentle, insidious 'perfume' gives way to something else altogether. At the most extreme, it is incorporated into Jacobin ideology, with its ritual cult accompanying the Terror. In which case,

> the *beyond* of ['pure insight' rendered totalitarian] hovers over the corpse of the vanished independence of real Being, or the Being of faith, merely as the exhalation of a stale gas, of the vacuous *être suprême*.[29]

And, truly, what more desperate expression of a felt deficiency in *Sittlichkeit* could there ever be, than that cult of the *être suprême*?

The chapter then concludes with a parade of further declassé types of conscientious individual, outside *Sittlichkeit*; the exact inverse, thus, to what we find in *Antigoné*. First: the Kantian, or Fichtean, moral philosopher. Next: shedding the imaginatively impoverished abstraction of Kantian / Fichtean theology, the 'beautiful soul'. Next: the confrontation, which I have already discussed, of the other-worldly 'beautiful soul' with the professedly conscientious, but perhaps hypocritical, political realist; and the mutation of the former into the unforgiving, 'hard-hearted' judge. And, finally: the breaking of that 'hard heart', in reconciliatory forgiveness.

§

What the breaking of the 'hard heart' at the end of Chapter 6 / Section C. BB signifies is pure pathos of shaken-ness, as the inspiration of the 'beautiful soul', reaching out *after all* towards incorporation into politically realistic solidarity-strategy; and, in the first instance, towards catholic religion, as the sacralization of such strategy.

Accordingly, Chapter 6 / Section C. BB opens into Chapter 7 / Section C. CC on the comparative history of religions.

This is a chapter in three sections, corresponding to three basic genera of religion: 'natural religion', 'art-religion' and 'revealed religion'. The first, rather brief section is illustrated by allusions to Zoroastrianism; early Indian sacred tradition; early Egyptian sacred tradition; and the veneration of the Kaaba in Mecca, from pre-Islamic antiquity onwards. The second section is illustrated by allusions to ancient Greek sacred tradition. The third is illustrated by allusions to Christianity. These allusions are somewhat random, and sketchy in nature; Hegel develops a much more encyclopaedic classification of traditions in his later Berlin *Lectures on the Philosophy of Religion*. But never mind. What really counts here is the capacity of certain sacred traditions to articulate *sacralized isothymotic humanism*. That is, conversely, to *de*-sacralize traditional class-segregation. This does not happen at the level of 'natural religion', as Hegel sees it. But it is already, to some extent, a feature both of true 'art-religion'; and, in more confrontational fashion, also of true 'revealed religion'. Hegel's philosophic thinking in this Chapter is comparable to Hölderlin's poetic thought in the provocative way he juxtaposes Ancient Greek paganism to Christian faith.[30] The sculptors of Ancient Greece portrayed their gods in heroic human form; but, crucially, *without any particular markers of social class*. In religious festivals featuring athletic competition, the Ancient Greeks, he argues, were symbolically honouring universal humanity purely and simply as such. Hegel sees these as anticipatory stirrings of *Geist*, on its way towards the Christian dogma of the Incarnation. Meanwhile, he further suggests, in the ecstatic worship of Démétér (Ceres) – goddess of bread, of the grain harvest, of poppies and opium, of the earth – and of Dionysos (Bacchus), the god of wine, of the grape harvest, of fertility, fruit and vegetation of every kind, the Ancient Greeks knew their existence, precisely as a whole community transcending any class-distinction, to be itself a direct manifestation of the divine. And what they thus knew in 'the mystery of bread and wine' is then sublated into the Christian eucharistic 'mystery of flesh and blood'; the Church's knowledge of itself as 'the body of Christ'.

How, then, can the humanist sacrament, in either case, peaceably co-exist with anti-humanist, segregationist class prejudice? Such co-existence is only possible thanks to an essentially thoughtless superficiality of participation, disguising the implicit tension here. So, the full contribution of religion to the solidarity of the shaken comes just where that latent tension is rendered explicit: where implicitly humanist liturgy, in consequence, becomes in the fullest sense catholic, flooded with pathos of shaken-ness.

In the domain of Greek art-religion, this is the work of drama, in the annual Athenian festivals of the Great (or City) Dionysia, and the Lénaia; both of which were dedicated to the worship of Dionysos.[31] The prizes for which the dramatists competed were, so to speak, a secular element in these festivals: focusing attention on the surface technical skills displayed. But, at the same time, the liturgical context served to amplify the underlying pathos of shaken-ness at work. There was, indeed, something sacred being aimed at. So, the cult of Dionysos became, by virtue of its drama, a great class-transcendent celebration of truth-as-openness: tragedy evoking truth-as-openness in compassion for the anguish of noble-minded victims; and comedy arousing scorn for arrogance, hypocrisy, self-deceit, all that closes truth-as-openness down.

The art of 'revealed religion', however, surpasses that of 'art-religion' not least inasmuch as, at this level, both tragedy and comedy are so very much more intimately integrated into liturgy. As regards tragedy: the turn from pure myth and legend to actual history adds to the political intensity involved; with the memory of Christ's death mediated through the commemoration of martyrs. And, as regards comedy: Hegel sees the comedic spirit essentially as a disruptive energy at work within the paganism of classic antiquity; laughing at false piety, to the point of seeming to discredit all piety.[32] Eventually it flips, and merges with the unhappiness of *das unglückliche Bewußtsein*, in pagan form, at its most self-aware – 'the grief that expresses itself in the harsh words: *God is dead*.'[33] Here is the spiritual void for Christianity to fill. For, unlike 'art-religion', Christianity has resources to *contain* the negativity, the scorn, the grief, expressed in those harsh words, and to *sublate* it. God is dead – but is also risen and ascended – and God will come again. Such is the 'divine comedy' of the gospel. It is 'comedic' truth of a far more universal kind than is attainable within the limits of 'art-religion': 'comedic' truth, mockery of all enemies of truth-as-openness, adapted now for catholic evangelism, right to the very ends of the earth.

As I have said, I am inclined to quarrel with Hegel's elevation of Christianity, *alone*, onto the pedestal of 'revealed religion'. Surely, what counts as the highest level of possible religious truth is just maximum catholicity plus maximum pathos of shaken-ness; a practical ideal which may, in principle, be achieved within all sorts of confessional tradition, Christian and non-Christian alike. Whatever *poetic advantages* a particular tradition may have over others, it still does need to be insisted that such advantages are not, *in themselves*, the proper criterion of revelation; that criterion is truth-as-openness alone, which no advantage can ever guarantee.

Nor am I persuaded by the interpretation of the dogma of the Trinity giving shape to Hegel's discussion of 'revealed religion' as such. Hegel is fascinated by the dogma's promise of logical flexibility; which is fair enough. But his account fails, in my view, because it remains, after all, fundamentally de-contextualized. He makes no attempt (as I have done above) to understand the dogma's origins in the historic context of the Early Church; or its evolution, especially in the immediate aftermath of the Constantinian Revolution.[34] This does seem to me to be quite a major flaw.

Note, however, how *das unglückliche Bewußtsein* has now reappeared: no longer, as in Chapter 4 / Section B, illustrated by examples of corrupted Christianity; but – on the contrary! – in the form of a decadent paganism, ripe for conversion to Christianity. So, in the section of Chapter 7/Chapter C. CC entitled 'Revealed Religion', Hegel presents Christian faith not as manifesting the *problem* that is *das unglückliche Bewußtsein*, but precisely as a potential *solution* to that problem.[35] What *das unglückliche Bewußtsein* splits apart, the Christian dogma of the Incarnation in principle poetically re-unites with great expressive power. On the one hand: the true '*Self*'; a depth of individuality capable, by nature, of participation in *Geist*. In Chapter 4 / Section B this was called 'the changeable consciousness'. On the other hand: '*the absolute essence*'; the domain of the sacred, which in Chapter 4 / Section B had as it were been captured by the malign self-projection of the '*un*-changeable consciousness', that is, the rigidified, herd-morality-enforcing, closed-minded gang-member ego.[36] *Das unglückliche Bewußtsein* separates these two, enslaving the former to the latter. But now, in Chapter 7 / Section C. CC, Hegel has finally arrived at the speculative proposition that

the Self *is* the absolute essence.

Or, conversely, that

The absolute essence is the Self.[37]

In place of the rigid opposition of the two maintained by *das unglückliche Bewußtsein*, Hegel here affirms a complex relationship of identity-in-difference between them; a whole live force-field of ideas. The solidarity-building truth of the truly sacred, the true 'absolute essence', *is* the truth of one's being true to one's own true 'Self', as a shaken individual.

The abstract nature of these speculative propositions allows for the capacity of other belief-systems, besides Christianity, to appropriate the underlying wisdom that they encapsulate. But, as a Christian, Hegel is primarily concerned with the sense in which the identity of the 'Self' with the 'absolute essence' is represented in the person of Christ, as both paradigmatic human individual and Son of God. (Compare Sebastian Moore on Christ as the paradigmatic 'self', in *The Crucified Is No Stranger*.)[38] At the beginning of the section on 'revealed religion' we hear 'the harsh words: *God is dead*' as an utterance of despairing paganism; at the end of the section the same 'harsh words' recur, with reference however to Christ's death on the cross.[39] And for Hegel there really are *two* deaths involved here: first, the redemptive death of Christ the 'mediator' – and second, the death of the false 'God', the mere projection of *das unglückliche Bewußtsein*, whose mendacious power Christ's 'mediation', properly understood, overthrows.[40]

In Hegelian terms, the Roman institution of the cross may be said to symbolize the fate of 'the Self' at the hands of *das unglückliche Bewußtsein*, generally. The resurrection of Christ, the crucified dissident, however, symbolically negates the initial triumph of *das unglückliche Bewußtsein*, inasmuch as it represents precisely the identity of 'the Self' with 'the absolute essence' – which is what *das unglückliche Bewußtsein*, by definition, fails to see.

From Hegel to Patočka: The transition to 'third modernity'

Unfortunately, the actual concept of '*das unglückliche Bewußtsein*' drops out of Hegel's work after the *Phenomenology of Spirit*. It is, in my view, a crucial loss. Nevertheless, one might well say that it still persists, in latent form, at the heart of his grand narrative. For, he frames his 'philosophy of world history' as, in essence, a story of evolving 'freedom'. And what else, at the deepest level, is the 'freedom' in question if not, precisely, freedom from *das unglückliche Bewußtsein*? First of all: increasingly self-aware subjective freedom from *das unglückliche Bewußtsein* on the part of megalothymotic individuals as such. And second: isothymotically demanded objective freedom from any socio-political order dependent for its survival on a prevalence of *das unglückliche Bewußtsein* amongst those that it governs, inhibiting dissent.

Thus, in terms of its basic structure, the logic of this 'philosophy of world history' represents a systematic mixing of megalothymia and isothymia. The isothymia is there in the tri-partite progress Hegel famously posits from (a) cultures which 'only know that *one* is free' – through (b) cultures which have grown aware that '*some* are free' – to (c) cultures which 'know that *all* human beings are intrinsically free, that the *human being* as *human* is free'.[41] And the megalothymia is there as the energy then translating isothymotic theory into practice: the dissident pride involved in rejecting, and overcoming *das unglückliche Bewußtsein*. For, what does it mean to know freedom only as the vocation of '*one*', the single overlord? Surely, it means that everyone other than that overlord is prescribed a dose of *das unglückliche Bewußtsein*. Or what does it mean to know freedom only as the vocation of '*some*'? Again, it means that whole classes of the population are being prescribed a dose of *das unglückliche Bewußtsein*. But a truly rational political order will, by definition, be dedicated to healing everyone from their addiction to this poison; as will a truly catholic religious community.

Admittedly, the absence of the concept of '*das unglückliche Bewußtsein*' in Hegel's later work does tend to render 'freedom', there, a somewhat flickering ideal; as Hegel himself, at times, lapses into an altogether more superficial notion of its demands. Yet, such is his greatness as a thinker that it is not – as it would be with almost any other thinker among his contemporaries – simply *anachronistic* to judge his stance on such issues as the relationship between the sexes, or the politics of colonialism, by the standards of a later age.

Of course, he is scarcely to be criticized for failing to foresee the way in which gender roles were, over the following centuries, to evolve. He admires Sophoklés' drama *Antigoné* for the way it depicts a clash between the 'law of woman', that is, family piety, and 'public law', the ethos of the political realm, reserved for men; with Antigoné represented, very much, as a heroine.[42] But, whilst he empathizes with Antigoné's rebellion, he shows no sympathy, in principle, for the more generally rebellious free-spiritedness of such intellectual erstwhile Jacobins of his own acquaintance as Caroline Schelling, or Meta Forkel-Liebeskind; who, rather than just upholding the 'law of woman', might precisely be seen as having laid claim, as women, to the freedom, in his own phrase, 'intrinsic' to 'the human being as human'.[43] Their Jacobinism (which pre-dated the Terror) was no doubt a misjudgement. Yet, there surely was already an implicit challenge here, which Hegel, simply as a matter of logical consistency, might have registered; but, disappointingly, never did.[44]

So too, in his *Lectures on the Philosophy of World History*, there clearly is quite grievous mischief in his labelling the first 'stage' of world history, in which freedom is reserved to the head of state alone, the '*Oriental* World'; the second 'stage', in which it is known only that *some* are meant to be free, the '*Greek and Roman* World'; and the third 'stage', in which it is finally recognized that *all* are by vocation free, the '*Germanic* World'.[45] By 'Germanic' he, in effect, simply means 'Christian European'; the racist connotations of the term, in his usage, are minimal.[46] Nevertheless, here we surely do have a set of illustrative allusions over-stepping their properly subordinate role; in just the way he so scrupulously tries to avoid in the *Phenomenology*. For, after all, examples of all three understandings of 'freedom' might be found in all sorts of geographical locations, at different periods. And the trouble with this dogmatic establishment of European civilization, *as such*, right at the centre of world history is that it then facilitates his theoretic acquiescence in the various enterprises of European colonialism.[47] If the culminating insight of European civilization is that '*all* human beings are [by rights] intrinsically free, that the *human being* as *human* is free' – then how, one might well ask, is that reconcilable with European rule over non-Europeans, which by its very nature can only succeed by promoting, and rewarding, the unfreedom of *das unglückliche Bewußtsein* amongst those non-European subjects, on a grand scale? In Hegel's world it was not eccentric to argue for the abolition of slavery; and he does so. But it *would* have been eccentric to go much further, along the same general lines. The essential logic of his theory surely *is* pressing him to do so. Yet, he holds back.[48]

§

What, then, do we still have to learn from Hegel?

Not least, I would argue: an elaborate grand-narrative mode of thought which – notwithstanding his own backslidings and datedness – still does provide a significant platform on which to build, more or less following his lead.

So, consider the history of grand narrative, as a genre. Every grand narrative may be said to advocate a certain socio-political ideal of 'modernity', envisaged as the logical culmination of world history. (Here I am simply following the terminological implications of Lyotard's definition of '*post*-modernity', as 'incredulity towards grand narratives' ...) And for every grand-narrative ideal there is a particular carrier-community, or set of carrier-communities, to which the narrators address themselves, communities they seek to inspire, with globally applicable modernizing zeal. *But there are, I would argue, three distinct possible types of grand-narrative carrier-community; corresponding to three basic species of 'modernity'.*[49] Three species of 'modernity', in this sense: each originating in a different era, and yet all three now co-existing, and interacting.

'*First modernity*' is the grand-narrative ideal whose carrier-communities are the liturgically constituted communities of evangelistic Abrahamic religion; Jewish, Christian and Muslim. And '*second modernity*' is the grand-narrative ideal whose carrier-communities are the advocates, the executive agencies and the political parties of the secular state as such. Hegel, the great mediator between philosophy and religion, is also the great mediator between 'second modernity', in this sense, and 'first modernity'.

Without the combined work of 'first' and 'second modernity', we would never have arrived at the strength we now have, critically to confront forms of *das unglückliche Bewußtsein* embedded within pre-modern patriarchal tradition and folk-superstition. These two 'modernities' are indeed always liable to be at loggerheads with one another. But they surely cannot be allowed to remain so. 'First modernity' simply rejecting 'second modernity' is nothing but a formula for aggressive theocracy. Whilst, as for 'second modernity' determined to do away with 'first modernity': that was Jacobin policy, Stalinist policy, latent Nazi policy, overt Mexican fascist policy, Maoist policy. So many recipes for misery! Hegel, more than any other thinker, gives us a systematic first sketch of the kind of grand-narrative theory required in order to negotiate a proper accommodation between the two.

But he died in 1831. And over the two centuries following his death something quite new has emerged. Something that he never foresaw, at all; a complete game-changer. Precisely: another, distinct, *third species of 'modernity'*.

§

By 'third modernity' I mean the grand-narrative ideal whose carrier-communities are the public conscience movements of secular civil society.

That is to say: non-violent campaigning organizations, unlike those of 'first modernity' in that they welcome participation of people from all sorts of religious or non-religious backgrounds – and, at the same time, unlike the organizations of 'second modernity' in that they are quite independent of political parties, not seeking, either in the short or in the long term, any direct share of state power – crucially therefore uninhibited by the strategic requirements of such ambition, but just aiming to shift public opinion, awakening awareness of social wrongs and encouraging a sense that some real change might be possible, building solidarity on that basis of shaken hope, shifting the moral context of politics.

By contrast, the liturgical organizations of 'first modernity', insofar as their grand-narrative notion of salvation is corrupted by evangelistic impatience, mix an appeal to the public conscience sometimes with outright coercion, sometimes with manipulative rhetoric around the ideas of post-mortem rewards and punishments, evoking *das unglückliche Bewußtsein*.

The secularizing organizations of 'second modernity' – and especially the quasi-messianic political parties of later 'second modernity' – insofar as these are corrupted by the philosophic impatience of their intellectual leadership, mix an appeal to the public conscience not only with outright coercion, but also with dogma evoking *das unglückliche Bewußtsein*, propaganda appeals to the greed, the fears and the conceit of the public's collective ego.

But the public conscience movements of 'third modernity' largely appeal to the public conscience *alone*. Surrounded by a penumbra of civil-society charitable initiatives, they are the polemic aspect of the public conscience, liberated from both evangelistic and philosophic impatience. *And is not 'third modernity', therefore, the prime natural habitat for the 'solidarity of the shaken'?* The solidarity which public conscience movements in general incubate transcends both the confessional restrictions intrinsic to 'first modernity' and the partisan manoeuvrings intrinsic to 'second modernity'. Jan Patočka, who first coined the term 'solidarity of the shaken', was himself one of the prime initiators of a public conscience movement. It is his term for the intended ethos of Charter 77. Moreover, as remarked above, Václav Havel, co-founder with him of the Charter 77 movement, also uses Patočka's term in the same sense.[50]

Yes, there are also radically corrupted public conscience movements: 'animal rights' protesters, for example, resorting to terrorist tactics; 'pro-life' activists picketing abortion clinics. Not much truth-as-openness there! But, in talking about the truth-potential of 'third modernity', I am thinking of public conscience movements strictly insofar as they do *not* indulge in self-righteous bullying. And *such* public conscience movements surely are the most efficient of all agencies for translating pure pathos of shaken-ness into anti-political action.

For my part, I share Hannah Arendt's admiration (akin to Hegel's) for Ancient Greek isonomy; and her closely related appreciation for the 'lost treasure of the revolutionary tradition', that spontaneous ferment at the beginning of modern revolutions, before political parties, eventually, get a tight grip on them. What I witnessed in Prague, back in January 1990, was a situation in which a classic public conscience movement had just morphed into revolutionary activism, to ephemerally beautiful effect. But the 'velvet' beauty of that moment largely derived from the thirteen-year labour of the Charter 77 movement which had prepared the way for it; providing the revolution with a ready-made, coherent, initial leadership. Public conscience movements in general are natural cultures of isonomy.

What, then, does it mean to try and re-do now, for the twenty-first century, what Hegel did for the early nineteenth? I would argue that, above all else, it means to supplement his narrative account of *Geist* with an affirmation of 'third modernity', plus an analysis of what 'third modernity' ideally requires, by way of theoretic support. Each individual public conscience movement being focused on its own single issue naturally tends to obscure the underlying coherence of 'third modernity' *as a whole*. Hence the need, in principle, for grand narrative here: 'third modernity' needs its own grand narrative, essentially, in order to reinforce its fundamental claim, as a whole, to sacred authority. And just as Hegel may be said to have worked at reconciling 'first' and 'second modernity', so *we* therefore need to work at reconciling the elements of truth in all three 'modernities'.

Twenty-first-century Geist

The kingdom of God = the solidarity of the shaken.
The solidarity of the shaken = the kingdom of God.

The name, the 'kingdom of God' – as a confessional term – has all the advantages, and all the disadvantages, proper to its being-at-home in a particular catholic culture. And the name, the 'solidarity of the shaken' – as a secular, humanistic term – has all the advantages, and all the disadvantages, proper to its transcendence of confessional particularity. But to grasp the full truth of 'third modernity', it seems to me, one has, above all, to grasp the essential complementarity of the two. On the one hand: catholic rootedness. On the other hand: cosmopolitical alliance-building. It is a matter of giving due weight to both, as two aspects of the same.

'First modernity' at its best is catholicity reaching out, ultimately, towards the solidarity of the shaken. But that initial out-stretch is negated by evangelistic impatience. 'Second modernity' at its best, then, begins as political negation of the negation here; and in Hegel's thought still, in fact, remains pure negation of the negation, once again reaching out towards catholic solidarity of the shaken. Philosophic impatience, however, negates the negation of the negation, as classically developed by the likes of Hegel. I have cited Heidegger, Strauss and Adorno by way of examples. These three represent (anti-Hegelian) philosophic impatience, in the context of second modernity, at its most sophisticated. Again, however, the disease itself is widespread, often in much cruder forms: whether in the bitterness of militantly secularist party-political ideologues, or in the angst of ivory-tower nihilists – indeed, in intellectual outlooks of every kind – all with just this one thing in common, that they are, in effect, barred shut against catholicity.

'Third modernity' at its truest – secular humanism reaching out towards catholicity – is, in short, the negation of the philosophically impatient negation of the (true) negation of the evangelistically impatient negation of the original, converse outreach of Abrahamic catholicity – towards the solidarity of the shaken.

§

There are however two further aspects of the matter, finally, to be considered.

- 'Second modernity' in its most lethally corrupt later forms is devised by philosophic impatience with populist political parties as its instruments. We need, accordingly, to consider the critical relationship of 'third modernity's' public conscience movements to political parties, in particular.
- But then, on the other hand, we also need a movement of *self*-critique, to balance this: reining in any tendency towards what, setting it alongside 'evangelistic impatience' and 'philosophic impatience', one might call 'impatient *innocence*'.

§

Thus, the public conscience movements of 'third modernity' address a wide range of diverse issues. Historically, the earliest such movement – welcoming participation by all and sundry, quite regardless either of 'first modernity' religious identity or of 'second modernity' party membership – was the campaign for the abolition of the trans-Atlantic slave trade; properly organized for the first time, in Britain, in 1787. Nowadays, there is of course an especially urgent proliferation of campaigns for the protection of nature – against the threats of climate change and the mass extinction of species. These campaigns are, also, 'third modernity' phenomena. To the same category there belong, as well, all sorts of peace campaign: against specific wars; against the weaponry of mass destruction; against the internationally proliferating arms trade. Then, campaigns in solidarity with marginalized and exploited groups of every kind: feminist campaigns; LGBT campaigns; child protection campaigns; campaigns championing the cause of refugees, or of those made homeless by poverty; campaigns against all sorts of bullying and cruelty; against the use of torture; against the death penalty; campaigns for free speech. The establishment of Amnesty International, in 1961, was a key milestone in the history of 'third modernity': inasmuch as Amnesty's advocacy for 'prisoners of conscience' amounts to a defence of the very possibility of public conscience movement activism, internationally.

It is of course always a cause for gratitude when political parties, lobbied and encouraged by public conscience movements, take up the same causes. But my concern here is with the question: What is properly to be regarded as *sacred*? The equation,

the kingdom of God = the solidarity of the shaken;

the solidarity of the shaken = the kingdom of God

is, in essence, a twofold formula, both catholic and secular, for the sacred; which I am intent on filling out and clarifying, in conversation with tradition. And I would argue that, whereas public conscience movements are, by nature, organizations to a unique degree transparent to the properly sacred, political parties will on the contrary always be a threat to it. Party-political activism has the obvious advantage, over public conscience movement activism, of its more immediate potential sheer effectiveness; especially if the party in question is successful in gaining governmental power. And yet, of course, a governing political party's ability to act in accordance with the properly sacred will, inevitably, be more or less impeded by all the various moral compromises involved in actually arriving at that position.

A plurality of political parties is no doubt necessary, for the civilized management of a mass democracy. I by no means wish to deny the importance of democratic legitimacy in the drafting of legislation. Given that everyone is liable to obey the law, every adult should enjoy at least some felt share in the electing of legislators; and yes, I fully acknowledge our need for political parties, in the organizing of this process. However, the power of public conscience movements is, in a sense, a necessary moral counter-balance to democracy. One might say: it is not so much 'democratic' (compounded from the Greek, *demos*, 'common people' + *kratos*, 'sovereign power') as 'agapacratic' (compounded from *agapé*, 'overflowing, compassionate love, or charity', + *kratos*). Balancing the power inherent in democratic legitimacy, agapacracy is the power inherent, precisely, in *moral authority*. It presses ahead, way beyond the already established collective will of the majority; forever further, towards the (sacred) dictates of perfect truth-as-openness.

Political parties, by definition, seek to obtain coercive power. To arrive at it, they need, in the first place, to placate a sufficient number of the already powerful; not to seem to threaten their vested interests. And secondly, they need to manipulate the masses, as such, with their propaganda: flattering, promising, evoking third-party threats and scapegoating. Populist political parties, moreover, tend to generate their own idolatrous, *ersatz* versions of the sacred: personality-cults of their leaders; sacralizing conceptions of national history and the national self-interest; glorification, in grand-narrative terms, of the revolutionary Party itself. All the greatest crimes of recent history have been either initiated by political parties, or at least involved party-political collusion.

The agencies of 'third modernity', very differently, do not seek any direct share in coercive power. On the contrary (I repeat) they seek to get things done solely by appeal to the public conscience – an appeal that would, straight away, be sabotaged by attempts at coercion, and which also absolutely precludes manipulative propaganda.

At its most authentic, in other words, their sense of the sacred is profoundly *anarcho-pacifist* in character.[51]

§

An anarcho-pacifist form of catholicity: think, for example, of Dorothy Day! But: anarcho-pacifism, crucially, tempered by *apocalyptic patience* …

By 'apocalyptic patience' I mean the patience ideally required in order to appreciate divine revelation. Here, I have sought to analyse it (a) in the context of 'first modernity', as resistance to evangelistic impatience; and (b) primarily in the context of 'second modernity', as resistance to evolved philosophic impatience. But evangelistic impatience and philosophic impatience are just two modifications of a yet more fundamental phenomenon: the impatience that belongs to original sin itself. That is to say, the impatient desire, quite simply, to feel oneself innocent, of all offence. For true innocence is one thing, the desire to *feel* oneself innocent is quite another. It is not innocent at all.[52]

In the contemporary context of 'third modernity', this desire mutates into what might be termed 'woke impatience'; 'woke' in its more recent, pejorated sense. Which is by no means to say that I am any more enamoured of *anti*-'woke' impatience. Far from it! 'Woke' impatience is a not uncommon potential failing of 'third modernity'. Anti-'woke' impatience is a wholesale closure to the underlying truth-potential of 'third modernity', right from the outset; equally, for the sake of feeling innocent. But, in any case – setting aside that dialogue of the deaf – I think the classic literary distillation of impatient innocence is actually to be found in the work of *Jean-Jacques Rousseau* (1712–78).

Thus: what *in essence* constitutes moral wisdom? Rousseau's distinctive answer takes the form of a vast, extended parable. In *Émile*, he tells the tale of what he sees as a child's ideal education, extending from birth to marriage; an education ideally calculated, he thinks, to inculcate the very purest wisdom in an otherwise quite ordinary young man.[53] The eponymous hero is given into the exclusive care of a young tutor. His parents withdraw from the scene, as soon as he is weaned. The tutor has no other occupation than to care for the education of this one child. Nor does he impose any pedagogic discipline upon him. His activity is confined to encouraging Émile's curiosity, and pleasure in acquiring technical skills; answering his questions; and, above all, keeping him solitary, right up until late adolescence, when he is ready to be introduced to his future bride, Sophie. In this way, Émile is precisely to be kept innocent: perfectly preserved, through his formative years, from the corruption of the surrounding world *by virtue of a strict withdrawal from any form of belonging*. He is, so far as possible, to remain an innocent child of nature. And Sophie is herself a similarly innocent girl.

Rousseau, great thinker that he is, more or less acknowledges that there may be drawbacks with such an upbringing, once the adult pair are fully exposed to the social world around them. In the sequel to *Émile*, left incomplete at his death, Sophie confesses to having committed adultery, or (more likely) been raped.[54] We learn of this in a letter written by Émile to his now retired tutor. It is entirely unclear whether she is in any way culpable – rather shockingly, Émile does not trouble to find out, just assumes the worst. At any rate, knowing him, Sophie sees no prospect of ever being forgiven. She is deeply depressed. There is no wisdom in Émile's wildly intemperate response: he simply flees. And rages, full of self-pity. True, he blames himself, for having brought her to the wicked city, Paris, in the first place; and toys with thoughts of forgiveness on that basis. But what he loved in Sophie had, it seems, always been the reflection, in her, of his own innocence; and now, as he puts it, 'the delightful charm of innocence has vanished'.[55] Nor had his solitary upbringing done anything to inculcate in him the discipline of patience, with imperfect other people, so clearly necessary for his and Sophie's relationship to recover.

Compare the little story told in Chapter 8 of *The Gospel According to John*, verses 3-11:

> And the scribes and the Pharisees brought a woman who had been caught in adultery and, making her stand before everyone in the open, Say to him, "Teacher, this woman has been caught in the very act of committing adultery; Now, in the Law Moses enjoined us to stone such a person; so what do you say?" (And they said this to test him, so that they might have some accusation to bring against him.) Jesus, however, bending down, wrote upon the ground with his finger. But, when they continued to question him, he stood up straight and said to them, "Let whosoever among you who is without sin be the first to cast a stone at her." And again, bending down, he wrote upon the ground. And, hearing this, they departed one by one, beginning with the older of them, and he was left alone with the woman before him. And, Jesus, standing up straight, said to her, "Madam, where are they? Does no one condemn you?" And she said, "No one, Lord." And Jesus said, "Neither do I condemn you; go, from now on sin no longer."[56]

The unforgiving crowd consists of people fired with impatient desire to feel innocent, in the sense of having not only the right, but also a positive duty, to cast stones. They have, initially therefore, no effective sense of belonging-together with the sinful woman, in common human frailty: just the same lack of real moral empathy that we also see exemplified by Émile, when tested by the crisis in his relationship to Sophie.

Here, we come back to Hegel's evocation of the 'beautiful soul', in the *Phenomenology of Spirit*.[57] For, the impatience in question is typical of the 'beautiful soul': resulting as it does, first, in timid inability to act in true collaboration with others, inasmuch as collaboration means compromise; but then also, in the angry censoriousness of the 'hard heart', the condition into which the 'beautiful soul' evolves. Hegel's whole political doctrine, in the *Philosophy of Right*, is premised not least on his critique of the 'beautiful soul'. Hence, his well-known speculative formula, in the Preface to that work:

> What is rational is actual and what is actual is rational.

In the *Philosophy of Right* Hegel is systematically holding in balance these two opposing energies: on the one hand, the energy of appreciation for 'the rational', which involves stepping outside what is actually there, in order to criticize it; and, on the other hand, the energy of appreciation for 'the actual', which on the contrary involves restraining one's critical instinct, with a view to, first, understanding the plight of those one is inclined to criticize – in all of its actuality – and so empathizing with them, after all. In the politics of *Geist*, as he sees it, these two energies flow together, and become one.

The *rational principle* of the solidarity of the shaken, its purest, is a spirit of anarcho-pacifism. Once upon a time, such a spirit could come to expression only in sheer raging defiance of political *actuality*. But my claim is that the development of 'third modernity' – the proliferation, now, of 'third modernity's' public conscience movement organizations, as *actual* centres of *rational* activism – potentially changes everything, in this regard.

Note, however, the completely opposite nature of Rousseau's political philosophy, as set out in *The Social Contract*. Rousseau published *The Social Contract* the same year as *Émile*, in 1762. And here the role that the tutor plays in *Émile* is, *mutatis mutandis*, replicated on an altogether different scale, by the ideal lawgiver of Book II, Chapter 7. For Rousseau, the 'rational' – far from being conjugated with the currently 'actual', as Hegel would have it – is far rather to be identified, instead, with distant dream-memories of the more or less mythic lawgiver, and his decrees. The lawgiver: that absolute outsider, belonging nowhere, in any social 'actuality'! Rousseau describes this fantastic, utopian figure as

> a superior intelligence, who could understand the passions of men without feeling any of them, who had no affinity with our nature but knew it to the full, whose happiness was independent of ours, but who would nevertheless make our happiness his concern, who would be content to wait in the fullness of time for a distant glory, and to labour in one age to enjoy the fruits in another. [58]

In short: he would be the most sublime imaginable embodiment of pure wisdom-as-innocence.

Is not the lawgiver, in essence, a projection of Rousseau's own, impatiently non-belonging, 'beautiful-soul' ego; pondering, as he is here, the basis of good law? In his autobiographical *Confessions*, Rousseau parades a record of, at times, quite scandalously delinquent behaviour, with unique shamelessness, concealing nothing. One may admire such honesty. And yet, one has to wonder about the exhibitionism involved. He appears to confuse guilt with shame. So that – hey presto! – his shame-less-ness equates to innocence, after all. These *Confessions* are the story of a man who, with no tutor other than himself, has nevertheless miraculously managed to preserve his inner Émile. The tragic tale, increasingly paranoid in tone, of an innocent outsider to society, whose innocence has led to his being victimized, is intended first and foremost as vindication of his *narcissistic moral impatience*.

O, how those Revolutionaries, the first totalitarians, adored the memory of Rousseau! They loved his innocence. Wanted a share of it ...

§

What constitutes very deepest-rooted obstacle to solidarity of the shaken, in the human heart? Such solidarity involves a fundamental shared commitment to honesty, truth-as-openness. Therefore, it confronts, not least, that core element of original sin: precisely, the impatient *will to feel innocent.*

Impatient evangelists, for their part, tend to manipulate those they address, whipping up in them acute guilt-feelings, then offering relief, in the form of a renewed sense of innocence, on condition of conversion and subsequent loyalty.

Impatient philosophers pre-emptively guard against such manipulation by cultivating a proud, *a priori* sense of innocence, well-padded with argument.

These are two very different strategies. But, look, they are both of them, equally, manifestations of one and the same underlying, impatient will to feel innocent.

I am a priest, one of 'them'. And I am a privileged intellectual, one of 'them'. God help me, in both regards alike, I am determined patiently to *own*, not only the elements of beauty in my people's history, but also the elements of ugliness, the corruption. To own the whole thing: the whole rich mixture, in it, of the pleasing with the repulsive. With nothing discreetly downplayed.

I aspire to be a theologian. Which, as I understand it, means, not least: one who, systematically, *scours* their own – their most cherished, their tightest clung-onto – delusions of corporate innocence, before God. One who scrapes away spin.

NOTES

Introduction

1 Václav Havel, 'Politics and Conscience', translated from Czech by Erazim Kohák and Roger Scruton, in Jan Vladislav, ed., *Living in Truth* (London: Faber and Faber, 1987), 157. My italics. The original Czech term translated as 'solidarity of the shaken' is '*solidarita otřesených*'.
   For a participant's account of Czech dissident life in the church context, see Tomáš Halík, *From the Underground Church to Freedom*, translated from Czech by Gerald Turner (Notre Dame, IN: University of Notre Dame Press, 2019).
2 Francis Fukuyama, *The End of History and the Last Man* (London: Penguin, 1992), xiv–xix.
3 Alexandre Kojève, *Introduction to the Reading of Hegel: Lectures on the Phenomenology of Spirit*, assembled by Raymond Queneau and first published in French in 1947; English translation by James H. Nichols, edited by Allan Bloom (New York: Basic Books, 1969; Ithaca NY: Cornell University Press, 1980).
4 G. W. F. Hegel, *The Letters*, translated by Clark Butler and Christiane Seiler (Bloomington: University of Indiana Press, 1984), letter to Niethammer.
5 Kojève, *Introduction to the Reading of Hegel*, 69–70.
6 The crucial passage, for Kojève, is *Phenomenology of Spirit*, paragraphs 178–96, the schematic drama of 'lord and bondsman'. This is Hegel's famous analysis of the lust for domination in general; its intrinsic futility, inasmuch as what the individual human spirit most deeply needs is the affirmation of being 'recognized' by others for whom one has real respect. But the domineering lord has foolishly devalued the recognition he receives from his bondsman, whom he fails to respect …
7 Kojève ended up working for the French diplomatic service, and played a significant role in the original formation of the European Economic Community, the nascent European Union. But he was Russian-born, and had an ambivalent attitude to the USSR. He used ironically to describe himself as a 'Stalinist', and it has been suggested that he maintained some relationship with the KGB, although it is not at all clear what, if anything, this amounted to. At the same time, he professed to be quite contemptuous of Soviet propaganda, especially the claim that the USSR had already become a classless state. He was a strange man; evidently somewhat psychopathic. At all events, his philosophic interest in the notion of universal human rights was, to say the least, not tender-hearted. His 'Stalinism' appears, in fact, to have been above all an affirmation of principled callousness; a callousness also apparent in his attitude to the French Revolutionary Terror.
8 This tripartite scheme is discussed at greatest length in *Republic* Book IV, 435c–441c. The concept of '*thymos*', or '*thymoeides*', is introduced in Book II, 375a–375e, 376c; and then recurs repeatedly, passim.
9 Václav Havel, 'The Power of the Powerless', translated by P. Wilson, in Vladislav, ed., *Living in Truth*, 41–2; italics added by Fukuyama, *The End of History and the*

Last Man, 166–7. This text of Havel's was originally written in 1978, soon after the founding of Charter 77; it is dedicated to the memory of Jan Patočka.
10   Ibid., 55.
11   Nietzsche, *Thus Spoke Zarathustra*, translated from German by R. J. Hollingdale (London: Penguin, 2nd edition, 1969), 46–7.
12   Hegel, *Lectures on the Philosophy of World History*, Vol. 1 *Manuscripts of the Introduction and the Lectures of 1822-3*, edited and translated by Robert F. Brown and Peter C. Hodgson with the assistance of William G. Geuss (Oxford University Press, 2011), 503.
13   Fukuyama, *The End of History and the Last Man*, 197.
14   Hegel, *Phenomenology of Spirit*, paras. 206–30. C.f. Kojève, *Introduction to the Reading of Hegel*, 64–7! The main translators of the Phenomenology – Michael Inwood (Oxford University Press, 2018), Terry Pinkard (Cambridge University Press, 2018) and A. V. Miller (Oxford University Press, 1977) – all stick with 'Unhappy Consciousness' here. But see Shanks, *Hegel and Religious Faith* (London: T&T Clark, 2011). The connotations of the word *Bewußtsein*, 'consciousness', have shifted, since Hegel's day, with the emergence of the new opposing concept, *Unterbewußtsein* 'sub-consciousness'. What Hegel calls *das unglückliche Bewußtsein*, insofar as it is a stable condition, is necessarily a sub-conscious one. As it grows self-conscious, it starts to dissolve. And, although objectively unhappy, it may well on the conscious surface manifest as quite joyful: think of the participants in those highly choreographed North Korean propaganda performances, say; or the compulsory jubilation of certain rather creepy religious sects! (These are just extreme examples – the basic concept surely covers a very wide spectrum of phenomena.) In what follows I therefore stick with the German.
15   Jan Patočka, 'The Obligation to Resist Injustice', 3 January 1977, in Erazim Kohák, ed., *Jan Patočka: Philosophy and Selected Writings* (University of Chicago Press, 1989), 340.

Chapter 1

1   Jan Patočka, *Heretical Essays in the Philosophy of History*, 1977, translated by Erazim Kohák, edited by James Dodd (Chicago: Open Court, 1996).
    Notable discussions of Patočka's work include Kohák, 1989; Derrida, 1995 (a); Tucker, 2000; Findlay, 2002; Tava, 2015.
2   C. f. Jan Patočka, *Le monde naturel et le movement de l'existence humaine*, translation into French by Erika Abrams (Dordrecht: Kluwer Academic Publishers, 1988); a collection of Patočka's essays.
3   Hannah Arendt, *The Human Condition* (University of Chicago Press, 1958); *On Revolution* (Harmondsworth: Penguin, 1973).
4   Patočka, *Heretical Essays*, 1996, 44 (emphasis added). Patočka had been first a student, then a friend and colleague, of Edmund Husserl; self-identifying as a practitioner of Husserlian 'phenomenology', whilst at the same time admiring the work of that other 'phenomenologist' colleague of Husserl's, Martin Heidegger.
5   Edmund Husserl, *The Crisis of European Sciences and Transcendental Phenomenology: An Introduction to Phenomenological Philosophy*, translated from German by David Carr (Evanston, IL: Northwestern University Press, 1970).

6 Andrew Shanks, *The Other Calling: Theology, Intellectual Vocation and Truth* (Oxford: Blackwell, 2007), Chapters 3–4.
7 Herakleitos B 80 (fragment cited in Origen, *Against Celsus* VI xlii).
8 C.f. fragment B2 (from Sextus Empiricus, *Against the Professors* VII 132–3): 'For that reason you must follow what is common. But although the *logos* is common, most men live as though they had an understanding of their own.'
9 Patočka, *Heretical Essays*, 43.
10 Ibid.,
11 Ibid., 62.
12 Ibid., 75. *Metanoein* [Greek]: change of mind; inner transformation through acceptance of the will of God.
13 Ibid., 77.
14 The reference is to Hegel, 'The German Constitution', edited and translated by T. M. Knox, in *Hegel's Political Writings* (Oxford University Press, 1964). This essay remained unpublished in Hegel's lifetime. Hegel ceased work on it in 1801; the Holy Roman Empire was formally wound up in 1806, in consequence of the Napoleonic War.
15 Václav Havel proposes the term 'post-totalitarianism' for what Charter 77 had to confront: *Living in Truth*, 40. It was still largely totalitarian; but came after the full-on totalitarianism of Stalin's day, in which a phenomenon like Charter 77 would not have been possible at all.
16 Patočka, *Heretical Essays*, 83.
17 Ibid.
18 Ibid., 125.
19 Ibid., 126–7.
20 Ibid., 129.
21 Ibid., 130.
22 Ibid., 131. Italics added.
23 Ibid., 134.
24 Ibid., 135. He cites Pierre Teilhard de Chardin, 'La nostalgie du front'; in *Ecrits du temps de la guerre* (Paris: Grasset, 1965), an essay originally written in 1917; and Ernst Jünger, 'Der Kampf als inneres Erlebnis'; in *Sämtliche Werke*, II, Vol. 7: essays, 1: *Betrachtungen zur Zeit* (Stuttgart: Klett Cotta, 1980), originally written in 1922.
25 Patočka, *Heretical Essays*, 135.
26 Ibid., 136.
27 Kohák, ed., *Jan Patočka: Philosophy and Selected Writings*, 16–17.
28 Patočka, *Heretical Essays*, 106–11.
29 Ibid., 108.
30 English translation in Kohák, *Jan Patočka: Philosophy and Selected Writings*, 327–39.
31 Ibid., 339.
32 Bultmann invokes the authority of Heidegger – as a supposed ally – simply, it would appear, so as to exempt himself from having to have any further dealings with philosophy, in general.
33 See especially Patočka, *Plato and Europe*, translated by Petr Lom (Redwood City CA: Stanford University Press, 2002), 85–90 and passim.
34 Iain McGilchrist, *The Master and His Emissary: The Divided Brain and the Making of the Western World* (New Haven and London: Yale University Press, 2009); *The Matter with Things*, 2 vols. (London: Perspectiva Press, 2021).
35 C.f. in particular McGilchrist, 2021, Vol. I, Chapter 10.

36 To be sure, composure of mind depends upon a certain degree of closure. Prejudices may well be useful, in this regard; up to a point, we do need them. However, sacralizing something because it is useful to do so is one thing. Truly responding to sacred revelation, as such, is quite another. Revelatory truth has nothing to do with utility. On the contrary! What is useful serves its user, the ego. But revelatory truth is, by nature, sheer threat to the egotism of the ego. Hence, it is a form of the very purest truth-as-openness.

Chapter 2

1 Andrew Shanks, *Hegel versus 'Inter-Faith Dialogue': A General Theory of True Xenophilia* (Cambridge University Press, 2015), Part II. The same threefold distinction is also developed in another way by Roberto Mangabeira Unger, *The Religion of the Future* (Cambridge, MA: Harvard University Press, 2014).
2 I am indebted to conversation with Carlos Medina Labayru for this conception.
3 See for instance Girard, *I See Satan Fall Like Lightning*, translated from French by James G. Williams (Maryknoll, NY: Orbis, 2001), Chapter 9. Girard also contrasts the Oedipus story, as a classic case of a legend implicitly vindicating the 'scapegoat mechanism', with the Joseph story in *Genesis* 37–50, in which it is shown as being altogether rejected by God.
4 See Heath D. Dewrell, *Child Sacrifice in Ancient Israel* (University Park, PA: Pennsylvania State University Press, 2017).
5 Or is the story as we have it in *Genesis* the corrective tweaking of an earlier version in which Abraham is allowed to follow through with the sacrifice? See Margaret Barker, *The Mother of the Lord*, Vol. 1, *The Lady in the Temple* (London: Bloomsbury, 2012), 131. As she notes, in *Genesis* 22: 19 Isaac is not mentioned as part of the band accompanying Abraham home …
6 *Taanit* 4a.
7 Kierkegaard, *Fear and Trembling: Dialectical Lyric by Johannes de Silentio*, translated by Alastair Hannay (London: Penguin Classics, 2003), Problem III: 'Was Abraham ethically defensible in keeping silent before Sarah, before Eleazar, before Isaac?' (Eleazar is the name traditionally attributed to Abraham's servant, unnamed in *Genesis*.)
8 Jacques Derrida, *The Gift of Death* (2nd edition) and *Literature in Secret*, translated from French by David Wills (University of Chicago Press, 2008).
9 Jeroboam II reigned over the northern kingdom of Israel from approximately 787 to approximately 747; Uzziah reigned over the southern kingdom of Judah from approximately 783 to perhaps as late as 736. As for the earthquake: archaeologists have traced the occurrence of a major such event in the region to, very roughly, around the year 760.

    Note that the specific predictions in 7.10-17 were not in fact fulfilled: Jeroboam was *not* killed on the battlefield; in his day, Israel was *not* conquered; the imminent catastrophes predicted for the high priest Amaziah and his family, along with the rest of the northern kingdom's ruling class, did *not* materialize. In *Amos* 6.14 we read:

    > Indeed, I am raising up against you a nation,
    > O house of Israel, says the Lord, the God of hosts,
    > and they shall oppress you from Lebohamath [in the north]
    > to the Wadi Arabah [in the south].

It is a distinctive geographical formulation. But, as is wryly noted in *2 Kings* 14.25, in actual fact king Jeroboam, on the contrary, '*restored the border of Israel* from Lebohamath as far as the Sea of the Arabah'. The historian does not refer to Amos by name, but he cites by way of contrast the now lost original prophecy of Jonah, son of Amittai, which he says predicted just such military success for Jeroboam. This seems to be strong evidence that the story of Amos's clash with Amaziah records a genuine historic event; for why should a later loyal contributor to the Amos tradition, knowing better, invent a story of the prophet getting it wrong? And presumably (for the mistaken prophecy to have been plausible) the clash happened quite a while before Jeroboam's eventual demise, from old age.

On the other hand, *Amos* 6.2 in particular appears to date from a period after Jeroboam's reign, and right towards the end of Uzziah's. Thus, it alludes to the conquest of Calneh, in northern Syria, and Hamath, in central Syria, by Tiglath-Pileser III, emperor of Assyria, which we know from Assyrian texts to have occurred in 738; also, to Uzziah's (undated) conquest of Gath, and his destruction of its city walls, recorded in *2 Chronicles* 26.6. *Amos* is, for the most part, a poetic evocation of imminent disaster for the kingdom of Israel; which was indeed finally destroyed by the Assyrians in 722/21. The process leading up to this disaster was initiated by Tiglath-Pileser, who came to power in 745; created the world's first-ever professional standing army; and proceeded systematically to extend Assyrian power throughout the region. *Amos* 1.3–2.16 consists of a series of threats, against Damascus, Gaza, Tyre, Edom, Ammon, Moab, Judah and finally Israel; Assyria is not named, but the threat envisaged in each case alike is presumably from the invading Assyrian army.

Amos's career may well have spanned several decades. Either that, or else these later verses come from the school of his admirers. See Petrus D. F. Strijdom, 'Reappraising the Historical Context of Amos', in *Old Testament Essays* 24/1; 2011; 221–54.

So, why such an epochal religious breakthrough just at that point? I guess the formation of the Amos-school depended on the coincidence of two factors: *first* (notwithstanding his predictive errors) the religious genius of the prophet; but then *also* the epochal breakthrough in military logistics under Tiglath-Pileser. In response to this shocking step-change in the human capacity for evil, the early Amos-school was, in effect, demanding an equivalent step-change in the corporate practice of good, at any rate amongst the Hebrew people.

10 Andrew Shanks, *Faith in Honesty: The Essential Nature of Theology* (Aldershot: Ashgate, 2005).

11 Again, for another angle on the Trinitarian dynamics of Christian theology, consider for instance how it plays out in relation to *Marian dogma*.

In the first place, the Mother of God's 'perpetual virginity' surely serves as legendary metaphor enshrining her as an ultimate symbol of liberation with regard to patriarchal convention. A maiden, supposed to be of the very lowest status according to the manipulative norms of that order, she is symbolically lifted by divine grace right out of her conventional place within it. This is what 'Second-Person theology' properly focuses on, here. As the resurrection of the crucified – her son – represents truth-as-openness renascent in the political domain, so Mary's 'virginity' is the authority behind the primarily domestic free-spiritedness which explodes in the Magnificat (*Luke* 1.46-55).

Secondly, however, the dogma of her 'immaculate conception' transfers her into the domain of 'First-Person theology'. As I understand it, she is properly declared exempt from original sin, inasmuch as original sin is transmitted down the generations in and through every form of banally divisive ethnic identity, class identity, religious or partisan identity; whatever in short may tend to generate prejudice, mistrust, closure between people. In the context of 'First-Person theology', Mary, the 'immaculately conceived', is lifted out of all this, and comes to symbolize the most radical humanism.

And then in the context of 'Third Person theology' what comes to the fore is the fundamental contrast between Mary's authentic innocence and the all-too-natural craving of a corrupted Church to disown its corporate sin, and misrepresent *itself* as innocent. 'Third Person theology' is indeed essentially a struggle against such delusions of innocence. Whereas Mary, on the other hand, represents the inextinguishable possibility of reformation: truth-as-openness triumphant, after all ...

Chapter 3

1   The confusion was enshrined in the biography written in 835 by the abbot of the great abbey of St. Denis near Paris, Hilduin, in honour of his abbey's patron. And the resultant muddle was only effectively unmasked by the scholarship of the Renaissance.

As regards the dates of the Dionysian texts: in general, their author clearly seems to have read the works of Proclus (412–85); and, more specifically, in the *Ecclesiastical Hierarchy* he refers to the liturgical singing of the creed, an innovation in the practice of Syrian Monophysite churches from around the year 476. On the other hand, his writing must at the very latest pre-date 528, when it is referred to in the Syriac translation of Severus of Antioch, *Adversus apologiam Juliani*. And the report of a debate in 532 between Orthodox theologians and Monophysites under the leadership of Severus also records the Monophysites appealing to the authority of Dionysius's 'Fourth Letter'.

Notwithstanding this association with the Monophysite 'heresy', however, in the Greek-speaking East Dionysius's various writings were mediated to subsequent generations above all through the interpretative work, and advocacy, of (the after all entirely Orthodox) Saint Maximus the Confessor (d. 662). And the notion of 'mystical theology' flourished accordingly. In the West, by contrast, Dionysian 'mystical theology' took rather longer to establish itself. Dionysius's writings were first translated into Latin by Hilduin; but then, in what became the definitive version, by John Scottus Eriugena. This latter translation, commissioned by the Carolingian Emperor Charles the Bald, was completed in 862. Nevertheless, it was not until 1125 that a Parisian scholar, the Augustinian Canon Regular, Hugh of St. Victor, wrote the first Latin commentary, after Eriugena's, on one of Dionysius's works, *The Celestial Hierarchy*; and not until the thirteenth century that Dionysius's *Mystical Theology* itself became a major influence within the Western tradition. The Victorine, Thomas Gallus (d. 1246) played a pioneering role in this regard; along with Robert Grosseteste, Bishop of Lincoln (d. 1253) who produced a new Latin translation of all Dionysius's work, with a commentary. But then, in the following period, there came something of a Dionysian surge: with the work of Bonaventure (d. 1274); Hugh of Balma (d. 1304/5); Meister Eckhart (d. 1327, and discussed below); Johannes Tauler (d. 1361); Henry Suso (d. 1366); Jan van Ruysbroeck (d. 1381); the anonymous fourteenth-century author of *The Cloud of Unknowing* who also translated *The Mystical Theology* into Middle English; the fourteenth-century author of the *Theologia Deutsch*; Jean Gerson (d. 1429); Nicholas of Cusa (d. 1464); Denis the Carthusian (d. 1471); Hendrik Herp (d. 1477); Marsilio Ficino (d. 1499); Bernardino of Laredo (d. 1540); Francisco of Osuna (d. 1540); Pedro of Alcántara (d. 1562); Louis of Blois (d. 1566); John of Ávila (d. 1569); Luis of Granada (d. 1588); John of the Cross (d. 1591); and others.

2   Salvian's history book is entitled *De gubernatione Dei*; his book on almsgiving and inheritance, *Ad ecclesiam*; there are also nine letters of his that are extant. For English translations see Jeremiah Francis O'Sullivan, *The Writings of Salvian, the Presbyter* (Baltimore, MD: Catholic University Press, 1947).

3   Alexander Golitzin, *Mystagogy: A Monastic Reading of Dionysius Areopagita* (Collegeville, MN: Cistercian Publications and Liturgical Press, 2014), Chapter 1, sections 1–2; Chapter 6, section 3. On the purpose of his pseudonymity: pages 11–12. Dionysius's *8th Epistle* is addressed to a monk called 'Demophilus', which Golitzin suggests is a made-up name (in English one might render it as 'beloved of the mob') rebuking him for his insolent fanaticism. 'Demophilus' has, it appears, interrupted the sacramental confession of a notorious sinner; has beaten the man up; has chased the priest-confessor out of the sanctuary of the church; and now stands, symbolically, guard over the reserved sacrament there, to prevent its being, in his view, profaned any more, by the lax conduct of the clergy. Here, then, we have just the type of individual who might be called a 'Messalian'. But, Dionysius protests, it is simply not for lay monks, in any circumstances, to go trespassing into the sanctuary; let alone interfere with the sacramental activity of the clergy there. It is notable that in the *Ecclesiastical Hierarchy* he sees bishops (or 'hierarchs'), in the first instance, as supervising the monks. The supreme authority of bishops is correlated to what Dionysius evidently sees as the Church's prime disciplinary need.

4   For a thoroughgoing account of Dionysius as a philosopher: see Eric D. Perl, *Theophany: The Neoplatonic Philosophy of Dionysius the Areopagite* (Albany, NY: State University of New York Press, 2007.)

5   Plato, *Republic* 6, 509 b 7–10. English translation by T. Griffith (Cambridge University Press, 2000).

6   Quotations from the English translation of *The Enneads* by Stephen MacKenna, second edition revised by B. S. Page (London: Faber and Faber, 1956). Here: V. 2. 1; page 380.

7   Ibid., VI. 5. 6; page 408; italics added, and simply removing MacKenna's capitalization of 'The One', for the reasons suggested by Michael Sells, namely that there is no equivalent in the original, and that it immediately suggests just the sort of emphasis on this particular name that Plotinus is seeking to avoid. See Sells, *Mystical Languages of Unsaying* (University of Chicago Press, 1994), 226–7.

8   *The Enneads* VI. 8. 9; page 603. Capitalization removed.

9   Ibid., Capitalization removed.

10 Ibid., VI. 4. 7; page 524.

11 *The Life of Moses*, §163; Gregory of Nyssa, 1978, 94.

12 Dionysius the Areopagite, *The Mystical Theology*, Chapter II; my translation.

13 'Toward Perpetual Peace', in Immanuel Kant, *Practical Philosophy*, translated from German by Mary J. Gregor (Cambridge University Press, 1996) conclusion of the second supplement, 'The Secret Article'.

14 *Republic* 414 b–c. I discuss this further in Chapter 7, 166–7.

15 The closing words of *The Enneads*: VI. 9. 11; page 625.
16 Iamblichus, *On the Mysteries*, translated from Greek by Emma C. Clarke, John M. Dillon and Jackson P. Hershbell (Atlanta, GA: Society of Biblical Literature, 2003). It appears that at one stage Porphyry had been his teacher. However, Porphyry's *Letter to Anebo*, even though it does not name Iamblichus, seems to have been a widely circulated attack, aimed at him.
17 See *Pseudo Dionysius: The Complete Works*, translated from Greek by C. Luibheid (New York: Paulist Press, 1987).
18 Ibid.
19 Edited by T. W. Adorno, Else Frenkel-Brunswick, Daniel J. Levinson, and R. Nevitt Sanford (New York: The Norton Library,1969), 1. This study was first in fact published in 1950. The individuals interviewed were a representative sample primarily of 'non-Jewish, white, native-born, middle-class Americans' (page 23).
    Seeking to rescue the word 'authoritarian' from this derogatory usage, I would prefer to speak of 'the idolatrous personality'.
20 Hannah Arendt, 'What Is Authority?' in *Between Past and Future* (London: Penguin, 1977), 92–3.
21 Ibid., 95–104.
22 The Franco regime in Spain and the Salazar regime in Portugal were both semi-totalitarian, and both sought to build alliances with the Church, reducing it politically to the status of a mere front organization for their rule, but by the same token rewarding it with their patronage. And in both cases the clerical hierarchy was, for the most part, willing at first to accept the Faustian pact. This, though, was only because the authoritarian integrity of their institutions had been so severely warped by the trauma of earlier anti-clerical persecution. The Spanish Church had been damaged by the persecution it suffered under the Second Republic beginning in 1931, and in the ensuing civil war. And the Portuguese Church had been damaged by the persecution it suffered under the First Republic, beginning in 1910. In order to function well, authoritarian regimes do require a degree of self-confidence, in their authoritarianism, which these churches, alas, had altogether lost.
23 David Graeber, *Debt: The First 5,000 Years* (Brooklyn & London: Melville House, 2014), chapter 5.
24 See Chapter 2, 44–6.
25 *Meister Eckhart: The Essential Sermons, Commentaries, Treatises and Defense*, edited and translated, from Latin and medieval German, by Edmund Colledge O.S.A. and Bernard McGinn (Mahwah, NJ: Paulist Press, 1981), 199–203. This is Sermon no. 12 in the numbering of Eckhart's primary twentieth-century editor, Josef Quint. But see also *The Complete Mystical Works of Meister Eckhart*, edited and translated by Maurice O'C. Walshe, Vol. 1 (New York: Crossroad Publishing Co., 1979, revised edition 2009). Here the same Sermon appears as no. 87, pages 420–6.
26 *Meister Eckhart: The Essential Sermons, Commentaries, Treatises and Defense*, 199. On the echoes – not only in this particular formula but in various other features, as well, especially of this sermon – of Marguerite Porete's *Mirror of Simple Souls*: see Sells, *Mystical Languages of Unsaying*, 180–3. Porete's work had been condemned as heretical, and in 1310 she herself, refusing to disown it, had been burned at the stake in Paris. The very next year, as it happened, Eckhart returned to Paris to teach at the university, and became a fellow-resident in the same Dominican house there as William Humbert, who had led the judicial investigation into Porete's work. This will presumably have given him direct access to a copy of the *Mirror*. But it renders

the parallels in his text all the more striking: parallels that, as Sells remarks, 'range from central conceptual resonances to precise correspondences in rhetoric and terminology'.
27 *Meister Eckhart: The Essential Sermons, Commentaries, Treatises and Defense*, 199.
28 Ibid., 200–1. My italics.
29 Ibid., 202.
30 Ibid., 201.
31 Simone Weil, *Gravity and Grace*, translated from French by Emma Craufurd (London: Routledge & Kegan Paul, 1952), 28–34.
32 Sells, *Mystical Languages of Unsaying*, 184. C.f. *Meister Eckhart: The Essential Sermons, Commentaries, Treatises and Defense*, sermon 52, page 200.
33 C.f. note 7, above. Also: Sells, *Mystical Languages of Unsaying*, 1–4, 10–13, 187–92.
34 Ibid., 188. C.f. *Meister Eckhart: The Essential Sermons, Commentaries, Treatises and Defense*, 200.
35 *Meister Eckhart: The Essential Sermons, Commentaries, Treatises and Defense*, 202–3.
36 Ibid., 203.
37 Ibid.
38 Ibid., 187. *The Complete Mystical Works of Meister Eckhart*, Sermon 65, pages 330–1.
39 *Meister Eckhart: The Essential Sermons, Commentaries, Treatises and Defense*, 187. Italicization added.
40 Ibid., 434. (In Walshe's enumeration this is Sermon no. 89.)
41 Here are just three examples; in Walshe's translation.
   (a) Sermon 25 *Moyses orabat dominum suum*; Walshe no. 10, page 92:
   'When the will is so unified that it forms a single *one*, then the heavenly Father bears his only-begotten Son in himself – in me. Why in himself, in me? Because then I am one with him, he cannot shut me out, and in that act the Holy Ghost receives his being, his becoming, from me as from God. Why? Because I am *in* God. If he does not receive it from me, he does not receive it from God.'
   (b) Sermon 75 *Mandatum novum do vobis ut diligatis invicem sicut dilexi vos*; Walshe no. 88, page 429:
   'And what would it profit me that the Father gives birth to his Son unless I bear him too? God begets his Son in a perfect soul and is brought to bed there so that she [the divinised soul!] may bear him forth again in all her works.'
   (c) Sermon 22 *Ave, gratia plena*; Walshe, no. 53, page 281:
   '*In principio*. Here we are given to understand that we are an only son whom the Father has been eternally begetting out of the hidden darkness of eternal concealment, indwelling in the first beginning of the primal purity which is the plenitude of all purity. There I have been eternally at rest and asleep in the hidden understanding of the eternal Father, immanent and unspoken. Out of that purity he has been ever begetting me, his only-begotten son, in the very image of his eternal Fatherhood that I may be father and beget him of whom I am begotten[!]'.
42 Athanasius, *On the Incarnation of the Word* (online: newadvent.org), 54: 3.
43 *Meister Eckhart: The Essential Sermons, Commentaries, Treatises and Defense*, 188.
44 It is the ninth article condemned in the Bull *In agro dominico*: ibid., 78.
45 Marguerite Porete, *The Mirror of Simple Souls*, translated from medieval French by Ellen Babinsky (Mahwah, NJ: Paulist Press, 1993).
46 English translation by Elvira Borgstädt, in Bernard McGinn, ed., *Meister Eckhart Teacher and Preacher* (Mahwah, NJ: Paulist Press, 1986), 347–88.

47 Eckhart, intent on affirming the redeemed individual's fundamental dignity, as an individual – that is, their transcendence of the herd / the gang / the mob, and consequent immunity from manipulation by impatient evangelists – turns, polemically, to the Christmas story as a source of metaphor. For this purpose, he might just as well, or even better, have turned to the Easter story. C.f. Sebastian Moore, *The Crucified Is No Stranger* (London: Darton, Longman & Todd, 1977): a remarkable meditation on one's 'crucifixion' of one's true self, and on 'resurrection' considered in that light. – Why does Eckhart's strategy historically precede Moore's? Why the greater, delaying resistance, in the latter case?

   I suppose it is just because the Easter story is so much more heavily freighted than the Christmas one is, with the authoritarian concerns of church ideology. The ecclesiastical authorities of Meister Eckhart's day were troubled enough by *his* mystical exegesis of the Christmas story. But, to the ideologues, it is of course the Easter story which has always really mattered most. The authority of the church hierarchy has traditionally derived, in ideological terms, from its 'apostolic' heritage. And the original authority of the apostles themselves is grounded in their status as having been the original witnesses to Christ's resurrection. In Roman Catholic or Orthodox tradition, especially, the authority of the clergy in general stems, above all, from their role as celebrants of the Eucharist, re-enacting the Last Supper, the event with which the Easter story starts to build towards its climax. So too, the Church has done everything it could to reinforce its authority by invoking the memory of its martyrs; each of whose deaths re-enacts that of Christ himself. Whenever the protagonists of church ideology have found themselves, in whatever way, embattled against the counter-vailing values of the 'earthly city' they have naturally tended to see themselves as carrying forward the struggle which brought Christ to the cross. And how, then, would that fit the frankly *anarchistic* implications of an argument like Moore's?

   Christmas, by contrast, has always been far more of an innocent folk-religious affair.

48 Michael Sells, trans. and ed., *Early Islamic Mysticism: Sufi, Qur'an, Mi'raj, Poetic and Theological Writings* (New York: Paulist Press, 1996), 78–84.

49 Ibid., 242–50; and c.f. 47–56.

50 Ibid., 254.

51 Muhammad Ibn 'Abdi 'l-Jabbár Al-Niffarí, *The Mawáqif and Mukhátabát*, edited and translated from Arabic into English by Arthur John Arberry, E. J. Gibb Memorial Trust 1935 (reissued by Cambridge University Press, 1978). This is a dual language edition, with detailed critical apparatus.

52 Sells, *Early Islamic Mysticism*, Chapter 10.

53 The first of these is by Maati Kabbal (Paris: Editions de l'Eclat, 1989); the second, by Mahmoud Sami-Ali (Paris: Fata Morgana, 1995); the third, by Adonis (Paris: Les Belles Lettres, 2017). Adonis – contributor to the first of these, and chief author of the third, in partnership with the philologist Donatien Grau – is one of the leading figures in modern Arabic literature. Niffarí had, it seems, largely been forgotten in the Arab world, when in 1965 Adonis, browsing in the library of the American University in Beirut, happened, quite by chance, to come across a copy of Arberry's edition; which had never been borrowed, perhaps never even been read, by anyone; but which introduced him to a poet of whom he had hitherto known little or nothing.

54 Although I am not an Arabist, the translations, or rather imitations, here are my own; working from Arberry's text, but seeking, with the aid both of Sells's and of Adonis's versions, to free up what I take to be the underlying sense. Arberry, very helpfully,

seeks to provide the most literal translation possible – never mind that it is, as a result, altogether removed from natural English. But Niffarí did not write in unnatural Arabic! And he aims at memorability, to facilitate recitation, as with the Qur'an. To reproduce this, I have rendered his work here into primarily anapaestic English, laid out in short, irregular lines. Neither that rhythm nor that lay-out is there in the original Arabic. But the anapaests are intended to concentrate, and so to energize, the swift flow of words; whilst the irregularity of the lines, on the contrary, resists, and breaks up, the flow (like the placement of rocks or other obstacles in a riverbed) with a view to minimizing aural monotony.

55 Seventy-five in most manuscripts; plus, two more in another manuscript, which Arberry also includes in his edition.
56 *Awqafni*, 'he stopped me', in this or that guise; *wa qal' li … waqal' li … wa qal' li …* 'and he said to me … and he said to me … and he said to me …'
57 Sells, *Early Islamic Mysticism*, 285–6; page 31 in Arberry's edition.
58 I am thinking in particular of the story of 'Abdullah the Fisherman and Abdullah the Merman' in the *Thousand and One Nights*; with its evocation of a deep underwater utopia.
59 Arberry translates *'álim* as 'the knower', *'ilm* as 'science'; *'árif* as 'the gnostic', *ma'rifa* as 'gnosis'. But 'knower' seems to me too vague here; 'science', surely misleading. And the prevailing connotations of 'gnosis' render it in my view quite inappropriate (see Chapter 5, below). For my part, I prefer 'the (metaphorical) grammarian' for *'álim*; 'the evangelist' for *'árif*.

The translation of *wáqif* is also problematic. The closest rendering, 'one who has been stopped in their tracks', is obviously, for most purposes, too cumbersome. Arberry (in accordance with his translation of *Kitáb al-Mawáqif* as the 'Book of the Spiritual Stayings') has 'the stayer'. This, though, does not in itself convey the necessary connotation of shocked amazement. If an English term is required, I would suggest a fresh coinage: 'the confrontee'.

60 This is the Islamic year 354. For evidence internal to the original manuscripts of the *Mawáqif* themselves suggesting a slightly later date, see Arberry, *The Mawáqif and Mukhátabát*, 227.
61 It is unclear whether this is Egypt (*Misr*) the country, or more likely the Mesopotamian region around a large canal, leading from, and back to, the Euphrates, locally called 'the Egypt Nile' (*Níl Misr*). C.f. Arberry, *The Mawáqif and Mukhátabát*, 4–5. Niffarí's original home town of Niffar (ancient Nippur) was bisected by this canal.
62 Arberry, 8–11.
63 See Louis Massignon, *The Passion of al-Halláj: Mystic and Martyr of Islam*, 4 vols., translated from French by Herbert Mason (Princeton University Press, 1982): a monumental work, which remains *the* great classic of Christian scholarly engagement with Islam.
64 Sells, *Early Islamic Mysticism*, 213–26.
65 Arberry, *The Mawáqif and Mukhátabát*, 77. And c.f. his note describing this as 'perhaps the most striking passage in the whole of Niffarí, for it exhibits in the clearest possible way his complete absorption in God and his insight into the worthlessness of everything other than Him': pages 227–8.

Chapter 4

1. Evelyn Underhill, *Mysticism: A Study of the Nature and Development of Man's Spiritual Consciousness* (London: Methuen, 1911). (This was the first religious book I ever read; as a precocious child, encouraged by my mother.)
2. Bernard of Clairvaux, *Sermons on the 'Song of Songs'*, English translation from Latin by Kilian Walsh and Irene Edmonds, in 4 vol. (Kalamazoo, MI: Cistercian Publications, 1971, 1976, 1979, 1980).
3. *Pseudo-Dionysius: The Complete Works*, ed. C. Luibheid, Letter Nine, page 282.
4. The exact dates of Hadewijch of Antwerp are unknown; Mechtild of Magdeburg died in 1282(?); Mechtild of Hackeborn died in 1298; Gertrude of Helfta died in 1302. Other notable visionaries include: Elisabeth of Schönau (d. 1165); Hildegard of Bingen (d. 1179); Mary of Oignies (d. 1213); Beatrijs of Nazareth (d. 1268); Angela of Foligno (d. 1309); Marguerite d'Oingt (d. 1310); Margareta Ebner (d. 1351); Bridget of Sweden (d. 1373); Catherine of Siena (d. 1380); Dorothea of Montau (d. 1394); Julian of Norwich (d. 1416); Margery Kempe (d. 1438?); Catherine of Genoa (d. 1510).
5. Teresa of Jesus, *Complete Works*, Vol. 2, translated from Spanish by E. Allison Peers, *The Interior Castle* (New York and London: Sheed and Ward, 1946).
6. A number of Dominicans, after her death, expressed anxiety lest Teresa become a heroine for so-called '*alumbrados*', 'enlightened ones' or crypto-Protestants. From the 1540s onwards the Inquisition, which the Dominicans ran – having eased off from their original persecution of forcibly converted Muslims and Jews suspected of backsliding – had turned instead to a focus on the supposed *alumbrado* threat.
7. Dom Cuthbert Butler, *Western Mysticism: The Teaching of Augustine, Gregory and Bernard on Contemplation and the Contemplative Life* (London: Constable, 2nd edition, 1926), xxiii–lxxii.
8. Ibid., xxxv.
9. This phrase is perhaps best known today as the title of Aldous Huxley's book, *The Perennial Philosophy* (London: Chatto & Windus 1946); although Huxley's thought actually remains something of an out-rider to the wider tendency I have in mind.

    It was originally coined by the Italian humanist scholar Agostino Steuco (1497–1549), who eventually rose to be, not only the absentee Bishop of Chisamo in Crete, but also a most industrious Director of the Vatican Library. In addition to writing various works of anti-Protestant polemic, Steuco was the author of a substantial volume entitled *De Perenni Philosophia* (*On the Perennial Philosophy*), dedicated to Pope Paul III. This is remembered today, for the most part, only for its title; it remains untranslated into English. Steuco's scholarship is of course very out-dated. But the basic argument is in accord with what one also finds in the earlier writings of Marsilio Ficino (1433–99) and Pico Della Mirandola (1463–94). Ficino, Pico and Steuco, although remaining loyal Catholic Christians, were keen students of pagan Neo-Platonist literature, and especially the work of Iamblichus. They were interested, as well, in what remained of the sacred literature produced by the 'mystery cults' celebrated by Iamblichus: fragmentary hymns from the cult of Orpheus, for instance; also, the so-called 'Chaldean Oracles'. And, above all: the great mass of second- or third-century CE Greco-Egyptian texts attributed to 'Hermes Trismegistus', which Ficino translated into Latin, in fourteen volumes, as the *Corpus Hermeticum*. These they took to be much older, in their final written form, than they actually are. What Steuco called the '*philosophia perennis*', Ficino had earlier termed the '*prisca theologia*', 'the primordial theology'. Hermes, he thought, had brought it, in one form, to the Egyptians; Zoroaster, in another form, to the Persians; and Pythagoras, to the Greeks. But in principle the 'primordiality' of the 'primordial theology' is, *ultimately*, that of the Garden of Eden. For here, in these various forms of pagan literature, Ficino thought to detect an actual surviving trace of Adam and Eve's original wisdom, from before the Fall. Pico developed the same view; with supplementary recognition of the Kabbalah, as another source. And the whole purpose of Steuco's work was then to try and demonstrate the essential complementarity of 'perennial philosophy', originally stemming from humanity's original innocence, to the remedial, redemptive wisdom of the Gospel.

In the later seventeenth century Steuco's coinage was significantly adopted, but also adapted, by Leibniz. For Leibniz, very differently from Ficino, Pico and Steuco, 'the perennial philosophy' is a term for the ideal religious ethos to accompany his own essentially *deist* metaphysics. Meanwhile, he was also wrestling with the newly emergent challenge of Chinese thought; now for the first time being relayed to European intellectuals. Leibniz seizes upon the essential metaphysical modesty of classical Confucianism and Taoism as an opportunity to project his own more developed metaphysical doctrine onto the Chinese texts: controversially, in particular, identifying Zhu Xi's modest Neo-Confucian notion of '*li*' with 'God'. As Leibniz sees it, 'the perennial philosophy' is pre-eminently the resultant bridge between Chinese wisdom and Western philosophical enlightenment.

Then, in the twentieth century, the concept mutates and becomes associated with the notion of 'mystical experience'.

10 Amongst Guénon's many writings, perhaps his masterpiece is *La crise du monde moderne*, 1927, translated from French by A. Osborne as *The Crisis of the Modern World* (River Road, CT: Lawrence Verry Inc., 1975).

For an account of the whole 'Traditionalist' tradition, see Mark Sedgwick, *Against the Modern World: Traditionalism and the Secret Intellectual History of the Twentieth Century* (Oxford University Press, 2004). This is an entertaining book: entertainingly sly, gossipy, amused. It is in fact an altogether irreverent study of a guru culture which of course, like all guru cultures, very much depends upon the devotee's reverence for their spiritual master. So, it has been fiercely attacked by loyal 'Traditionalists', objecting to the inevitable omissions in such a broad overview of the topic, and quibbling over details. For my part, I must confess that I rather warm to Sedgwick's irreverence. But, for the sake of balance, one might also consult three lengthy reviews collected together in the web edition of *Studies in Comparative Religion*, 2009: by Michael Fitzgerald (originally published in *Sacred Web*, Vol. 13, 2004); Wilson Eliot Poindexter (originally published in *Sophia*, Vol. 11, no. 1, Summer 2005); and Róbert Horváth.

11 See for example Coomaraswamy, *A New Approach to the Vedas: An Essay in Translation and Exegesis* (London: Luzac, 1933); *The Transformation of Nature in Art* (Cambridge, MA: Harvard University Press, 1934); *Hinduism and Buddhism* (New York: Philosophical Library, 1941).

These are his major 'Traditionalist' works. He had a significant influence on Guénon especially with regard to his advocacy of the truth-potential of Buddhism; of which Guénon had hitherto been somewhat dismissive.

Mircea Eliade (1907–86) may be said to have been another highly influential representative of the same. Thus, Sedgwick (op. cit. page 189) speaks of Eliade's 'soft Traditionalism'.

12 For a flavour of Schuon's own writing: see Seyyed Hossein Nasr, ed., *The Essential Frithjof Schuon* (Bloomington, IN: World Wisdom Books, 2006). And for a loyally Schuonian introduction to his work: Harry Oldmeadow, *Frithjof Schuon and the Perennial Philosophy* (Bloomington, IN: World Wisdom Books, 2010). His most significant allies included Seyyed Hossein Nasr, Martin Lings, Huston Smith. Another leading Schuonian, Marco Pallis, entered into a promising correspondence with Thomas Merton; cut short however by Merton's sudden death in 1968.

Schuon first met Guénon in 1938. However, their initial alliance began to fall apart some ten years later, as Guénon became increasingly alarmed by what he saw as Schuon's challenge to his authority within the 'Traditionalist' movement globally.

13 For an account of the other three, apart from Schuon's order, see Sedgwick, *Against the Modern World*, 131–42.

14 Evola's central work, *Revolt against the Modern World* first appeared in 1934; translated into English by Guido Stucco (Rochester, VT: Inner Traditions International, 1995). See also, most notably for instance, Evola, *Ride the Tiger: A Survival Manual for Aristocrats of the Soul*, translated by Joscelyn Godwin and Constance Fontana (Rochester, VT: Inner Traditions, 2003); and his 1963 intellectual autobiography: *The Path of Cinnabar*, translated by John Morgan (London: Arktos Media, 2010).

15 This was in a journal, *La Torre*, which Evola edited. It was actually closed down by the Fascist authorities after the fifth issue, the one in which this formulation appeared.

16 Evola, *Revolt against the Modern World*, 68. On Charlemagne, see ibid., 69–70: here, for Evola, we see the essential lost potential-for-truth in Christianity.

17 Sedgwick, *Against the Modern World*, 221–37: an account of the early influence of Traditionalism on the development of Dugin's thinking. In the topsy-turvy world of Russian politics in the 1990s Dugin opportunistically at first allied himself with the remnant of the Communist Party, under Gennady Zyuganov, as this had mutated into an essentially nationalistic enterprise; but subsequently became a qualified – at times however quite sycophantic – supporter of Vladimir Putin. Sedgwick traces the story up to the early years of the Putin regime. Since then, Dugin has been a leading advocate of Russian military expansionism: in the Caucasus, in Syria, in the Ukraine.

18 Walter T. Stace, *The Teachings of the Mystics* (New York: Mentor Books, 1960); *Mysticism and Philosophy* (London: Macmillan, 1961).

For subsequent developments of the basic Stacean philosophical argument, see for instance William Wainwright, *Mystical Experience* (Madison, WI: University of Wisconsin Press, 1982); Richard H. Jones, *Philosophy of Mysticism: Raids on the Ineffable* (Albany, NY: State University of New York Press, 2016).

(In his youth, Stace – whilst, as it happens, working as a civil servant for the British Raj in Ceylon – had notably published a book-length study of *The Philosophy of Hegel*. But this work seems to me to be rather more a study of the letter, than of the true critical spirit informing Hegel's thought: Stace is so entirely preoccupied, here, with the paedagogic architecture of the Hegelian 'system' as such. One can only admire the thoroughness of the pull-out 'Diagram of the Hegelian system' he provides, mapping over 200 items of Hegelian terminology as such. Yet, the net effect is of a supremely desiccated work!).

19 Stace, *The Teachings of the Mystics*, 9.

20 See R. C. Zaehner, *Concordant Discord: The Interdependence of Faiths* (Oxford University Press, 1971), 200. Zaehner's critique here is in fact a counter-attack: Stace having, in particular, attacked Zaehner's book *Mysticism Sacred and Profane* on the basis of its character as an apologia for the Roman Catholic tradition from a comparison-of-religions point of view. See Stace, *Mysticism and Philosophy*, 97.

21 Stace, *Mysticism and Philosophy*, 18–22.
22 C.f. Maggie Ross, *Silence: A User's Guide*, Volume 1, *Process* (London: Darton, Longman and Todd, 2014), 79.
23 R. M. Bucke, *Cosmic Consciousness: A Study in the Evolution of the Human Mind* (Boston, MA: E. P. Dutton & Co., 1901).
24 Stace, *Mysticism and Philosophy*, 33.
25 William James, *The Varieties of Religious Experience: A Study in Human Nature* (London: Collins, 1960.)
26 Ibid., Lecture 2.
27 This is strikingly apparent, for instance, in James's damning verdict on Teresa of Ávila. She above all represents the turn within Christian theology towards a concern with his own topic, 'religious experience' as such; indeed, he acknowledges that she is 'the expert of experts' in this regard (ibid., Lecture 17, page 394). He is also keen to defend Teresa from the assaults of 'medical materialist' critics, who would dismiss her 'experience' as merely being symptomatic of 'hysteria' (ibid., Lecture 1). Nevertheless, he is repelled by her loyalty to the Church.

Accordingly, he develops a breezy *ad feminam* attack on Teresa: 'In spite of the sufferings which she endured,' he writes, 'there is a curious flavour of *superficiality* about her genius' (ibid., Lecture 14, pages 338). He alludes to a recent work of popular psychology:

> A Birmingham anthropologist, Dr. Jordan, has divided the human race into two types, whom he calls 'shrews' and non-shrews' respectively. The shrew-type is defined as possessing an 'active unimpassioned temperament'. In other words, shrews are the 'motors', rather than the 'sensories', and their expressions are as a rule more energetic than the feelings which appear to prompt them. Saint Teresa, paradoxical as such a judgment may sound, was a typical shrew, in this sense of the term. The bustle of her style, as well as of her life, proves it. Not only must she receive unheard-of personal favours and spiritual graces from her Saviour, but she must immediately write about them and *exploiter* them professionally, and use her expertness to give instruction to those less privileged. Her voluble egotism; her sense, not of radical bad being, as the really contrite have it, but of her 'faults' and 'imperfections' in the plural; her stereotyped humility and return upon herself, as covered with 'confusion' at each new manifestation of God's singular partiality for a person so unworthy, are typical of shrewdom: a paramountly feeling nature would be objectively lost in gratitude, and silent. She had some public instincts, it is true; she hated the Lutherans, and longed for the church's triumph over them; but in the main her idea of religion seems to have been that of an endless amatory flirtation – if one may say so without irreverence – between the devotee and the deity; and apart from helping the younger nuns to go in this direction by the inspiration of her example and instruction, there is absolutely no human use in her, or sign of any general human interest. Yet the spirit of her age, far from rebuking her, exalted her as superhuman. (Ibid., 338–9)

Teresa is amongst the most interesting of Christian religious writers, according to James's criteria. And yet, he judges that 'there is absolutely no human use in her'. Her testimony is in no way *useful*, as an example to be followed.

At the end of Lecture XV, James describes his method in *The Varieties of Religious Experience* as an 'abandonment of theological criteria', in favour of 'practical common sense and the empirical method': page 364. Lectures XIV and XV, on 'The Value of Saintliness', feature several invocations of 'utility' as a criterion, in this context: pages 339, 340, 345 (twice), 352, 364. 'Utility', however, seems to me quite a superficial, in fact absolutely *useless*, criterion for religious truth! For how, after all, is it more than mere cover for arbitrary prejudice?

The institutional Church to which Teresa belonged was of course singularly oppressive. Her expressions of 'stereotyped humility' and 'flirtatious' talk of divine 'favours' surely have to be understood as tactics, necessary to her successful out-manoeuvring of its extreme patriarchy. James, however, does not consider this. Nor does he consider the difference between *this* ecclesiastical context and others, more benign. His hostility to institutional religion thus remains no more than an over-generalized prejudice.

28 Gordon Allport, *The Individual and his Religion* (New York: Macmillan, 1950). C.f. Adorno et al., *The Authoritarian Personality*. Note that both books originally appeared the same year.

29 Abraham Maslow, *Religions, Values and Peak-Experiences* (Indianapolis, IN: Kappa Delta Pi, 1964). By 'peak experiences', in the title of this seminal lecture, is meant every form of ecstatic experience, not only those explicitly framed as religious. Maslow's research suggested to him that almost everyone has such experiences; although some refuse to attribute what he regards as proper significance to them. He calls such people 'non-peakers'. 'Mystics', by contrast, are the supreme 'peakers'. 'Organised religion', he argues (page 24), 'can [essentially] be thought of as an effort to communicate peak-experiences to non-peakers, to teach them, to apply them, etc. Often, to make it more difficult, this job falls into the hands of non-peakers'. And he goes on to argue (page 25) that there are two basic sorts of religion: the (good) left-wing sort and the (bad) right-wing sort, the left-wing constituted by 'the peakers, the mystics, the transcenders, *or the privately religious people*', and the right-wing by 'those who take the organisation, the church, as primary and as more important to them than the prophet and his original revelation'. (The italics in that quotation are mine.) Maslow also cites with warm approval Marghanita Laski's 1961 study of *Ecstasy in Secular and Religious Experience*. In fact, he saw himself as contributing to two major new disciplines: 'third force psychology' and 'fourth force psychology'. In this scheme, the first two 'forces' are psychoanalysis in the Freudian sense and behaviourism. 'Third force psychology', then, is the study, not of mental disorder, but of what makes for mental health and well-being in general; whilst 'fourth force psychology' is another name for 'transpersonal psychology', which differs from 'third force psychology' simply inasmuch as it is a study, not just of *ordinary* well-being, but of *optimal* well-being, the supreme fulfilment of human potential through cultivated ecstasy.

30 Stace, *Mysticism and Philosophy*, 79.
31 Ibid., 278.
32 Ibid., 305. Italics and exclamation mark added.
33 Katz, ed., *Mysticism and Philosophical Analysis* (London: Sheldon Press, 1978); *Mysticism and Religious Traditions* (Oxford University Press, 1983); *Mysticism and Language* (Oxford University Press, 1992); *Mysticism and Sacred Scripture* (Oxford University Press, 2000). For Katz's direct discussion of Stace, see his essay in the first of these collections, 'Language, Epistemology and Mysticism'.
34 See also Wayne Proudfoot, *Religious Experience* (Berkeley, CA: University of California Press, 1985).
35 Nicholas Lash, *Easter in Ordinary* (Charlottesville, VA: University Press of Virginia, 1988).

36 Rowan Williams, 'Butler's *Western Mysticism*: Towards an Assessment', *Downside Review* 102; 1984; discussing Butler, 1926. See note 12. Other relevant texts by Williams are listed in the bibliography.
37 Denys Turner, *The Darkness of God* (Cambridge University Press, 1995).
    As regards Augustine, by the way, consider his struggle against Pelagius: isn't the key issue here that – whereas Pelagius prioritizes the (often bullying) puritanical principle, '*No excuses!*' – Augustine prioritizes, precisely, '*No boasting!*'?
38 For a comprehensive history of scholarly literature on 'mysticism', up to that date: see Bernard McGinn, *The Presence of God: A History of Christian Mysticism*, Volume 1, *The Foundations of Mysticism: Origins to 5th Century* (New York: Crossroads, 1991); Appendix, 'Theoretical Foundations: The Modern Study of Mysticism', 265–343. Later volumes in the same series are listed in the bibliography.
39 Turner, *The Darkness of God*, 262–5.
40 Grace Jantzen, *Power, Gender and Christian Mysticism* (Cambridge University Press, 1995) And see also her two earlier articles: 'Mysticism and Experience', *Religious Studies* 25; 1989; 'Could There Be a Mystical Core of Religion?', *Religious Studies* 26; 1990.
41 Ross, *Silence: A User's Guide*.
42 Gerson, *De mystica theologica*, 1. 28. 4–7; André Combes, ed., *Ioannis Carlerii de Gerson: De Mystica Theologia*, Lugano: Thesaurus Mundi, 1958.
43 Harmless, *Mystics* (Oxford University Press, 2008), 5.
44 Ross, *Silence: A User's Guide*, Vol. I; 90–1.
45 Ibid., 78. Italics added.

Chapter 5

1 *Theaetetus* 155d.
2 *Metaphysics* 982 b12, 18–19.
3 Julian of Norwich, *Revelations of Divine Love*, edited by Barry Windeatt (Oxford University Press, 2015), Chapter 27.
4 C.f. Cyril O'Regan, *Gnostic Return in Modernity* (Albany, NY: State University of New York, 2001), Chapter 3 on the six-fold-ness specifically of Valentinian narrative. But the same basic shape also recurs in Sethian and Basilidean classical gnostic narrative; in Kabbalah; in Böhme's thought.
5 Amin Maalouf, *The Gardens of Light*, translated from French by Dorothy S. Blair (London: Abacus, 1997). Maalouf indeed represents Mani as a model of proper evangelistic patience. In Chapter 18, he imagines a scene in which the Sassanian King of Kings Shapur I offers to convert, and help spread Mani's gospel by armed force, if only Mani will make this possible by relaxing his strict pacifism. But Mani refuses.
6 In the mid-twentieth century the study of early gnosticism was transformed above all by the work of the philosopher *Hans Jonas*. During the 1920s Jonas was a student of both Martin Heidegger and Rudolf Bultmann in Marburg; (also a friend of his fellow-student Hannah Arendt). He was much influenced by the grand-narrative thought of Oswald Spengler; then hot off the press; and developed an interest in 'the Gnostic religion' essentially as representing, in his view, the very purest and most radical expression of the innovatory truth-potential inherent in what he calls the 'Spirit of late antiquity'. Thus, for him, early 'Gnosticism' is first and foremost a

product of '*Entweltlichung*', 'un-worldly-ing'. That is: a rebellious supposed unmasking of the corruption of the entire metaphysical world-order – a wholesale nihilistic repudiation, therefore, of all existing popular religion, as reflecting that world-order, accompanied by intense existential anxiety and insecurity – but, at the same time, also an apocalyptic sense of euphoria, as 'Gnostic' groups set to work rebuilding spiritual communion afresh, from scratch. Jonas sees in this a remote anticipation, in mythic form, of the dialectic of 'authenticity' developed in Heidegger's *Being and Time*. It is, after all, quite closely akin to what Bultmann finds in the Johannine and Pauline New Testament texts. And it is at the core of what Spengler calls 'Arabian Culture', in its spring-time, penetrating the world of Hellenistic antiquity to subvert it.

Unfortunately, however, Jonas's account is somewhat vitiated by the paucity of original sources available to him. His notion of 'Gnosticism' was especially dependent on ancient Mandean and Manichean texts, in particular. But, of course, this whole field of study was revolutionized by the discovery of the fourth-century Coptic-language library hidden in a cave near Nag Hammadi in Upper Egypt, in 1945.

The first volume of Jonas's great treatise on *Gnosis und spätantiker Geist* appeared in 1934; and, although the second volume was delayed until 1954, he did not himself read Coptic, and proper translations of the Nag Hammadi texts had still not been made. Even his later work on *The Gnostic Religion*, published in 1958, suffers from the same problem. Jonas's evaluation of early 'Gnosticism' may have evolved – in later years he became more critical of what he had at first affirmed, as he also became more critical of Heidegger – but his essential understanding of its meaning remained more fixed. And subsequent scholarship, based on the Nag Hammadi texts, has increasingly tended to reject that understanding as being, after all, far too monolithic. See for instance Michael Waldstein, 'Hans Jonas's Construct "Gnosticism": Analysis and Critique', *Journal of Early Christian Studies* 8 (3), 2000.

At any rate, what I mean by 'gnosticism' is by no means what Jonas means.

7   Tertullian, *Against the Valentinians* (online: newadvent.org).
8   There were minority Christian groups around, in the world of early Islam, 'docetists' denying that Christ truly suffered in the flesh. This teaching did play a role in helping release the special genius of Islam from the orbit of Christianity (*Qur'an*, Sura 4: 157–8). And, it is true, docetist thought swirled around in the same general thought-world as early gnosticism. But common or garden docetism, in itself, by no means automatically equates to gnosticism, in the strict sense. Indeed, insofar as it correlates to *a boast* – 'We, the enlightened, are at one with Christ in our spiritual elevation above the domain of fleshly existence; you, our rivals, are not' – it may well be regarded as representing, in the first instance, a counter-current of quite crude evangelistic impatience.
9   Irenaeus lived *c.* 130–*c.* 202. His major work, a treatise *Against Heresies* written at some point in the years 174–89, is largely an attack on the gnostic teacher Ptolemy, who was evangelizing in his diocese. For an English translation, see Bentley Layton, ed., *The Gnostic Scriptures: A New Translation with Annotations and Introductions* (London: SCM Press, 1987), 281–302.
10 Rabbi Meir ben Simeon of Narbonne, in the early thirteenth century, denounced the book *Bahir* in particular. Later anti-Kabbalist polemicists include Leon Modena in early seventeenth-century Venice, and Rabbi Jacob Emden of Altona, Hamburg, in the mid-eighteenth century.
11 Gershom Scholem, *Major Trends in Jewish Mysticism* (Jerusalem: Schocken Publishing House, 1941); *On the Kabbalah and Its Symbolism*, translated from German by Ralph Mannheim (New York: Schocken Books, 1965).

For a defence of Graetz's work: see George Y. Kohler, 'Heinrich Graetz and the Kabbalah', in *Kabbalah – Journal for the Study of Jewish Mystical Texts*, 2018; 111–35.

Scholem's great successor is Moshe Idel. See especially his breakthrough work: Idel, *Kabbalah: New Perspectives* (New Haven and London: Yale University Press, 1988).

12 James M. Robinson, ed., *The Nag Hammadi Library in English*, translated and introduced by members of the Coptic Gnostic Library Project of the Institute for Antiquity and Christianity (Claremont, CA; Leiden: E. J. Brill, 1996), 104–23. Also: Layton, ed. *The Gnostic Scriptures: A New Translation*; where the title is rendered '*The Secret Book According to John*'. This is a key Nag Hammadi text.

13 Robinson, ed., *The Nag Hammadi Library in English*, 58–103. Another key Nag Hammadi text.

14 See Alan Unterman, ed., *The Kabbalist Tradition* (London: Penguin Classics, 2008).

15 Literally: 'the Short Face'. See Scholem, *Major Trends in Jewish Mysticism*, 270. *Zeir Anpin* is counterposed in the Lurianic scheme to *Arikh Anpin*, the highest Partsuf: literally 'the Long Face', but more exactly 'the Long-Suffering' or 'Infinitely Patient One'.

16 The chief pastor of Böhme's home town, Görlitz, one Gregorius Richter, did, it is true, react with fierce hostility to the appearance, in his congregation, of this unauthorized prophetic layman. (Böhme was a shoemaker, who subsequently became a linen and glove-merchant by trade.) In 1612, after he had written his first book *Aurora*, and people had started making copies of it, Böhme went to church one Sunday only to find himself being personally denounced from the pulpit. For six years he was silenced. But then he began again. On New Year's Day 1624 his first published work, *The Way to Christ*, appeared. And shortly afterwards Richter actually prevailed upon the Town Council of Görlitz to expel him. However, Böhme readily found shelter, and enthusiastic Lutheran patronage, elsewhere. He was never in any sort of serious danger; and was never driven publicly to lash out, in any dramatic gesture. Eventually, indeed, Richter's own son was to edit a collection of extracts from Böhme's writings, which was published in Amsterdam.

17 John Wesley and other Evangelicals of his day were great admirers of Law's 1729 work, *A Serious Call to a Devout and Holy Life*. But that was written before Law's turn towards Böhme, which dates from 1737. Unsurprisingly, Wesley the great evangelist was dismayed by this; and in 1756 issued an open letter deploring it.

18 Valentin Weigel was a key predecessor in this regard. See Andrew Weeks, ed., *Valentin Weigel: Selected Spiritual Writings* (Mahwah, NJ: Paulist Press, 2003); *Valentin Weigel (1533–1588): German Religious Dissenter, Speculative Theorist and Advocate of Tolerance* (Albany, NY: State University of New York Press, 1999).

Also: Steven Osment, *Mysticism and Dissent* (New Haven, CT: Yale University Press, 1973); Alexandre Koyré, *Mystiques, spirituels, alchemistes du xvi siècle* (Paris: Gallimard, 1961).

19 *De Electione Gratiae (1623)*.

20 Böhme, in fact, correlates the taking of Eve out of the body of Adam to the breaking of Christ's body on the cross; and especially – since Eve is said to have been taken from one of Adam's ribs – the centurion's spear-thrust into Christ's side: *Magnum Mysterium* 19: 2, 6. So, then, the resurrection of the crucified becomes not least a symbol representing the ideal reintegration of the feminine with the masculine.

21 Hegel, *Lectures on the History of Philosophy*, Vol. 3, *Medieval and Modern Philosophy, 1819–31*, translated by Robert F. Brown (Oxford University Press, 2009), 99–103. (This characterization of Böhme is first in fact to be found in a letter from Hegel

to his Dutch former student P. G. van Ghert dated 29 July 1811.) For a meticulous study of Hegel's developing response to Böhme throughout his career, see Cecilia Muratori, *The First German Philosopher: The Mysticism of Jakob Böhme as Interpreted by Hegel*, translated from Italian by Richard Dixon and Raphaëlle Burns (Dordrecht: Springer, 2016).

22 F. W. J. Schelling, *Philosophical Investigations into the Essence of Human Freedom and Matters Connected Therewith*, 1809, translated from German by Jeff Love and Johannes Schmidt (Albany, NY: State University of New York Press, 2012). See also Robert Brown, *The Later Philosophy of Schelling: The Influence of Böhme on the Works of 1809–1815* (Lewisburg, PA: Bucknell University Press, 1977); Andrew Shanks, *Theodicy Beyond the Death of 'God': The Persisting Problem of Evil* (London and New York: Routledge, 2018).

23 William Blake, 'Letters', in Sir Geoffrey Keynes, ed. *Complete Writings of William Blake* (Oxford University Press, revised edition, 1966), 799. For examples of Blake's borrowings from Böhme, see Kathleen Raine, *Blake and Tradition*, 2 vols. (Princeton University Press, 1968).

As for that other great poet of apocalypse, John Milton: it seems likely that he will have had at least some knowledge of Böhme. He had a number of German friends, refugees from the Thirty Years War; could read German; and may well have read the original English translations. There is no conclusive evidence that he actually did. But see Margaret Lewis Bailey, *Milton and Jakob Boehme: A Study of German Mysticism in Seventeenth Century England* (Oxford University Press, 1914). In Chapter 5 she goes looking for possible echoes of Böhme in Milton's work.

24 F. C. Baur, *Die christliche Gnosis; oder die christliche Religions-Philosophie in ihrer geschichtlicher Entwicklung* (Tübingen: Osiander, 1835), 557–635.

25 Hans Lassen Martensen, *Jacob Böhme, His Life and Teaching, or, Studies in Theosophy*, translated from Danish by Thomas Rhys Evans (London: Hodder and Stoughton, 1885).

26 Nikolai Berdyaev, 'Studies Concerning Jacob Boehme: Etude 1, The Teaching about the Ungrund and Freedom', *Put'* 20; Feb. 1930; 'Etude 2, The Teaching about Sophia and the Androgyne. J. Boehme and the Russian Sophiological Current', *Put'* 21; April 1930. The first of these texts also appears as the Introduction to John Rolleston Earle's edition of Böhme, *Six Theosophic Points and Other Writings* (New York: Knopf, 1920).

27 Thomas J. J. Altizer, *The Genesis of God: A Theological Genealogy* (Louisville, KY: Westminster/John Knox Press, 1993), 15–16, 108–9, 118; *Genesis and Apocalypse: A Theological Voyage Toward Authentic Christianity* (Louisville KY: Westminster/John Knox Press, 1990), 163.

28 For extended accounts: see Cyril O'Regan, *Gnostic Apocalypse: Jacob Boehme's Haunted Narrative* (Albany, NY: State University of New York Press, 2002); Andrew Weeks, *Boehme: An Intellectual Biography of the Seventeenth-Century Philosopher and Mystic* (Albany, NY: State University of New York Press, 1991); David Walsh, *The Mysticism of Innerworldly Fulfilment: A Study of Jacob Boehme* (Gainesville: University Presses of Florida, 1983); Ernst Benz, *Mystical Sources of German Romantic Philosophy*, translated from German by Blair R. Reynolds and Eunice M. Paul (Allison Park, PA: Pickwick Publications, 1983); John Joseph Stoudt, *From Sunrise to Eternity* (Philadelphia: University of Pennsylvania Press, 1957). Alexandre Koyré, *La Philosophie de Jacob Böhme* (Paris: Vrin, 1929).

29 All the translations from Böhme in what follows are my own.

John Ellistone, the original translator, renders Böhme's German terms '*der Ungrund*' and '*der Grund*' as 'Abyss' and 'Byss'.
30 Ellistone, in his English translation, rather curiously renders it by the Latinate term 'lubet'.
31 C.f. also *Mysterium Magnum* Chapter 7.
32 'Proto-Trinity' is not a Böhmean term; it is my coinage, as are 'proto-God the Father', 'proto-God the Son', 'proto-God the Holy Spirit'. But, in general, it seems to me that Böhme's thought does need a certain amount of experimental reformulation, if it is to be brought to renewed life.
33 Again, Ellistone renders Böhme's antique term '*Schracke*' with the Latin 'flagrat' ('it blazes').
34 As its title indicates, another key text in this regard is the 1619 book *Concerning the Three Principles of the Divine Essence*.
    Note: only the Second Principle is truly divine (ibid., 10: 36). As the First remains deficient specifically because of its admixture of impatience, so the Third is a veiling of true divinity by ineradicable human ignorance and stupidity in general.
35 *The Aurora* 1612. This was the work of Böhme's that was most important to Hegel; who was especially intrigued by the dialectical role Böhme allots to Lucifer. Muratori, op. cit., discusses Hegel's response at some length.
36 These include: *Concerning the Three Principles of the Divine Essence*; *Of the Incarnation of Christ*; *De Electione Gratiae* and *Questiones Theosophicae*.
37 Eric Voegelin, *Order in History*, 5 vols. (Baton Rouge: Louisiana University Press, 1956–2000).
38 See Chapter 3, 57–8.
39 *Republic* 414 b–c. Voegelin discusses this in *Order and History* Vol. 3; 104–8.
40 Altizer, 'A New History and a New but Ancient God' review essay on Voegelin's *The Ecumenic Age*', in Ellis Sandoz, ed., *Eric Voegelin's Thought: A Critical Appraisal* (Durham, NC: Duke University Press, 1982), 184.
41 Voegelin himself acknowledges the significant influence that Kojève had on his thinking about Hegel: see his response to Altizer, ibid., 193.
42 Ibid., 183. *The Ecumenic Age* is Vol. 4 of *Order and History*. Vol. 5, *in Search of Order*, also includes discussion of Hegel. And see, as well, his 1971 essay 'On Hegel: A Study in Sorcery': *Studium Generale*, 24; 335–68.
43 Sandoz, ed., *Eric Voegelin's Thought*, 184. My italics.
44 For Voegelin's notion of 'modern Gnosticism', see also for instance, besides his texts specifically on Hegel, the following: *Science, Politics and Gnosticism: Two Essays* (Chicago: Regnery, 1968), 40–4, 67–70; *The New Science of Politics: An Introduction* (Baton Rouge: Louisiana State University Press, 1982), 112–13, 124; his contribution to John H. Hallowell, ed., *From Enlightenment to Revolution* (Durham, NC: Duke University Press, 1975), 240–302; *The Ecumenic Age* (Baton Rouge: Louisiana State University Press, 1974), 121–2; *In Search of Order* (Baton Rouge: Louisiana State University Press, 1987), 48–70; *Published Essays, 1966–1985*, edited by Ellis Sandoz (Baton Rouge: Louisiana State University Press, 1990), 293–303, 333–4; and *What Is History? And Other Late Unpublished Writings*, edited by Thomas A. Hollweck and Paul Caringella (Baton Rouge: Louisiana State University Press, 1990), 143–4.
    It should however be noted that his friend Eugene Webb reports a conversation in which Voegelin, late on in his career, confessed that, were he starting again, he probably would not in fact use the word 'Gnosticism' the way he had, but would

search for some less burdened, alternative term instead: Webb, *Eric Voegelin: Philosopher of History* (Seattle and London: University of Washington Press, 1981), 200.
45 Glenn Alexander Magee, *Hegel and the Hermetic Tradition* (Ithaca and London: Cornell University Press, 2001).
46 The term refers, in the first instance, to the reappropriation, in the Renaissance, of the *Corpus Hermeticum*. See Chapter 4, 224–5 n. 9.
47 Op. cit., page 8.
48 Ibid., page 1.
49 Böhme's 1622 treatise *De Signatura Rerum* is the prime text for this: Böhme, 1969.
50 O'Regan, *The Heterodox Hegel* (Albany, NY: State University of New York Press, 1994).
51 O'Regan, *Gnostic Return in Modernity*.
52 O'Regan, *Gnostic Apocalypse: Jacob Boehme's Haunted Narrative*.
53 Published to date: O'Regan, *Anatomy of Misremembering: Von Balthasar's Response to Modernity*, Vol. 1 *Hegel* (Chestnut Ridge, NY: Crossroad Publishing, 2014).
54 In Part 3 of his Böhme book, *Gnostic Apocalypse*, as a whole, O'Regan is weighing up the significance of each of these various elements in turn.
55 His use of the term 'metalepsis' in this sense runs through his work, as does the metaphor of intellectual 'swerving'. For 'vicious torquing': see O'Regan, *Gnostic Return in Modernity*, 58.
56 See above: Introduction, note 14.
57 On the understanding of First-Person theology/Second-Person theology/Third-Person theology operative here: see Chapter 2, 43–6.
58 In no form of church life is the Holy Spirit more fervently invoked than in the churches of the Pentecostalist tradition. And yet, I confess, it is not there that I find 'Third-Person theology' at its most penetrating. Pentecostalist theology generally seems to me to be snared in relatively superficial critique of mere lukewarmness; whilst I am afraid that Pentecostalist mega-churches look to me like fresh monuments to evangelistic impatience, run amok.

But whereas, on the other hand, those mega-churches represent evangelistic impatience at its most successful, the dominant institutional culture of my own church, the contemporary Church of England, exemplifies it at its most panicky, in a context of long-term church shrinkage. Here, alas – again in the name of the Holy Spirit – it manifests as an ethos of self-harming desperation. See Alison Milbank, *The Once and Future Parish* (London: SCM Press, 2023); Andrew Davison and Alison Milbank, *For the Parish* (London: SCM Press, 2010).
59 When I speak of 'regular preaching', obviously I do not mean anything like the quite extraordinary preaching of a Meister Eckhart!

Chapter 6

1 See above: Chapter 2, 33–5.
2 In the context of pre-political religion – or where an ethos deriving from such a culture has entered into anti-political religious tradition – the highest wisdom tends to be identified, not with a form of pathos, but on the contrary, with *apatheia*, impassivity. That is to say: shakenness out of egotistically distractive passion. But Kierkegaard, Levinas and Løgstrup are purely Abrahamic, prophetic thinkers;

primarily concerned, therefore, with wisdom in its (complementary) character as shakenness out of egotistically distractive indifference.
3   Søren Kierkegaard, *Concluding Unscientific Postscript to the Philosophical Fragments*, translated from Danish by David F. Swenson and Walter Lowrie (Princeton University Press, 1941). The crucial chapter in this regard is Part Two, Chapter 2, entitled 'The Subjective Truth, Inwardness; Truth Is Subjectivity'.
4   The two works are published together in Kierkegaard, *Philosophical Fragments / Johannes Climacus*, translated by Howard V. Hong and Edna H. Hong (Princeton University Press, 1985).
5   Kierkegaard, *Concluding Unscientific Postscript*, 165–6.
6   Ibid., 178.
7   Ibid., 181.
8   Ibid., 182.
9   Kierkegaard, *The Concept of Anxiety: A Simple Psychologically Oriented Deliberation in View of the Dogmatic Problem of Hereditary Sin*, translated by Alastair Hannay (New York & London: Liveright Publishing Corp., 2014). Previously translated as *The Concept of Dread*.
10 Kierkegaard, *The Sickness unto Death: A Christian Psychological Exposition for Edification and Awakening*, translated by Alastair Hannay (London: Penguin, 1989); *Practice in Christianity*, translated by Howard V. Hong and Edna H. Hong (Princeton University Press, 1991). The latter was also previously translated as *Training in Christianity*.
11 Kierkegaard, *The Sickness unto Death*, 109.
12 Kierkegaard, *Concluding Unscientific Postscript*, 493–8.
13 Ibid., 494.
14 Ibid., 495. (But c.f. 497–8, where it is especially associated, at its best, with a heightened '*guilt-consciousness*'; which, in terms of Vigilius Haufniensis's stereotyped comparison of sacred cultures in *The Concept of Anxiety*, would appear to bring it closer to 'Judaism' than to 'paganism'!).
15 Kierkegaard, *Concluding Unscientific Postscript*, 496.
16 See the various references to the Middle Ages strung through Kierkegaard, *Concluding Unscientific Postscript*, Part 2, Chapter IV, Section II A, 'Existential Pathos'. The category of 'religiousness A' is introduced with a view to summing up this whole stage of the argument.
17 Ibid., 345–6; 493–4.
18 Merold Westphal, *Levinas and Kierkegaard in Dialogue* (Bloomington: Indiana University Press, 2008), 134–7.
19 Westphal finds hints of 'Religiousness C', as he understands it, in some of Kierkegaard's later writings: *Two Ages*, *Works of Love*, and *Practice in Christianity*. But he himself concedes that they are no more than hints.
20 See Introduction, 6–10.
21 Kierkegaard, *Works of Love: Some Christian Reflections in the Form of Discourses*, translated by Howard and Edna Hong (New York: Harper & Row, 1962).
22 Ibid., 70–2. (But c.f. for instance the fiercely explicit affirmation of megalothymia, as opposed to isothymia, in *Two Ages*: the attack there on the 'diabolical principle of the levelling process', which Kierkegaard sees at work in his world.)
23 This is the main thesis of *Levinas and Kierkegaard in Dialogue*. And see also J. Aaron Simmons and David Wood, eds., *Kierkegaard and Levinas: Ethics, Politics and Religion* (Bloomington: Indiana University Press, 2008).

24 See in particular 'Phenomenon and Enigma', in Levinas, *Collected Philosophical Papers*, translated from French by Alphonso Lingis (Dordrecht: Nijhoff, 1987).
25 Levinas, *Totality and Infinity: An Essay on Exteriority*, translated from French by Alphonso Lingis (Dordrecht: Nijhoff, 1969); *Otherwise than Being or Beyond Essence*, translated by Alphonso Lingis (Dordrecht: Nijhoff, 1978).
26 'Á propos of "Kierkegaard vivant"', in Levinas, *Proper Names*, translated by Michael B. Smith (London: The Athlone Press, 1996), 77–8.
27 As regards Levinas's extravagantly extended use of the term 'persecution': see also *Otherwise than Being*, 75, 102, 111–12, 114, 121, 126, 127.
28 Levinas, *Proper Names*, 78.
29 Ibid., 76.
30 Ibid.
31 Kierkegaard, *Fear and Trembling*.
32 'Kierkegaard: Existence and Ethics', in Levinas, *Proper Names* 74. (And c.f. Chapter 2, 36–9.)
33 See Howard Caygill, *Levinas and the Political* (London and New York: Routledge, 2002). In Levinas's own terms, the problem is: how to reconcile his biblically inspired notion of 'prophetic' or 'messianic politics' with his concrete response, as a prominent public intellectual, to specific events.

　The most notorious case in point is his participation in a radio discussion, on the 28 September 1982, immediately after the horrific massacre of Palestinians in the Sabra and Chatila refugee camps, in West Beirut. It was Lebanese Christian soldiers of the Phalangist Militia who carried out the massacre, over a period of three days. However, the Israeli Defence Force, occupying the area, had not only, on the orders of Defence Minister Ariel Sharon, admitted them to the camp; but had then done nothing to stop the killing, although they certainly could have. It was a spectacular war crime, prompting a great public outcry of protest both in Israel and in the Jewish diaspora. The full text of the discussion is to be found, translated into English, in Hand, ed., 1989. Levinas deplores the slaughter, as who could not? And he applauds the public outcry, seeing it as evidence of the basic moral good health of Israeli society. But he is primarily concerned to reaffirm his commitment to Zionism, after all. His interlocutors appear, in fact, to be quite taken aback by his contribution: so cold it seems towards the victims; so irritably defensive; so lacking, one is even tempted to say, in any real thoughtfulness, beyond the mere reiteration of his own jargon …

　In general, Levinas is much more compelling as a pure ethicist than he is as a political thinker.

　(Caygill also draws attention, for example, to his repeated inclination to advocate a grand Judaeo-Christian cultural alliance against the supposed threat from the East, which in one place he actually terms 'the yellow peril'; and to his marked ambivalence towards Islam. There is not much apparent historical research behind these enemy-images of his! See Caygill, op. cit., 182–90.)
34 See 'Martin Buber and the Theory of Knowledge' and 'Dialogue with Martin Buber', in Levinas, *Proper Names*, 17–39.

　For Buber's dissident Zionism, see especially his *Paths in Utopia*, written in 1945; also, the discussion of Buber, Hans Kohn and Ahad Ha'am in Jacqueline Rose, *The Question of Zion* (Princeton University Press, 2005), Chapter 2.
35 The concept of '*illeity*' first emerges into Levinas's thought in the 1963 essay 'The Trace of the Other': '*La trace de l'autre*', in Levinas, *En decouvrant l'existence avec Husserl et Heidegger* (Paris: Vrin, 1974).

36 Martin Buber, *I and Thou*, 1923, translated from German by Walter Kaufmann (New York: Scribner, 1970). Walter Kaufmann, in the Prologue to this translation, makes clear that he accepted the already well-established translation of the title only under protest. He is surely right that 'I – You' is in fact a more appropriate rendering of '*Ich – Du*'.
37 *Otherwise than Being*, 147.
38 Ibid., 148.
39 Westphal, *Levinas and Kierkegaard in Dialogue*, 71–2.
40 See David Bentley Hart, *The Beauty of the Infinite: The Aesthetics of Christian Truth* (Grand Rapids, MI: William B. Eerdmans Publishing Company, 2003), Part One, II, 43–93, 'The Veil of the Sublime'; where he discusses Levinas alongside Jean-François Lyotard, Jacob Rogozinski, Jacques Derrida, Gilles Deleuze, Michel Foucault, and Jean-Luc Nancy.
41 Ibid., 75.
42 Ibid., 84.
43 Ibid., 82.
44 Levinas, *En decouvrant l'existence avec Husserl et Heidegger* (Paris: Vrin, 1974); Løgstrup, *Kierkegaards und Heideggers Existenzanalyse und ihr Verhältnis zür Verkündigung* (Berlin: Eric Blaschker Verlag, 1950).
45 It may well be that they both attended Jean Héring's classes at Strasbourg University in 1930, but we do not know. See Robert Stern, *The Radical Demand in Løgstrup's Ethics* (Oxford University Press, 2019), 248.
46 Besides Stern's admirable monograph, other pioneering works in this regard are Hans Fink and Robert Stern, eds., *What Is Ethically Demanded? K. E. Løgstrup's Philosophy of Moral Life* (Notre Dame, IN: University of Notre Dame Press, 2017); Svend Andersen and Kees van Kooten Niekerk, *Concern for the Other: Perspectives on the Ethics of K. E. Løgstrup* (Notre Dame, IN: University of Notre Dame Press, 2007).
47 English translation by Theodor I. Jensen and Gary Puckering, ed. Hans Fink and Alasdair MacIntyre, (Notre Dame, IN: University of Notre Dame Press, 1997).
48 Ibid., 5, 160, 164, 207 and passim.
49 See note 44.
50 Løgstrup, *Opgør med Kierkegaard* (Aarhus: Klim, new edition, 2013). A portion of this work is available in English translation by Susan Dew and Heidi Flegal, and alongside an introduction by Kees van Kooten Niekerk, in Løgstrup, *Beyond the Ethical Demand* (Notre Dame, IN: University of Notre Dame, 2007). See below: note 58. Although *Controverting Kierkegaard* is the standard English rendering of the title, Stern remarks that '*opgør*' in fact 'means something more like "showdown" or "confrontation", making "controverting" sound rather tame': Stern, *The Radical Demand in Løgstrup's Ethics*, 10.
51 The leading *Tidehverv* contributor Kristoffer Olesen Larsen, for example, was an especially notable Kierkegaardian thinker.
52 *The Ethical Demand*, page 1; italics added. The formula is repeated in Chapter 5, page 108, where he is asking the question: 'Is there a Christian ethics'? [That is, as distinct from humane ethics in general.] To which, in effect, his answer is: at the deepest level, *no*.
53 Løgstrup, *Beyond the Ethical Demand*, 28–9; and see also ibid., 71.
    Løgstrup was fundamentally opposed to the notion of 'Christian Democratic' political parties. Church ideology fails adequately to distinguish between the supreme authority of the ethical demand, which does indeed belong to the gospel, albeit not

exclusively, and the lesser authority of social norms which – however well they may be embedded in church tradition, and however worthwhile they may be – do not. So-called 'Christian Democracy' embodies that confusion, inasmuch as its programme is all about the implementation of certain such norms, misleadingly baptised.

54 C.f. for instance Stephen Darwall, 'Løgstrup on Morals and "the Sovereign Expressions of Life"', in Fink and Stern, eds., *What Is Ethically Demanded?* 35–53.
55 I use the translation of the New Testament by David Bentley Hart (New Haven & London: Yale University Press, 2017), which, by aiming at a quite literal rendering, helps bring out its original freshness, to its first readers.
56 Kierkegaard, *Works of Love,* 119; and c.f. 113. It is this discourse as a whole, Part 1, III A 'Love Is the Fulfilling of the Law', which crucially sets out the standpoint which Løgstrup is criticizing.
57 Ibid., 113–14.
58 From *Opgør med Kierkegaard*: 'The Sovereign Expressions of Life', 49–82. From *Norm og spontaneitet*: 'Sovereign Expressions of Life, the Golden Rule, Character Traits and Norms', 83–122. From *System og symbol*: 'Norms and Expressions of Life', 123–40, and 'Expressions of Life and Ideas', 149–65.
59 Løgstrup, *Beyond the Ethical Demand*, 83–5.
60 Ibid., 84.
61 Ibid., 50–3.
62 Ibid., 115.
63 Ibid., 77.
64 Ibid., 53.
65 Kierkegaard, *Concluding Unscientific Postscript*, 412.
66 Løgstrup, *Beyond the Ethical Demand*, 70–1.

Chapter 7

1 'Anti-political' in the sense of activism designed to influence governmental power only ever from the outside: as in what I have also termed 'anti-political religion'. C.f. György Konrád, *Antipolitics*, 1982, translated from Hungarian by Richard E. Allen (New York: Henry Holt, 1987); also, Gustav Landauer, *Revolution and Other Writings: A Political Reader* (Oakland, CA: PM Press, 2010), 79.
2 Shanks, *'What Is Truth?' Towards a Theological Poetics* (London: Routledge, 2001).
3 David Bentley Hart's translation.
4 C.f. also Shanks, *The Other Calling*.
5 Heidegger, *Being and Time*, 1927, translated from the German 7th edition by John Macquarrie and Edward Robinson (Oxford: Blackwell, 1962). Page references, hereafter, both to the English pagination and to that in the German 7th edition (Tübingen: Niemeyer), which appears in the margin of the translation; the latter indicated with a preceding H.
6 He does not himself speak in terms of 'wonder' in *Being and Time*. But c.f. in particular his 1937/38 lectures entitled *Grundfragen der Philosophie: Ausgewählte 'Probleme' der 'Logik'*, sections 36–8; *Gesamtausgabe* Vol. 45, ed. Friedrich Wilhelm von Herrman (Frankfurt: Vittorio Klostermann, 1984).
7 *Being and Time* consists of an Introduction followed by two roughly equal 'Divisions'. The concepts of 'care' (*Sorge*) and 'anxiety' (*Angst*) emerge to the fore at the end of

Division One. And the concept of 'Being-towards-death' (*Sein zum Tode*) emerges to the fore at the beginning of Division Two.

8   Heidegger, *Phenomenological Interpretations of Aristotle: Initiation into Phenomenological Research*, 1921–22, translated by Richard Rojcewicz (Bloomington & Indianapolis: Indiana University Press, 2001), 148.
9   George Kovacs, *The Question of God in Heidegger's Phenomenology* (Evanston, Illinois: Northwestern University Press, 1990), 201–2.
10 Heidegger, *Being and Time*, 219–20; H175.
11 Ibid., 211; H167.
12 The transition to grand narrative is most directly anticipated in II, Chapter 5.
13 It was published in 1942. Translated as 'Plato's Doctrine of Truth' by Thomas Sheehan; in Heidegger, *Pathmarks*, edited by William McNeill (Cambridge University Press, 1998).
14 Heidegger, *Plato's Sophist*, translated by Richard Rojcewicz and André Schuwer (Bloomington & Indianapolis: Indiana University Press, 1997); and *The Essence of Truth: On Plato's Cave Allegory and Theaetetus*, translated by Ted Sadler (London & New York: Continuum, 2002).
15 See Chapter 3, 52–6.

Early on in his career, in the Summer Semester of 1921, Heidegger did deliver a lecture series on 'Augustine and Neoplatonism'. And he did write notes, and an introduction, to a course, scheduled for the Winter Semester of 1918–19 but never actually delivered, on 'The Philosophical Fundamentals of Mediaeval Mysticism'. After that, however, his interest in these topics evidently waned.

16 Heidegger, *Identity and Difference*, translated by Joan Stambaugh (New York: Harper & Row, 1969), 72. For Heidegger's remark on the importance of this work, see the Introduction by Joan Stambaugh, page 7.
17 Heidegger, 'Nur noch ein Gott kann uns retten', *Der Spiegel*, Nr. 23/1976; 193–219. English translation, 'Only a God Can Save Us', in Thomas Sheehan, ed., *Heidegger: The Man and the Thinker* (London & New York: Routledge, 2017), 45–68; quote on page 57.
18 The literature on this is extensive. But the work I myself have found most helpful is Miguel de Beistegui, *Heidegger and the Political: Dystopias* (London and New York: Routledge, 1998).
19 English translation in Gunther Neske and Emil Kettering, eds., *Martin Heidegger and National Socialism* (New York: Paragon House, 1990), 5–13.
20 Heidegger's own most extended, direct retrospective account is to be found in a document written in 1945, 'The Rectorate 1933/4: Facts and Thoughts', first published posthumously in 1983, and included in Heidegger, *Reden und andere Zeugnisse eines Lebensweges (1910–1976)*, *Gesamtausgabe* Vol. 16, edited by Hermann Heidegger (Frankfurt: Vittorio Klostermann, 2000).
21 C.f. Beistegui, *Heidegger and the Political*, Chapter 3.
22 Patočka, 'Heroes of Our Time', translated from Czech by Paul Wilson, *International Journal of Politics* 11 (1), (Spring, 1981), 10–15.
23 The *Einsatzgruppen* started systematically massacring Jews in the East in June 1941, the gassings at Auschwitz began in September that year and the genocidal process then continued in full swing until the collapse of the Third Reich in the spring of 1945. During this period, in Freiburg University, Heidegger lectured on Schelling (summer 1941); on 'Basic Concepts' (summer 1941); on Hölderlin (winter 1941–2, summer 1942, and June 1943); on Parmenides (winter 1942–3); on Herakleitos

(summer 1943, summer 1944); and on Nietzsche (winter 1944–5, part of an incomplete course entitled 'Introduction to Philosophy: Thinking and Poetry', which in the *Spiegel* interview he describes as a continuation of his 'critical reckoning with National Socialism'). He also published a collection of poetic texts, *Winke* (1941); the essay referred to above, on *Plato's Doctrine of Truth* (1942); and *Elucidations of Hölderlin's Poetry* (1944). And he wrote a number of essays.

24 Eventually, in the autumn of 1944, he was drafted for compulsory national service, construction work on fortifications in Alsace. As he points out in the *Spiegel* interview, many academics were exempted from this, but his being drafted was very much a mark of his being out of favour.

25 He was banned from 1951 to 1968, and then again from 1972 onwards. For a 'Philosophical Biography' of Patočka, see Erazim Kohák's essay under that title, Part 1 of Kohák, *Jan Patočka: Philosophy and Selected Writings*.

26 See Heidegger, *Discourse on Thinking*, translated by John M. Anderson and E. Hans Freund (New York: Harper & Row, 1966). The German original is entitled *Gelassenheit*; and this is the central theme. It is a slim volume, containing a 'Memorial Address' of 1949, for the hundredth anniversary of the death of the composer Conradin Kreutzer, and a dialogue, written in the spooky (un-mentioned) context of 1944-5, 'Conversation on a Country Path about Thinking'. This dialogue is a weird text, in that, although divided between three voices, it does not really read like a dialogue at all; but more like the inner ruminations of a single mind. (Meister Eckhart is invoked on pages 61–2; only for his catholic piety, at once, to be rejected.)

27 On the relationship of Strauss's thought to Heidegger's, see for instance Richard L. Velkley, *Heidegger, Strauss, and the Premises of Philosophy* (University of Chicago Press, 2011).

28 Strauss, 'Philosophy as a Rigorous Science and Political Philosophy', in *Studies in Platonic Political Philosophy* (University of Chicago Press, 1983), 30.

29 Ibid., page 34.

30 Cited in Velkley, *Heidegger, Strauss, and the Premises of Philosophy*, 179; translating from Strauss, *Gesammelte Schriften*, edited by H. Meier, Vol. 3 (Stuttgart & Weimar: J. B. Metzler, 2001), 769–70.

31 Strauss, 'An Introduction to Heideggerian Existentialism', in T. Pangle, ed., *The Rebirth of Classical Political Rationalism: Essays and Lectures by Leo Strauss* (University of Chicago Press, 1989), 29.

32 Strauss, 'Living Issues in German Postwar Philosophy', in H. Meier, *Leo Strauss and the Theologico-Political Problem* (Cambridge University Press, 2006), 115–39.
    On the Nietzsche half of this statement, see Lampert, 1996.

33 Strauss, 'An Unspoken Prologue to a Public Lecture at St. John's College in Honor of Jacob Klein', in Strauss, *Jewish Philosophy and the Crisis of Modernity* edited by K. H. Green (Albany, NY: State University of New York Press, 1997), 450. (Strauss had attended Heidegger's lectures with Klein for company.)

34 Velkley, *Heidegger, Strauss, and the Premises of Philosophy*, Chapter Two.

35 In Strauss's commentary on the *Republic*, he remarks:
> The doctrine of ideas which Socrates expounds to his interlocutors is very hard to understand; to begin with, it is utterly incredible, not to say that it appears to be fantastic. ... No one has ever succeeded in giving a satisfactory or clear account of this doctrine of ideas.

Strauss, *The City and Man* (Chicago: Rand McNally, 1964), 119.

36 *Republic* 336b–354c. On Thrasymachus: see Strauss, *The City and Man*, 75 ff.

37 *Republic* 498c.
38 Ibid., *414c*. The whole sentence runs something like this:

> So, I said, I wonder how we might contrive one of those salutary lies that we were talking about just now – a big one – aiming to convince the whole city, even if possible the Guardians themselves.

I for my part prefer 'Big Lie' here to any more euphemistic translation; basically, for the way that it captures the tone of jokey bumptiousness in the passage. The reference back is to 382c, where Socrates discusses the occasional usefulness of lying, either to deceive the enemies of the city, or else to restrain friends led astray by madness or folly; and to 389b, where he speaks of such lies as a 'medicine', generally only to be applied by the rulers. In 414c the context is a discussion of potential corruption among the trainee philosopher-rulers, especially when still young. Ideally, it appears, they too are to be dupes of the salutary 'Big Lie'. To what extent their elders also are is unclear. But at all events the readers of the *Republic* are, to say the least, clearly encouraged to be somewhat sceptical.

39 Ibid., 415a–c.
40 Strauss, *Persecution and the Art of Writing* (University of Chicago Press, 1988), 'Introduction', 21.
41 Ibid., 17.
42 Al-Fárábí, *The Attainment of Happiness*, translated from Arabic in Muhsin Mahdi, ed., *Alfarabi's Philosophy of Plato and Aristotle* (New York: Free Press of Glencoe, 1962); § 60; in Muhsin Mahdi, ed. *Alfarabi's Philosophy of Plato and Aristotle*, translated from Arabic (New York: Free Press of Glencoe, 1962).
43 For Strauss's reading of Maimonides, in relation to Fárábí and Averroes: see Kenneth Hart Green, ed., *Leo Strauss on Maimonides: The Complete Writings* (University of Chicago Press, 2013).
44 C.f. Velkley, *Heidegger, Strauss and the Premises of Philosophy*, Chapter 7.
45 Strauss, *Natural Right and History* (University of Chicago Press, 2nd edition, 1965), 12–13.
46 C.f. ibid., 29.
47 That Heidegger is not named here is partly attributable to his actual thought not yet having attained much currency in the United States.; and partly to his notoriety as a one-time collaborator with Nazism, a distractingly over-specific context for the more general point that Strauss wants to make about 'historicism'.
48 Strauss, *Natural Right and History*, 27; c.f. Heidegger, *Being and Time*, 437–8; H385 – 6.
49 Strauss, *Natural Right and History*, 18.
50 Ibid., 140–3.
51 Ibid., 142.
52 Ibid.
53 Ibid., 143.
54 On Adorno's style: see for instance Gillian Rose, *The Melancholy Science: An Introduction to the Thought of Theodor W. Adorno* (New York and London: Verso, 2014), Chapter 2.
55 Adorno, *Negative Dialectics*, 1966, translated by E. B. Ashton (London: Routledge & Kegan Paul, 1973), Part One is the prime text for this critique; *The Jargon of Authenticity*, 1964, translated from German by Knut Tarnowski and Frederic Will (London: Routledge & Kegan Paul, 1973) is a polemical analysis of the widespread

intellectual neediness, the appetite, to which, as Adorno sees it, Heidegger and his followers are catering.
56 Martin Jay, *Adorno* (London: Fontana, 1984), 11–12; quoting Adorno, *The Jargon of Authenticity*, 93.
57 Op. cit. 3. The allusion, of course, is to Marx's 11th Thesis on Feuerbach: 'The philosophers have only *interpreted* the world, in various ways; the point is to *change* it.'
58 Ernst Bloch, *The Principle of Hope* 3 vols., 1954, 1955, 1959, translated from German by Neville Plaice, Stephen Plaice, Paul Knight (Cambridge: MIT Press, 1986).
59 For a spirited defence of Arendt in this regard, see Dana R. Villa, *Arendt and Heidegger: The Fate of the Political* (Princeton University Press, 1996).
60 Thomas Pangle, *The Spirit of Modern Republicanism: The Moral Vision of the American Founders and the Philosophy of John Locke* (University of Chicago Press, 1988).
   Other attacks on the Heideggerian element in Arendt's thought include Luc Ferry, *The System of Philosophies of History*, translated from French by Franklin Philip (University of Chicago Press, 1992); Luc Ferry and Alain Renaut, *Heidegger and Modernity*, translated by Franklin Philip (University of Chicago Press, 1990); John Gunnell, *Between Philosophy and Politics: The Alienation of Political Theory* (Amherst, MA: University of Massachusetts Press, 1986), and *The Descent of Political Theory: The Genealogy of an American Vocation* (University of Chicago Press, 1993); Martin Jay, 'Political Existentialism of Hannah Arendt', in *Permanent Exiles: Essays on the Intellectual Migration from Germany to America* (New York: Columbia University Press, 1985); Richard Wolin, *The Politics of Being: The Political Thought of Martin Heidegger* (New York: Columbia University Press, 1990). A heterogeneous group!
61 Patočka, *Heretical Essays on the Philosophy of History*, 135.
62 Arendt, *The Origins of Totalitarianism*, 1951 (New York: Schocken Books, 2004).
63 Ibid., xii.
64 The term 'plutocracy' first appears in English in 1631. 'Bureaucracy', in French '*bureaucratie*', is a French-Greek hybrid originating in the mid-eighteenth century, its coinage being anecdotally attributed to the economist J. C. M. V. de Gournay. 'Kleptocracy' is a term dating back to 1819. 'Meritocracy', a Latin-Greek hybrid, first appeared in print in 1958, the coinage of the sociologist Michael Young.
65 Herodotus, *The Histories*, translated by Aubrey de Sélincourt (London: Penguin Classics, 2003), Book III, 80–3.
66 Arendt, *On Revolution* (Harmondsworth: Penguin, 1973), 30–1.
67 Thucydides, *History of the Peloponnesian Wars*, translated by Rex Warner (Harmondsworth: Penguin Classics, 1974); 3. 82. 8: referring in fact to two sorts of demagogue, both the upholders of isonomy and the upholders of moderate aristocracy.
68 Op. cit. 32.
69 Arendt at one point considered giving what eventually became *The Human Condition* the title *Amor Mundi*.
70 Tertullian, *Apology* (online: newadvent.org); 38.
71 English translation, incorporating extensive authorial revisions: Arendt, *Love and Saint Augustine*, ed. Joanna Vecchiarelli Scott and Judith Chelius Stark (University of Chicago Press, 1996).
72 *City of God* XIV. 28.
73 Arendt, *The Human Condition*, 53–4; quoting from Augustine, *Contra Faustum Manichaeum* V. 5.

74 Hobbes, Hobbes, *Leviathan*, 1651, edited by C. B. Macpherson (London: Penguin Classics, 1982), Introduction.
75 At the beginning of Chapter 3, page 79, Arendt writes: 'In the following chapter, Karl Marx will be criticized. This is unfortunate at a time when so many writers … have decided to become professional anti-Marxists.' And she quotes Benjamin Constant's remarks about Rousseau: 'Certainly, I shall avoid the detractors of a great man. If I happen to agree with them on a single point, I grow suspicious of myself; and in order to console myself for having seemed to be of their opinion … I feel I must disavow and keep these false friends away from me as much as I can.'
76 Arendt, *On Revolution*, 248; quoting Jefferson's letter to the English political reformer John Cartwright, dated 5 June 1824.
77 Arendt allows that 'there are certain paragraphs in the writings of the Utopian Socialists, especially in Proudhon and Bakunin, into which it has been relatively easy to read an awareness of the council system'. But (perhaps a little unfairly) she goes on: 'the truth is that these essentially anarchist political thinkers were singularly unequipped to deal with a phenomenon which demonstrated so clearly how a revolution did not end with the abolition of state and government but, on the contrary, aimed at the foundation of a new state and the establishment of a new form of government.' Arendt, *On Revolution*, 261.
78 Ibid., 257–8.
79 Arendt, *Between Past and Future*, 91–2. And c.f. Chapter 3, 59–62.
80 Arendt, *Between Past and Future*, 91.
81 Ibid., 92.
82 C.f. her remark, made at a conference in Toronto: 'I am perfectly sure that this totalitarian catastrophe would not have happened if people still had believed in God, or in hell rather – that is, if there were still ultimates.' Melvyn Hill, ed., *Hannah Arendt: The Recovery of the Public World* (New York: St. Martin's Press, 1979), 313–14.

Chapter 8

1 Desmond, *Being and the Between* (Albany, NY: State University of New York Press, 1995); *Ethics and the Between* (Albany, NY: State University of New York Press, 2001); *God and the Between* (Oxford: Blackwell, 2008).
2 Desmond, *Hegel's God: A Counterfeit Double?* (Aldershot: Ashgate, 2003).
3 Ibid., 55–6.
4 There are translations by Michael Inwood (Oxford University Press, 2018), which is what I shall quote from; Terry Pinkard (Cambridge University Press, 2018); A. V. Miller (Oxford University Press, 1977); and J. B. Baillie, who renders the title as *The Phenomenology of Mind* (London: George Allen and Unwin, 1910). Pinkard's numbering of the paragraphs diverges slightly from Inwood's and Miller's; they split at paragraphs 402–3 (Inwood, Miller)/403 (Pinkard), rejoin one another at paragraph 541. Pinkard also, unlike Inwood, gives pride of place to Hegel's lettered division of the text, rather than to his chapter numbering.
5 Commentators have often suggested that Hegel, in speaking of the 'beautiful soul', chiefly has the figure of Novalis in mind; and, in this description of a community, is thinking of the Moravian Church, to which Novalis's father had belonged. Inwood, in his notes, repeats this suggestion. I am, however, instinctively somewhat resistant

to interpretations of the *Phenomenology* that appear to de-code it by particularizing, in this fashion. Never mind what Hegel may or may not have had at the back of his mind! What he is describing remains, in principle, a very general species of mentality.

Novalis's novel *Heinrich von Ofterdingen* (1802) portrays a 'beautiful soul'. So does Jacobi's novel *Woldemar* (1779). And Goethe's novel *Wilhelm Meisters Lehrjahre* (1795) includes a section with the actual title 'Confessions of a Beautiful Soul'.

6   This is not to say that Hegel had any great knowledge of Eckhart's thought (certainly far less than Franz von Baader); nor that Böhme's actual texts were a major formative influence on his thought. (He did not actually *own* any until 1811.) But rather: that his enthusiasm for what he learnt, regarding Eckhart, from Baader in a series of conversations in 1823-4, is indeed of a piece with his enthusiastic discussion of Böhme in the *Lectures on the History of Philosophy*. Again, see Muratori, *The First German Philosopher: The Mysticism of Jakob Böhme as Interpreted by Hegel*.

7   Adams, *Eclipse of Grace: Divine and Human Action in Hegel* (Oxford: Blackwell, 2013). The title of this work is perhaps a little misleading: it is anything but an anti-Hegelian polemic. The passages discussed are the concluding chapter of the *Phenomenology of Spirit*, on 'Absolute Knowing'; the concluding chapter of the *Science of Logic*, on 'The Absolute Idea'; and various excerpts from Volume 3 of the Berlin *Lectures on the Philosophy of Religion*, discussing the vocation of the Christian Church.

8   At this point (ibid., 6), Adams acknowledges that he is echoing the insight of Martin Wendte, in *Gottmenschliche Einheit bei Hegel: eine logische und theologische Untersuchung* (Berlin: de Gruyter, 2007), 2-9. And he cites the latter part of the Chalcedonian formula (451 CE), declaring the orthodox Church's faith in

one and the same Christ, Son, Lord, Only-begotten, recognized in two natures, without confusion, without change, without division, without separation; the distinction of natures being in no way annulled by the union, but rather the characteristics of each nature being preserved and coming together to form one person and subsistence, not as parted and separated into two persons, but one and the same Son and Only-begotten God the Word, Lord Jesus Christ.

9   He did briefly discuss the metaphysical proofs of the existence of God in his *Lectures on the Philosophy of Religion*; and also devoted a whole series of sixteen lectures, in 1829, to these proofs. But these lectures are very much something of a late afterthought.

10 Hegel, *The Science of Logic*, 1833, translated by George di Giovanni (Cambridge University Press, 2010), 29. In the earlier translation by A. Miller (London: George Allen and Unwin, 1969) the same passage is rendered on page 50.

11 *Hegel's Logic: being Part One of the Encyclopaedia of the Philosophical Sciences (1830)*, edited and translated by William Wallace (Oxford University Press, 1975), 113-21.

12 See Introduction, 11-12; and 214, n.14. Also, Chapter 1, 30-1.

13 *Phenomenology of Spirit*, paragraphs 202-6.

14 Ibid., paragraphs 197-201.

15 Hegel, *Early Theological Writings*, translated by T. M. Knox (Philadelphia: University of Pennsylvania Press, 1971), 67-181.

16 Ibid., 182-301.

17 Desmond, *God and the Between*, 93.

18 *Phenomenology of Spirit*, paragraphs 446-76 (Inwood, Miller)/445-75 (Pinkard).

19 Ibid., paragraphs 582-95.

20 Ibid., paragraphs 488-526 (Inwood, Miller)/487-525 (Pinkard).

21 Ibid., paragraphs 527 (Inwood, Miller)/526 (Pinkard)–581 (both).
22 Ibid., paragraph 503 (Inwood, Miller)/502 (Pinkard).
23 Ibid., paragraph 511 (Inwood, Miller)/510 (Pinkard).
24 Denis Diderot's dialogue *Rameau's Nephew* features two characters, 'Moi' ('Me'), roughly based on Diderot himself, and 'Lui' ('Him'), roughly based on Jean-François Rameau, nephew of the composer Rameau. It was written in 1761–2, revised 1773–4; but unpublished by Diderot; first appearing in Goethe's German translation, in 1805, at a key stage in Hegel's work on the *Phenomenology of Spirit*. Hegel inserts quotations from Goethe's translation in paragraphs 489 (Inwood, Miller)/488 (Pinkard), 522 (Inwood, Miller)/521 (Pinkard) and 545. But the whole of paragraphs 519–26 (Inwood, Miller)/518–25 (Pinkard) is permeated with allusions to the work. The 'sniggering' comes in paragraph 525 (Inwood, Miller)/524 (Pinkard).
25 Ibid., paragraph 541. Here 'pure insight' is said to be 'initially devoid of content'; only subsequently 'giving itself a content' in the course of its struggle. I take this to mean the sort of imaginative/commemorative/legislative 'content' intrinsic to 'faith', which 'stoicism' and 'scepticism' lack.
26 Ibid., paragraphs 528–9 (Inwood, Miller)/527–8 (Pinkard).
27 Ibid., paragraph 561.
28 Ibid., paragraph 545; quoting from *Rameau's Nephew*.
29 Ibid., paragraph 586.
30 See especially ibid., paragraphs 724–5.
31 The Great Dionysia was held in March or April. Dramas premiered there might then be repeated in the various smaller towns of Attica, as part of the Rural Dionysia in December to January, the following winter. The Lénaia festival, held in January, was smaller. And whereas the Dionysia originally featured only tragedies, only later including comedies as well, with the Lénaia it was the other way round.

Hegel begins his discussion of the third mode of 'art-religion', *Phenomenology* paragraphs 727–47, with some remarks on epic poetry. But it is with drama that he is principally concerned.
32 Ibid., paragraphs 744–7.
33 Ibid., paragraph 752.
34 See Chapter 2, 43–6.
35 *Phenomenology of Spirit*, paragraphs 751–4.
36 Ibid., paragraphs 207–9.
37 Ibid., paragraphs 748–9.
38 See above, Chapter 3, note 47.
39 *Phenomenology of Spirit*, paragraph 785.
40 Hegel had already deployed the concept of the 'death of God' in his 1802 essay *Faith and Knowledge*; English translation by Walter Cerf and H. S. Harris (Albany, NY: State University of New York Press, 1977), 190. There it evokes pagan despair, modern loss of faith, and the need for a radically philosophic re-appropriation of the gospel, all at once.
41 Hegel, *Lectures on the Philosophy of World History*, Vol. 1, *Manuscripts of the Introduction and the Lectures of 1822–3*, translated by Robert F. Brown and Peter C. Hodgson, with the assistance of William G. Geuss (Oxford University Press, 2011), 88. This formulation, in fact, comes from the 1830–1 Introduction, in Vol. 3. C.f., also, pages 110–11, in the same text. And *Elements of the Philosophy of Right*, English translation ed. Allen W. Wood (Cambridge University Press, 1991), §§ 354–60.

42 Besides the discussion in the *Phenomenology of Spirit*, see also, on gender roles in general, *Elements of the Philosophy of Right* §166.
43 Hegel first met Caroline Michaelis Böhmer Schlegel, as she then was, when he moved to Jena in 1801. She divorced Auguste Schlegel and married Hegel's old friend Schelling in 1803. The mutual antipathy between Hegel and her was a major factor in the ensuing cooling, and then breakdown, of Hegel's friendship with Schelling. He met Meta Forkel-Liebeskind in 1806 when he moved to Bamberg, as a local newspaper editor. And during the year and a half that he lived in Bamberg, she and her husband J. H. Liebeskind appear to have been his closest friends in the town.

Both women were the daughters of academics at Göttingen University. They had come to share a house together in Mainz, just before the arrival of the French Revolutionary army there in October 1792; and were part of the milieu around the Jacobin Club established in Mainz at that time. So too was the then Therese Forster (later Huber); who was likewise the daughter of a Göttingen academic, and a childhood friend of Caroline, and whose husband Georg Forster (famous as having been a scientist on Captain Cook's second expedition to the Pacific) was one of the Club's co-founders. In April 1793, when Prussian troops briefly recaptured Mainz, both Caroline and Meta were captured and imprisoned.

Caroline Schelling is known for her extensive correspondence with notable figures belonging to the world of German romanticism. Meta Forkel-Liebeskind was both a novelist and a translator from English.
44 See Kimberly Hutchings and Tuija Pulkkinnen, eds., *Hegel's Philosophy and Feminist Thought: Beyond Antigone* (London: Palgrave Macmillan, 2010).
45 Hegel, *Lectures on the Philosophy of World History*, Vol. 1, 87–8.
46 In Hegel's German, the term is '*germanisch*'; not '*deutsch*'.
47 See Alison Stone, 'Hegel and Colonialism', *Hegel Bulletin* 83; Summer 2020, 247–70.
48 For such an extremely sophisticated, and generally very well-intentioned, thinker, it has to be admitted that Hegel could on occasion be quite surprisingly naïve. Of sub-Saharan Africa, for instance, in his *Lectures on the Philosophy of World History* he remarks that 'it has not yet entered into history' – and yes, that, in itself, is fair enough. Given that by 'history' here he just means the grand narrative of the emergence of the possibility of the philosophic insights he himself is attempting to articulate, he is after all merely confessing the lack of any adequate literature on African affairs, available to an early nineteenth century German philosophic enquirer like himself. But then, in a throwaway remark, he also entertains his student audience with *this* prejudicial stereotype: 'The Negroes display great strength of body and a highly sensual nature along with affability but also a shocking and inconceivable ferocity … ' Hegel, *Philosophy of World History*, Vol. 1, page 197.

It is, to my mind, somewhat comically unclear which *particular* individuals he has in mind here. The cannibals in *Robinson Crusoe*, perhaps? (Defoe's book was immensely popular, in German translation.) How remote the political correctness of our world is, now that sub-Saharan Africa has so completely 'entered into history', from the intellectual *mores* of Berlin, in 1822–3; when Hegel was speaking!

His racism is not of the most stupid, biological kind. Nor is it a significant aspect of his originality, or his influence. Yet, there it nevertheless is; laid bare by his remarkable desire to express an opinion on pretty much everything possible. Others among his contemporaries (e.g., Blumenbach) were, in fact, more enlightened in this regard.

49 As I have argued before: see in particular *God and Modernity: A New and Better Way to Do Theology* (London: Routledge, 2000).
50 See Introduction, 3.
51 The spirit of 'third modernity', at its core, is anarchist – but let us also consider, how the state might best be constituted, for the purpose of systematically opening up to its critique.

    Given the widespread call, in Britain, for constitutional reform, abolishing and replacing the present House of Lords, I for my part would suggest a bicameral system fundamentally designed to reflect the distinction between democracy and agapacracy: a lower chamber elected as now by universal suffrage, to give democratic legitimacy to the laws – but complemented by an essentially agapacratic upper chamber. The upper chamber would, then, require a different method of election: a more restricted electorate, from that involved in choosing members of the lower chamber. Thus, the aim would simply be to establish an institution of maximum moral authority, for the debating and revising of laws. But – where is the greatest store of already institutionalized moral authority in our society? Is it not in the *charitable sector*, as a whole? Therefore, my proposal is that the present 'House of Lords', primarily selected as it is by a system of party-political patronage, be replaced by a representative 'House of Charities', elections to which would be regulated by the Charity Commissioners; the electorate being representatives of the charities.

    Hopefully, the ethos of such an upper house would be as friendly as that of any state institution could be, to public conscience movements.
52 C.f., here, the related discussion of deracinated 'mysticism' in Chapter 4, 93–9.
53 Jean-Jacques Rousseau, *Émile, or On Education*, 1762, edited and translated by Christopher Kelly and Allan Bloom (Hanover, NH: Dartmouth College Press, 2010).
54 A translation of *Émile and Sophie, or the Solitaries* is included in Kelly and Bloom's edition of *Émile*.
55 Ibid., 703.
56 Translation by David Bentley Hart. (This passage is generally recognized to be an interpolation into *John*.)
57 See Chapter 8, 187–8.
58 Rousseau, *The Social Contract*, 1762, translated by Maurice Cranston (London: Penguin, 1968), Book 2, Chapter 7, page 84.

BIBLIOGRAPHY

Adams, Nicholas, *Eclipse of Grace: Divine and Human Action in Hegel*, Oxford: Blackwell, 2013.
Adorno, T. W., with Else Frenkel-Brunswik, Daniel J. Levinson, R. Nevitt Sanford, *The Authoritarian Personality*, New York: W. W. Norton & Co., 1969.
Adorno, T. W., with Else Frenkel-Brunswik, Daniel J. Levinson, R. Nevitt Sanford, *The Jargon of Authenticity*, 1964, translated from German by Knut Tarnowski and Frederic Will, London: Routledge & Kegan Paul, 1973.
Adorno, T. W., with Else Frenkel-Brunswik, Daniel J. Levinson, R. Nevitt Sanford, *Negative Dialectics*, 1966, translated by E. B. Ashton, London: Routledge & Kegan Paul, 1973.
Al-Fárábí, Abu Nasr Muhammad, 'The Attainment of Happiness', in Muhsin Mahdi, ed., *Alfarabi's Philosophy of Plato and Aristotle*, translated from Arabic, New York: Free Press of Glencoe, 1962.
Al-Niffarí, Muhammad Ibn 'Abdi 'l-Jabbár, *The Mawáqif and Mukhátabát*, edited and translated from Arabic into English by Arthur John Arberry, E. J. W. Gibb, Memorial Trust, 1935; reissued, Cambridge University Press, 1978.
Al-Niffarí, Muhammad Ibn 'Abdi 'l-Jabbár, *Livre des Stations*, French translation of the *Mawáqif* by Maati Kabbal, Paris: Editions de l'Eclat, 1989.
Al-Niffarí, Muhammad Ibn 'Abdi 'l-Jabbár, *Les Haltes*, French translation of the *Mawáqif* by Mahmoud Sami-Ali, Paris: Fata Morgana, 1995.
Al-Niffarí, Muhammad Ibn 'Abdi 'l-Jabbár, *Livre des Ecstases*, French translation of the *Mawáqif* by Adonis (and Donatien Grau), Paris: Les Belles Lettres, 2017.
Allport, Gordon, *The Individual and His Religion*, New York: Macmillan, 1950.
Altizer, Thomas J. J., *Genesis and Apocalypse: A Theological Voyage toward Authentic Christianity*, Louisville, KY: Westminster / John Knox Press, 1990.
Altizer, Thomas J. J., *The Genesis of God: A Theological Genealogy*, Louisville, KY: Westminster / John Knox Press, 1993.
Andersen, Svend and Kees van Kooten Niekerk, *Concern for the Other: Perspectives on the Ethics of K. E. Løgstrup*, Notre Dame, IN: University of Notre Dame Press, 2007.
Arendt, Hannah, *The Human Condition*, University of Chicago Press, 1958.
Arendt, Hannah, *On Revolution*, Harmondsworth: Penguin, 1973.
Arendt, Hannah, 'What Is Authority?', in *Between Past and Future*, London: Penguin, 1977.
Arendt, Hannah, *Love and Saint Augustine*, edited by Joanna Vecchiarelli Scott and Judith Chelius Stark, University of Chicago Press, 1996.
Arendt, Hannah, *The Origins of Totalitarianism*, 1951, New York: Schocken Books, 2004.
Aristotle, *Metaphysics*, translated from Greek by Hugh Tredennik, Loeb Classical Library, Cambridge, MA: Harvard University Press, 1933.
Aristotle, *The Art of Rhetoric*, translated by Robin Waterfield, Oxford University Press, 2018.
Athanasius, *On the Incarnation*, translated from Greek by Sr. Penelope Lawson CSMV, New York: MacMillan Company, 1951.

Augustine, *City of God*, translated from Latin by Henry Bettenson, London: Penguin Classics, 1984.
Bailey, Margaret Lewis, *Milton and Jakob Boehme: A Study of German Mysticism in Seventeenth Century England*, Oxford University Press, 1914.
Barker, Margaret, *The Mother of the Lord*, Vol. 1, *The Lady in the Temple*, London: Bloomsbury, 2012.
Barth, Karl, *The Epistle to the Romans*, translated from German by Edwyn C. Hoskins, Oxford University Press, 1933.
Baur, F. C., *Die christliche Gnosis; oder die christliche Religions-Philosophie in ihrer geschichtlicher Entwicklung*, Tübingen: Osiander, 1835.
Beistegui, Miguel de, *Heidegger and the Political: Dystopias*, London and New York: Routledge, 1998.
Benz, Ernst, *Mystical Sources of German Romantic Philosophy*, translated from German by Blair R. Reynolds and Eunice M. Paul, Allison Park: Pickwick Publications, 1983.
Berdyaev, Nikolai, 'Studies Concerning Jacob Boehme: Etude 1, The Teaching about the Ungrund and Freedom', *Put'* vol. 20 (February 1930a).
Berdyaev, Nikolai, 'Etude 2, The Teaching about Sophia and the Androgyne. J. Boehme and the Russian Sophiological Current', *Put'* vol. 21 (April 1930b).
Bernard of Clairvaux, *Sermons on the "Song of Songs"*, English translation, from Latin, in 4 volumes, Kalamazoo, Michigan: Cistercian Publications; Vol. 1 translated by Kilian Walsh, 1971; Vol. 2 translated by Kilian Walsh, 1976; Vol. 3 translated by Kilian Walsh and Irene Edmonds, 1979; Vol. 4 translated by Irene Edmonds, 1980.
Blake, William, 'Letters', in Sir Geoffrey Keynes, ed. *Complete Writings of William Blake*, Oxford University Press, revised edition 1966.
Bloch, Ernst, *The Principle of Hope*, 3 vols., 1954, 1955, 1959, translated from German by Neville Plaice, Stephen Plaice and Paul Knight, Cambridge, MA: MIT Press, 1986.
Böhme, Jakob, *Three Principles of the Divine Essence*, 1619, original English translation by John Sparrow 1648; reissued by C. J. Barker, London: J. M. Watkins, 1909.
Böhme, Jakob, *De Signatura Rerum*, 1622, anonymously translated into English as *The Signature of All Things*, London: J. M. Dent, 1912.
Böhme, Jakob, *The Aurora*, 1612, original English translation from German by John Sparrow 1656, edited by C. J. Barker and D. S. Hefner, London: J. M. Watkins, 1914.
Böhme, Jakob, *Six Theosophic Points* [1620] *and Other Writings*, translated by John Rolleston Earle, New York: Knopf, 1920.
Böhme, Jakob, *Mysterium Magnum*, 1623, original English translation by John Ellistone 1654, edited by C. J. Barker in two volumes, London: John M. Watkins, 1924.
Böhme, Jakob, *De Electione Gratiae and Questiones Theosophicae*, 1623 / 1624, translated by John Rolleston Earle, London: Constable, 1930.
Böhme, Jakob, *Of the Incarnation of Christ* (original title *De Incarnatione Verbi, oder Von der Menschwerdung Jesu Christi*), 1620, translated by John Rolleston Earle, London: Constable, 1934.
Brown, Robert, *The Later Philosophy of Schelling: The Influence of Böhme on the Works of 1809–1815*, Lewisburg, PA: Bucknell University Press, 1977.
Buber, Martin, *Paths in Utopia*, translated from Hebrew by R. F. C. Hull, Boston: Beacon Press, 1958.
Buber, Martin, *I and Thou*, 1923, translated from German by Walter Kaufmann, New York: Scribner, 1970.
Bucke, R. M., *Cosmic Consciousness: A Study in the Evolution of the Human Mind*, Boston, MA: E. P. Dutton & Co., 1901.

Butler, Dom Cuthbert, *Western Mysticism: The Teaching of Augustine, Gregory and Bernard on Contemplation and the Contemplative Life*, London: Constable, 2nd edition, 1926.
Caygill, Howard, *Levinas and the Political*, London and New York: Routledge, 2002.
Combes, André, ed., *Ioannis Carlerii de Gerson: De Mystica Theologia*, Lugano: Thesaurus Mundi, 1958.
Coomaraswamy, Ananda, *A New Approach to the Vedas: An Essay in Translation and Exegesis*, London: Luzac, 1933.
Coomaraswamy, Ananda, *The Transformation of Nature in Art*, Cambridge, MA: Harvard University Press, 1934.
Coomaraswamy, Ananda, *Hinduism and Buddhism*, New York: Philosophical Library, 1941.
Davison, Andrew and Alison Milbank, *For the Parish*, London: SCM Press, 2010.
Derrida, Jacques, *The Gift of Death* (2nd edition) and *Literature in Secret*, translated from French by David Wills, University of Chicago Press, 2008.
Desmond, William, *Being and the Between*, Albany: State University of New York Press, 1995.
Desmond, William, *Ethics and the Between*, Albany: State University of New York Press, 2001.
Desmond, William, *Hegel's God: A Counterfeit Double?*, Aldershot: Ashgate, 2003.
Desmond, William, *God and the Between*, Oxford: Blackwell, 2008.
Dewrell, Heath D., *Child Sacrifice in Ancient Israel*, University Park, PA: Pennsylvania State University Press, 2017.
Diderot, Denis, *Rameau's Nephew and D'Alembert's Dream*, translated from French by Leonard Tancock, London: Penguin Classics, 1976.
Eckhart, Meister Johannes, *Meister Eckhart: The Essential Sermons, Commentaries, Treatises and Defense*, edited and translated, from Latin and medieval German, by Edmund Colledge O. S. A. and Bernard McGinn, Mahwah, NJ: Paulist Press, 1981.
Eckhart, Meister Johannes, *The Complete Mystical Works of Meister Eckhart*, edited and translated by Maurice O'C. Walshe, NY: Crossroad Publishing Co., 1979, revised edition 2009.
Evola, Julius, *Revolt against the Modern World*, translated from Italian by Guido Stucco, Rochester, Vermont: Inner Traditions International, 1995.
Evola, Julius, *Ride the Tiger: A Survival Manual for Aristocrats of the Soul*, translated by Joscelyn Godwin and Constance Fontana, Rochester: Vermont: Inner Traditions, 2003.
Evola, Julius, *The Path of Cinnabar*, translated by John Morgan, London: Arktos Media, 2010.
Evola, Julius, *Fascism Viewed from the Right*, translated by John Morgan, London: Arktos Media, 2013.
Evola, Julius, *Notes on the Third Reich*, translated by John Morgan, London: Arktos Media, 2013.
Evola, Julius, *A Traditionalist Confronts Fascism*, translated by John Morgan, London: Arktos Media, 2015.
Ferry, Luc, *The System of Philosophies of History*, translated from French by Franklin Philip, University of Chicago Press, 1992.
Ferry, Luc, with Alain Renaut, *Heidegger and Modernity*, translated by Franklin Philip, University of Chicago Press, 1990.
Findlay, Edward F., *Caring for the Soul in a Postmodern Age: Politics and Phenomenology in the Thought of Jan Patočka*, Albany: State University of New York Press, 2002.

Fink, Hans, and Robert Stern, eds., *What Is Ethically Demanded? K. E. Løgstrup's Philosophy of Moral Life*, Notre Dame, IN: University of Notre Dame Press, 2017.
Fukuyama, Francis, *The End of History and the Last Man*, London: Penguin, 1992.
Girard, René, *I See Satan Fall like Lightning*, translated from French by James G. Williams, Maryknoll, NY: Orbis, 2001.
Goethe, J. W. von, *Wilhelm Meister's Apprenticeship*, 1795, translated from German by Eric A. Blackall, in *Goethe: The Collected Works*, Vol. 9, Princeton University Press, 1994.
Golitzin, Alexander, *Mystagogy: A Monastic Reading of Dionysius Areopagita*, Collegeville, MN: Cistercian Publications and Liturgical Press, 2014.
Graeber, David, *Debt: The First 5,000 Years*, Brooklyn & London: Melville House, 2014.
Gregory of Nyssa, *The Life of Moses*, translated from Greek by Abraham J. Malherbe and Everett Ferguson, New York: Paulist Press, 1978.
Guénon, René, *The Crisis of the Modern World*, translated from French by A. Osborne, River Road, CT: Lawrence Verry Inc., 1975.
Gunnell, John, *Between Philosophy and Politics: The Alienation of Political Theory*, Amherst: University of Massachusetts Press, 1986.
Gunnell, John, *The Descent of Political Theory: The Genealogy of an American Vocation*, University of Chicago Press, 1993.
Halík, Tomáš, *From the Underground Church to Freedom*, translated from Czech by Gerald Turner, Notre Dame, IN: University of Notre Dame Press, 2019.
Hand, Seán, ed., *The Levinas Reader*, Oxford: Blackwell, 1989.
Harmless, William, *Mystics*, Oxford University Press, 2008.
Hart, David Bentley, *The Beauty of the Infinite: The Aesthetics of Christian Truth*, Grand Rapids, MI: William B. Eerdmans Publishing Company, 2003.
Hart, David Bentley, *The New Testament: A Translation*, New Haven & London: Yale University Press, 2017.
Havel, Václav, 'Politics and Conscience', translated from Czech by E. Kohák and R. Scruton, in Jan Vladislav, ed., *Living in Truth*, London: Faber and Faber, 1987 (a).
Havel, Václav, 'The Power of the Powerless', translated by P. Wilson, in Jan Vladislav, ed., *Living in Truth*, London: Faber and Faber, 1987 (b).
Hegel, G. W. F., *Philosophy of Right*, 1821, translated from German by T. M. Knox, Oxford University Press, 1952.
Hegel, G. W. F., 'The German Constitution', edited and translated by T. M. Knox, in *Hegel's Political Writings*, Oxford University Press, 1964.
Hegel, G. W. F., *Early Theological Writings*, translated by T. M. Knox, Philadelphia: University of Pennsylvania Press, 1971.
Hegel, G. W. F., *Hegel's Logic: being Part One of the Encyclopaedia of the Philosophical Sciences (1830)*, edited and translated by William Wallace, Oxford University Press, 1975.
Hegel, G. W. F., *Faith and Knowledge*, 1802, translated by Walter Cerf and H. S. Harris, Albany, NY: State University of New York Press, 1977.
Hegel, G. W. F., *The Letters*, translated by Clark Butler and Christiane Seiler, Bloomington: University of Indiana Press, 1984.
Hegel, G. W. F., *Lectures on the Philosophy of Religion*, 1821, 1824, 1827, 1831, 3 Volumes, English translation edited by Peter C. Hodgson, Oxford University Press, 2007.
Hegel, G. W. F., *Lectures on the Proofs of the Existence of God*, edited and translated by Peter C. Hodgson, Oxford University Press, 2007.
Hegel, G. W. F., *Lectures on the History of Philosophy*, 3 vols., 1819–31, translated by Robert F. Brown, Oxford University Press, 2011, 2006, 2009.

Hegel, G. W. F., *The Science of Logic*, 1833, English translations by A. V. Miller, London: George Allen & Unwin, 1969; George di Giovanni, Cambridge University Press, 2010.

Hegel, G. W. F., *Lectures on the Philosophy of World History*, Vol. 1 *Manuscripts of the Introduction and the Lectures of 1822–3*, edited and translated by Robert F. Brown and Peter C. Hodgson with the assistance of William G. Geuss, Oxford University Press, 2011.

Hegel, G. W. F., *Phenomenology of Spirit*, 1807, English translations by A. V. Miller, Oxford University Press, 1977; Michael Inwood, Oxford University Press, 2018; Terry Pinkard, Cambridge University Press, 2018.

Heidegger, Martin, *Being and Time*, 1927, translated from the German 7th edition by John Macquarrie and Edward Robinson, Oxford: Blackwell, 1962.

Heidegger, Martin, *Discourse on Thinking*, translated by John M. Anderson and E. Hans Freund, New York: Harper & Row, 1966.

Heidegger, Martin, *Identity and Difference*, translated by Joan Stambaugh, New York: Harper & Row, 1969.

Heidegger, Martin, 'Nur noch ein Gott kann uns retten', *Der Spiegel*, Nr. 23 / 1976.

Heidegger, Martin, *Grundfragen der Philosophie: Ausgewählte 'Probleme' der 'Logik'* (Winter Semester 1937 / 38), edited by Friedrich Wilhelm von Herrman, *Gesamtausgabe* 45, Frankfurt: Vittorio Klostermann, 1984.

Heidegger, Martin, *Plato's Sophist*, translated by Richard Rojcewicz and André Schuwer, Bloomington & Indianapolis: Indiana University Press, 1997.

Heidegger, Martin, *Pathmarks*, edited and translated by William McNeill, Cambridge University Press, 1998.

Heidegger, Martin, *Reden und andere Zeugnisse eines Lebensweges (1910–1976)*, *Gesamtausgabe* Vol. 16, edited by Hermann Heidegger, Frankfurt: Vittorio Klostermann, 2000.

Heidegger, Martin, *Phenomenological Interpretations of Aristotle: Initiation into Phenomenological Research*, 1921–22, translated by Richard Rojcewicz, Bloomington & Indianapolis: Indiana University Press, 2001.

Heidegger, Martin, *The Essence of Truth: On Plato's Cave Allegory and Theaetetus*, translated by Ted Sadler, London & New York: Continuum, 2002.

Hengel, Martin, *Crucifixion*, translated from German by John Bowden, London: SCM Press, 1977.

Heraclitus / Herakleitos, *Fragments*, translated from Greek by Brooks Haxton, London: Penguin, 2003.

Herodotus, *The Histories*, translated from Greek by Aubrey de Sélincourt, Harmondsworth: Penguin, 1954.

Hill, Melvyn, ed., *Hannah Arendt: The Recovery of the Public World*, New York: St. Martin's Press, 1979.

Hobbes, Thomas, *Leviathan*, 1651, edited by C. B. Macpherson, London: Penguin Classics, 1982.

Husserl, Edmund, *The Crisis of European Sciences and Transcendental Phenomenology: An Introduction to Phenomenological Philosophy*, translated from German by David Carr, Evanston, IL: Northwestern University Press, 1970.

Hutchings, Kimberley and Tuija Pulkkinnen, eds., *Hegel's Philosophy and Feminist Thought: Beyond Antigone*, London: Palgrave Macmillan, 2010.

Huxley, Aldous, *The Perennial Philosophy*, London: Chatto & Windus, 1946.

Iamblichus, *On the Mysteries*, translated from Greek by Emma C. Clarke, John M. Dillon and Jackson P. Hershbell, Atlanta, GA: Society of Biblical Literature, 2003.

Idel, Moshe, *Kabbalah: New Perspectives*, New Haven and London: Yale University Press, 1988.
Jacobi, F. H., *Woldemar: Eine Seltenheit aus der Naturgeschichte*, 1779, Berlin: Contumax, 2013.
James, William, *The Varieties of Religious Experience: A Study in Human Nature*, London: Collins, 1960.
Jantzen, Grace, 'Mysticism and Experience', *Religious Studies* vol. 25, no. 3: (1989), 295–315.
Jantzen, Grace, 'Could There Be a Mystical Core of Religion?', *Religious Studies* vol. 26, no. 1: (1990), 59–71.
Jantzen, Grace, *Power, Gender and Christian Mysticism*, Cambridge University Press, 1995.
Jay, Martin, *Adorno*, London: Fontana, 1984.
Jay, Martin, 'Political Existentialism of Hannah Arendt', in *Permanent Exiles: Essays on the Intellectual Migration from Germany to America*, New York: Columbia University Press, 1985.
Jeremias, Jörg, *The Book of Amos: A Commentary*, translated from German by Douglas W. Stott, Louisville, KY: Westminster John Knox Press, 1998.
Jonas, Hans, *The Gnostic Religion: The Message of the Alien God and the Beginnings of Christianity*, Boston, MA: Beacon Press, 1958, 1963.
Jonas, Hans, *Gnosis und spätantiker Geist*, Vol. 1, *Die mythologische Gnosis*, Göttingen: Vandenhoeck & Ruprecht, 1934, 1954, 1964.
Jonas, Hans, Vol. 2, *Von der Mythologie zur mystische Philosophie, 1 Hälfte*, Göttingen: Vandenhoeck & Ruprecht, 1954, 1966; *1 & 2 Hälfte*, ed. K. Rudolph, Göttingen: Vandenhoeck & Ruprecht, 1993.
Jones, Richard H., *Philosophy of Mysticism: Raids on the Ineffable*, Albany: State University of New York Press, 2016.
Julian of Norwich, *Revelations of Divine Love*, edited by Barry Windeatt, Oxford University Press, 2015.
Jünger, Ernst, 'Der Kampf als inneres Erlebnis', in *Sämtliche Werke*, II, Vol. 7: essays 1: *Betrachtungen zur Zeit*, Stuttgart: Klett Cotta, 1980.
Kant, Immanuel, 'Toward Perpetual Peace', in *Practical Philosophy*, translated from German by Mary J. Gregor, Cambridge University Press, 1996.
Katz, Steven T., ed., *Mysticism and Philosophical Analysis*, London: Sheldon Press, 1978.
Katz, Steven T., *Mysticism and Religious Traditions*, Oxford University Press, 1983.
Katz, Steven T., *Mysticism and Language*, Oxford University Press, 1992.
Katz, Steven T., *Mysticism and Sacred Scripture*, Oxford University Press, 2000.
Kierkegaard, Søren, *Concluding Unscientific Postscript to the Philosophical Fragments*, translated from Danish by David F. Swenson and Walter Lowrie, Princeton University Press, 1941.
Kierkegaard, Søren, *Works of Love: Some Christian Reflections in the Form of Discourses*, translated by Howard and Edna Hong, New York: Harper & Row, 1962.
Kierkegaard, Søren, *Attack upon 'Christendom'*, 1854–55, translated by Walter Lowrie, Princeton University Press, 1968.
Kierkegaard, Søren, *Two Ages: The Age of Revolution and the Present Age, A Literary Review*, translated by Howard V. Hong and Edna H. Hong, Princeton University Press, 1978.
Kierkegaard, Søren, *Philosophical Fragments / Johannes Climacus*, translated by Howard V. Hong and Edna H. Hong, Princeton University Press, 1985.

Kierkegaard, Søren, *The Sickness unto Death: A Christian Psychological Exposition for Edification and Awakening*, translated by Alastair Hannay, London: Penguin, 1989.
Kierkegaard, Søren, *Practice in Christianity*, translated by Howard V. Hong and Edna H. Hong, Princeton University Press, 1991.
Kierkegaard, Søren, *Fear and Trembling: Dialectical Lyric by Johannes de Silentio*, translated by Alastair Hannay, London: Penguin Classics, 2003.
Kierkegaard, Søren, *The Concept of Anxiety: A Simple Psychologically Oriented Deliberation in View of the Dogmatic Problem of Hereditary Sin*, translated by Alastair Hannay, New York & London: Liveright Publishing Corp., 2014.
Kohák, Erazim, ed., *Jan Patočka: Philosophy and Selected Writings*, University of Chicago Press, 1989.
Kohler, George Y., 'Heinrich Graetz and the Kabbalah', *Kabbalah – Journal for the Study of Jewish Mystical Texts*, 2018.
Kojève, Alexandre, *Introduction to the Reading of Hegel: Lectures on the Phenomenology of Spirit*, assembled by Raymond Queneau and first published in French in 1947; English translation by James H. Nichols, edited by Allan Bloom, NY: Basic Books, 1969; Ithaca, NY: Cornell University Press, 1980.
Konrád, György, *Antipolitics*, 1982, translated from Hungarian by Richard E. Allen, New York: Henry Holt, 1987.
Kovacs, George, *The Question of God in Heidegger's Phenomenology*, Evanston, IL: Northwestern University Press, 1990.
Koyré, Alexandre, *La Philosophie de Jacob Böhme*, Paris: Vrin, 1929.
Koyré, Alexandre, *Mystiques, spirituels, alchemistes du xvi siècle*, Paris: Gallimard, 1961.
Lampert, Laurence, *Leo Strauss and Nietzsche*, University of Chicago Press, 1996.
Landauer, Gustav, *Revolution and Other Writings: A Political Reader*, Oakland, CA: PM Press, 2010.
Lash, Nicholas, *Easter in Ordinary*, Charlottesville: University Press of Virginia, 1988.
Laski, Marghanita, *Ecstasy in Secular and Religious Experience*, London: Cresset Press, 1961.
Layton, Bentley, ed., *The Gnostic Scriptures: A New Translation with Annotations and Introductions*, London: SCM Press, 1987.
Levinas, Emmanuel, *Totality and Infinity: An Essay on Exteriority*, translated from French by Alphonso Lingis, Dordrecht: Nijhoff, 1969.
Levinas, Emmanuel, *En decouvrant l'existence avec Husserl et Heidegger*, Paris: Vrin, 1974.
Levinas, Emmanuel, *Otherwise than Being or beyond Essence*, translated by Alphonso Lingis, Dordrecht: Nijhoff, 1978.
Levinas, Emmanuel, 'Phenomenon and Enigma', in *Collected Philosophical Papers*, translated by Alphonso Lingis, Dordrecht: Nijhoff, 1987.
Levinas, Emmanuel, *Proper Names*, translated by Michael B. Smith, London: The Athlone Press, 1996.
Løgstrup, Knud E., *Kierkegaards und Heideggers Existenzanalyse und ihr Verhältnis zür Verkündigung*, Berlin: Eric Blaschker Verlag, 1950.
Løgstrup, Knud E., *Norm og spontaneitet*, Copenhagen: Gyldendal, 1972.
Løgstrup, Knud E., *System og symbol*, Copenhagen: Gyldendal, 1982.
Løgstrup, Knud E., *The Ethical Demand*, translated from Danish by Theodor I. Jensen and Gary Puckering, edited by Hans Fink and Alasdair MacIntyre, Notre Dame, IN: University of Notre Dame Press, 1997.
Løgstrup, Knud E., *Beyond the Ethical Demand*, translated by Susan Dew and Heidi Flegal, Notre Dame, IN: University of Notre Dame Press, 2007.

Løgstrup, Knud E., *Opgør med Kierkegaard*, Aarhus: Klim, new edition 2013.
Luther, Martin, *Selections*, English translation edited by John Dillenberger, New York: Anchor Books, 1961.
Lyotard, Jean-François, *The Postmodern Condition: A Report on Knowledge*, translated from French by Geoff Bennington and Brian Massumi, Minneapolis, MN: University of Minnesota Press, 1984.
Maalouf, Amin, *The Gardens of Light*, translated from French by Dorothy S. Blair, London: Abacus, 1997.
Magee, Glenn Alexander, *Hegel and the Hermetic Tradition*, Ithaca and London: Cornell University Press, 2001.
Martensen, Hans Lassen, *Jacob Böhme, His Life and Teaching, or, Studies in Theosophy*, translated from Danish by Thomas Rhys Evans, London: Hodder and Stoughton, 1885.
Maslow, Abraham, *Religions, Values and Peak-Experiences*, Indianapolis, IN: Kappa Delta Pi, 1964.
Massignon, Louis, *The Passion of al-Hallāj: Mystic and Martyr of Islam*, 4 vols., translated from French by Herbert Mason, Princeton University Press, 1982.
McGilchrist, Iain, *The Master and His Emissary: The Divided Brain and the Making of the Western World*, New Haven and London: Yale University Press, 2009.
McGilchrist, Iain, *The Matter with Things*, 2 vols., London: Perspectiva Press, 2021.
McGinn, Bernard, ed., *Meister Eckhart Teacher and Preacher*, Mahwah, NJ: Paulist Press, 1986.
McGinn, Bernard, *The Presence of God: A History of Christian Mysticism*, Volume 1, *The Foundations of Mysticism: Origins to 5th Century*, New York: Crossroads, 1991.
McGinn, Bernard, *The Growth of Mysticism: Gregory the Great through the 12th century*, New York: Crossroads, 1994.
McGinn, Bernard, *The Flowering of Mysticism: Men and Women in the New Mysticism (1200-1350)*, New York: Crossroads, 1998.
McGinn, Bernard, *The Harvest of Mysticism in Medieval Germany (1300-1500)*, New York: Crossroads, 2005.
McGinn, Bernard, *The Varieties of Vernacular Mysticism (1350-1550)*, New York: Crossroads, 2013.
McGinn, Bernard, *Mysticism in the Golden Age of Spain (1500-1650)*, New York: Crossroads, 2017.
McGinn, Bernard, *Mysticism in the Reformation (1500-1650)*, New York: Crossroads, 2017.
Milbank, Alison, *The Once and Future Parish*, London: SCM Press, 2023.
Moore, Sebastian, *The Crucified Is No Stranger*, London: Darton, Longman & Todd, 1977.
Muratori, Cecilia, *The First German Philosopher: The Mysticism of Jakob Böhme as Interpreted by Hegel*, translated from Italian by Richard Dixon and Raphaëlle Burns, Dordrecht: Springer, 2016.
Nasr, Seyyed Hossein, ed., *The Essential Frithjof Schuon*, Bloomington, IN: World Wisdom Books, 2006.
Neske, Gunther and Emil Kettering, eds., *Martin Heidegger and National Socialism*, New York: Paragon House, 1990.
Nietzsche, Friedrich, *Thus Spoke Zarathustra*, translated from German by R. J. Hollingdale, London: Penguin, 2nd edition, 1969.
Novalis (F. L. Freiherr von Hardenberg), *Henry of Ofterdingen*, 1802, translated from German by John Owen, Whithorn: Anodos, 2019.
Oldmeadow, Harry, *Frithjof Schuon and the Perennial Philosophy*, Bloomington, IN: World Wisdom Books, 2010.

O'Regan, Cyril, *The Heterodox Hegel*, Albany, NY: State University of New York Press, 1994.
O'Regan, Cyril, *Gnostic Return in Modernity*, Albany, NY: State University of New York, 2001.
O'Regan, Cyril, *Gnostic Apocalypse: Jacob Boehme's Haunted Narrative*, Albany, NY: State University of New York Press, 2002.
O'Regan, Cyril, *Anatomy of Misremembering: Von Balthasar's Response to Modernity*, Vol. 1, Chestnut Ridge, NY: Crossroad Publishing, 2014.
Osment, Steven, *Mysticism and Dissent*, New Haven: Yale University Press, 1973.
O'Sullivan, Jeremiah Francis, *The Writings of Salvian, the Presbyter*, Baltimore, MD: Catholic University Press, 1947.
Pagels, Elaine, *The Gnostic Gospels*, New York: Vintage Books, 1979.
Pangle, Thomas, *The Spirit of Modern Republicanism: The Moral Vision of the American Founders and the Philosophy of John Locke*, University of Chicago Press, 1988.
Patočka, Jan, 'Heroes of Our Time', translated from Czech by Paul Wilson, *The International Journal of Politics* vol. 11, no. 1: (Spring 1981).
Patočka, Jan, *Le monde naturel et le movement de l'existence humaine*, translation into French by Erika Abrams, Dordrecht: Kluwer Academic Publishers, 1988.
Patočka, Jan, 'The Obligation to Resist Injustice', 3 January 1977, in Erazim Kohák, ed., *Jan Patočka: Philosophy and Selected Writings*, University of Chicago Press, 1989.
Patočka, Jan, *Heretical Essays in the Philosophy of History*, 1977, translated by Erazim Kohák, edited by James Dodd, Chicago: Open Court, 1996.
Patočka, Jan, *Plato and Europe*, translated by Petr Lom, Redwood City, CA: Stanford University Press, 2002.
Perl, Eric D., *Theophany: The Neoplatonic Philosophy of Dionysius the Areopagite*, Albany, NY: State University of New York Press, 2007.
Plato, *Theaetetus*, translated from Greek by Harold N. Fowler, Loeb Classical Library, Cambridge, MA: Harvard University Press, 1921.
Plato, *Theaetetus, Phaedo*, translated by Hugh Tredennick, in *The Last Days of Socrates*, London: Penguin, 1954.
Plato, *Theaetetus, Republic*, translated by Desmond Lee, London: Penguin, 1955.
Plotinus, *The Enneads*, translated from Greek by Stephen MacKenna, second edition revised by B. S. Page, London: Faber and Faber, 1956.
Porete, Marguerite, *The Mirror of Simple Souls*, translated from medieval French by Ellen Babinsky, Mahwah, NJ: Paulist Press, 1993.
Proudfoot, Wayne, *Religious Experience*, Berkeley, CA: University of California Press, 1985.
Pseudo-Dionysius the Areopagite, *Pseudo-Dionysius: The Complete Works*, edited by C. Luibheid, NY: Paulist Press, 1987.
Raine, Kathleen, *Blake and Tradition*, 2 vols., Princeton University Press, 1968.
Raine, Kathleen, *Selected Poems*, Ipswich: Golgonooza Press, 1988.
Robinson, James M., ed., *The Nag Hammadi Library in English*, translated and introduced by members of the Coptic Gnostic Library Project of the Institute for Antiquity and Christianity, Claremont, CA; Leiden: E. J. Brill, 1996.
Rose, Gillian, *The Melancholy Science: An Introduction to the Thought of Theodor W. Adorno*, New York and London: Verso, 2014.
Ross, Maggie, *Silence: A User's Guide*, Volume 1, *Process*, London: Darton, Longman and Todd, 2014.
Rousseau, *The Confessions*, 1781, translated from French by J. M. Cohen, London: Penguin, 1953.

Rousseau, *The Social Contract*, 1762, translated by Maurice Cranston, London: Penguin, 1968.
Rousseau, *Émile, or on Education*, 1762 (including *Émile and Sophie, or The Solitaries*) edited and translated by Christopher Kelly and Allan Bloom, Hanover, NH: Dartmouth College Press, 2010.
Sandoz, Ellis, ed., *Eric Voegelin's Thought: A Critical Appraisal*, Durham, NC: Duke University Press, 1982.
Schelling, F. W. J., *Philosophical Investigations into the Essence of Human Freedom and Matters Connected Therewith*, 1809, translated from German by Jeff Love and Johannes Schmidt, Albany, NY: State University of New York Press, 2012.
Scholem, Gershom, *Major Trends in Jewish Mysticism*, Jerusalem: Schocken Publishing House, 1941.
Scholem, Gershom, *On the Kabbalah and Its Symbolism*, translated from German by Ralph Mannheim, New York: Schocken Books, 1965.
Sedgwick, Mark, *Against the Modern World: Traditionalism and the Secret Intellectual History of the Twentieth Century*, Oxford University Press, 2004.
Sells, Michael, *Mystical Languages of Unsaying*, University of Chicago Press, 1994.
Sells, Michael, trans. and ed., *Early Islamic Mysticism: Sufi, Qur'an, Mi'raj, Poetic and Theological Writings*, New York: Paulist Press, 1996.
Shanks, Andrew, *Hegel's Political Theology*, Cambridge University Press, 1991.
Shanks, Andrew, *God and Modernity: A New and Better Way to Do Theology*, London: Routledge, 2000.
Shanks, Andrew, *'What Is Truth?' Towards a Theological Poetics*, London: Routledge, 2001.
Shanks, Andrew, *Faith in Honesty: The Essential Nature of Theology*, Aldershot: Ashgate, 2005.
Shanks, Andrew, *The Other Calling: Theology, Intellectual Vocation and Truth*, Oxford: Blackwell, 2007.
Shanks, Andrew, *Hegel and Religious Faith*, London: T. & T. Clark, 2011.
Shanks, Andrew, *Hegel versus 'Inter-Faith Dialogue': A General Theory of True Xenophilia*, Cambridge University Press, 2015.
Shanks, Andrew, *Theodicy Beyond the Death of 'God': The Persisting Problem of Evil*, London and New York: Routledge, 2018.
Sheehan, Thomas, ed., *Heidegger: The Man and the Thinker*, London & New York: Routledge, 2017.
Simmons, J. Aaron and David Wood, eds., *Kierkegaard and Levinas: Ethics, Politics and Religion*, Bloomington: Indiana University Press, 2008.
Stace, Walter T., *The Teachings of the Mystics*, New York: Mentor Books, 1960.
Stace, Walter T., *Mysticism and Philosophy*, London: Macmillan, 1961.
Staudenmaier, Franz Anton, *Zum Religiösen Frieden der Zukunft*, Vol. 3, Freiburg im Breisgau: Friedrich Wagner'sche Buchhandlung, 1851.
Staudenmaier, Franz Anton, *Die Philosophie des Christentums oder Metaphysik der heiligen Schrift als Lehre von den göttlichen Ideen in ihrer Entwicklung in Natur, Geist und Geschichte. 1. Bd. Die Lehre von der Idee; in Verbindung mit einer Entwicklungsgeschichte der Ideenlehre und der Lehre von göttlichen Logos* (1840), Frankfurt am Main: Minerva, 1966.
Stern, Robert, *The Radical Demand in Løgstrup's Ethics*, Oxford University Press, 2019.
Stone, Alison, 'Hegel and Colonialism', *Hegel Bulletin* 83 (Summer 2020).
Stoudt, John Joseph, *From Sunrise to Eternity*, Philadelphia: University of Pennsylvania Press, 1957.

Strauss, D. F., *The Life of Jesus Critically Examined*, 1840, translated from German by George Eliot, edited by Peter C. Hodgson, London: SCM Press, 4th edition, 1973.
Strauss, Leo, *The City and Man*, Chicago: Rand McNally, 1964.
Strauss, Leo, *Natural Right and History*, University of Chicago Press, 2nd edition, 1965.
Strauss, Leo, 'Philosophy as a Rigorous Science and Political Philosophy', in *Studies in Platonic Political Philosophy*, University of Chicago Press, 1983.
Strauss, Leo, *Persecution and the Art of Writing*, University of Chicago Press, 1988.
Strauss, Leo, 'An Introduction to Heideggerian Existentialism', in T. Pangle, ed., *The Rebirth of Classical Political Rationalism: Essays and Lectures by Leo Strauss*, University of Chicago Press, 1989.
Strauss, Leo, 'An Unspoken Prologue to a Public Lecture at St. John's College in Honour of Jacob Klein', in K. H. Green, ed., *Jewish Philosophy and the Crisis of Modernity*, Albany: State University of New York Press, 1997.
Strauss, Leo, *Gesammelte Schriften*, edited by H. Meier, Vol. 3, Stuttgart & Weimar: J. B. Metzler, 2001.
Strauss, Leo, 'Living Issues in German Postwar Philosophy', in H. Meier, *Leo Strauss and the Theologico-Political Problem*, Cambridge University Press, 2006.
Strauss, Leo, Kenneth Hart Green, ed., *Leo Strauss on Maimonides: The Complete Writings*, University of Chicago Press, 2013.
Strijdom, Petrus D. F., 'Reappraising the Historical Context of Amos', *Old Testament Essays* vol. 24, no. 1: (2011), 221–54.
Tava, Francesco, *The Risk of Freedom: Phenomenology and Freedom in Jan Patočka*, London: Rowman and Littlefield, 2015.
Teilhard de Chardin, Pierre, 'La nostalgie du front', in *Ecrits du temps de la guerre*, Paris: Grasset, 1965.
Teresa of Jesus, *Complete Works*, Vol. 2, translated from Spanish by E. Allison Peers, *The Interior Castle*, New York and London: Sheed and Ward, 1946.
Thucydides, *History of the Peloponnesian War*, translated from Greek by Rex Warner, London: Penguin, revised edition, 2000.
Tucker, Aviezer, *The Philosophy and Politics of Czech Dissidence from Patočka to Havel*, University of Pittsburgh Press, 2000.
Turner, Denys, *The Darkness of God*, Cambridge University Press, 1995.
Underhill, Evelyn, *Mysticism: A Study of the Nature and Development of Man's Spiritual Consciousness*, London: Methuen, 1911.
Unger, Roberto Mangabeira, *The Religion of the Future*, Cambridge, MA: Harvard University Press, 2014.
Unterman, Alan, ed., *The Kabbalist Tradition*, London: Penguin Classics, 2008.
Velkley, Richard L., *Heidegger, Strauss, and the Premises of Philosophy*, University of Chicago Press, 2011.
Villa, Dana R., *Arendt and Heidegger: The Fate of the Political*, Princeton University Press, 1996.
Voegelin, Eric, *Science, Politics and Gnosticism: Two Essays*, Chicago: Regnery, 1968.
Voegelin, Eric, 'On Hegel: A Study in Sorcery', *Studium Generale* vol. 24: (1971), 335–68.
Voegelin, Eric, *The Ecumenic Age*, Baton Rouge: Louisiana State University Press, 1974.
Voegelin, Eric, *From Enlightenment to Revolution*, edited by John H. Hallowell, Durham NC: Duke University Press, 1975.
Voegelin, Eric, *The New Science of Politics: An Introduction*, Baton Rouge: Louisiana State University Press, 1982.
Voegelin, Eric, *In Search of Order*, Baton Rouge: Louisiana State University Press, 1987.

Voegelin, Eric, *Published Essays, 1966–1985*, edited by Ellis Sandoz, Baton Rouge: Louisiana State University Press, 1990.
Voegelin, Eric, *What Is History? And Other Late Unpublished Writings*, edited by Thomas A. Hollweck and Paul Caringella, Baton Rouge: Louisiana State University Press, 1990.
Voegelin, Eric, *Order in History*, 5 vols., Baton Rouge: Louisiana University Press, 1956, 1957, 1957, 1974, 2000.
Wainwright, William, *Mystical Experience*, Madison: University of Wisconsin Press, 1982.
Waldstein, Michael, 'Hans Jonas's Construct "Gnosticism": Analysis and Critique', *The Journal of Early Christian Studies* vol. 8, no. 3: (2000).
Walsh, David, *The Mysticism of Innerworldly Fulfilment: A Study of Jacob Boehme*, Gainesville: University Presses of Florida, 1983.
Webb, Eugene, *Eric Voegelin: Philosopher of History*, Seattle and London: University of Washington Press, 1981.
Weeks, Andrew, *Boehme: An Intellectual Biography of the Seventeenth-Century Philosopher and Mystic*, Albany, NY: State University of New York Press, 1991.
Weeks, Andrew, *Valentin Weigel, (1533–1588): German Religious Dissenter, Speculative Theorist and Advocate of Tolerance*, Albany, NY: State University of New York Press, 1999.
Weeks, Andrew, ed., *Valentin Weigel: Selected Spiritual Writings*, Mahwah, NJ: Paulist Press, 2003.
Weil, Simone, *Gravity and Grace*, translated from French by Emma Craufurd, London: Routledge & Kegan Paul, 1952.
Wendte, Martin, *Gottmenschliche Einheit bei Hegel: eine logische und theologische Untersuchung*, Berlin: de Gruyter, 2007.
Westermann, Claus, *Isaiah 40–66*, translated from German by David M. G. Stalker, London: SCM, 1969.
Westphal, Merold, *Levinas and Kierkegaard in Dialogue*, Bloomington: Indiana University Press, 2008.
Williams, Rowan, 'The Prophetic and the Mystical: Heiler Revisited', *New Blackfriars* vol. 64, no. 757: (July / August 1983), 330–47.
Williams, Rowan, 'Butler's *Western Mysticism*: Towards an Assessment', *Downside Review* vol. 102: (1984).
Williams, Rowan, *Teresa of Avila*, London: Bloomsbury, 1991.
Winstanley, Gerrard, *The Law of Freedom and Other Writings*, edited by Christopher Hill, Harmondsworth: Penguin, 1973.
Winstanley, Gerrard, *Gerrard Winstanley: A Common Treasury*, edited by Andrew Hopton, London: Verso, 2011.
Wolin, Richard, *The Politics of Being: The Political Thought of Martin Heidegger*, New York: Columbia University Press, 1990.
Wycliffe, John, *Writings*, Philadelphia: Presbyterian Board of Publication, 1842.
Zaehner, R. C., *Mysticism Sacred and Profane*, Oxford University Press, 1957.
Zaehner, R. C., *Concordant Discord: The Interdependence of Faiths*, Oxford University Press, 1971.

INDEX

abolitionism 203, 207
Abraham 36–9, 139
Abrahamic tradition 13, 14, 35–42, 45, 49, 50, 72, 101, 121, 123, 127, 141, 144, 161, 172, 204, 206
'absolute knowing' 43, 185, 190, 192
Abú Yazíd *see* Bistámí
Adams, N. 190–1
Adonis 222 n.53
Adorno, T. W. 15, 172–4, 206, 220 n.19
'agapacracy' 208, 247 n.51
agapé 186–7
akedah 36–9
Albert the Great 71
Allport, G. 96
'almightiness' 103–5
Altizer, T. J. J. 110, 118
Alumbrados 224 n.6
Amos 39–41, 42, 49, 68, 71, 127, 128–9, 134–5, 138, 140–1, 145, 216–17 n.9
'*Amos* impulse, the' 42, 44, 50–1, 61–3, 68, 71, 72, 122, 137, 140, 144, 150, 154, 183
anarcho-pacifism 208, 211
Anaximandros 159
Angela of Foligno 224 n.4
Antigoné 195–6, 203
'anti-politics' 154, 155, 183, 188, 238 n.1
Apocryphon of John 107–8, 116
Aqiba, rabbi 86
Arberry, A. J. 75, 84, 222–3 n.54, 223 n.59, 223 n.65
Arendt, H. 20, 60, 174–83, 187, 188, 205
  Love and Saint Augustine 178, 187
  On Revolution 177, 181
  The Human Condition 177–81
  The Origins of Totalitarianism 175–6
  'What Is Authority?' 60, 182–3
Arianism 45
Aristotle 22, 101, 117, 159, 168–9
'art-religion' 199–200, 245 n.31

Assagioli, R. 96
Athanasius 71
atheism 101–2, 147, 157–8, 189–90, 191, 197
Augustine 52, 178–9, 187, 229 n.37
'authority' 59–62, 63, 182–3, 208, 220 n.19, 220 n.22
Averroes (Ibn Rushd) 168–9
Axial Age 33–5, 43, 127
  'Second' Axial Age 35

Baader, F. X. von 109, 244 n.6
Bahir 107
Bakunin, M. 243 n.77
Balthasar, Fr. H. U. von 120, 142, 190, 191
Barth, K. 44, 190, 191
Basil of Caesarea 52
Basilides 106, 107
Bäumler, A. 161
Baur, F. C. 110, 117, 119–20
'beautiful soul', the 187–8, 198–9, 210, 211
Beatrijs of Nazareth 224 n.4
Berdyaev, N. 110
Bernard of Clairvaux 86–7
Bernardino of Laredo 219 n.1
Besse, Père L. de 88
'Big Lie', the *see gennaion pseudos*
Bistámí, Abú Yazíd 73–4, 80–1
Blake, William 109–10, 155
Bloch, E. 173–4
Blumenbach, J. F. 246 n.48
Bogomilism 106
Böhme, J. 14, 109–21, 190, 231 n.16, 244 n.6
  Aurora 115
  Mysterium Magnum 110–15, 231 n.20
  Three Principles 233 n.34
Bonaventure 218 n.1
Brecht, B. 173
Brethren of the Free Spirit 71–2
Bridget of Sweden 224 n.4
Buber, M. 140–1, 157, 158, 236 n.34

Index

Bucke, R. 95–6, 98
Buddhism 34
Bultmann, R. 28, 44, 215 n.32, 229 n.6
Butler, Dom C. 88, 98

'care for the soul' 29
Catharism 106
Catherine of Genoa 224 n.4
Catherine of Siena 224 n.4
'catholicity' 14, 15, 21, 57, 62, 85, 127,
  130, 143, 144, 146, 150, 154, 155–6,
  160–1, 167, 168, 171–2, 173, 174,
  178, 183, 185, 195, 199, 200, 202,
  206, 207
Chamberlain, H. S. 176
Charter 77 1–3, 6, 12, 19, 25, 26, 28, 205
Clement of Alexandria 52
Cloud of Unknowing, The 219 n.1
Comte, A. 118
Condorcet, Marquis de 155
Confucianism 33–4, 225 n.9
Coomaraswamy, A. 91, 225 n.11
Cordovero, rabbi Moses 107

Darius I 177
Day, Dorothy 208
'death of God' 201–2, 245 n.40
deism 198
Denis the Carthusian 86, 219 n.1
Derrida, J. 38
Descartes, René 159, 180, 189
Desmond, W. 186–8, 194–5
Deutero-Isaiah 36, 138
'Dialectic' 192–4
Diderot, D. 245 n.24
'Dionysius the Areopagite' 14, 50–2,
  56–62, 63, 65, 68, 73, 85, 86, 94, 95,
  98–9, 219 n.3
Dionysos 199–200
docetism 230 n.8
Dorothea of Montau 224 n.4
Drury, S. 167
Dugin, A. 93, 226 n.17

Eckhart, Meister Johannes 14, 63–73,
  74, 85, 94, 164, 173, 190, 218 n.1,
  220–1 n.26, 221 n.41, 240 n.26,
  244 n.6
Egyptian antiquity 199

Eliade, M. 225 n.11
Elijah 41
Elisabeth of Schönau 224 n.4
Emden, rabbi Jacob 230 n.10
Eriugena, John Scottus 218 n.1
eros, political 143, 186–7
'ethical phenomenology' 14, 124, 128
Evagrius 52
'evangelistic impatience' 13, 14, 49–50, 51,
  52, 54, 55, 56, 59, 64, 66–8, 72, 78,
  80, 83, 84, 85, 86, 102–3, 104–5,
  106, 108, 119, 120–1, 122, 127, 128,
  130, 144, 182–3, 185, 206, 207, 209,
  212
Evola, Julius 91–3

fanā' wa baqā' 74, 77, 95, 135
Fárábí, Abú Nasr al-167–9, 171
Farges, Monsignor A. 88
Feuerbach, L. 189, 191
Fichte, J. G. 120, 155, 189, 198
Ficino, Marsilio 219 n.1, 224–5 n.9
Forkel-Liebeskind, Meta 203, 246 n.43
Forster, Therese 246 n.43
Francis of Assisi 186
Francisco of Osuna 219 n.1
Franck, Sebastian 120
Fukuyama, F. 4–7, 9–12, 50
fundamentalism 197

Galileo 179
Gallus, Thomas 86, 218 n.1
Gandhi, Mahatma 34
'gang' 36–7, 38, 39, 49, 50, 64, 71, 74, 77,
  85, 101–2, 122, 135, 150, 152, 187
Gardeil, Père A. 88
Garrigou-Lagrange, Père R. 88
Geist 21, 28–30, 42–3, 45, 121, 185, 186,
  187–8, 189, 190, 191, 192, 195, 199,
  205–6, 211
gennaion pseudos 57–8, 118, 119, 166–7,
  241 n.38
Gerson, Jean 86, 98–9, 219 n.1
Gertrude of Helfta 87, 224 n.4
Giorgi, Francesco 109
Girard, R. 36, 216 n.3
'gnosticism' 14, 72, 73, 101–24, 127,
  233–4 n.44
Gobineau, A. de 176

Goethe, J. W. von 244 n.5, 245 n.24
Graeber, D. 61
Graetz, H. 107
'grand narrative' 4–6, 26, 35–6, 123, 146,
    155, 158–9, 163, 174, 178, 183, 185,
    186, 188, 202, 203–12, 246 n.48
Gregory the Great 88
Gregory of Nazianzus 52
Gregory of Nyssa 52, 56, 69, 73, 86
Grosseteste, Robert 86, 218 n.1
Guénon, R. 90–1, 226 n.12

Hadewijch of Antwerp 87, 224 n.4
Halík, T. 213 n.1
Halláj, Husayn ibn Mansúr al-80–1
Harmless, W. 99
Hart, D. B. 142–4
Hasidism 133
Havel, V. 1, 3, 7–8, 205
Hegel, G. W. F. 5–6, 7, 10, 15, 21, 22,
    28–9, 30, 35, 43, 109, 117, 118, 119,
    120, 121, 130, 137, 169, 185–204,
    205–6
  early writings 194
  Faith and Knowledge 245 n.40
  *Lectures on the Philosophy of
    Religion*,35, 191, 199, 244 n.9
  *Lectures on the Philosophy of World
    History* 10–1, 203, 246 n.48
  Phenomenology of Spirit 5–6, 11–2,
    121, 185, 187–8, 189, 190, 191,
    192–4, 195–202, 203, 210
  Philosophy of Right 210–1
  Science of Logic 190–1
Heidegger, M. 15, 19, 20, 27, 52, 118, 120,
    137, 144, 156–65, 169–72, 173,
    174–5, 206, 214 n.4, 229 n.6
  Being and Time 156–8
  'Conversation on a Country Path about
    Thinking' 240 n.26
  Der Spiegel interview 161, 240 n.23,
    240 n.24
  Elucidations of Hölderlin's Poetry
    239–40 n.23
  Freiburg University rectorate 161–3
  Identity and Difference 160–1
  Plato's Doctrine of Truth 239–40 n.23
  Winke 239–40 n.23
hemispheres, cerebral 29–30, 53

Herakleitos 20–1, 22
'herd' 36–7, 38, 39, 49, 50, 55, 64, 71, 73,
    74, 77, 85, 101–2, 129, 130, 135,
    139, 150, 152, 158
Héring, J. 237 n.45
'Hermeticism' 118–19, 224–5 n.9
Herodotus 177
Herp, Hendrik 219 n.1
hierarchy 50, 57–62, 63, 72
Hildegard of Bingen 224 n.4
Hippolytus of Rome 86
Hobbes, T. 179–80
Hölderlin, J. C. F. 120, 155, 160, 162, 199
Hosea 41, 42, 145
Hugh of Balma 218 n.1
Hugh of St. Victor 218 n.1
Husserl, E. 20, 27, 137, 163, 214 n.4
Hussites 2

Iamblichus 58–9, 224 n.9
Ibn 'Arabí, Muhyiddín 73, 80
Idel, M. 231 n.11
Incarnation, the doctrine of the 199,
    200–2
Indian antiquity 199
innocence 207, 209–12
'inwardness' *see* 'subjectivity'
Irenaeus of Lyons 106, 118, 230 n.9
'isonomy' 15, 177–9, 183, 205
'isothymia' 7–10, 15, 40, 44, 50–1, 61,
    62–3, 135–6, 139, 148, 150, 157,
    158, 174, 182, 199, 235 n.22

Ja'afar ibn Muhammad as-Sádiq 73–4
Jacobi, F. H. 244 n.5
Jacobins 176, 189, 203, 204, 211
James, W. 96, 98, 227–8 n.27
Jantzen, G. 98
Jaspers, K. 33
Jefferson, Thomas 181
Joachim of Fiore 102, 117, 118
Job 103
John of Ávila 219 n.1
John of the Cross 86, 88, 219 n.1
Jonas, H. 229–30 n.6
Joret, Père F. 88
Julian of Norwich 103–4, 224 n.4
Junayd, Abúl-Qásim al-73, 74–5, 81
Jung, C. 96

Index

Jünger, E. 25
Justin Martyr 52

Kaaba, the 199
Kabbalah 14, 73, 106–7, 108, 110, 118–19, 120, 122, 225 n.9
Kant, I. 4, 57, 159, 189, 194, 198
Katz, S. K. 98
Kempe, Margery 224 n.4
Kierkegaard, S. 15, 38, 110, 128–37, 138–40, 142, 144, 146–50, 153, 154, 155, 157–8, 186, 188
    attack upon Christendom 128–9, 130, 134–5
    Concluding Unscientific Postscript 128, 129, 153
    Fear and Trembling 38
    Johannes Climacus 129
    Philosophical Fragments 129
    Practice in Christianity 131, 132
    The Concept of Anxiety 131–2
    The Sickness unto Death 131–2
    Works of Love 135, 146, 148–9
'kingdom of God' 1–3, 11, 13, 30, 42, 49, 128, 155, 206, 207 *see also* Abrahamic tradition
Klein, J. 240 n.33
Kojève, A. 5–6, 9–12, 189, 213 n.6, 213 n.7, 233 n.41
Korsch, K. 173

Larsen, K. O. 237 n.51
Lash, N. 98
Law, William 109, 231 n.17
Leibniz, G. W. 225 n.9
Lenin, V. I. 181
Levinas, E. 15, 128, 134, 136–45, 150, 153, 154, 155, 157, 174, 186, 188
    'epiphany of the face' 137–8
    'illeity' 140–2
    'persecution' 138
    Sabra and Chatila massacres 236 n.33
    'the said' / 'the saying' 136
Lings, M. 226 n.12
Løgstrup, K. E. 15, 128, 134, 136, 144–54, 155, 157
    against Christian Democracy 237–8 n.53
    'sovereign expressions of life' 150–4
    The Ethical Demand 146–50

Louis of Blois 219 n.1
Lucifer 115–16, 121
Luis of Granada 219 n.1
Lukács, G. 173
Luria, rabbi Isaac 107, 108
Luther, Martin 10–1, 189
Lyotard. J.-F. 4, 6, 204

Maalouf, A. 229 n.5
Magee, G. A. 118–19, 121
Maimonides (Moses ben Maimon) 168–9
Malý, Fr. V. 2
Mandaeism 106
Manicheanism 106
Marcionism 105–6
Maréchal, Père J. 88
Margareta Ebner 224 n.4
Marguerite d'Oignt 224 n.4
Marie d'Oignies 224 n.4
Martensen, H. L. 110, 135
Marxism 4, 6, 19, 22, 118, 155, 164, 172–4, 180–1, 188–9
Mary, Mother of God 172, 217–18 n.11
Maslow, A. 96, 228 n.29
Maximus the Confessor 218 n.1
McGilchrist, I. 29–30
McGinn, B. 98
Mechtild of Hackeborn 87, 224 n.4
Mechtild of Magdeburg 87, 224 n.4
Megabyzus 177
'megalothymia' 7, 9–10, 40, 44, 50–1, 62–3, 122, 135–6, 139, 146, 150, 157, 158, 164, 166, 169, 172, 174, 182, 235 n.22
Meir ben Simeon of Narbonne, rabbi 230 n.10
Merton, T. 226 n.12
Messalianism 51, 59, 62, 63, 72, 219 n.3
'metaphysics' 159–61, 167, 169, 172, 186, 191, 225 n.9
Milbank, A. 234 n.58
Milton, John 232 n.23
'mob' 49, 50, 64, 71, 74, 77, 101–2, 122, 135, 152
Modena, rabbi Leon 230 n.10
'modernity', three species of
    'first modernity' 204, 205, 206, 209
    'second modernity' 204, 205, 207–8, 209
    'third modernity' 204–6, 207–8, 209, 211

Index

Montanism 63
Moore, Dom S. 201, 222 n.47
Moses 41, 56, 94
Moses de Leon, rabbi 107
Mynster, Bishop J. P. 135
'mystical theology' 14, 50, 52, 56, 57, 61, 63, 68, 72, 73, 85, 86, 88, 97, 99, 101, 102–3, 122–4, 128, 130, 133
'mysticism' 14, 85–99, 101, 109

Nag Hammadi library, the 230 n.6
Napoleon 5–6, 132
Nasr, Seyyed Hossein 226 n.12
'negative revelation' 163
Neo-Platonism 14, 52–9, 62, 63, 65, 69, 73, 120, 121, 122–3, 130, 133, 159, 225 n.9
New Labour 197
Nicholas of Cusa 219 n.1
Nietzsche, F. 6, 9–10, 93, 118, 139, 162, 164, 165, 189
Niffarí, Muhammad ibn 'Abd al-Jabbár an- 14, 72, 75–84, 85, 94, 95, 223 n.61
'Novalis' (G. P. F. von Hardenberg) 120, 243–4 n.5

Občanské Fórum (Civic Forum) 1
O'Regan, C. 119–21
Origen 45, 52, 86
Otanes 177–8

Pallis, M. 226 n.12
Pangle, T. 174
Paracelsus 109, 119, 120
Parmenides 159
'pathos of shakenness' 15, 21–2, 25, 102, 128, 130, 132, 136, 139–40, 144, 145, 146–7, 154, 155, 157–8, 163, 183, 186, 187, 194, 195, 200, 234–5 n.2
Patočka, J. 3, 12, 13, 19–28, 29, 127, 146, 162–3, 164, 172, 174, 175, 205, 214 n.4, 240 n.25
Heretical Essays 19–26
Paul 88–90, 97, 156
Paulicianism 106
Pedro of Alcántara 219 n.1
Pelagius 229 n.37
Pentecostalism 234 n.58

'perennial philosophy' 224–5 n.9 *see also* 'Traditionalism'
Philo of Alexandria 45–6
'philosophic impatience' 13, 15, 20, 21, 57–8, 127, 156, 158–9, 161–2, 165–72, 174, 185, 206, 207, 209, 212
Pico della Mirandola 109, 224–5 n.9
Platonism 6–7, 15, 20, 22, 23, 27, 46, 52–9, 66, 101, 117–18, 122, 156, 158–9, 165–9, 170, 175, 178, 179
Plotinus 14, 52–5, 56, 58, 65, 94, 95, 121, 124
political parties 175, 181, 205, 206, 207–8
Popper, K. 167
Porete, Marguerite 71–2, 220–1 n.22
Porphyry 58
postmodernism 4, 6, 188, 204
Poulain, Père A. 88
Proclus 52, 56, 58–9, 218 n.1
Proudhon, P.-J. 243 n.77
Ptolemy (Valentinian teacher) 230 n.9
'public conscience movements' 205–6, 207–8, 211
Pythagoras 57, 225 n.9

Rameau's Nephew (Diderot) 197, 245 n.24
religion
    'anti-political' 34, 35–6, 39–41, 127
    'intra-political' 33–4, 127, 133
    'pre-political' 34, 35, 127, 133, 234–5 n.2
religiousness 'A' / 'B' / 'C' 132–4, 136
Reuchlin, Johannes 109
'revealed religion' 190, 199, 200–2
'revelation, negative' 163, 164, 174–5, 176, 178, 189
Revelation of John, The 120
Rosenberg, A. E. 161
Rosmini, Fr. A. 190
Ross, M. 98–9
Rousseau, Jean-Jacques 196, 209–10, 211
Ruysbroeck, Jan van 86, 218 n.1

Sabbatianism 107
Sabellianism 43
Sachs, Nelly 155
Saint-Martin, Louis-Claude de 109

Salvian 51
Sarráj, Abú Nasr as-73
Saudreau, Abbé A. 88
'scepticism' 22, 197
Schelling, Caroline 203, 246 n.43
Schelling, F. W. J. von 109, 117, 120, 189, 246 n.43
Schleiermacher, F. 117
Schmitt, C. 161
Scholem, G. 107, 165
Schuon, Frithjof 91–2, 226 n.12
Schwenkfeld, Caspar 120
Sells, M. 67
Sethianism 106, 107–8, 116, 122
'Sister Catherine' 72
Sittlichkeit 195–9
Smith, H. 226 n.12
Sobornost 156
Socrates 26, 29, 52, 53, 57, 66, 101, 129, 136–7, 166–7, 168, 175, 178
Søe, N. H. 147
'solidarity of the shaken' 3, 13, 14, 15, 20, 21, 22, 25–6, 33, 35, 36, 41, 42, 43, 49, 50, 61–2, 102, 124, 127–8, 132, 134, 144, 155, 156, 163–4, 171–2, 175, 183, 185, 186–7, 192, 200, 201, 205, 206, 207, 211–2
Solomon, R. C. 189
Song of Songs 86
Sophoklés 195–6, 203
'Speculative Reason' 192–4
Spengler, O. 229–30 n.6
Spinoza, Baruch de 160, 189
Spirit *see Geist*
Spiritual Franciscans 186
Stace, W. T. 93–5, 96–8, 226 n.18
Steuco, Agostino 224 n.9
'stoicism' 22, 197
Strauss, L. 15, 20, 118, 119, 156, 164–72, 173, 174, 178, 185, 206
'subjectivity' 128, 130–1, 133
Sufism 73–84, 133
Sulamí, Abú 'Abd ar-Rahman as-73
Suso, Henry 86, 218 n.1

Taoism 33, 225 n.9
Tauler, Johannes 218 n.1
Teilhard de Chardin, Fr. P. 25
Teresa of Avila 87–8, 224 n.6, 227–8 n.27

Tertullian 106, 178
Thatcherism 197
Tholuck, F. A. G. 190
Thrasymachus 166
thymos 6–10 *see also* isothymia, megalothymia
Tiglath-Pileser III 217 n.9
Tilimsání, 'Afif ad-Dín at-80
totalitarianism 23, 26, 59–61, 161–4, 153, 174, 175–83, 189, 211, 215 n.15, 220 n.22, 243 n.82
'Traditionalism' 90–3
Trinity, the doctrine of the
    'First-Person theology' 43–6, 62–3, 102, 124
    in Böhme's thought 111, 115
    in Eckhart's thought 69–70
    in Hegel's thought 200–1
    in Joachim's thought 102
    'Second-Person theology' 44–6, 62, 102, 123
    'Third-Person theology' 44–6, 62–3, 102–3, 123–4, 234 n.58
Tripartite Tractate 108, 116
truth, the nature of
    'truth-as-correctness' 29–31, 49–50, 52–4, 56, 63, 64, 70–1, 72, 88, 110, 127, 129, 133, 141, 155, 159–60, 167, 171, 172, 175, 185, 190–1
    'truth-as-openness' 20, 28–31, 42–3, 45, 49, 52–4, 56, 59, 61, 63, 64, 70–1, 72, 78, 88, 95, 99, 104, 110, 127, 128, 133, 136, 141, 155, 159–60, 171, 172, 175, 185, 190, 200, 211–2, 216 n.36
    'truth is subjectivity' *see* 'subjectivity'
Turner, D. 98

Underhill E. 86
unglückliche Bewußtsein, das 11–2, 30–1, 33, 34–5, 38, 40, 45, 50, 61, 64, 66, 71, 80, 104, 121, 187, 192–4, 197–8, 200, 201–2, 203, 204, 205, 214 n.14
Upanishadic Hinduism 34
Usurpation, the 30–1, 33, 34, 35, 105, 121 *and see also* '*unglückliche Bewußtsein, das*'

Valentinianism 106, 107, 108, 116
Verstand 30, 192–3
Voegelin, E. 117–18, 121, 233 n.41, 233–4 n.44

Weigel, Valentin 120
Weil, S. 66
Wesley, John 231 n.17
Westphal, M. 134, 136, 142, 143
Wilber, K. 96
Williams, R. 98

'woke impatience' 209
'wonder' 101–2, 157, 174
Wycliffe, John 2

Yahweh-alone-ism 40–1, 42

Zaehner, R. C. 94, 226 n.20
Zhu Xi 225 n.9
Zohar 107
Zoroastrianism 199, 225 n.9

www.ingramcontent.com/pod-product-compliance
Lightning Source LLC
Chambersburg PA
CBHW071814300426
44116CB00009B/1317